Aristotle

The Ethics and Politics According to Aristotle

OK Publishing 2021

Aristotle

The Ethics and Politics According to Aristotle

Published by
MUSAICUM
Books

- Advanced Digital Solutions & High-Quality book Formatting -

musaicumbooks@okpublishing.info

2021 OK Publishing

ISBN 978-80-272-7331-7

Contents

Ethics

Introduction

The *Ethics* of Aristotle is one half of a single treatise of which his *Politics* is the other half. Both deal with one and the same subject. This subject is what Aristotle calls in one place the "philosophy of human affairs;" but more frequently Political or Social Science. In the two works taken together we have their author's whole theory of human conduct or practical activity, that is, of all human activity which is not directed merely to knowledge or truth. The two parts of this treatise are mutually complementary, but in a literary sense each is independent and self-contained. The proem to the *Ethics* is an introduction to the whole subject, not merely to the first part; the last chapter of the *Ethics* points forward to the *Politics*, and sketches for that part of the treatise the order of enquiry to be pursued (an order which in the actual treatise is not adhered to).

The principle of distribution of the subject-matter between the two works is far from obvious, and has been much debated. Not much can be gathered from their titles, which in any case were not given to them by their author. Nor do these titles suggest any very compact unity in the works to which they are applied: the plural forms, which survive so oddly in English (Ethic*s*, Politic*s*), were intended to indicate the treatment within a single work of a *group* of connected questions. The unity of the first group arises from their centring round the topic of character, that of the second from their connection with the existence and life of the city or state. We have thus to regard the *Ethics* as dealing with one group of problems and the *Politics* with a second, both falling within the wide compass of Political Science. Each of these groups falls into sub-groups which roughly correspond to the several books in each work. The tendency to take up one by one the various problems which had suggested themselves in the wide field obscures both the unity of the subject-matter and its proper articulation. But it is to be remembered that what is offered us is avowedly rather an enquiry than an exposition of hard and fast doctrine.

Nevertheless each work aims at a relative completeness, and it is important to observe the relation of each to the other. The distinction is not that the one treats of Moral and the other of Political Philosophy, nor again that the one deals with the moral activity of the individual and the other with that of the State, nor once more that the one gives us the theory of human conduct, while the other discusses its application in practice, though not all of these misinterpretations are equally erroneous. The clue to the right interpretation is given by Aristotle himself, where in the last chapter of the *Ethics* he is paving the way for the *Politics*. In the *Ethics* he has not confined himself to the abstract or isolated individual, but has always thought of him, or we might say, in his social and political context, with a given nature due to race and heredity and in certain surroundings. So viewing him he has studied the nature and formation of his character-all that he can make himself or be made by others to be. Especially he has investigated the various admirable forms of human character and the mode of their production. But all this, though it brings more clearly before us what goodness or virtue is, and how it is to be reached, remains mere theory or talk. By itself it does not enable us to become, or to help others to become, good. For this it is necessary to bring into play the great force of the Political Community or State, of which the main instrument is Law. Hence arises the demand for the necessary complement to the *Ethics*, *i.e.*, a treatise devoted to the questions which centre round the enquiry; by what organisation of social or political forces, by what laws or institutions can we best secure the greatest amount of good character?

We must, however, remember that the production of good character is not the end of either individual or state action: that is the aim of the one and the other because good character is the indispensable condition and chief determinant of happiness, itself the goal of all human doing. The end of all action, individual or collective, is the greatest happiness of the greatest number. There is, Aristotle insists, no difference of kind between the good of one and the good of many or all. The sole difference is one of amount or scale. This does not mean simply that the State exists to secure in larger measure the objects of degree which the isolated individual attempts, but is too feeble, to secure without it. On the contrary, it rather insists that whatever goods society alone enables a man to secure have always had to the individual-whether he realised it or not-the value which, when so secured, he recognises them to possess. The best and happiest life for the individual is that which the State renders possible, and this it does mainly by revealing to him the value of new objects of desire and educating him to appreciate them. To Aristotle or to Plato the State is, above all, a large and powerful educative agency which gives the individual increased opportunities of self-development and greater capacities for the enjoyment of life.

Looking forward, then, to the life of the State as that which aids support, and combines the efforts of the individual to obtain happiness, Aristotle draws no hard and fast distinction between the spheres of action of Man as individual and Man as citizen. Nor does the division of his discussion into the *Ethics* and the *Politics* rest upon any such distinction. The distinction implied is rather between two stages in the life of the civilised man-the stage of preparation for the full life of the adult citizen, and the stage of the actual exercise or enjoyment of citizenship. Hence the *Ethics*, where his attention is directed upon the formation of character, is largely and centrally a treatise on Moral Education. It discusses especially those admirable human qualities which fit a man for life in an organised civic community, which makes him "a good citizen," and considers how they can be fostered or created and their opposites prevented.

This is the kernel of the *Ethics*, and all the rest is subordinate to this main interest and purpose. Yet "the rest" is not irrelevant; the whole situation in which character grows and operates is concretely conceived. There is a basis of what we should call Psychology, sketched in firm outlines, the deeper presuppositions and the wider issues of human character and conduct are not ignored, and there is no little of what we should call Metaphysics. But neither the Psychology nor the Metaphysics is elaborated, and only so much is brought forward as appears necessary to put the main facts in their proper perspective and setting. It is this combination of width of outlook with close observation of the concrete facts of conduct which gives its abiding value to the work, and justifies the view of it as containing Aristotle's Moral Philosophy. Nor is it important merely as summing up the moral judgments and speculations of an age now long past. It seizes and dwells upon those elements and features in human practice which are most essential and permanent, and it is small wonder that so much in it survives in our own ways of regarding conduct and speaking of it. Thus it still remains one of the classics of Moral Philosophy, nor is its value likely soon to be exhausted.

As was pointed out above, the proem (Book I, cc. i-iii.) is a prelude to the treatment of the whole subject covered by the *Ethics* and the *Politics* together. It sets forth the purpose of the enquiry, describes the spirit in which it is to be undertaken and what ought to be the expectation of the reader, and lastly states the necessary conditions of studying it with profit. The aim of it is the acquisition and propagation of a certain kind of knowledge (science), but this knowledge and the thinking which brings it about are subsidiary to a practical end. The knowledge aimed at is of what is best for man and of the conditions of its realisation. Such knowledge is that which in its consumate form we find in great statesmen, enabling them to organise and administer their states and regulate by law the life of the citizens to their advantage and happiness, but it is the same kind of knowledge which on a smaller scale secures success in the management of the family or of private life.

It is characteristic of such knowledge that it should be deficient in "exactness," in precision of statement, and closeness of logical concatenation. We must not look for a mathematics of conduct. The subject-matter of Human Conduct is not governed by necessary and uniform laws. But this does not mean that it is subject to no laws. There are general principles at work in it, and these can be formulated in "rules," which rules can be systematised or unified. It is all-important to remember that practical or moral rules are only general and always admit of exceptions, and that they arise not from the mere complexity of the facts, but from the liability of the facts to a certain unpredictable variation. At their very best, practical rules state probabilities, not certainties; a relative constancy of connection is all that exists, but it is enough to serve as a guide in life. Aristotle here holds the balance between a misleading hope of reducing the subject-matter of conduct to a few simple rigorous abstract principles, with conclusions necessarily issuing from them, and the view that it is the field of operation of inscrutable forces acting without predictable regularity. He does not pretend to find in it absolute uniformities, or to deduce the details from his principles. Hence, too, he insists on the necessity of experience as the source or test of all that he has to say. Moral experience-the actual possession and exercise of good character-is necessary truly to understand moral principles and profitably to apply them. The mere intellectual apprehension of them is not possible, or if possible, profitless.

The *Ethics* is addressed to students who are presumed both to have enough general education to appreciate these points, and also to have a solid foundation of good habits. More than that is not required for the profitable study of it.

If the discussion of the nature and formation of character be regarded as the central topic of the *Ethics*, the contents of Book I, cc. iv-xii may be considered as still belonging to the introduction and setting, but these chapters contain matter of profound importance and have exercised an enormous influence upon subsequent thought. They lay down a principle which governs all Greek thought about human life, viz. that it is only intelligible when viewed as directed towards some end or good. This is the Greek way of expressing that all human life involves an ideal element-something which it is not yet and which under certain conditions it is to be. In that sense Greek Moral Philosophy is essentially idealistic. Further it is always assumed that all human practical activity is directed or "oriented" to a *single* end, and that that end is knowable or definable in advance of its realisation. To know it is not merely a matter of speculative interest, it is of the highest practical moment for only in the light of it can life be duly guided, and particularly only so can the state be properly organised and administered. This explains the stress laid throughout by Greek Moral Philosophy upon the necessity of knowledge as a condition of the best life. This knowledge is not, though it includes knowledge of the nature of man and his circumstances, it is knowledge of what is best-of man's supreme end or good.

But this end is not conceived as presented to him by a superior power nor even as something which *ought* to be. The presentation of the Moral Ideal as Duty is almost absent. From the outset it is identified with the object of desire, of what we not merely judge desirable but actually do desire, or that which would, if realised, satisfy human desire. In fact it is what we all, wise and simple, agree in naming "Happiness" (Welfare or Well-being).

In what then does happiness consist? Aristotle summarily sets aside the more or less popular identifications of it with abundance of physical pleasures, with political power and honour, with the mere possession of such superior gifts or attainments as normally entitle men to these, with wealth. None of these can constitute the end or good of man as such. On the other hand, he rejects his master Plato's conception of a good which is the end of the whole universe, or at least dismisses it as irrelevant to his present enquiry. The good towards which all human desires and practical activities are directed must be one conformable to man's special nature and circumstances and attainable by his efforts. There is in Aristotle's theory of human conduct no trace of Plato's "other worldliness"; he brings the moral ideal in Bacon's phrase down to "right earth"—and so closer to the facts and problems of actual human living. Turning from criticism of others he states his own positive view of Happiness, and, though he avowedly states it merely in outline, his account is pregnant with significance. Human Happiness lies in activity or energising, and that in a way peculiar to man with his given nature and his given circumstances, it is not theoretical, but practical: it is the activity not of reason but still of a being who possesses reason and applies it, and it presupposes in that being the development, and not merely the natural possession, of certain relevant powers and capacities. The last is the prime condition of successful living and therefore of satisfaction, but Aristotle does not ignore other conditions, such as length of life, wealth and good luck, the absence or diminution of which render happiness not impossible, but difficult of attainment.

It is interesting to compare this account of Happiness with Mill's in *Utilitarianism*. Mill's is much the less consistent: at times he distinguishes and at times he identifies, happiness, pleasure, contentment, and satisfaction. He wavers between belief in its general attainability and an absence of hopefulness. He mixes up in an arbitrary way such ingredients as "not expecting more from life than it is capable of bestowing," "mental cultivation," "improved laws," etc., and in fact leaves the whole conception vague, blurred, and uncertain. Aristotle draws the outline with a firmer hand and presents a more definite ideal. He allows for the influence on happiness of conditions only partly, if at all, within the control of man, but he clearly makes the man positive determinant of man's happiness lie in himself, and more particularly in what he makes directly of his own nature, and so indirectly of his circumstances. "'Tis in ourselves that we are thus or thus." But once more this does not involve an artificial or abstract isolation of the individual moral agent from his relation to other persons or things, from his context in society and nature, nor ignore the relative dependence of his life upon a favourable environment.

The main factor which determines success or failure in human life is the acquisition of certain powers, for Happiness is just the exercise or putting forth of these in actual living; everything else is secondary and subordinate. These powers arise from the due development of certain natural aptitudes which belong (in various degrees) to human nature as such and therefore to all normal human beings. In their developed form they are known as virtues (the Greek means simply "goodnesses," "perfections," "excellences," or "fitnesses"), some of them are physical, but others are psychical, and among the latter some, and these distinctively or peculiarly human, are "rational," *i.e.*, presuppose the possession and exercise of mind or intelligence. These last fall into two groups, which Aristotle distinguishes as Goodnesses of Intellect and Goodnesses of Character. They have in common that they all excite in us admiration and praise of their possessors, and that they are not natural endowments, but acquired characteristics. But they differ in important ways: (1) the former are excellences or developed powers of the reason as such-of that in us which sees and formulates laws, rules, regularities, systems, and is content in the vision of them, while the latter involve a submission or obedience to such rules of something in us which is in itself capricious and irregular, but capable of regulation, viz. our instincts and feelings; (2) the former are acquired by study and instruction, the latter by discipline. The latter constitute "character," each of them as a "moral virtue" (literally "a goodness of character"), and upon them primarily depends the realisation of happiness. This is the case at least for the great majority of men, and for all men their possession is an indispensable basis of the best, *i.e.*, the most desirable life. They form the chief or central subject-matter of the *Ethics*.

Perhaps the truest way of conceiving Aristotle's meaning here is to regard a moral virtue as a form of obedience to a maxim or rule of conduct accepted by the agent as valid for a class of recurrent situations in human life. Such obedience requires knowledge of the rule and acceptance of it *as the rule* of the agent's own actions, but not necessarily knowledge of its ground or of its systematic connexion with other similarly known and similarly accepted rules. (It may be remarked that the Greek word usually translated "reason," means in almost all cases in the *Ethics* such a rule, and not the faculty which apprehends, formulates, considers them).

The "moral virtues and vices" make up what we call character, and the important questions arise: (1) What is character? and (2) How is it formed? (for character in this sense is not a natural endowment; it is formed or produced). Aristotle deals with these questions in the reverse order. His answers are peculiar and distinctive-not that they are absolutely novel (for they are anticipated in Plato), but that by him they are for the first time distinctly and clearly formulated.

(1.) Character, good or bad, is produced by what Aristotle calls "habituation," that is, it is the result of the repeated doing of acts which have a similar or common quality. Such repetition acting upon natural aptitudes or propensities gradually fixes them in one or other of two opposite directions, giving them a bias towards good or evil. Hence the several acts which determine goodness or badness of character must be done in a certain way, and thus the formation of good character requires discipline and direction from without. Not that the agent himself contributes nothing to the formation of his character, but that at first he needs guidance. The point is not so much that the process cannot be safely left to Nature, but that it cannot be entrusted to merely intellectual instruction. The process is one of assimilation, largely by imitation and under direction and control. The result is a growing understanding of what is done, a choice of it for its own sake, a fixity and steadiness of purpose. Right acts and feelings become, through habit, easier and more pleasant, and the doing of them a "second nature." The agent acquires the power of doing them freely, willingly, more and more "of himself."

But what are "right" acts? In the first place, they are those that conform to a rule-to the right rule, and ultimately to reason. The Greeks never waver from the conviction that in the end moral conduct is essentially reasonable conduct. But there is a more significant way of describing their "rightness," and here for the first time Aristotle introduces his famous "Doctrine of the Mean." Reasoning from the analogy of "right" physical acts, he pronounces that rightness always means adaptation or adjustment to the special requirements of a situation. To this adjustment he gives a quantitative interpretation. To do (or to feel) what is right in a given situation is to do or to feel just the amount required-neither more nor less: to do wrong is to do or to feel too much or too little-to fall short of or over-shoot, "a mean" determined by the situation. The repetition of acts which lie in the mean is the cause of the formation of each and every "goodness of character," and for this "rules" can be given.

(2) What then is a "moral virtue," the result of such a process duly directed? It is no mere mood of feeling, no mere liability to emotion, no mere natural aptitude or endowment, it is a permanent *state* of the agent's self, or, as we might in modern phrase put it, of his will, it consists in a steady self-imposed obedience to a rule of action in certain situations which frequently recur in human life. The rule prescribes the control and regulation within limits of the agent's natural impulses to act and feel thus and thus. The situations fall into groups which constitute the "fields" of the several "moral virtues", for each there is a rule, conformity to which secures rightness in the individual acts. Thus the moral ideal appears as a code of rules, accepted by the agent, but as yet *to him* without rational justification and without system or unity. But the rules prescribe no mechanical uniformity: each within its limits permits variety, and the exactly right amount adopted to the requirements of the individual situation (and every actual situation is individual) must be determined by the intuition of the moment. There is no attempt to reduce the rich possibilities of right action to a single monotonous type. On the contrary, there are acknowledged to be many forms of moral virtue, and there is a long list of them, with their correlative vices enumerated.

The Doctrine of the Mean here takes a form in which it has impressed subsequent thinkers, but which has less importance than is usually ascribed to it. In the "Table of the Virtues and Vices," each of the virtues is flanked by two opposite vices, which are respectively the excess and defect of that which in due measure constitutes the virtue. Aristotle tries to show that this is the case in regard to every virtue named and recognised as such, but his treatment is often forced and the endeavour is not very successful. Except as a convenient principle of arrangement of the various forms of praiseworthy or blameworthy characters, generally acknowledged as such by Greek opinion, this form of the doctrine is of no great significance.

Books III-V are occupied with a survey of the moral virtues and vices. These seem to have been undertaken in order to verify in detail the general account, but this aim is not kept steadily in view. Nor is there any well-considered principle of classification. What we find is a sort of portrait-gallery of the various types of moral excellence which the Greeks of the author's age admired and strove to encourage. The discussion is full of acute, interesting and sometimes profound observations. Some of the types are those which are and will be admired at all times, but others are connected with peculiar features of Greek life which have now passed away. The most important is that of Justice or the Just Man, to which we may later return. But the discussion is preceded by an attempt to elucidate some difficult and obscure points in the general account of moral virtue and action (Book III, cc. i-v). This section is concerned with the notion of Responsibility. The discussion designedly excludes what we may call the metaphysical issues of the problem, which here present themselves, it moves on the level of thought of the practical man, the statesman, and the legislator. Coercion and ignorance of relevant circumstances render acts involuntary and exempt their doer from responsibility, otherwise the act is voluntary and the agent responsible, choice or preference of what is done, and inner consent to the deed, are to be presumed. Neither passion nor ignorance of the right rule can extenuate responsibility. But there is a difference between acts done voluntarily and acts done of *set* choice or purpose. The latter imply Deliberation. Deliberation involves thinking, thinking out means to ends: in deliberate acts the whole nature of the agent consents to and enters into the act, and in a peculiar sense they are his, they *are* him in action, and the most significant evidence of what he is. Aristotle is unable wholly to avoid allusion to the metaphysical difficulties and what he does here say upon them is obscure and unsatisfactory. But he insists upon the importance in moral action of the agent's inner consent, and on the reality of his individual responsibility. For his present purpose the metaphysical difficulties are irrelevant.

The treatment of Justice in Book V has always been a source of great difficulty to students of the *Ethics*. Almost more than any other part of the work it has exercised influence upon mediæval and modern thought upon the subject. The distinctions and divisions have become part of the stock-in-trade of would be philosophic jurists. And yet, oddly enough, most of these distinctions have been misunderstood and the whole purport of the discussion misconceived. Aristotle is here dealing with justice in a restricted sense viz. as that special goodness of character which is required of every adult citizen and which can be produced by early discipline or habituation. It is the temper or habitual attitude demanded of the citizen for the due exercise of his functions as taking part in the administration of the civic community-as a member of the judicature and executive. The Greek citizen was only exceptionally, and at rare intervals if ever, a law-maker while at any moment he might be called upon to act as a judge (juryman or arbitrator) or as an administrator. For the work of a legislator far more than the moral virtue of justice or fairmindedness was necessary, these were requisite to the rarer and higher "intellectual virtue" of practical wisdom. Then here, too, the discussion moves on a low level, and the raising of fundamental problems is excluded. Hence "distributive justice" is concerned not with the large question of the distribution of political power and privileges among the constituent members or classes of the state but with the smaller questions of the distribution among those of casual gains and even with the division among private claimants of a common fund or inheritance, while "corrective justice" is concerned solely with the management of legal redress. The whole treatment is confused by the unhappy attempt to give a precise mathematical form to the principles of justice in the various fields distinguished. Still it remains an interesting first endeavour to give greater exactness to some of the leading conceptions of jurisprudence.

Book VI appears to have in view two aims: (1) to describe goodness of intellect and discover its highest form or forms; (2) to show how this is related to goodness of character, and so to conduct generally. As all thinking is either theoretical or practical, goodness of intellect has *two* supreme forms-Theoretical and Practical Wisdom. The first, which apprehends the eternal laws of the universe, has no direct relation to human conduct: the second is identical with that master science of human life of which the whole treatise, consisting of the *Ethics* and the *Politics*, is an exposition. It is this science which supplies the right rules of conduct. Taking them as they emerge in and from practical experience, it formulates them more precisely and organises them into a system where they are all seen to converge upon happiness. The mode in which such knowledge manifests itself is in the power to show that such and such rules of action follow from the very nature of the end or good for man. It presupposes and starts from a clear conception of the end and the wish for it as conceived, and it proceeds by a deduction which is deliberation writ large. In the man of practical wisdom this process has reached its perfect result, and the code of right rules is apprehended as a system with a single principle and so as something wholly rational or reasonable. He has not on each occasion to seek and find the right rule applicable to the situation, he produces it at once from within himself, and can at need justify it by exhibiting its rationale, *i.e.* , its connection with the end. This is the consummate form of reason applied to conduct, but there are minor forms of it, less independent or original, but nevertheless of great value, such as the power to think out the proper cause of policy in novel circumstances, or the power to see the proper line of treatment to follow in a court of law.

The form of the thinking which enters into conduct is that which terminates in the production of a rule which declares some means to the end of life. The process presupposes *(a)* a clear and just apprehension of the nature of that end-such as the *Ethics* itself endeavours to supply; *(b)* a correct perception of the conditions of action. *(a)* at least is impossible except to a man whose character has been duly formed by discipline; it arises only in a man who has acquired moral virtue. For such action and feeling as forms bad character, blinds the eye of the soul and corrupts the moral principle, and the place of practical wisdom is taken by that parody of itself which Aristotle calls "cleverness"—the "wisdom" of the unscrupulous man of the world. Thus true practical wisdom and true goodness of character are interdependent; neither is genuinely possible or "completely" present without the other. This is Aristotle's contribution to the discussion of the question, so central in Greek Moral Philosophy, of the relation of the intellectual and the passionate factors in conduct.

Aristotle is not an intuitionist, but he recognises the implication in conduct of a direct and immediate apprehension both of the end and of the character of his circumstances under which it is from moment to moment realised. The directness of such apprehension makes it analogous to sensation or sense-perception; but it is on his view in the end due to the existence or activity in man of that power in him which is the highest thing in his nature, and akin to or identical with the divine nature-mind, or intelligence. It is this which reveals to us what is best for us-the ideal of a happiness which is the object of our real wish and the goal of all our efforts. But beyond and above the practical ideal of what is best *for man* begins to show itself another and still higher ideal-that of a life not distinctively human or in a narrow sense practical, yet capable of being participated in by man even under the actual circumstances of this world. For a time, however, this further and higher ideal is ignored.

The next book (Book VII), is concerned partly with moral conditions, in which the agent seems to rise above the level of moral virtue or fall below that of moral vice, but partly and more largely with conditions in which the agent occupies a middle position between the two. Aristotle's attention is here directed chiefly towards the phenomena of "Incontinence," weakness of will or imperfect self-control. This condition was to the Greeks a matter of only too frequent experience, but it appeared to them peculiarly difficult to understand. How can a man know what is good or best for him, and yet chronically fail to act upon his knowledge? Socrates was driven to the paradox of denying the possibility, but the facts are too strong for him. Knowledge of the right rule may be present, nay the rightfulness of its authority may be acknowledged, and yet time after time it may be disobeyed; the will may be good and yet overmastered by the force of desire, so that the act done is contrary to the agent's will. Nevertheless the act may be the agent's, and the will therefore divided against itself. Aristotle is aware of the seriousness and difficulty of the problem, but in spite of the vividness with which he pictures, and the acuteness with which he analyses, the situation in which such action occurs, it cannot be said that he solves the problem. It is time that he rises above the abstract view of it as a conflict between reason and passion, recognising that passion is involved in the knowledge which in conduct prevails or is overborne, and that the force which leads to the wrong act is not blind or ignorant passion, but always has some reason in it. But he tends to lapse back into the abstraction, and his final account is perplexed and obscure. He finds the source of the phenomenon in the nature of the desire for bodily pleasures, which is not irrational but has something rational in it. Such pleasures are not necessarily or inherently bad, as has sometimes been maintained; on the contrary, they are good, but only in certain amounts or under certain conditions, so that the will is often misled, hesitates, and is lost.

Books VIII and IX (on Friendship) are almost an interruption of the argument. The subject-matter of them was a favourite topic of ancient writers, and the treatment is smoother and more orderly than elsewhere in the *Ethics*. The argument is clear, and may be left without comment to the readers. These books contain a necessary and attractive complement to the somewhat dry account of Greek morality in the preceding books, and there are in them profound reflections on what may be called the metaphysics of friendship or love.

At the beginning of Book X we return to the topic of Pleasure, which is now regarded from a different point of view. In Book VII the antagonists were those who over-emphasised the irrationality or badness of Pleasure: here it is rather those who so exaggerate its value as to confuse or identify it with the good or Happiness. But there is offered us in this section much more than criticism of the errors of others. Answers are given both to the psychological question, "What is Pleasure?" and to the ethical question, "What is its value?" Pleasure, we are told, is the natural concomitant and index of perfect activity, distinguishable but inseparable from it—"the activity of a subject at its best acting upon an object at its best." It is therefore always and in itself a good, but its value rises and falls with that of the activity with which it is conjoined, and which it intensifies and perfects. Hence it follows that the highest and best pleasures are those which accompany the highest and best activity.

Pleasure is, therefore, a necessary element in the best life, but it is not the whole of it nor the principal ingredient. The value of a life depends upon the nature and worth of the activity which it involves; given the maximum of full free action, the maximum of pleasure necessary follows. But on what sort of life is such activity possible? This leads us back to the question, What is Happiness? In what life can man find the fullest satisfaction for his desires? To this question Aristotle gives an answer which cannot but surprise us after what has preceded. True Happiness, great satisfaction, cannot be found by man in any form of "practical" life, no, not in the fullest and freest exercise possible of the "moral virtues," not in the life of the citizen or of the great soldier or statesman. To seek it there is to court failure and disappointment. It is to be found in the life of the onlooker, the disinterested spectator; or, to put it more distinctly, "in the life of the philosopher, the life of scientific and philosophic contemplation." The highest and most satisfying form of life possible to man is "the contemplative life"; it is only in a secondary sense and for those incapable of their life, that the practical or moral ideal is the best. It is time that such a life is not distinctively human, but it is the privilege of man to partake in it, and such participation, at however rare intervals and for however short a period, is the highest Happiness which human life can offer. All other activities have value only because and in so far as they render *this* life possible.

But it must not be forgotten that Aristotle conceives of this life as one of intense activity or energising: it is just this which gives it its supremacy. In spite of the almost religious fervour with which he speaks of it ("the most orthodox of his disciples" paraphrases his meaning by describing its content as "the service and vision of God"), it is clear that he identified it with the life of the philosopher, as he understood it, a life of ceaseless intellectual activity in which at least at times all the distractions and disturbances inseparable from practical life seemed to disappear and become as nothing. This ideal was partly an inheritance from the more ardent idealism of his master Plato, but partly it was the expression of personal experience.

The nobility of this ideal cannot be questioned; the conception of the end of man or a life lived for truth-of a life blissfully absorbed in the vision of truth-is a lofty and inspiring one. But we cannot resist certain criticisms upon its presentation by Aristotle: (1) the relation of it to the lower ideal of practice is left somewhat obscure; (2) it is described in such a way as renders its realisation possible only to a gifted few, and under exceptional circumstances; (3) it seems in various ways, as regards its content, to be unnecessarily and unjustifiably limited. But it must be borne in mind that this is a first endeavour to determine its principle, and that similar failures have attended the attempts to describe the "religious" or the "spiritual" ideals of life, which have continually been suggested by the apparently inherent limitations of the "practical" or "moral" life, which is the subject of Moral Philosophy. The Moral Ideal to those who have most deeply reflected on it leads to the thought of an Ideal beyond and above it, which alone gives it meaning, but which seems to escape from definite conception by man. The richness and variety of this Ideal ceaselessly invite, but as ceaselessly defy, our attempts to imprison it in a definite formula or portray it in detailed imagination. Yet the thought of it is and remains inexpungable from our minds.

This conception of the best life is not forgotten in the *Politics*. The end of life in the state is itself well-living and well-doing—a life which helps to produce the best life. The great agency in the production of such life is the State operating through Law, which is Reason backed by Force. For its greatest efficiency there is required the development of a science of legislation. The main drift of what he says here is that the most desirable thing would be that the best reason of the community should be embodied in its laws. But so far as that is not possible, it still is true that anyone who would make himself and others better must become a miniature legislator-must study the general principles of law, morality, and education. The conception of πολιτική [Greek: politikae] with which he opened the *Ethics* would serve as a guide to a father educating his children as well as to the legislator legislating for the state. Finding in his predecessors no developed doctrine on this subject, Aristotle proposes himself to undertake the construction of it, and sketches in advance the programme of the *Politics* in the concluding sentence of the *Ethics*. His ultimate object is to answer the questions, What is the best form of Polity, how should each be constituted, and what laws and customs should it adopt and employ? Not till this answer is given will "the philosophy of human affairs" be complete.

On looking back it will be seen that the discussion of the central topic of the nature and formation of character has expanded into a Philosophy of Human Conduct, merging at its beginning and end into metaphysics. The result is a Moral Philosophy set against a background of Political Theory and general Philosophy. The most characteristic features of this Moral Philosophy are due to the fact of its essentially teleological view of human life and action: (1) Every human activity, but especially every human practical activity, is directed towards a simple End discoverable by reflection, and this End is conceived of as the object of universal human desire, as something to be enjoyed, not as something which ought to be done or enacted. Anstotle's Moral Philosophy is not hedonistic but it is eudæmonistic; the end is the enjoyment of Happiness, not the fulfilment of Duty. (2) Every human practical activity derives its value from its efficiency as a means to that end, it is good or bad, right or wrong, as it conduces or fails to conduce to Happiness. Thus his Moral Philosophy is essentially utilitarian or prudential. Right action presupposes Thought or Thinking, partly on the development of a clearer and distincter conception of the end of desire, partly as the deduction from that of rules which state the normally effective conditions of its realisation. The thinking involved in right conduct is calculation-calculation of means to an end fixed by nature and foreknowable. Action itself is at its best just the realisation of a scheme preconceived and thought out beforehand, commending itself by its inherent attractiveness or promise of enjoyment.

This view has the great advantage of exhibiting morality as essentially reasonable, but the accompanying disadvantage of lowering it into a somewhat prosaic and unideal Prudentialism, nor is it saved from this by the tacking on to it, by a sort of after-thought, of the second and higher Ideal-an addition which ruins the coherence of the account without really transmuting its substance. The source of our dissatisfaction with the whole theory lies deeper than in its tendency to identify the end with the maximum of enjoyment or satisfaction, or to regard the goodness or badness of acts and feelings as lying solely in their efficacy to produce such a result. It arises from the application to morality of the distinction of means and end. For this distinction, for all its plausibility and usefulness in ordinary thought and speech, cannot finally be maintained. In morality-and this is vital to its character-everything is both means and end, and so neither in distinction or separation, and all thinking about it which presupposes the finality of this distinction wanders into misconception and error. The thinking which really matters in conduct is not a thinking which imaginatively forecasts ideals which promise to fulfil desire, or calculates means to their attainment-that is sometimes useful, sometimes harmful, and always subordinate, but thinking which reveals to the agent the situation in which he is to act, both, that is, the universal situation on which as man he always and everywhere stands, and the ever-varying and ever-novel situation in which he as this individual, here and now, finds himself. In such knowledge of given or historic fact lie the natural determinants of his conduct, in such knowledge alone lies the condition of his freedom and his good.

But this does not mean that Moral Philosophy has not still much to learn from Aristotle's *Ethics*. The work still remains one of the best introductions to a study of its important subject-matter; it spreads before us a view of the relevant facts, it reduces them to manageable compass and order, it raises some of the central problems, and makes acute and valuable suggestions towards their solution. Above all, it perpetually incites to renewed and independent reflection upon them.

J. A. SMITH

Book One

1

Every art and every inquiry, and similarly every action and pursuit, is thought to aim at some good; and for this reason the good has rightly been declared to be that at which all things aim. But a certain difference is found among ends; some are activities, others are products apart from the activities that produce them. Where there are ends apart from the actions, it is the nature of the products to be better than the activities. Now, as there are many actions, arts, and sciences, their ends also are many; the end of the medical art is health, that of shipbuilding a vessel, that of strategy victory, that of economics wealth. But where such arts fall under a single capacity- as bridle-making and the other arts concerned with the equipment of horses fall under the art of riding, and this and every military action under strategy, in the same way other arts fall under yet others- in all of these the ends of the master arts are to be preferred to all the subordinate ends; for it is for the sake of the former that the latter are pursued. It makes no difference whether the activities themselves are the ends of the actions, or something else apart from the activities, as in the case of the sciences just mentioned.

2

If, then, there is some end of the things we do, which we desire for its own sake (everything else being desired for the sake of this), and if we do not choose everything for the sake of something else (for at that rate the process would go on to infinity, so that our desire would be empty and vain), clearly this must be the good and the chief good. Will not the knowledge of it, then, have a great influence on life? Shall we not, like archers who have a mark to aim at, be more likely to hit upon what is right? If so, we must try, in outline at least, to determine what it is, and of which of the sciences or capacities it is the object. It would seem to belong to the most authoritative art and that which is most truly the master art. And politics appears to be of this nature; for it is this that ordains which of the sciences should be studied in a state, and which each class of citizens should learn and up to what point they should learn them; and we see even the most highly esteemed of capacities to fall under this, e.g. strategy, economics, rhetoric; now, since politics uses the rest of the sciences, and since, again, it legislates as to what we are to do and what we are to abstain from, the end of this science must include those of the others, so that this end must be the good for man. For even if the end is the same for a single man and for a state, that of the state seems at all events something greater and more complete whether to attain or to preserve; though it is worth while to attain the end merely for one man, it is finer and more godlike to attain it for a nation or for city-states. These, then, are the ends at which our inquiry aims, since it is political science, in one sense of that term.

3

Our discussion will be adequate if it has as much clearness as the subject-matter admits of, for precision is not to be sought for alike in all discussions, any more than in all the products of the crafts. Now fine and just actions, which political science investigates, admit of much variety and fluctuation of opinion, so that they may be thought to exist only by convention, and not by nature. And goods also give rise to a similar fluctuation because they bring harm to many people; for before now men have been undone by reason of their wealth, and others by reason of their courage. We must be content, then, in speaking of such subjects and with such premisses to indicate the truth roughly and in outline, and in speaking about things which are only for the most part true and with premisses of the same kind to reach conclusions that are no better. In the same spirit, therefore, should each type of statement be received; for it is the mark of an educated man to look for precision in each class of things just so far as the nature of the subject admits; it is evidently equally foolish to accept probable reasoning from a mathematician and to demand from a rhetorician scientific proofs.

Now each man judges well the things he knows, and of these he is a good judge. And so the man who has been educated in a subject is a good judge of that subject, and the man who has received an all-round education is a good judge in general. Hence a young man is not a proper hearer of lectures on political science; for he is inexperienced in the actions that occur in life, but its discussions start from these and are about these; and, further, since he tends to follow his passions, his study will be vain and unprofitable, because the end aimed at is not knowledge but action. And it makes no difference whether he is young in years or youthful in character; the defect does not depend on time, but on his living, and pursuing each successive object, as passion directs. For to such persons, as to the incontinent, knowledge brings no profit; but to those who desire and act in accordance with a rational principle knowledge about such matters will be of great benefit.

These remarks about the student, the sort of treatment to be expected, and the purpose of the inquiry, may be taken as our preface.

4

Let us resume our inquiry and state, in view of the fact that all knowledge and every pursuit aims at some good, what it is that we say political science aims at and what is the highest of all goods achievable by action. Verbally there is very general agreement; for both the general run of men and people of superior refinement say that it is happiness, and identify living well and doing well with being happy; but with regard to what happiness is they differ, and the many do not give the same account as the wise. For the former think it is some plain and obvious thing, like pleasure, wealth, or honour; they differ, however, from one another- and often even the same man identifies it with different things, with health when he is ill, with wealth when he is poor; but, conscious of their ignorance, they admire those who proclaim some great ideal that is above their comprehension. Now some thought that apart from these many goods there is another which is self-subsistent and causes the goodness of all these as well. To examine all the opinions that have been held were perhaps somewhat fruitless; enough to examine those that are most prevalent or that seem to be arguable.

Let us not fail to notice, however, that there is a difference between arguments from and those to the first principles. For Plato, too, was right in raising this question and asking, as he used to do, 'are we on the way from or to the first principles?' There is a difference, as there is in a race-course between the course from the judges to the turning-point and the way back. For, while we must begin with what is known, things are objects of knowledge in two senses- some to us, some without qualification. Presumably, then, we must begin with things known to us. Hence any one who is to listen intelligently to lectures about what is noble and just, and generally, about the subjects of political science must have been brought up in good habits. For the fact is the starting-point, and if this is sufficiently plain to him, he will not at the start need the reason as well; and the man who has been well brought up has or can easily get startingpoints. And as for him who neither has nor can get them, let him hear the words of Hesiod:

Far best is he who knows all things himself; Good, he that hearkens when men counsel right; But he who neither knows, nor lays to heart Another's wisdom, is a useless wight.

5

Let us, however, resume our discussion from the point at which we digressed. To judge from the lives that men lead, most men, and men of the most vulgar type, seem (not without some ground) to identify the good, or happiness, with pleasure; which is the reason why they love the life of enjoyment. For there are, we may say, three prominent types of life- that just mentioned, the political, and thirdly the contemplative life. Now the mass of mankind are evidently quite slavish in their tastes, preferring a life suitable to beasts, but they get some ground for their view from the fact that many of those in high places share the tastes of Sardanapallus. A consideration of the prominent types of life shows that people of superior refinement and of active disposition identify happiness with honour; for this is, roughly speaking, the end of the political life. But it seems too superficial to be what we are looking for, since it is thought to depend on those who bestow honour rather than on him who receives it, but the good we divine to be something proper to a man and not easily taken from him. Further, men seem to pursue honour in order that they may be assured of their goodness; at least it is by men of practical wisdom that they seek to be honoured, and among those who know them, and on the ground of their virtue; clearly, then, according to them, at any rate, virtue is better. And perhaps one might even suppose this to be, rather than honour, the end of the political life. But even this appears somewhat incomplete; for possession of virtue seems actually compatible with being asleep, or with lifelong inactivity, and, further, with the greatest sufferings and misfortunes; but a man who was living so no one would call happy, unless he were maintaining a thesis at all costs. But enough of this; for the subject has been sufficiently treated even in the current discussions. Third comes the contemplative life, which we shall consider later.

The life of money-making is one undertaken under compulsion, and wealth is evidently not the good we are seeking; for it is merely useful and for the sake of something else. And so one might rather take the aforenamed objects to be ends; for they are loved for themselves. But it is evident that not even these are ends; yet many arguments have been thrown away in support of them. Let us leave this subject, then.

6

We had perhaps better consider the universal good and discuss thoroughly what is meant by it, although such an inquiry is made an uphill one by the fact that the Forms have been introduced by friends of our own. Yet it would perhaps be thought to be better, indeed to be our duty, for the sake of maintaining the truth even to destroy what touches us closely, especially as we are philosophers or lovers of wisdom; for, while both are dear, piety requires us to honour truth above our friends.

The men who introduced this doctrine did not posit Ideas of classes within which they recognized priority and posteriority (which is the reason why they did not maintain the existence of an Idea embracing all numbers); but the term 'good' is used both in the category of substance and in that of quality and in that of relation, and that which is per se, i.e. substance, is prior in nature to the relative (for the latter is like an off shoot and accident of being); so that there could not be a common Idea set over all these goods. Further, since 'good' has as many senses as 'being' (for it is predicated both in the category of substance, as of God and of reason, and in quality, i.e. of the virtues, and in quantity, i.e. of that which is moderate, and in relation, i.e. of the useful, and in time, i.e. of the right opportunity, and in place, i.e. of the right locality and the like), clearly it cannot be something universally present in all cases and single; for then it could not have been predicated in all the categories but in one only. Further, since of the things answering to one Idea there is one science, there would have been one science of all the goods; but as it is there are many sciences even of the things that fall under one category, e.g. of opportunity, for opportunity in war is studied by strategics and in disease by medicine, and the moderate in food is studied by medicine and in exercise by the science of gymnastics. And one might ask the question, what in the world they mean by 'a thing itself', is (as is the case) in 'man himself' and in a particular man the account of man is one and the same. For in so far as they are man, they will in no respect differ; and if this is so, neither will 'good itself' and particular goods, in so far as they are good. But again it will not be good any the more for being eternal, since that which lasts long is no whiter than that which perishes in a day. The Pythagoreans seem to give a more plausible account of the good, when they place the one in the column of goods; and it is they that Speusippus seems to have followed.

But let us discuss these matters elsewhere; an objection to what we have said, however, may be discerned in the fact that the Platonists have not been speaking about all goods, and that the goods that are pursued and loved for themselves are called good by reference to a single Form, while those which tend to produce or to preserve these somehow or to prevent their contraries are called so by reference to these, and in a secondary sense. Clearly, then, goods must be spoken of in two ways, and some must be good in themselves, the others by reason of these. Let us separate, then, things good in themselves from things useful, and consider whether the former are called good by reference to a single Idea. What sort of goods would one call good in themselves? Is it those that are pursued even when isolated from others, such as intelligence, sight, and certain pleasures and honours? Certainly, if we pursue these also for the sake of something else, yet one would place them among things good in themselves. Or is nothing other than the Idea of good good in itself? In that case the Form will be empty. But if the things we have named are also things good in themselves, the account of the good will have to appear as something identical in them all, as that of whiteness is identical in snow and in white lead. But of honour, wisdom, and pleasure, just in respect of their goodness, the accounts are distinct and diverse. The good, therefore, is not some common element answering to one Idea.

But what then do we mean by the good? It is surely not like the things that only chance to have the same name. Are goods one, then, by being derived from one good or by all contributing to one good, or are they rather one by analogy? Certainly as sight is in the body, so is reason in the soul, and so on in other cases. But perhaps these subjects had better be dismissed for the present; for perfect precision about them would be more appropriate to another branch of philosophy. And similarly with regard to the Idea; even if there is some one good which is universally predicable of goods or is capable of separate and independent existence, clearly it could not be achieved or attained by man; but we are now seeking something attainable. Perhaps, however, some one might think it worth while to recognize this with a view to the goods that are attainable and achievable; for having this as a sort of pattern we shall know better the goods that are good for us, and if we know them shall attain them. This argument has some plausibility, but seems to clash with the procedure of the sciences; for all of these, though they aim at some good and seek to supply the deficiency of it, leave on one side the knowledge of the good. Yet that all the exponents of the arts should be ignorant of, and should not even seek, so great an aid is not probable. It is hard, too, to see how a weaver or a carpenter will be benefited in regard to his own craft by knowing this 'good itself', or how the man who has viewed the Idea itself will be a better doctor or general thereby. For a doctor seems not even to study health in this way, but the health of man, or perhaps rather the health of a particular man; it is individuals that he is healing. But enough of these topics.

7

Let us again return to the good we are seeking, and ask what it can be. It seems different in different actions and arts; it is different in medicine, in strategy, and in the other arts likewise. What then is the good of each? Surely that for whose sake everything else is done. In medicine this is health, in strategy victory, in architecture a house, in any other sphere something else, and in every action and pursuit the end; for it is for the sake of this that all men do whatever else they do. Therefore, if there is an end for all that we do, this will be the good achievable by action, and if there are more than one, these will be the goods achievable by action.

So the argument has by a different course reached the same point; but we must try to state this even more clearly. Since there are evidently more than one end, and we choose some of these (e.g. wealth, flutes, and in general instruments) for the sake of something else, clearly not all ends are final ends; but the chief good is evidently something final. Therefore, if there is only one final end, this will be what we are seeking, and if there are more than one, the most final of these will be what we are seeking. Now we call that which is in itself worthy of pursuit more final than that which is worthy of pursuit for the sake of something else, and that which is never desirable for the sake of something else more final than the things that are desirable both in themselves and for the sake of that other thing, and therefore we call final without qualification that which is always desirable in itself and never for the sake of something else.

Now such a thing happiness, above all else, is held to be; for this we choose always for self and never for the sake of something else, but honour, pleasure, reason, and every virtue we choose indeed for themselves (for if nothing resulted from them we should still choose each of them), but we choose them also for the sake of happiness, judging that by means of them we shall be happy. Happiness, on the other hand, no one chooses for the sake of these, nor, in general, for anything other than itself.

From the point of view of self-sufficiency the same result seems to follow; for the final good is thought to be self-sufficient. Now by self-sufficient we do not mean that which is sufficient for a man by himself, for one who lives a solitary life, but also for parents, children, wife, and in general for his friends and fellow citizens, since man is born for citizenship. But some limit must be set to this; for if we extend our requirement to ancestors and descendants and friends' friends we are in for an infinite series. Let us examine this question, however, on another occasion; the self-sufficient we now define as that which when isolated makes life desirable and lacking in nothing; and such we think happiness to be; and further we think it most desirable of all things, without being counted as one good thing among others- if it were so counted it would clearly be made more desirable by the addition of even the least of goods; for that which is added becomes an excess of goods, and of goods the greater is always more desirable. Happiness, then, is something final and self-sufficient, and is the end of action.

Presumably, however, to say that happiness is the chief good seems a platitude, and a clearer account of what it is still desired. This might perhaps be given, if we could first ascertain the function of man. For just as for a flute-player, a sculptor, or an artist, and, in general, for all things that have a function or activity, the good and the 'well' is thought to reside in the function, so would it seem to be for man, if he has a function. Have the carpenter, then, and the tanner certain functions or activities, and has man none? Is he born without a function? Or as eye, hand, foot, and in general each of the parts evidently has a function, may one lay it down that man similarly has a function apart from all these? What then can this be? Life seems to be common even to plants, but we are seeking what is peculiar to man. Let us exclude, therefore, the life of nutrition and growth. Next there would be a life of perception, but it also seems to be common even to the horse, the ox, and every animal. There remains, then, an active life of the element that has a rational principle; of this, one part has such a principle in the sense of being obedient to one, the other in the sense of possessing one and exercising thought. And, as 'life of the rational element' also has two meanings, we must state that life in the sense of activity is what we mean; for this seems to be the more proper sense of the term. Now if the function of man is an activity of soul which follows or implies a rational principle, and if we say 'so-and-so-and 'a good so-and-so' have a function which is the same in kind, e.g. a lyre, and a good lyre-player, and so without qualification in all cases, eminence in respect of goodness being idded to the name of the function (for the function of a lyre-player is to play the lyre, and that of a good lyre-player is to do so well): if this is the case, and we state the function of man to be a certain kind of life, and this to be an activity or actions of the soul implying a rational principle, and the function of a good man to be the good and noble performance of these, and if any action is well performed when it is performed in accordance with the appropriate excellence: if this is the case, human good turns out to be activity of soul in accordance with virtue, and if there are more than one virtue, in accordance with the best and most complete.

But we must add 'in a complete life.' For one swallow does not make a summer, nor does one day; and so too one day, or a short time, does not make a man blessed and happy.

Let this serve as an outline of the good; for we must presumably first sketch it roughly, and then later fill in the details. But it would seem that any one is capable of carrying on and articulating what has once been well outlined, and that time is a good discoverer or partner in such a work; to which facts the advances of the arts are due; for any one can add what is lacking. And we must also remember what has been said before, and not look for precision in all things alike, but in each class of things such precision as accords with the subject-matter, and so much as is appropriate to the inquiry. For a carpenter and a geometer investigate the right angle in different ways; the former does so in so far as the right angle is useful for his work, while the latter inquires what it is or what sort of thing it is; for he is a spectator of the truth. We must act in the same way, then, in all other matters as well, that our main task may not be subordinated to minor questions. Nor must we demand the cause in all matters alike; it is enough in some cases that the fact be well established, as in the case of the first principles; the fact is the primary thing or first principle. Now of first principles we see some by induction, some by perception, some by a certain habituation, and others too in other ways. But each set of principles we must try to investigate in the natural way, and we must take pains to state them definitely, since they have a great influence on what follows. For the beginning is thought to be more than half of the whole, and many of the questions we ask are cleared up by it.

8

We must consider it, however, in the light not only of our conclusion and our premisses, but also of what is commonly said about it; for with a true view all the data harmonize, but with a false one the facts soon clash. Now goods have been divided into three classes, and some are described as external, others as relating to soul or to body; we call those that relate to soul most properly and truly goods, and psychical actions and activities we class as relating to soul. Therefore our account must be sound, at least according to this view, which is an old one and agreed on by philosophers. It is correct also in that we identify the end with certain actions and activities; for thus it falls among goods of the soul and not among external goods. Another belief which harmonizes with our account is that the happy man lives well and does well; for we have practically defined happiness as a sort of good life and good action. The characteristics that are looked for in happiness seem also, all of them, to belong to what we have defined happiness as being. For some identify happiness with virtue, some with practical wisdom, others with a kind of philosophic wisdom, others with these, or one of these, accompanied by pleasure or not without pleasure; while others include also external prosperity. Now some of these views have been held by many men and men of old, others by a few eminent persons; and it is not probable that either of these should be entirely mistaken, but rather that they should be right in at least some one respect or even in most respects.

With those who identify happiness with virtue or some one virtue our account is in harmony; for to virtue belongs virtuous activity. But it makes, perhaps, no small difference whether we place the chief good in possession or in use, in state of mind or in activity. For the state of mind may exist without producing any good result, as in a man who is asleep or in some other way quite inactive, but the activity cannot; for one who has the activity will of necessity be acting, and acting well. And as in the Olympic Games it is not the most beautiful and the strongest that are crowned but those who compete (for it is some of these that are victorious), so those who act win, and rightly win, the noble and good things in life.

Their life is also in itself pleasant. For pleasure is a state of soul, and to each man that which he is said to be a lover of is pleasant; e.g. not only is a horse pleasant to the lover of horses, and a spectacle to the lover of sights, but also in the same way just acts are pleasant to the lover of justice and in general virtuous acts to the lover of virtue. Now for most men their pleasures are in conflict with one another because these are not by nature pleasant, but the lovers of what is noble find pleasant the things that are by nature pleasant; and virtuous actions are such, so that these are pleasant for such men as well as in their own nature. Their life, therefore, has no further need of pleasure as a sort of adventitious charm, but has its pleasure in itself. For, besides what we have said, the man who does not rejoice in noble actions is not even good; since no one would call a man just who did not enjoy acting justly, nor any man liberal who did not enjoy liberal actions; and similarly in all other cases. If this is so, virtuous actions must be in themselves pleasant. But they are also good and noble, and have each of these attributes in the highest degree, since the good man judges well about these attributes; his judgement is such as we have described. Happiness then is the best, noblest, and most pleasant thing in the world, and these attributes are not severed as in the inscription at Delos-

Most noble is that which is justest, and best is health; But pleasantest is it to win what we love.

For all these properties belong to the best activities; and these, or one- the best- of these, we identify with happiness.

Yet evidently, as we said, it needs the external goods as well; for it is impossible, or not easy, to do noble acts without the proper equipment. In many actions we use friends and riches and political power as instruments; and there are some things the lack of which takes the lustre from happiness, as good birth, goodly children, beauty; for the man who is very ugly in appearance or ill-born or solitary and childless is not very likely to be happy, and perhaps a man would be still less likely if he had thoroughly bad children or friends or had lost good children or friends by death. As we said, then, happiness seems to need this sort of prosperity in addition; for which reason some identify happiness with good fortune, though others identify it with virtue.

9

For this reason also the question is asked, whether happiness is to be acquired by learning or by habituation or some other sort of training, or comes in virtue of some divine providence or again by chance. Now if there is any gift of the gods to men, it is reasonable that happiness should be god-given, and most surely god-given of all human things inasmuch as it is the best. But this question would perhaps be more appropriate to another inquiry; happiness seems, however, even if it is not god-sent but comes as a result of virtue and some process of learning or training, to be among the most godlike things; for that which is the prize and end of virtue seems to be the best thing in the world, and something godlike and blessed.

It will also on this view be very generally shared; for all who are not maimed as regards their potentiality for virtue may win it by a certain kind of study and care. But if it is better to be happy thus than by chance, it is reasonable that the facts should be so, since everything that depends on the action of nature is by nature as good as it can be, and similarly everything that depends on art or any rational cause, and especially if it depends on the best of all causes. To entrust to chance what is greatest and most noble would be a very defective arrangement.

The answer to the question we are asking is plain also from the definition of happiness; for it has been said to be a virtuous activity of soul, of a certain kind. Of the remaining goods, some must necessarily pre-exist as conditions of happiness, and others are naturally co-operative and useful as instruments. And this will be found to agree with what we said at the outset; for we stated the end of political science to be the best end, and political science spends most of its pains on making the citizens to be of a certain character, viz. good and capable of noble acts.

It is natural, then, that we call neither ox nor horse nor any other of the animals happy; for none of them is capable of sharing in such activity. For this reason also a boy is not happy; for he is not yet capable of such acts, owing to his age; and boys who are called happy are being congratulated by reason of the hopes we have for them. For there is required, as we said, not only complete virtue but also a complete life, since many changes occur in life, and all manner of chances, and the most prosperous may fall into great misfortunes in old age, as is told of Priam in the Trojan Cycle; and one who has experienced such chances and has ended wretchedly no one calls happy.

10

Must no one at all, then, be called happy while he lives; must we, as Solon says, see the end? Even if we are to lay down this doctrine, is it also the case that a man is happy when he is dead? Or is not this quite absurd, especially for us who say that happiness is an activity? But if we do not call the dead man happy, and if Solon does not mean this, but that one can then safely call a man blessed as being at last beyond evils and misfortunes, this also affords matter for discussion; for both evil and good are thought to exist for a dead man, as much as for one who is alive but not aware of them; e.g. honours and dishonours and the good or bad fortunes of children and in general of descendants. And this also presents a problem; for though a man has lived happily up to old age and has had a death worthy of his life, many reverses may befall his descendants- some of them may be good and attain the life they deserve, while with others the opposite may be the case; and clearly too the degrees of relationship between them and their ancestors may vary indefinitely. It would be odd, then, if the dead man were to share in these changes and become at one time happy, at another wretched; while it would also be odd if the fortunes of the descendants did not for some time have some effect on the happiness of their ancestors.

But we must return to our first difficulty; for perhaps by a consideration of it our present problem might be solved. Now if we must see the end and only then call a man happy, not as being happy but as having been so before, surely this is a paradox, that when he is happy the attribute that belongs to him is not to be truly predicated of him because we do not wish to call living men happy, on account of the changes that may befall them, and because we have assumed happiness to be something permanent and by no means easily changed, while a single man may suffer many turns of fortune's wheel. For clearly if we were to keep pace with his fortunes, we should often call the same man happy and again wretched, making the happy man out to be chameleon and insecurely based. Or is this keeping pace with his fortunes quite wrong? Success or failure in life does not depend on these, but human life, as we said, needs these as mere additions, while virtuous activities or their opposites are what constitute happiness or the reverse.

The question we have now discussed confirms our definition. For no function of man has so much permanence as virtuous activities (these are thought to be more durable even than knowledge of the sciences), and of these themselves the most valuable are more durable because those who are happy spend their life most readily and most continuously in these; for this seems to be the reason why we do not forget them. The attribute in question, then, will belong to the happy man, and he will be happy throughout his life; for always, or by preference to everything else, he will be engaged in virtuous action and contemplation, and he will bear the chances of life most nobly and altogether decorously, if he is 'truly good' and 'foursquare beyond reproach'.

Now many events happen by chance, and events differing in importance; small pieces of good fortune or of its opposite clearly do not weigh down the scales of life one way or the other, but a multitude of great events if they turn out well will make life happier (for not only are they themselves such as to add beauty to life, but the way a man deals with them may be noble and good), while if they turn out ill they crush and maim happiness; for they both bring pain with them and hinder many activities. Yet even in these nobility shines through, when a man bears with resignation many great misfortunes, not through insensibility to pain but through nobility and greatness of soul.

If activities are, as we said, what gives life its character, no happy man can become miserable; for he will never do the acts that are hateful and mean. For the man who is truly good and wise, we think, bears all the chances life becomingly and always makes the best of circumstances, as a good general makes the best military use of the army at his command and a good shoemaker makes the best shoes out of the hides that are given him; and so with all other craftsmen. And if this is the case, the happy man can never become miserable; though he will not reach blessedness, if he meet with fortunes like those of Priam.

Nor, again, is he many-coloured and changeable; for neither will he be moved from his happy state easily or by any ordinary misadventures, but only by many great ones, nor, if he has had many great misadventures, will he recover his happiness in a short time, but if at all, only in a long and complete one in which he has attained many splendid successes.

When then should we not say that he is happy who is active in accordance with complete virtue and is sufficiently equipped with external goods, not for some chance period but throughout a complete life? Or must we add 'and who is destined to live thus and die as befits his life'? Certainly the future is obscure to us, while happiness, we claim, is an end and something in every way final. If so, we shall call happy those among living men in whom these conditions are, and are to be, fulfilled- but happy men. So much for these questions.

11

That the fortunes of descendants and of all a man's friends should not affect his happiness at all seems a very unfriendly doctrine, and one opposed to the opinions men hold; but since the events that happen are numerous and admit of all sorts of difference, and some come more near to us and others less so, it seems a long- nay, an infinite- task to discuss each in detail; a general outline will perhaps suffice. If, then, as some of a man's own misadventures have a certain weight and influence on life while others are, as it were, lighter, so too there are differences among the misadventures of our friends taken as a whole, and it makes a difference whether the various suffering befall the living or the dead (much more even than whether lawless and terrible deeds are presupposed in a tragedy or done on the stage), this difference also must be taken into account; or rather, perhaps, the fact that doubt is felt whether the dead share in any good or evil. For it seems, from these considerations, that even if anything whether good or evil penetrates to them, it must be something weak and negligible, either in itself or for them, or if not, at least it must be such in degree and kind as not to make happy those who are not happy nor to take away their blessedness from those who are. The good or bad fortunes of friends, then, seem to have some effects on the dead, but effects of such a kind and degree as neither to make the happy unhappy nor to produce any other change of the kind.

12

These questions having been definitely answered, let us consider whether happiness is among the things that are praised or rather among the things that are prized; for clearly it is not to be placed among potentialities. Everything that is praised seems to be praised because it is of a certain kind and is related somehow to something else; for we praise the just or brave man and in general both the good man and virtue itself because of the actions and functions involved, and we praise the strong man, the good runner, and so on, because he is of a certain kind and is related in a certain way to something good and important. This is clear also from the praises of the gods; for it seems absurd that the gods should be referred to our standard, but this is done because praise involves a reference, to something else. But if if praise is for things such as we have described, clearly what applies to the best things is not praise, but something greater and better, as is indeed obvious; for what we do to the gods and the most godlike of men is to call them blessed and happy. And so too with good things; no one praises happiness as he does justice, but rather calls it blessed, as being something more divine and better.

Eudoxus also seems to have been right in his method of advocating the supremacy of pleasure; he thought that the fact that, though a good, it is not praised indicated it to be better than the things that are praised, and that this is what God and the good are; for by reference to these all other things are judged. Praise is appropriate to virtue, for as a result of virtue men tend to do noble deeds, but encomia are bestowed on acts, whether of the body or of the soul. But perhaps nicety in these matters is more proper to those who have made a study of encomia; to us it is clear from what has been said that happiness is among the things that are prized and perfect. It seems to be so also from the fact that it is a first principle; for it is for the sake of this that we all do all that we do, and the first principle and cause of goods is, we claim, something prized and divine.

13

Since happiness is an activity of soul in accordance with perfect virtue, we must consider the nature of virtue; for perhaps we shall thus see better the nature of happiness. The true student of politics, too, is thought to have studied virtue above all things; for he wishes to make his fellow citizens good and obedient to the laws. As an example of this we have the lawgivers of the Cretans and the Spartans, and any others of the kind that there may have been. And if this inquiry belongs to political science, clearly the pursuit of it will be in accordance with our original plan. But clearly the virtue we must study is human virtue; for the good we were seeking was human good and the happiness human happiness. By human virtue we mean not that of the body but that of the soul; and happiness also we call an activity of soul. But if this is so, clearly the student of politics must know somehow the facts about soul, as the man who is to heal the eyes or the body as a whole must know about the eyes or the body; and all the more since politics is more prized and better than medicine; but even among doctors the best educated spend much labour on acquiring knowledge of the body. The student of politics, then, must study the soul, and must study it with these objects in view, and do so just to the extent which is sufficient for the questions we are discussing; for further precision is perhaps something more laborious than our purposes require.

Some things are said about it, adequately enough, even in the discussions outside our school, and we must use these; e.g. that one element in the soul is irrational and one has a rational principle. Whether these are separated as the parts of the body or of anything divisible are, or are distinct by definition but by nature inseparable, like convex and concave in the circumference of a circle, does not affect the present question.

Of the irrational element one division seems to be widely distributed, and vegetative in its nature, I mean that which causes nutrition and growth; for it is this kind of power of the soul that one must assign to all nurslings and to embryos, and this same power to fullgrown creatures; this is more reasonable than to assign some different power to them. Now the excellence of this seems to be common to all species and not specifically human; for this part or faculty seems to function most in sleep, while goodness and badness are least manifest in sleep (whence comes the saying that the happy are not better off than the wretched for half their lives; and this happens naturally enough, since sleep is an inactivity of the soul in that respect in which it is called good or bad), unless perhaps to a small extent some of the movements actually penetrate to the soul, and in this respect the dreams of good men are better than those of ordinary people. Enough of this subject, however; let us leave the nutritive faculty alone, since it has by its nature no share in human excellence.

There seems to be also another irrational element in the soul-one which in a sense, however, shares in a rational principle. For we praise the rational principle of the continent man and of the incontinent, and the part of their soul that has such a principle, since it urges them aright and towards the best objects; but there is found in them also another element naturally opposed to the rational principle, which fights against and resists that principle. For exactly as paralysed limbs when we intend to move them to the right turn on the contrary to the left, so is it with the soul; the impulses of incontinent people move in contrary directions. But while in the body we see that which moves astray, in the soul we do not. No doubt, however, we must none the less suppose that in the soul too there is something contrary to the rational principle, resisting and opposing it. In what sense it is distinct from the other elements does not concern us. Now even this seems to have a share in a rational principle, as we said; at any rate in the continent man it obeys the rational principle and presumably in the temperate and brave man it is still more obedient; for in him it speaks, on all matters, with the same voice as the rational principle.

Therefore the irrational element also appears to be two-fold. For the vegetative element in no way shares in a rational principle, but the appetitive and in general the desiring element in a sense shares in it, in so far as it listens to and obeys it; this is the sense in which we speak of 'taking account' of one's father or one's friends, not that in which we speak of 'accounting for a mathematical property. That the irrational element is in some sense persuaded by a rational principle is indicated also by the giving of advice and by all reproof and exhortation. And if this element also must be said to have a rational principle, that which has a rational principle (as well as that which has not) will be twofold, one subdivision having it in the strict sense and in itself, and the other having a tendency to obey as one does one's father.

Virtue too is distinguished into kinds in accordance with this difference; for we say that some of the virtues are intellectual and others moral, philosophic wisdom and understanding and practical wisdom being intellectual, liberality and temperance moral. For in speaking about a man's character we do not say that he is wise or has understanding but that he is good-tempered or temperate; yet we praise the wise man also with respect to his state of mind; and of states of mind we call those which merit praise virtues.

Book Two

1

Virtue, then, being of two kinds, intellectual and moral, intellectual virtue in the main owes both its birth and its growth to teaching (for which reason it requires experience and time), while moral virtue comes about as a result of habit, whence also its name (ethike) is one that is formed by a slight variation from the word ethos (habit). From this it is also plain that none of the moral virtues arises in us by nature; for nothing that exists by nature can form a habit contrary to its nature. For instance the stone which by nature moves downwards cannot be habituated to move upwards, not even if one tries to train it by throwing it up ten thousand times; nor can fire be habituated to move downwards, nor can anything else that by nature behaves in one way be trained to behave in another. Neither by nature, then, nor contrary to nature do the virtues arise in us; rather we are adapted by nature to receive them, and are made perfect by habit.

Again, of all the things that come to us by nature we first acquire the potentiality and later exhibit the activity (this is plain in the case of the senses; for it was not by often seeing or often hearing that we got these senses, but on the contrary we had them before we used them, and did not come to have them by using them); but the virtues we get by first exercising them, as also happens in the case of the arts as well. For the things we have to learn before we can do them, we learn by doing them, e.g. men become builders by building and lyreplayers by playing the lyre; so too we become just by doing just acts, temperate by doing temperate acts, brave by doing brave acts.

This is confirmed by what happens in states; for legislators make the citizens good by forming habits in them, and this is the wish of every legislator, and those who do not effect it miss their mark, and it is in this that a good constitution differs from a bad one.

Again, it is from the same causes and by the same means that every virtue is both produced and destroyed, and similarly every art; for it is from playing the lyre that both good and bad lyre-players are produced. And the corresponding statement is true of builders and of all the rest; men will be good or bad builders as a result of building well or badly. For if this were not so, there would have been no need of a teacher, but all men would have been born good or bad at their craft. This, then, is the case with the virtues also; by doing the acts that we do in our transactions with other men we become just or unjust, and by doing the acts that we do in the presence of danger, and being habituated to feel fear or confidence, we become brave or cowardly. The same is true of appetites and feelings of anger; some men become temperate and good-tempered, others self-indulgent and irascible, by behaving in one way or the other in the appropriate circumstances. Thus, in one word, states of character arise out of like activities. This is why the activities we exhibit must be of a certain kind; it is because the states of character correspond to the differences between these. It makes no small difference, then, whether we form habits of one kind or of another from our very youth; it makes a very great difference, or rather all the difference.

2

Since, then, the present inquiry does not aim at theoretical knowledge like the others (for we are inquiring not in order to know what virtue is, but in order to become good, since otherwise our inquiry would have been of no use), we must examine the nature of actions, namely how we ought to do them; for these determine also the nature of the states of character that are produced, as we have said. Now, that we must act according to the right rule is a common principle and must be assumed-it will be discussed later, i.e. both what the right rule is, and how it is related to the other virtues. But this must be agreed upon beforehand, that the whole account of matters of conduct must be given in outline and not precisely, as we said at the very beginning that the accounts we demand must be in accordance with the subject-matter; matters concerned with conduct and questions of what is good for us have no fixity, any more than matters of health. The general account being of this nature, the account of particular cases is yet more lacking in exactness; for they do not fall under any art or precept but the agents themselves must in each case consider what is appropriate to the occasion, as happens also in the art of medicine or of navigation.

But though our present account is of this nature we must give what help we can. First, then, let us consider this, that it is the nature of such things to be destroyed by defect and excess, as we see in the case of strength and of health (for to gain light on things imperceptible we must use the evidence of sensible things); both excessive and defective exercise destroys the strength, and similarly drink or food which is above or below a certain amount destroys the health, while that which is proportionate both produces and increases and preserves it. So too is it, then, in the case of temperance and courage and the other virtues. For the man who flies from and fears everything and does not stand his ground against anything becomes a coward, and the man who fears nothing at all but goes to meet every danger becomes rash; and similarly the man who indulges in every pleasure and abstains from none becomes self-indulgent, while the man who shuns every pleasure, as boors do, becomes in a way insensible; temperance and courage, then, are destroyed by excess and defect, and preserved by the mean.

But not only are the sources and causes of their origination and growth the same as those of their destruction, but also the sphere of their actualization will be the same; for this is also true of the things which are more evident to sense, e.g. of strength; it is produced by taking much food and undergoing much exertion, and it is the strong man that will be most able to do these things. So too is it with the virtues; by abstaining from pleasures we become temperate, and it is when we have become so that we are most able to abstain from them; and similarly too in the case of courage; for by being habituated to despise things that are terrible and to stand our ground against them we become brave, and it is when we have become so that we shall be most able to stand our ground against them.

3

We must take as a sign of states of character the pleasure or pain that ensues on acts; for the man who abstains from bodily pleasures and delights in this very fact is temperate, while the man who is annoyed at it is self-indulgent, and he who stands his ground against things that are terrible and delights in this or at least is not pained is brave, while the man who is pained is a coward. For moral excellence is concerned with pleasures and pains; it is on account of the pleasure that we do bad things, and on account of the pain that we abstain from noble ones. Hence we ought to have been brought up in a particular way from our very youth, as Plato says, so as both to delight in and to be pained by the things that we ought; for this is the right education.

Again, if the virtues are concerned with actions and passions, and every passion and every action is accompanied by pleasure and pain, for this reason also virtue will be concerned with pleasures and pains. This is indicated also by the fact that punishment is inflicted by these means; for it is a kind of cure, and it is the nature of cures to be effected by contraries.

Again, as we said but lately, every state of soul has a nature relative to and concerned with the kind of things by which it tends to be made worse or better; but it is by reason of pleasures and pains that men become bad, by pursuing and avoiding these- either the pleasures and pains they ought not or when they ought not or as they ought not, or by going wrong in one of the other similar ways that may be distinguished. Hence men even define the virtues as certain states of impassivity and rest; not well, however, because they speak absolutely, and do not say 'as one ought' and 'as one ought not' and 'when one ought or ought not', and the other things that may be added. We assume, then, that this kind of excellence tends to do what is best with regard to pleasures and pains, and vice does the contrary.

The following facts also may show us that virtue and vice are concerned with these same things. There being three objects of choice and three of avoidance, the noble, the advantageous, the pleasant, and their contraries, the base, the injurious, the painful, about all of these the good man tends to go right and the bad man to go wrong, and especially about pleasure; for this is common to the animals, and also it accompanies all objects of choice; for even the noble and the advantageous appear pleasant.

Again, it has grown up with us all from our infancy; this is why it is difficult to rub off this passion, engrained as it is in our life. And we measure even our actions, some of us more and others less, by the rule of pleasure and pain. For this reason, then, our whole inquiry must be about these; for to feel delight and pain rightly or wrongly has no small effect on our actions.

Again, it is harder to fight with pleasure than with anger, to use Heraclitus' phrase', but both art and virtue are always concerned with what is harder; for even the good is better when it is harder. Therefore for this reason also the whole concern both of virtue and of political science is with pleasures and pains; for the man who uses these well will be good, he who uses them badly bad.

That virtue, then, is concerned with pleasures and pains, and that by the acts from which it arises it is both increased and, if they are done differently, destroyed, and that the acts from which it arose are those in which it actualizes itself- let this be taken as said.

4

The question might be asked,; what we mean by saying that we must become just by doing just acts, and temperate by doing temperate acts; for if men do just and temperate acts, they are already just and temperate, exactly as, if they do what is in accordance with the laws of grammar and of music, they are grammarians and musicians.

Or is this not true even of the arts? It is possible to do something that is in accordance with the laws of grammar, either by chance or at the suggestion of another. A man will be a grammarian, then, only when he has both done something grammatical and done it grammatically; and this means doing it in accordance with the grammatical knowledge in himself.

Again, the case of the arts and that of the virtues are not similar; for the products of the arts have their goodness in themselves, so that it is enough that they should have a certain character, but if the acts that are in accordance with the virtues have themselves a certain character it does not follow that they are done justly or temperately. The agent also must be in a certain condition when he does them; in the first place he must have knowledge, secondly he must choose the acts, and choose them for their own sakes, and thirdly his action must proceed from a firm and unchangeable character. These are not reckoned in as conditions of the possession of the arts, except the bare knowledge; but as a condition of the possession of the virtues knowledge has little or no weight, while the other conditions count not for a little but for everything, i.e. the very conditions which result from often doing just and temperate acts.

Actions, then, are called just and temperate when they are such as the just or the temperate man would do; but it is not the man who does these that is just and temperate, but the man who also does them as just and temperate men do them. It is well said, then, that it is by doing just acts that the just man is produced, and by doing temperate acts the temperate man; without doing these no one would have even a prospect of becoming good.

But most people do not do these, but take refuge in theory and think they are being philosophers and will become good in this way, behaving somewhat like patients who listen attentively to their doctors, but do none of the things they are ordered to do. As the latter will not be made well in body by such a course of treatment, the former will not be made well in soul by such a course of philosophy.

5

Next we must consider what virtue is. Since things that are found in the soul are of three kinds- passions, faculties, states of character, virtue must be one of these. By passions I mean appetite, anger, fear, confidence, envy, joy, friendly feeling, hatred, longing, emulation, pity, and in general the feelings that are accompanied by pleasure or pain; by faculties the things in virtue of which we are said to be capable of feeling these, e.g. of becoming angry or being pained or feeling pity; by states of character the things in virtue of which we stand well or badly with reference to the passions, e.g. with reference to anger we stand badly if we feel it violently or too weakly, and well if we feel it moderately; and similarly with reference to the other passions.

Now neither the virtues nor the vices are passions, because we are not called good or bad on the ground of our passions, but are so called on the ground of our virtues and our vices, and because we are neither praised nor blamed for our passions (for the man who feels fear or anger is not praised, nor is the man who simply feels anger blamed, but the man who feels it in a certain way), but for our virtues and our vices we are praised or blamed.

Again, we feel anger and fear without choice, but the virtues are modes of choice or involve choice. Further, in respect of the passions we are said to be moved, but in respect of the virtues and the vices we are said not to be moved but to be disposed in a particular way.

For these reasons also they are not faculties; for we are neither called good nor bad, nor praised nor blamed, for the simple capacity of feeling the passions; again, we have the faculties by nature, but we are not made good or bad by nature; we have spoken of this before. If, then, the virtues are neither passions nor faculties, all that remains is that they should be states of character.

Thus we have stated what virtue is in respect of its genus.

6

We must, however, not only describe virtue as a state of character, but also say what sort of state it is. We may remark, then, that every virtue or excellence both brings into good condition the thing of which it is the excellence and makes the work of that thing be done well; e.g. the excellence of the eye makes both the eye and its work good; for it is by the excellence of the eye that we see well. Similarly the excellence of the horse makes a horse both good in itself and good at running and at carrying its rider and at awaiting the attack of the enemy. Therefore, if this is true in every case, the virtue of man also will be the state of character which makes a man good and which makes him do his own work well.

How this is to happen we have stated already, but it will be made plain also by the following consideration of the specific nature of virtue. In everything that is continuous and divisible it is possible to take more, less, or an equal amount, and that either in terms of the thing itself or relatively to us; and the equal is an intermediate between excess and defect. By the intermediate in the object I mean that which is equidistant from each of the extremes, which is one and the same for all men; by the intermediate relatively to us that which is neither too much nor too little- and this is not one, nor the same for all. For instance, if ten is many and two is few, six is the intermediate, taken in terms of the object; for it exceeds and is exceeded by an equal amount; this is intermediate according to arithmetical proportion. But the intermediate relatively to us is not to be taken so; if ten pounds are too much for a particular person to eat and two too little, it does not follow that the trainer will order six pounds; for this also is perhaps too much for the person who is to take it, or too little- too little for Milo, too much for the beginner in athletic exercises. The same is true of running and wrestling. Thus a master of any art avoids excess and defect, but seeks the intermediate and chooses this- the intermediate not in the object but relatively to us.

If it is thus, then, that every art does its work well- by looking to the intermediate and judgling its works by this standard (so that we often say of good works of art that it is not possible either to take away or to add anything, implying that excess and defect destroy the goodness of works of art, while the mean preserves it; and good artists, as we say, look to this in their work), and if, further, virtue is more exact and better than any art, as nature also is, then virtue must have the quality of aiming at the intermediate. I mean moral virtue; for it is this that is concerned with passions and actions, and in these there is excess, defect, and the intermediate. For instance, both fear and confidence and appetite and anger and pity and in general pleasure and pain may be felt both too much and too little, and in both cases not well; but to feel them at the right times, with reference to the right objects, towards the right people, with the right motive, and in the right way, is what is both intermediate and best, and this is characteristic of virtue. Similarly with regard to actions also there is excess, defect, and the intermediate. Now virtue is concerned with passions and actions, in which excess is a form of failure, and so is defect, while the intermediate is praised and is a form of success; and being praised and being successful are both characteristics of virtue. Therefore virtue is a kind of mean, since, as we have seen, it aims at what is intermediate.

Again, it is possible to fail in many ways (for evil belongs to the class of the unlimited, as the Pythagoreans conjectured, and good to that of the limited), while to succeed is possible only in one way (for which reason also one is easy and the other difficult- to miss the mark easy, to hit it difficult); for these reasons also, then, excess and defect are characteristic of vice, and the mean of virtue;

For men are good in but one way, but bad in many.

Virtue, then, is a state of character concerned with choice, lying in a mean, i.e. the mean relative to us, this being determined by a rational principle, and by that principle by which the man of practical wisdom would determine it. Now it is a mean between two vices, that which depends on excess and that which depends on defect; and again it is a mean because the vices respectively fall short of or exceed what is right in both passions and actions, while virtue both finds and chooses that which is intermediate. Hence in respect of its substance and the definition which states its essence virtue is a mean, with regard to what is best and right an extreme.

But not every action nor every passion admits of a mean; for some have names that already imply badness, e.g. spite, shamelessness, envy, and in the case of actions adultery, theft, murder; for all of these and suchlike things imply by their names that they are themselves bad, and not the excesses or deficiencies of them. It is not possible, then, ever to be right with regard to them; one must always be wrong. Nor does goodness or badness with regard to such things depend on committing adultery with the right woman, at the right time, and in the right way, but simply to do any of them is to go wrong. It would be equally absurd, then, to expect that in unjust, cowardly, and voluptuous action there should be a mean, an excess, and a deficiency; for at that rate there would be a mean of excess and of deficiency, an excess of excess, and a deficiency of deficiency. But as there is no excess and deficiency of temperance and courage because what is intermediate is in a sense an extreme, so too of the actions we have mentioned there is no mean nor any excess and deficiency, but however they are done they are wrong; for in general there is neither a mean of excess and deficiency, nor excess and deficiency of a mean.

7

We must, however, not only make this general statement, but also apply it to the individual facts. For among statements about conduct those which are general apply more widely, but those which are particular are more genuine, since conduct has to do with individual cases, and our statements must harmonize with the facts in these cases. We may take these cases from our table. With regard to feelings of fear and confidence courage is the mean; of the people who exceed, he who exceeds in fearlessness has no name (many of the states have no name), while the man who exceeds in confidence is rash, and he who exceeds in fear and falls short in confidence is a coward. With regard to pleasures and pains- not all of them, and not so much with regard to the pains- the mean is temperance, the excess self-indulgence. Persons deficient with regard to the pleasures are not often found; hence such persons also have received no name. But let us call them 'insensible'.

With regard to giving and taking of money the mean is liberality, the excess and the defect prodigality and meanness. In these actions people exceed and fall short in contrary ways; the prodigal exceeds in spending and falls short in taking, while the mean man exceeds in taking and falls short in spending. (At present we are giving a mere outline or summary, and are satisfied with this; later these states will be more exactly determined.) With regard to money there are also other dispositions- a mean, magnificence (for the magnificent man differs from the liberal man; the former deals with large sums, the latter with small ones), an excess, tastelessness and vulgarity, and a deficiency, niggardliness; these differ from the states opposed to liberality, and the mode of their difference will be stated later. With regard to honour and dishonour the mean is proper pride, the excess is known as a sort of 'empty vanity', and the deficiency is undue humility; and as we said liberality was related to magnificence, differing from it by dealing with small sums, so there is a state similarly related to proper pride, being concerned with small honours while that is concerned with great. For it is possible to desire honour as one ought, and more than one ought, and less, and the man who exceeds in his desires is called ambitious, the man who falls short unambitious, while the intermediate person has no name. The dispositions also are nameless, except that that of the ambitious man is called ambition. Hence the people who are at the extremes lay claim to the middle place; and we ourselves sometimes call the intermediate person ambitious and sometimes unambitious, and sometimes praise the ambitious man and sometimes the unambitious. The reason of our doing this will be stated in what follows; but now let us speak of the remaining states according to the method which has been indicated.

With regard to anger also there is an excess, a deficiency, and a mean. Although they can scarcely be said to have names, yet since we call the intermediate person good-tempered let us call the mean good temper; of the persons at the extremes let the one who exceeds be called irascible, and his vice irascibility, and the man who falls short an inirascible sort of person, and the deficiency inirascibility.

There are also three other means, which have a certain likeness to one another, but differ from one another: for they are all concerned with intercourse in words and actions, but differ in that one is concerned with truth in this sphere, the other two with pleasantness; and of this one kind is exhibited in giving amusement, the other in all the circumstances of life. We must therefore speak of these too, that we may the better see that in all things the mean is praise-worthy, and the extremes neither praiseworthy nor right, but worthy of blame. Now most of these states also have no names, but we must try, as in the other cases, to invent names ourselves so that we may be clear and easy to follow. With regard to truth, then, the intermediate is a truthful sort of person and the mean may be called truthfulness, while the pretence which exaggerates is boastfulness and the person characterized by it a boaster, and that which understates is mock modesty and the person characterized by it mock-modest. With regard to pleasantness in the giving of amusement the intermediate person is ready-witted and the disposition ready wit, the excess is buffoonery and the person characterized by it a buffoon, while the man who falls short is a sort of boor and his state is boorishness. With regard to the remaining kind of pleasantness, that which is exhibited in life in general, the man who is pleasant in the right way is friendly and the mean is friendliness, while the man who exceeds is an obsequious person if he has no end in view, a flatterer if he is aiming at his own advantage, and the man who falls short and is unpleasant in all circumstances is a quarrelsome and surly sort of person.

There are also means in the passions and concerned with the passions; since shame is not a virtue, and yet praise is extended to the modest man. For even in these matters one man is said to be intermediate, and another to exceed, as for instance the bashful man who is ashamed of everything; while he who falls short or is not ashamed of anything at all is shameless, and the intermediate person is modest. Righteous indignation is a mean between envy and spite, and these states are concerned with the pain and pleasure that are felt at the fortunes of our neighbours; the man who is characterized by righteous indignation is pained at undeserved good fortune, the envious man, going beyond him, is pained at all good fortune, and the spiteful man falls so far short of being pained that he even rejoices. But these states there will be an opportunity of describing elsewhere; with regard to justice, since it has not one simple meaning, we shall, after describing the other states, distinguish its two kinds and say how each of them is a mean; and similarly we shall treat also of the rational virtues.

8

There are three kinds of disposition, then, two of them vices, involving excess and deficiency respectively, and one a virtue, viz. the mean, and all are in a sense opposed to all; for the extreme states are contrary both to the intermediate state and to each other, and the intermediate to the extremes; as the equal is greater relatively to the less, less relatively to the greater, so the middle states are excessive relatively to the deficiencies, deficient relatively to the excesses, both in passions and in actions. For the brave man appears rash relatively to the coward, and cowardly relatively to the rash man; and similarly the temperate man appears self-indulgent relatively to the insensible man, insensible relatively to the self-indulgent, and the liberal man prodigal relatively to the mean man, mean relatively to the prodigal. Hence also the people at the extremes push the intermediate man each over to the other, and the brave man is called rash by the coward, cowardly by the rash man, and correspondingly in the other cases.

These states being thus opposed to one another, the greatest contrariety is that of the extremes to each other, rather than to the intermediate; for these are further from each other than from the intermediate, as the great is further from the small and the small from the great than both are from the equal. Again, to the intermediate some extremes show a certain likeness, as that of rashness to courage and that of prodigality to liberality; but the extremes show the greatest unlikeness to each other; now contraries are defined as the things that are furthest from each other, so that things that are further apart are more contrary.

To the mean in some cases the deficiency, in some the excess is more opposed; e.g. it is not rashness, which is an excess, but cowardice, which is a deficiency, that is more opposed to courage, and not insensibility, which is a deficiency, but self-indulgence, which is an excess, that is more opposed to temperance. This happens from two reasons, one being drawn from the thing itself; for because one extreme is nearer and liker to the intermediate, we oppose not this but rather its contrary to the intermediate. E.g. since rashness is thought liker and nearer to courage, and cowardice more unlike, we oppose rather the latter to courage; for things that are further from the intermediate are thought more contrary to it. This, then, is one cause, drawn from the thing itself; another is drawn from ourselves; for the things to which we ourselves more naturally tend seem more contrary to the intermediate. For instance, we ourselves tend more naturally to pleasures, and hence are more easily carried away towards self-indulgence than towards propriety. We describe as contrary to the mean, then, rather the directions in which we more often go to great lengths; and therefore self-indulgence, which is an excess, is the more contrary to temperance.

9

That moral virtue is a mean, then, and in what sense it is so, and that it is a mean between two vices, the one involving excess, the other deficiency, and that it is such because its character is to aim at what is intermediate in passions and in actions, has been sufficiently stated. Hence also it is no easy task to be good. For in everything it is no easy task to find the middle, e.g. to find the middle of a circle is not for every one but for him who knows; so, too, any one can get angry- that is easy- or give or spend money; but to do this to the right person, to the right extent, at the right time, with the right motive, and in the right way, that is not for every one, nor is it easy; wherefore goodness is both rare and laudable and noble.

Hence he who aims at the intermediate must first depart from what is the more contrary to it, as Calypso advises-

Hold the ship out beyond that surf and spray.

For of the extremes one is more erroneous, one less so; therefore, since to hit the mean is hard in the extreme, we must as a second best, as people say, take the least of the evils; and this will be done best in the way we describe. But we must consider the things towards which we ourselves also are easily carried away; for some of us tend to one thing, some to another; and this will be recognizable from the pleasure and the pain we feel. We must drag ourselves away to the contrary extreme; for we shall get into the intermediate state by drawing well away from error, as people do in straightening sticks that are bent.

Now in everything the pleasant or pleasure is most to be guarded against; for we do not judge it impartially. We ought, then, to feel towards pleasure as the elders of the people felt towards Helen, and in all circumstances repeat their saying; for if we dismiss pleasure thus we are less likely to go astray. It is by doing this, then, (to sum the matter up) that we shall best be able to hit the mean.

But this is no doubt difficult, and especially in individual cases; for or is not easy to determine both how and with whom and on what provocation and how long one should be angry; for we too sometimes praise those who fall short and call them good-tempered, but sometimes we praise those who get angry and call them manly. The man, however, who deviates little from goodness is not blamed, whether he do so in the direction of the more or of the less, but only the man who deviates more widely; for he does not fail to be noticed. But up to what point and to what extent a man must deviate before he becomes blameworthy it is not easy to determine by reasoning, any more than anything else that is perceived by the senses; such things depend on particular facts, and the decision rests with perception. So much, then, is plain, that the intermediate state is in all things to be praised, but that we must incline sometimes towards the excess, sometimes towards the deficiency; for so shall we most easily hit the mean and what is right.

Book Three

1

Since virtue is concerned with passions and actions, and on voluntary passions and actions praise and blame are bestowed, on those that are involuntary pardon, and sometimes also pity, to distinguish the voluntary and the involuntary is presumably necessary for those who are studying the nature of virtue, and useful also for legislators with a view to the assigning both of honours and of punishments. Those things, then, are thought-involuntary, which take place under compulsion or owing to ignorance; and that is compulsory of which the moving principle is outside, being a principle in which nothing is contributed by the person who is acting or is feeling the passion, e.g. if he were to be carried somewhere by a wind, or by men who had him in their power.

But with regard to the things that are done from fear of greater evils or for some noble object (e.g. if a tyrant were to order one to do something base, having one's parents and children in his power, and if one did the action they were to be saved, but otherwise would be put to death), it may be debated whether such actions are involuntary or voluntary. Something of the sort happens also with regard to the throwing of goods overboard in a storm; for in the abstract no one throws goods away voluntarily, but on condition of its securing the safety of himself and his crew any sensible man does so. Such actions, then, are mixed, but are more like voluntary actions; for they are worthy of choice at the time when they are done, and the end of an action is relative to the occasion. Both the terms, then, 'voluntary' and 'involuntary', must be used with reference to the moment of action. Now the man acts voluntarily; for the principle that moves the instrumental parts of the body in such actions is in him, and the things of which the moving principle is in a man himself are in his power to do or not to do. Such actions, therefore, are voluntary, but in the abstract perhaps involuntary; for no one would choose any such act in itself.

For such actions men are sometimes even praised, when they endure something base or painful in return for great and noble objects gained; in the opposite case they are blamed, since to endure the greatest indignities for no noble end or for a trifling end is the mark of an inferior person. On some actions praise indeed is not bestowed, but pardon is, when one does what he ought not under pressure which overstrains human nature and which no one could withstand. But some acts, perhaps, we cannot be forced to do, but ought rather to face death after the most fearful sufferings; for the things that 'forced' Euripides Alcmaeon to slay his mother seem absurd. It is difficult sometimes to determine what should be chosen at what cost, and what should be endured in return for what gain, and yet more difficult to abide by our decisions; for as a rule what is expected is painful, and what we are forced to do is base, whence praise and blame are bestowed on those who have been compelled or have not.

What sort of acts, then, should be called compulsory? We answer that without qualification actions are so when the cause is in the external circumstances and the agent contributes nothing. But the things that in themselves are involuntary, but now and in return for these gains are worthy of choice, and whose moving principle is in the agent, are in themselves involuntary, but now and in return for these gains voluntary. They are more like voluntary acts; for actions are in the class of particulars, and the particular acts here are voluntary. What sort of things are to be chosen, and in return for what, it is not easy to state; for there are many differences in the particular cases.

But if some one were to say that pleasant and noble objects have a compelling power, forcing us from without, all acts would be for him compulsory; for it is for these objects that all men do everything they do. And those who act under compulsion and unwillingly act with pain, but those who do acts for their pleasantness and nobility do them with pleasure; it is absurd to make external circumstances responsible, and not oneself, as being easily caught by such attractions, and to make oneself responsible for noble acts but the pleasant objects responsible for base acts. The compulsory, then, seems to be that whose moving principle is outside, the person compelled contributing nothing.

Everything that is done by reason of ignorance is not voluntary; it is only what produces pain and repentance that is involuntary. For the man who has done something owing to ignorance, and feels not the least vexation at his action, has not acted voluntarily, since he did not know what he was doing, nor yet involuntarily, since he is not pained. Of people, then, who act by reason of ignorance he who repents is thought an involuntary agent, and the man who does not repent may, since he is different, be called a not voluntary agent; for, since he differs from the other, it is better that he should have a name of his own.

Acting by reason of ignorance seems also to be different from acting in ignorance; for the man who is drunk or in a rage is thought to act as a result not of ignorance but of one of the causes mentioned, yet not knowingly but in ignorance.

Now every wicked man is ignorant of what he ought to do and what he ought to abstain from, and it is by reason of error of this kind that men become unjust and in general bad; but the term 'involuntary' tends to be used not if a man is ignorant of what is to his advantage- for it is not mistaken purpose that causes involuntary action (it leads rather to wickedness), nor ignorance of the universal (for that men are blamed), but ignorance of particulars, i.e. of the circumstances of the action and the objects with which it is concerned. For it is on these that both pity and pardon depend, since the person who is ignorant of any of these acts involuntarily.

Perhaps it is just as well, therefore, to determine their nature and number. A man may be ignorant, then, of who he is, what he is doing, what or whom he is acting on, and sometimes also what (e.g. what instrument) he is doing it with, and to what end (e.g. he may think his act will conduce to some one's safety), and how he is doing it (e.g. whether gently or violently).

Now of all of these no one could be ignorant unless he were mad, and evidently also he could not be ignorant of the agent; for how could he not know himself? But of what he is doing a man might be ignorant, as for instance people say 'it slipped out of their mouths as they were speaking', or 'they did not know it was a secret', as Aeschylus said of the mysteries, or a man might say he 'let it go off when he merely wanted to show its working', as the man did with the catapult. Again, one might think one's son was an enemy, as Merope did, or that a pointed spear had a button on it, or that a stone was pumicestone; or one might give a man a draught to save him, and really kill him; or one might want to touch a man, as people do in sparring, and really wound him. The ignorance may relate, then, to any of these things, i.e. of the circumstances of the action, and the man who was ignorant of any of these is thought to have acted involuntarily, and especially if he was ignorant on the most important points; and these are thought to be the circumstances of the action and its end. Further, the doing of an act that is called involuntary in virtue of ignorance of this sort must be painful and involve repentance.

Since that which is done under compulsion or by reason of ignorance is involuntary, the voluntary would seem to be that of which the moving principle is in the agent himself, he being aware of the particular circumstances of the action. Presumably acts done by reason of anger or appetite are not rightly called involuntary. For in the first place, on that showing none of the other animals will act voluntarily, nor will children; and secondly, is it meant that we do not do voluntarily any of the acts that are due to appetite or anger, or that we do the noble acts voluntarily and the base acts involuntarily? Is not this absurd, when one and the same thing is the cause? But it would surely be odd to describe as involuntary the things one ought to desire; and we ought both to be angry at certain things and to have an appetite for certain things, e.g. for health and for learning. Also what is involuntary is thought to be painful, but what is in accordance with appetite is thought to be pleasant. Again, what is the difference in respect of involuntariness between errors committed upon calculation and those committed in anger? Both are to be avoided, but the irrational passions are thought not less human than reason is, and therefore also the actions which proceed from anger or appetite are the man's actions. It would be odd, then, to treat them as involuntary.

2

Both the voluntary and the involuntary having been delimited, we must next discuss choice; for it is thought to be most closely bound up with virtue and to discriminate characters better than actions do.

Choice, then, seems to be voluntary, but not the same thing as the voluntary; the latter extends more widely. For both children and the lower animals share in voluntary action, but not in choice, and acts done on the spur of the moment we describe as voluntary, but not as chosen.

Those who say it is appetite or anger or wish or a kind of opinion do not seem to be right. For choice is not common to irrational creatures as well, but appetite and anger are. Again, the incontinent man acts with appetite, but not with choice; while the continent man on the contrary acts with choice, but not with appetite. Again, appetite is contrary to choice, but not appetite to appetite. Again, appetite relates to the pleasant and the painful, choice neither to the painful nor to the pleasant.

Still less is it anger; for acts due to anger are thought to be less than any others objects of choice.

But neither is it wish, though it seems near to it; for choice cannot relate to impossibles, and if any one said he chose them he would be thought silly; but there may be a wish even for impossibles, e.g. for immortality. And wish may relate to things that could in no way be brought about by one's own efforts, e.g. that a particular actor or athlete should win in a competition; but no one chooses such things, but only the things that he thinks could be brought about by his own efforts. Again, wish relates rather to the end, choice to the means;

for instance, we wish to be healthy, but we choose the acts which will make us healthy, and we wish to be happy and say we do, but we cannot well say we choose to be so; for, in general, choice seems to relate to the things that are in our own power.

For this reason, too, it cannot be opinion; for opinion is thought to relate to all kinds of things, no less to eternal things and impossible things than to things in our own power; and it is distinguished by its falsity or truth, not by its badness or goodness, while choice is distinguished rather by these.

Now with opinion in general perhaps no one even says it is identical. But it is not identical even with any kind of opinion; for by choosing what is good or bad we are men of a certain character, which we are not by holding certain opinions. And we choose to get or avoid something good or bad, but we have opinions about what a thing is or whom it is good for or how it is good for him; we can hardly be said to opine to get or avoid anything. And choice is praised for being related to the right object rather than for being rightly related to it, opinion for being truly related to its object. And we choose what we best know to be good, but we opine what we do not quite know; and it is not the same people that are thought to make the best choices and to have the best opinions, but some are thought to have fairly good opinions, but by reason of vice to choose what they should not. If opinion precedes choice or accompanies it, that makes no difference; for it is not this that we are considering, but whether it is identical with some kind of opinion.

What, then, or what kind of thing is it, since it is none of the things we have mentioned? It seems to be voluntary, but not all that is voluntary to be an object of choice. Is it, then, what has been decided on by previous deliberation? At any rate choice involves a rational principle and thought. Even the name seems to suggest that it is what is chosen before other things.

3

Do we deliberate about everything, and is everything a possible subject of deliberation, or is deliberation impossible about some things? We ought presumably to call not what a fool or a madman would deliberate about, but what a sensible man would deliberate about, a subject of deliberation. Now about eternal things no one deliberates, e.g. about the material universe or the incommensurability of the diagonal and the side of a square. But no more do we deliberate about the things that involve movement but always happen in the same way, whether of necessity or by nature or from any other cause, e.g. the solstices and the risings of the stars; nor about things that happen now in one way, now in another, e.g. droughts and rains; nor about chance events, like the finding of treasure. But we do not deliberate even about all human affairs; for instance, no Spartan deliberates about the best constitution for the Scythians. For none of these things can be brought about by our own efforts.

We deliberate about things that are in our power and can be done; and these are in fact what is left. For nature, necessity, and chance are thought to be causes, and also reason and everything that depends on man. Now every class of men deliberates about the things that can be done by their own efforts. And in the case of exact and self-contained sciences there is no deliberation, e.g. about the letters of the alphabet (for we have no doubt how they should be written); but the things that are brought about by our own efforts, but not always in the same way, are the things about which we deliberate, e.g. questions of medical treatment or of money-making. And we do so more in the case of the art of navigation than in that of gymnastics, inasmuch as it has been less exactly worked out, and again about other things in the same ratio, and more also in the case of the arts than in that of the sciences; for we have more doubt about the former. Deliberation is concerned with things that happen in a certain way for the most part, but in which the event is obscure, and with things in which it is indeterminate. We call in others to aid us in deliberation on important questions, distrusting ourselves as not being equal to deciding.

We deliberate not about ends but about means. For a doctor does not deliberate whether he shall heal, nor an orator whether he shall persuade, nor a statesman whether he shall produce law and order, nor does any one else deliberate about his end. They assume the end and consider how and by what means it is to be attained; and if it seems to be produced by several means they consider by which it is most easily and best produced, while if it is achieved by one only they consider how it will be achieved by this and by what means this will be achieved, till they come to the first cause, which in the order of discovery is last. For the person who deliberates seems to investigate and analyse in the way described as though he were analysing a geometrical construction (not all investigation appears to be deliberation- for instance mathematical investigations- but all deliberation is investigation), and what is last in the order of analysis seems to be first in the order of becoming. And if we come on an impossibility, we give up the search, e.g. if we need money and this cannot be got; but if a thing appears possible we try to do it. By 'possible' things I mean things that might be brought about by our own efforts; and these in a sense include things that can be brought about by the efforts of our friends, since the moving principle is in ourselves. The subject of investigation is sometimes the instruments, sometimes the use of them; and similarly in the other cases- sometimes the means, sometimes the mode of using it or the means of bringing it about. It seems, then, as has been said, that man is a moving principle of actions; now deliberation is about the things to be done by the agent himself, and actions are for the sake of things other than themselves. For the end cannot be a subject of deliberation, but only the means; nor indeed can the particular facts be a subject of it, as whether this is bread or has been baked as it should; for these are matters of perception. If we are to be always deliberating, we shall have to go on to infinity.

The same thing is deliberated upon and is chosen, except that the object of choice is already determinate, since it is that which has been decided upon as a result of deliberation that is the object of choice. For every one ceases to inquire how he is to act when he has brought the moving principle back to himself and to the ruling part of himself; for this is what chooses. This is plain also from the ancient constitutions, which Homer represented; for the kings announced their choices to the people. The object of choice being one of the things in our own power which is desired after deliberation, choice will be deliberate desire of things in our own power; for when we have decided as a result of deliberation, we desire in accordance with our deliberation.

We may take it, then, that we have described choice in outline, and stated the nature of its objects and the fact that it is concerned with means.

4

That wish is for the end has already been stated; some think it is for the good, others for the apparent good. Now those who say that the good is the object of wish must admit in consequence that that which the man who does not choose aright wishes for is not an object of wish (for if it is to be so, it must also be good; but it was, if it so happened, bad); while those who say the apparent good is the object of wish must admit that there is no natural object of wish, but only what seems good to each man. Now different things appear good to different people, and, if it so happens, even contrary things.

If these consequences are unpleasing, are we to say that absolutely and in truth the good is the object of wish, but for each person the apparent good; that that which is in truth an object of wish is an object of wish to the good man, while any chance thing may be so the bad man, as in the case of bodies also the things that are in truth wholesome are wholesome for bodies which are in good condition, while for those that are diseased other things are wholesome- or bitter or sweet or hot or heavy, and so on; since the good man judges each class of things rightly, and in each the truth appears to him? For each state of character has its own ideas of the noble and the pleasant, and perhaps the good man differs from others most by seeing the truth in each class of things, being as it were the norm and measure of them. In most things the error seems to be due to pleasure; for it appears a good when it is not. We therefore choose the pleasant as a good, and avoid pain as an evil.

5

The end, then, being what we wish for, the means what we deliberate about and choose, actions concerning means must be according to choice and voluntary. Now the exercise of the virtues is concerned with means. Therefore virtue also is in our own power, and so too vice. For where it is in our power to act it is also in our power not to act, and vice versa; so that, if to act, where this is noble, is in our power, not to act, which will be base, will also be in our power, and if not to act, where this is noble, is in our power, to act, which will be base, will also be in our power. Now if it is in our power to do noble or base acts, and likewise in our power not to do them, and this was what being good or bad meant, then it is in our power to be virtuous or vicious.

The saying that 'no one is voluntarily wicked nor involuntarily happy' seems to be partly false and partly true; for no one is involuntarily happy, but wickedness is voluntary. Or else we shall have to dispute what has just been said, at any rate, and deny that man is a moving principle or begetter of his actions as of children. But if these facts are evident and we cannot refer actions to moving principles other than those in ourselves, the acts whose moving principles are in us must themselves also be in our power and voluntary.

Witness seems to be borne to this both by individuals in their private capacity and by legislators themselves; for these punish and take vengeance on those who do wicked acts (unless they have acted under compulsion or as a result of ignorance for which they are not themselves responsible), while they honour those who do noble acts, as though they meant to encourage the latter and deter the former. But no one is encouraged to do the things that are neither in our power nor voluntary; it is assumed that there is no gain in being persuaded not to be hot or in pain or hungry or the like, since we shall experience these feelings none the less. Indeed, we punish a man for his very ignorance, if he is thought responsible for the ignorance, as when penalties are doubled in the case of drunkenness; for the moving principle is in the man himself, since he had the power of not getting drunk and his getting drunk was the cause of his ignorance. And we punish those who are ignorant of anything in the laws that they ought to know and that is not difficult, and so too in the case of anything else that they are thought to be ignorant of through carelessness; we assume that it is in their power not to be ignorant, since they have the power of taking care.

But perhaps a man is the kind of man not to take care. Still they are themselves by their slack lives responsible for becoming men of that kind, and men make themselves responsible for being unjust or self-indulgent, in the one case by cheating and in the other by spending their time in drinking bouts and the like; for it is activities exercised on particular objects that make the corresponding character. This is plain from the case of people training for any contest or action; they practise the activity the whole time. Now not to know that it is from the exercise of activities on particular objects that states of character are produced is the mark of a thoroughly senseless person. Again, it is irrational to suppose that a man who acts unjustly does not wish to be unjust or a man who acts self-indulgently to be self-indulgent. But if without being ignorant a man does the things which will make him unjust, he will be unjust voluntarily. Yet it does not follow that if he wishes he will cease to be unjust and will be just. For neither does the man who is ill become well on those terms. We may suppose a case in which he is ill voluntarily, through living incontinently and disobeying his doctors. In that case it was then open to him not to be ill, but not now, when he has thrown away his chance, just as when you have let a stone go it is too late to recover it; but yet it was in your power to throw it, since the moving principle was in you. So, too, to the unjust and to the self-indulgent man it was open at the beginning not to become men of this kind, and so they are unjust and selfindulgent voluntarily; but now that they have become so it is not possible for them not to be so.

But not only are the vices of the soul voluntary, but those of the body also for some men, whom we accordingly blame; while no one blames those who are ugly by nature, we blame those who are so owing to want of exercise and care. So it is, too, with respect to weakness and infirmity; no one would reproach a man blind from birth or by disease or from a blow, but rather pity him, while every one would blame a man who was blind from drunkenness or some other form of self-indulgence. Of vices of the body, then, those in our own power are blamed, those not in our power are not. And if this be so, in the other cases also the vices that are blamed must be in our own power.

Now some one may say that all men desire the apparent good, but have no control over the appearance, but the end appears to each man in a form answering to his character. We reply that if each man is somehow responsible for his state of mind, he will also be himself somehow responsible for the appearance; but if not, no one is responsible for his own evildoing, but every one does evil acts through ignorance of the end, thinking that by these he will get what is best, and the aiming at the end is not self-chosen but one must be born with an eye, as it were, by which to judge rightly and choose what is truly good, and he is well endowed by nature who is well endowed with this. For it is what is greatest and most noble, and what we cannot get or learn from another, but must have just such as it was when given us at birth, and to be well and nobly endowed with this will be perfect and true excellence of natural endowment. If this is true, then, how will virtue be more voluntary than vice? To both men alike, the good and the bad, the end appears and is fixed by nature or however it may be, and it is by referring everything else to this that men do whatever they do.

Whether, then, it is not by nature that the end appears to each man such as it does appear, but something also depends on him, or the end is natural but because the good man adopts the means voluntarily virtue is voluntary, vice also will be none the less voluntary; for in the case of the bad man there is equally present that which depends on himself in his actions even if not in his end. If, then, as is asserted, the virtues are voluntary (for we are ourselves somehow partly responsible for our states of character, and it is by being persons of a certain kind that we assume the end to be so and so), the vices also will be voluntary; for the same is true of them.

With regard to the virtues in general we have stated their genus in outline, viz. that they are means and that they are states of character, and that they tend, and by their own nature, to the doing of the acts by which they are produced, and that they are in our power and voluntary, and act as the right rule prescribes. But actions and states of character are not voluntary in the same way; for we are masters of our actions from the beginning right to the end, if we know the particular facts, but though we control the beginning of our states of character the gradual progress is not obvious any more than it is in illnesses; because it was in our power, however, to act in this way or not in this way, therefore the states are voluntary.

Let us take up the several virtues, however, and say which they are and what sort of things they are concerned with and how they are concerned with them; at the same time it will become plain how many they are. And first let us speak of courage.

6

That it is a mean with regard to feelings of fear and confidence has already been made evident; and plainly the things we fear are terrible things, and these are, to speak without qualification, evils; for which reason people even define fear as expectation of evil. Now we fear all evils, e.g. disgrace, poverty, disease, friendlessness, death, but the brave man is not thought to be concerned with all; for to fear some things is even right and noble, and it is base not to fear them- e.g. disgrace; he who fears this is good and modest, and he who does not is shameless. He is, however, by some people called brave, by a transference of the word to a new meaning;

for he has in him something which is like the brave man, since the brave man also is a fearless person. Poverty and disease we perhaps ought not to fear, nor in general the things that do not proceed from vice and are not due to a man himself. But not even the man who is fearless of these is brave. Yet we apply the word to him also in virtue of a similarity; for some who in the dangers of war are cowards are liberal and are confident in face of the loss of money. Nor is a man a coward if he fears insult to his wife and children or envy or anything of the kind; nor brave if he is confident when he is about to be flogged. With what sort of terrible things, then, is the brave man concerned? Surely with the greatest; for no one is more likely than he to stand his ground against what is awe-inspiring. Now death is the most terrible of all things; for it is the end, and nothing is thought to be any longer either good or bad for the dead. But the brave man would not seem to be concerned even with death in all circumstances, e.g. at sea or in disease. In what circumstances, then? Surely in the noblest. Now such deaths are those in battle; for these take place in the greatest and noblest danger. And these are correspondingly honoured in city-states and at the courts of monarchs. Properly, then, he will be called brave who is fearless in face of a noble death, and of all emergencies that involve death; and the emergencies of war are in the highest degree of this kind. Yet at sea also, and in disease, the brave man is fearless, but not in the same way as the seaman; for he has given up hope of safety, and is disliking the thought of death in this shape, while they are hopeful because of their experience. At the same time, we show courage in situations where there is the opportunity of showing prowess or where death is noble; but in these forms of death neither of these conditions is fulfilled.

7

What is terrible is not the same for all men; but we say there are things terrible even beyond human strength. These, then, are terrible to every one- at least to every sensible man; but the terrible things that are not beyond human strength differ in magnitude and degree, and so too do the things that inspire confidence. Now the brave man is as dauntless as man may be. Therefore, while he will fear even the things that are not beyond human strength, he will face them as he ought and as the rule directs, for honour's sake; for this is the end of virtue. But it is possible to fear these more, or less, and again to fear things that are not terrible as if they were. Of the faults that are committed one consists in fearing what one should not, another in fearing as we should not, another in fearing when we should not, and so on; and so too with respect to the things that inspire confidence. The man, then, who faces and who fears the right things and from the right motive, in the right way and from the right time, and who feels confidence under the corresponding conditions, is brave; for the brave man feels and acts according to the merits of the case and in whatever way the rule directs. Now the end of every activity is conformity to the corresponding state of character. This is true, therefore, of the brave man as well as of others. But courage is noble. Therefore the end also is noble; for each thing is defined by its end. Therefore it is for a noble end that the brave man endures and acts as courage directs.

Of those who go to excess he who exceeds in fearlessness has no name (we have said previously that many states of character have no names), but he would be a sort of madman or insensible person if he feared nothing, neither earthquakes nor the waves, as they say the Celts do not; while the man who exceeds in confidence about what really is terrible is rash. The rash man, however, is also thought to be boastful and only a pretender to courage; at all events, as the brave man is with regard to what is terrible, so the rash man wishes to appear; and so he imitates him in situations where he can. Hence also most of them are a mixture of rashness and cowardice; for, while in these situations they display confidence, they do not hold their ground against what is really terrible. The man who exceeds in fear is a coward; for he fears both what he ought not and as he ought not, and all the similar characterizations attach to him. He is lacking also in confidence; but he is more conspicuous for his excess of fear in painful situations. The coward, then, is a despairing sort of person; for he fears everything. The brave man, on the other hand, has the opposite disposition; for confidence is the mark of a hopeful disposition. The coward, the rash man, and the brave man, then, are concerned with the same objects but are differently disposed towards them; for the first two exceed and fall short, while the third holds the middle, which is the right, position; and rash men are precipitate, and wish for dangers beforehand but draw back when they are in them, while brave men are keen in the moment of action, but quiet beforehand.

As we have said, then, courage is a mean with respect to things that inspire confidence or fear, in the circumstances that have been stated; and it chooses or endures things because it is noble to do so, or because it is base not to do so. But to die to escape from poverty or love or anything painful is not the mark of a brave man, but rather of a coward; for it is softness to fly from what is troublesome, and such a man endures death not because it is noble but to fly from evil.

8

Courage, then, is something of this sort, but the name is also applied to five other kinds.

First comes the courage of the citizen-soldier; for this is most like true courage. Citizen-soldiers seem to face dangers because of the penalties imposed by the laws and the reproaches they would otherwise incur, and because of the honours they win by such action; and therefore those peoples seem to be bravest among whom cowards are held in dishonour and brave men in honour. This is the kind of courage that Homer depicts, e.g. in Diomede and in Hector:

First will Polydamas be to heap reproach on me then; and

For Hector one day 'mid the Trojans shall utter his vaulting harangue: Afraid was Tydeides, and fled from my face.

This kind of courage is most like to that which we described earlier, because it is due to virtue; for it is due to shame and to desire of a noble object (i.e. honour) and avoidance of disgrace, which is ignoble. One might rank in the same class even those who are compelled by their rulers; but they are inferior, inasmuch as they do what they do not from shame but from fear, and to avoid not what is disgraceful but what is painful; for their masters compel them, as Hector does:

But if I shall spy any dastard that cowers far from the fight, Vainly will such an one hope to escape from the dogs.

And those who give them their posts, and beat them if they retreat, do the same, and so do those who draw them up with trenches or something of the sort behind them; all of these apply compulsion. But one ought to be brave not under compulsion but because it is noble to be so.

(2) Experience with regard to particular facts is also thought to be courage; this is indeed the reason why Socrates thought courage was knowledge. Other people exhibit this quality in other dangers, and professional soldiers exhibit it in the dangers of war; for there seem to be many empty alarms in war, of which these have had the most comprehensive experience; therefore they seem brave, because the others do not know the nature of the facts. Again, their experience makes them most capable in attack and in defence, since they can use their arms and have the kind that are likely to be best both for attack and for defence; therefore they fight like armed men against unarmed or like trained athletes against amateurs; for in such contests too it is not the bravest men that fight best, but those who are strongest and have their bodies in the best condition. Professional soldiers turn cowards, however, when the danger puts too great a strain on them and they are inferior in numbers and equipment; for they are the first to fly, while citizen-forces die at their posts, as in fact happened at the temple of Hermes. For to the latter flight is disgraceful and death is preferable to safety on those terms; while the former from the very beginning faced the danger on the assumption that they were stronger, and when they know the facts they fly, fearing death more than disgrace; but the brave man is not that sort of person.

(3) Passion also is sometimes reckoned as courage; those who act from passion, like wild beasts rushing at those who have wounded them, are thought to be brave, because brave men also are passionate; for passion above all things is eager to rush on danger, and hence Homer's 'put strength into his passion' and 'aroused their spirit and passion and 'hard he breathed panting' and 'his blood boiled'. For all such expressions seem to indicate the stirring and onset of passion. Now brave men act for honour's sake, but passion aids them; while wild beasts act under the influence of pain; for they attack because they have been wounded or because they are afraid, since if they are in a forest they do not come near one. Thus they are not brave because, driven by pain and passion, they rush on danger without foreseeing any of the perils, since at that rate even asses would be brave when they are hungry; for blows will not drive them from their food; and lust also makes adulterers do many daring things. (Those creatures are not brave, then, which are driven on to danger by pain or passion.) The 'courage' that is due to passion seems to be the most natural, and to be courage if choice and motive be added.

Men, then, as well as beasts, suffer pain when they are angry, and are pleased when they exact their revenge; those who fight for these reasons, however, are pugnacious but not brave; for they do not act for honour's sake nor as the rule directs, but from strength of feeling; they have, however, something akin to courage.

(4) Nor are sanguine people brave; for they are confident in danger only because they have conquered often and against many foes. Yet they closely resemble brave men, because both are confident; but brave men are confident for the reasons stated earlier, while these are so because they think they are the strongest and can suffer nothing. (Drunken men also behave in this way; they become sanguine). When their adventures do not succeed, however, they run away; but it was the mark of a brave man to face things that are, and seem, terrible for a man, because it is noble to do so and disgraceful not to do so. Hence also it is thought the mark of a braver man to be fearless and undisturbed in sudden alarms than to be so in those that are foreseen; for it must have proceeded more from a state of character, because less from preparation; acts that are foreseen may be chosen by calculation and rule, but sudden actions must be in accordance with one's state of character.

(5) People who are ignorant of the danger also appear brave, and they are not far removed from those of a sanguine temper, but are inferior inasmuch as they have no self-reliance while these have. Hence also the sanguine hold their ground for a time; but those who have been deceived about the facts fly if they know or suspect that these are different from what they supposed, as happened to the Argives when they fell in with the Spartans and took them for Sicyonians.

We have, then, described the character both of brave men and of those who are thought to be brave.

9

Though courage is concerned with feelings of confidence and of fear, it is not concerned with both alike, but more with the things that inspire fear; for he who is undisturbed in face of these and bears himself as he should towards these is more truly brave than the man who does so towards the things that inspire confidence. It is for facing what is painful, then, as has been said, that men are called brave. Hence also courage involves pain, and is justly praised; for it is harder to face what is painful than to abstain from what is pleasant.

Yet the end which courage sets before it would seem to be pleasant, but to be concealed by the attending circumstances, as happens also in athletic contests; for the end at which boxers aim is pleasant- the crown and the honours- but the blows they take are distressing to flesh and blood, and painful, and so is their whole exertion; and because the blows and the exertions are many the end, which is but small, appears to have nothing pleasant in it. And so, if the case of courage is similar, death and wounds will be painful to the brave man and against his will, but he will face them because it is noble to do so or because it is base not to do so. And the more he is possessed of virtue in its entirety and the happier he is, the more he will be pained at the thought of death; for life is best worth living for such a man, and he is knowingly losing the greatest goods, and this is painful. But he is none the less brave, and perhaps all the more so, because he chooses noble deeds of war at that cost. It is not the case, then, with all the virtues that the exercise of them is pleasant, except in so far as it reaches its end. But it is quite possible that the best soldiers may be not men of this sort but those who are less brave but have no other good; for these are ready to face danger, and they sell their life for trifling gains.

So much, then, for courage; it is not difficult to grasp its nature in outline, at any rate, from what has been said.

10

After courage let us speak of temperance; for these seem to be the virtues of the irrational parts. We have said that temperance is a mean with regard to pleasures (for it is less, and not in the same way, concerned with pains); self-indulgence also is manifested in the same sphere. Now, therefore, let us determine with what sort of pleasures they are concerned. We may assume the distinction between bodily pleasures and those of the soul, such as love of honour and love of learning; for the lover of each of these delights in that of which he is a lover, the body being in no way affected, but rather the mind; but men who are concerned with such pleasures are called neither temperate nor self-indulgent. Nor, again, are those who are concerned with the other pleasures that are not bodily; for those who are fond of hearing and telling stories and who spend their days on anything that turns up are called gossips, but not self-indulgent, nor are those who are pained at the loss of money or of friends.

Temperance must be concerned with bodily pleasures, but not all even of these; for those who delight in objects of vision, such as colours and shapes and painting, are called neither temperate nor self-indulgent; yet it would seem possible to delight even in these either as one should or to excess or to a deficient degree.

And so too is it with objects of hearing; no one calls those who delight extravagantly in music or acting self-indulgent, nor those who do so as they ought temperate.

Nor do we apply these names to those who delight in odour, unless it be incidentally; we do not call those self-indulgent who delight in the odour of apples or roses or incense, but rather those who delight in the odour of unguents or of dainty dishes; for self-indulgent people delight in these because these remind them of the objects of their appetite. And one may see even other people, when they are hungry, delighting in the smell of food; but to delight in this kind of thing is the mark of the self-indulgent man; for these are objects of appetite to him.

Nor is there in animals other than man any pleasure connected with these senses, except incidentally. For dogs do not delight in the scent of hares, but in the eating of them, but the scent told them the hares were there; nor does the lion delight in the lowing of the ox, but in eating it; but he perceived by the lowing that it was near, and therefore appears to delight in the lowing; and similarly he does not delight because he sees 'a stag or a wild goat', but because he is going to make a meal of it. Temperance and self-indulgence, however, are concerned with the kind of pleasures that the other animals share in, which therefore appear slavish and brutish; these are touch and taste. But even of taste they appear to make little or no use; for the business of taste is the discriminating of flavours, which is done by winetasters and people who season dishes; but they hardly take pleasure in making these discriminations, or at least self-indulgent people do not, but in the actual enjoyment, which in all cases comes through touch, both in the case of food and in that of drink and in that of sexual intercourse. This is why a certain gourmand prayed that his throat might become longer than a crane's, implying that it was the contact that he took pleasure in. Thus the sense with which self-indulgence is connected is the most widely shared of the senses; and self-indulgence would seem to be justly a matter of reproach, because it attaches to us not as men but as animals. To delight in such things, then, and to love them above all others, is brutish. For even of the pleasures of touch the most liberal have been eliminated, e.g. those produced in the gymnasium by rubbing and by the consequent heat; for the contact characteristic of the self-indulgent man does not affect the whole body but only certain parts.

11

Of the appetites some seem to be common, others to be peculiar to individuals and acquired; e.g. the appetite for food is natural, since every one who is without it craves for food or drink, and sometimes for both, and for love also (as Homer says) if he is young and lusty; but not every one craves for this or that kind of nourishment or love, nor for the same things. Hence such craving appears to be our very own. Yet it has of course something natural about it; for different things are pleasant to different kinds of people, and some things are more pleasant to every one than chance objects. Now in the natural appetites few go wrong, and only in one direction, that of excess; for to eat or drink whatever offers itself till one is surfeited is to exceed the natural amount, since natural appetite is the replenishment of one's deficiency. Hence these people are called belly-gods, this implying that they fill their belly beyond what is right. It is people of entirely slavish character that become like this. But with regard to the pleasures peculiar to individuals many people go wrong and in many ways. For while the people who are 'fond of so and so' are so called because they delight either in the wrong things, or more than most people do, or in the wrong way, the self-indulgent exceed in all three ways; they both delight in some things that they ought not to delight in (since they are hateful), and if one ought to delight in some of the things they delight in, they do so more than one ought and than most men do.

Plainly, then, excess with regard to pleasures is self-indulgence and is culpable; with regard to pains one is not, as in the case of courage, called temperate for facing them or self-indulgent for not doing so, but the selfindulgent man is so called because he is pained more than he ought at not getting pleasant things (even his pain being caused by pleasure), and the temperate man is so called because he is not pained at the absence of what is pleasant and at his abstinence from it.

The self-indulgent man, then, craves for all pleasant things or those that are most pleasant, and is led by his appetite to choose these at the cost of everything else; hence he is pained both when he fails to get them and when he is merely craving for them (for appetite involves pain); but it seems absurd to be pained for the sake of pleasure. People who fall short with regard to pleasures and delight in them less than they should are hardly found; for such insensibility is not human. Even the other animals distinguish different kinds of food and enjoy some and not others; and if there is any one who finds nothing pleasant and nothing more attractive than anything else, he must be something quite different from a man; this sort of person has not received a name because he hardly occurs. The temperate man occupies a middle position with regard to these objects. For he neither enjoys the things that the self-indulgent man enjoys most-but rather dislikes them-nor in general the things that he should not, nor anything of this sort to excess, nor does he feel pain or craving when they are absent, or does so only to a moderate degree, and not more than he should, nor when he should not, and so on; but the things that, being pleasant, make for health or for good condition, he will desire moderately and as he should, and also other pleasant things if they are not hindrances to these ends, or contrary to what is noble, or beyond his means. For he who neglects these conditions loves such pleasures more than they are worth, but the temperate man is not that sort of person, but the sort of person that the right rule prescribes.

12

Self-indulgence is more like a voluntary state than cowardice. For the former is actuated by pleasure, the latter by pain, of which the one is to be chosen and the other to be avoided; and pain upsets and destroys the nature of the person who feels it, while pleasure does nothing of the sort. Therefore self-indulgence is more voluntary. Hence also it is more a matter of reproach; for it is easier to become accustomed to its objects, since there are many things of this sort in life, and the process of habituation to them is free from danger, while with terrible objects the reverse is the case. But cowardice would seem to be voluntary in a different degree from its particular manifestations; for it is itself painless, but in these we are upset by pain, so that we even throw down our arms and disgrace ourselves in other ways; hence our acts are even thought to be done under compulsion. For the self-indulgent man, on the other hand, the particular acts are voluntary (for he does them with craving and desire), but the whole state is less so; for no one craves to be self-indulgent.

The name self-indulgence is applied also to childish faults; for they bear a certain resemblance to what we have been considering. Which is called after which, makes no difference to our present purpose; plainly, however, the later is called after the earlier. The transference of the name seems not a bad one; for that which desires what is base and which develops quickly ought to be kept in a chastened condition, and these characteristics belong above all to appetite and to the child, since children in fact live at the beck and call of appetite, and it is in them that the desire for what is pleasant is strongest. If, then, it is not going to be obedient and subject to the ruling principle, it will go to great lengths; for in an irrational being the desire for pleasure is insatiable even if it tries every source of gratification, and the exercise of appetite increases its innate force, and if appetites are strong and violent they even expel the power of calculation. Hence they should be moderate and few, and should in no way oppose the rational principle-and this is what we call an obedient and chastened state-and as the child should live according to the direction of his tutor, so the appetitive element should live according to rational principle. Hence the appetitive element in a temperate man should harmonize with the rational principle; for the noble is the mark at which both aim, and the temperate man craves for the things be ought, as he ought, as when he ought; and when he ought; and this is what rational principle directs.

Here we conclude our account of temperance.

Book Four

1

Let us speak next of liberality. It seems to be the mean with regard to wealth; for the liberal man is praised not in respect of military matters, nor of those in respect of which the temrate man is praised, nor of judicial decisions, but with regard to the giving and taking of wealth, and especially in respect of giving. Now by 'wealth' we mean all the things whose value is measured by money. Further, prodigality and meanness are excesses and defects with regard to wealth; and meanness we always impute to those who care more than they ought for wealth, but we sometimes apply the word 'prodigality' in a complex sense; for we call those men prodigals who are incontinent and spend money on self-indulgence. Hence also they are thought the poorest characters; for they combine more vices than one. Therefore the application of the word to them is not its proper use; for a 'prodigal' means a man who has a single evil quality, that of wasting his substance; since a prodigal is one who is being ruined by his own fault, and the wasting of substance is thought to be a sort of ruining of oneself, life being held to depend on possession of substance.

This, then, is the sense in which we take the word 'prodigality'. Now the things that have a use may be used either well or badly; and riches is a useful thing; and everything is used best by the man who has the virtue concerned with it; riches, therefore, will be used best by the man who has the virtue concerned with wealth; and this is the liberal man. Now spending and giving seem to be the using of wealth; taking and keeping rather the possession of it. Hence it is more the mark of the liberal man to give to the right people than to take from the right sources and not to take from the wrong. For it is more characteristic of virtue to do good than to have good done to one, and more characteristic to do what is noble than not to do what is base; and it is not hard to see that giving implies doing good and doing what is noble, and taking implies having good done to one or not acting basely. And gratitude is felt towards him who gives, not towards him who does not take, and praise also is bestowed more on him. It is easier, also, not to take than to give; for men are apter to give away their own too little than to take what is another's. Givers, too, are called liberal; but those who do not take are not praised for liberality but rather for justice; while those who take are hardly praised at all. And the liberal are almost the most loved of all virtuous characters, since they are useful; and this depends on their giving.

Now virtuous actions are noble and done for the sake of the noble. Therefore the liberal man, like other virtuous men, will give for the sake of the noble, and rightly; for he will give to the right people, the right amounts, and at the right time, with all the other qualifications that accompany right giving; and that too with pleasure or without pain; for that which is virtuous is pleasant or free from pain-least of all will it be painful. But he who gives to the wrong people or not for the sake of the noble but for some other cause, will be called not liberal but by some other name. Nor is he liberal who gives with pain; for he would prefer the wealth to the noble act, and this is not characteristic of a liberal man. But no more will the liberal man take from wrong sources; for such taking is not characteristic of the man who sets no store by wealth. Nor will he be a ready asker; for it is not characteristic of a man who confers benefits to accept them lightly. But he will take from the right sources, e.g. from his own possessions, not as something noble but as a necessity, that he may have something to give. Nor will he neglect his own property, since he wishes by means of this to help others. And he will refrain from giving to anybody and everybody, that he may have something to give to the right people, at the right time, and where it is noble to do so. It is highly characteristic of a liberal man also to go to excess in giving, so that he leaves too little for himself; for it is the nature of a liberal man not to look to himself. The term 'liberality' is used relatively to a man's substance; for liberality resides not in the multitude of the gifts but in the state of character of the giver, and this is relative to the giver's substance. There is therefore nothing to prevent the man who gives less from being the more liberal man, if he has less to give those are thought to be more liberal who have not made their wealth but inherited it; for in the first place they have no experience of want, and secondly all men are fonder of their own productions, as are parents and poets. It is not easy for the liberal man to be rich, since he is not apt either at taking or at keeping, but at giving away, and does not value wealth for its own sake but as a means to giving. Hence comes the charge that is brought against fortune, that those who deserve riches most get it least. But it is not unreasonable that it should turn out so; for he cannot have wealth, any more than anything else, if he does not take pains to have it. Yet he will not give to the wrong people nor at the wrong time, and so on; for he would no longer be acting in accordance with liberality, and if he spent on these objects he would have nothing to spend on the right objects. For, as has been said, he is liberal who spends according to his substance and on the right objects; and he who exceeds is prodigal. Hence we do not call despots prodigal; for it is thought not easy for them to give and spend beyond the amount of their possessions. Liberality, then, being a mean with regard to giving and taking of wealth, the liberal man will both give and spend the right amounts and on the right objects, alike in small things and in great, and that with pleasure; he will also take the right amounts and from the right sources. For, the virtue being a mean with regard to both, he will do both as he ought; since this sort of taking accompanies proper giving, and that which is not of this sort is contrary to it, and accordingly the giving and taking that accompany each other are present together in the same man, while the contrary kinds evidently are not. But if he happens to spend in a manner contrary to what is right and noble, he will be pained, but moderately and as he ought; for it is the mark of virtue both to be pleased and to be pained at the right objects and in the right way. Further, the liberal man is easy to deal with in money matters; for he can be got the better of, since he sets no store by money, and is more annoyed if he has not spent something that he ought than pained if he has spent something that he ought not, and does not agree with the saying of Simonides.

The prodigal errs in these respects also; for he is neither pleased nor pained at the right things or in the right way; this will be more evident as we go on. We have said that prodigality and meanness are excesses and deficiencies, and in two things, in giving and in taking; for we include spending under giving. Now prodigality exceeds in giving and not taking, while meanness falls short in giving, and exceeds in taking, except in small things.

The characteristics of prodigality are not often combined; for it is not easy to give to all if you take from none; private persons soon exhaust their substance with giving, and it is to these that the name of prodigals is applied- though a man of this sort would seem to be in no small degree better than a mean man. For he is easily cured both by age and by poverty, and thus he may move towards the middle state. For he has the characteristics of the liberal man, since he both gives and refrains from taking, though he does neither of these in the right manner or well. Therefore if he were brought to do so by habituation or in some other way, he would be liberal; for he will then give to the right people, and will not take from the wrong sources. This is why he is thought to have not a bad character; it is not the mark of a wicked or ignoble man to go to excess in giving and not taking, but only of a foolish one. The man who is prodigal in this way is thought much better than the mean man both for the aforesaid reasons and because he benefits many while the other benefits no one, not even himself.

But most prodigal people, as has been said, also take from the wrong sources, and are in this respect mean. They become apt to take because they wish to spend and cannot do this easily; for their possessions soon run short. Thus they are forced to provide means from some other source. At the same time, because they care nothing for honour, they take recklessly and from any source; for they have an appetite for giving, and they do not mind how or from what source. Hence also their giving is not liberal; for it is not noble, nor does it aim at nobility, nor is it done in the right way; sometimes they make rich those who should be poor, and will give nothing to people of respectable character, and much to flatterers or those who provide them with some other pleasure. Hence also most of them are self-indulgent; for they spend lightly and waste money on their indulgences, and incline towards pleasures because they do not live with a view to what is noble.

The prodigal man, then, turns into what we have described if he is left untutored, but if he is treated with care he will arrive at the intermediate and right state. But meanness is both incurable (for old age and every disability is thought to make men mean) and more innate in men than prodigality; for most men are fonder of getting money than of giving. It also extends widely, and is multiform, since there seem to be many kinds of meanness.

For it consists in two things, deficiency in giving and excess in taking, and is not found complete in all men but is sometimes divided; some men go to excess in taking, others fall short in giving. Those who are called by such names as 'miserly', 'close', 'stingy', all fall short in giving, but do not covet the possessions of others nor wish to get them. In some this is due to a sort of honesty and avoidance of what is disgraceful (for some seem, or at least profess, to hoard their money for this reason, that they may not some day be forced to do something disgraceful; to this class belong the cheeseparer and every one of the sort; he is so called from his excess of unwillingness to give anything); while others again keep their hands off the property of others from fear, on the ground that it is not easy, if one takes the property of others oneself, to avoid having one's own taken by them; they are therefore content neither to take nor to give.

Others again exceed in respect of taking by taking anything and from any source, e.g. those who ply sordid trades, pimps and all such people, and those who lend small sums and at high rates. For all of these take more than they ought and from wrong sources. What is common to them is evidently sordid love of gain; they all put up with a bad name for the sake of gain, and little gain at that. For those who make great gains but from wrong sources, and not the right gains, e.g. despots when they sack cities and spoil temples, we do not call mean but rather wicked, impious, and unjust. But the gamester and the footpad (and the highwayman) belong to the class of the mean, since they have a sordid love of gain. For it is for gain that both of them ply their craft and endure the disgrace of it, and the one faces the greatest dangers for the sake of the booty, while the other makes gain from his friends, to whom he ought to be giving. Both, then, since they are willing to make gain from wrong sources, are sordid lovers of gain; therefore all such forms of taking are mean.

And it is natural that meanness is described as the contrary of liberality; for not only is it a greater evil than prodigality, but men err more often in this direction than in the way of prodigality as we have described it.

So much, then, for liberality and the opposed vices.

2

It would seem proper to discuss magnificence next. For this also seems to be a virtue concerned with wealth; but it does not like liberality extend to all the actions that are concerned with wealth, but only to those that involve expenditure; and in these it surpasses liberality in scale. For, as the name itself suggests, it is a fitting expenditure involving largeness of scale. But the scale is relative; for the expense of equipping a trireme is not the same as that of heading a sacred embassy. It is what is fitting, then, in relation to the agent, and to the circumstances and the object. The man who in small or middling things spends according to the merits of the case is not called magnificent (e.g. the man who can say 'many a gift I gave the wanderer'), but only the man who does so in great things. For the magnificent man is liberal, but the liberal man is not necessarily magnificent. The deficiency of this state of character is called niggardliness, the excess vulgarity, lack of taste, and the like, which do not go to excess in the amount spent on right objects, but by showy expenditure in the wrong circumstances and the wrong manner; we shall speak of these vices later.

The magnificent man is like an artist; for he can see what is fitting and spend large sums tastefully. For, as we said at the begining, a state of character is determined by its activities and by its objects. Now the expenses of the magnificent man are large and fitting. Such, therefore, are also his results; for thus there will be a great expenditure and one that is fitting to its result. Therefore the result should be worthy of the expense, and the expense should be worthy of the result, or should even exceed it. And the magnificent man will spend such sums for honour's sake; for this is common to the virtues. And further he will do so gladly and lavishly; for nice calculation is a niggardly thing. And he will consider how the result can be made most beautiful and most becoming rather than for how much it can be produced and how it can be produced most cheaply. It is necessary, then, that the magnificent man be also liberal. For the liberal man also will spend what he ought and as he ought; and it is in these matters that the greatness implied in the name of the magnificent man-his bigness, as it were-is manifested, since liberality is concerned with these matters; and at an equal expense he will produce a more magnificent work of art. For a possession and a work of art have not the same excellence. The most valuable possession is that which is worth most, e.g. gold, but the most valuable work of art is that which is great and beautiful (for the contemplation of such a work inspires admiration, and so does magnificence); and a work has an excellence-viz. magnificence-which involves magnitude.

Magnificence is an attribute of expenditures of the kind which we call honourable, e.g. those connected with the gods-votive offerings, buildings, and sacrifices-and similarly with any form of religious worship, and all those that are proper objects of public-spirited ambition, as when people think they ought to equip a chorus or a trireme, or entertain the city, in a brilliant way. But in all cases, as has been said, we have regard to the agent as well and ask who he is and what means he has; for the expenditure should be worthy of his means, and suit not only the result but also the producer. Hence a poor man cannot be magnificent, since he has not the means with which to spend large sums fittingly; and he who tries is a fool, since he spends beyond what can be expected of him and what is proper, but it is right expenditure that is virtuous. But great expenditure is becoming to those who have suitable means to start with, acquired by their own efforts or from ancestors or connexions, and to people of high birth or reputation, and so on; for all these things bring with them greatness and prestige. Primarily, then, the magnificent man is of this sort, and magnificence is shown in expenditures of this sort, as has been said; for these are the greatest and most honourable. Of private occasions of expenditure the most suitable are those that take place once for all, e.g. a wedding or anything of the kind, or anything that interests the whole city or the people of position in it, and also the receiving of foreign guests and the sending of them on their way, and gifts and counter-gifts; for the magnificent man spends not on himself but on public objects, and gifts bear some resemblance to votive offerings. A magnificent man will also furnish his house suitably to his wealth (for even a house is a sort of public ornament), and will spend by preference on those works that are lasting (for these are the most beautiful), and on every class of things he will spend what is becoming; for the same things are not suitable for gods and for men, nor in a temple and in a tomb. And since each expenditure may be great of its kind, and what is most magnificent absolutely is great expenditure on a great object, but what is magnificent here is what is great in these circumstances, and greatness in the work differs from greatness in the expense (for the most beautiful ball or bottle is magnificent as a gift to a child, but the price of it is small and mean),-therefore it is characteristic of the magnificent man, whatever kind of result he is producing, to produce it magnificently (for such a result is not easily surpassed) and to make it worthy of the expenditure.

Such, then, is the magnificent man; the man who goes to excess and is vulgar exceeds, as has been said, by spending beyond what is right. For on small objects of expenditure he spends much and displays a tasteless showiness; e.g. he gives a club dinner on the scale of a wedding banquet, and when he provides the chorus for a comedy he brings them on to the stage in purple, as they do at Megara. And all such things he will do not for honour's sake but to show off his wealth, and because he thinks he is admired for these things, and where he ought to spend much he spends little and where little, much. The niggardly man on the other hand will fall short in everything, and after spending the greatest sums will spoil the beauty of the result for a trifle, and whatever he is doing he will hesitate and consider how he may spend least, and lament even that, and think he is doing everything on a bigger scale than he ought.

These states of character, then, are vices; yet they do not bring disgrace because they are neither harmful to one's neighbour nor very unseemly.

3

Pride seems even from its name to be concerned with great things; what sort of great things, is the first question we must try to answer. It makes no difference whether we consider the state of character or the man characterized by it. Now the man is thought to be proud who thinks himself worthy of great things, being worthy of them; for he who does so beyond his deserts is a fool, but no virtuous man is foolish or silly. The proud man, then, is the man we have described. For he who is worthy of little and thinks himself worthy of little is temperate, but not proud; for pride implies greatness, as beauty implies a goodsized body, and little people may be neat and well-proportioned but cannot be beautiful. On the other hand, he who thinks himself worthy of great things, being unworthy of them, is vain; though not every one who thinks himself worthy of more than he really is worthy of in vain. The man who thinks himself worthy of worthy of less than he is really worthy of is unduly humble, whether his deserts be great or moderate, or his deserts be small but his claims yet smaller. And the man whose deserts are great would seem most unduly humble; for what would he have done if they had been less? The proud man, then, is an extreme in respect of the greatness of his claims, but a mean in respect of the rightness of them; for he claims what is accordance with his merits, while the others go to excess or fall short.

If, then, he deserves and claims great things, and above all the great things, he will be concerned with one thing in particular. Desert is relative to external goods; and the greatest of these, we should say, is that which we render to the gods, and which people of position most aim at, and which is the prize appointed for the noblest deeds; and this is honour; that is surely the greatest of external goods. Honours and dishonours, therefore, are the objects with respect to which the proud man is as he should be. And even apart from argument it is with honour that proud men appear to be concerned; for it is honour that they chiefly claim, but in accordance with their deserts. The unduly humble man falls short both in comparison with his own merits and in comparison with the proud man's claims. The vain man goes to excess in comparison with his own merits, but does not exceed the proud man's claims.

Now the proud man, since he deserves most, must be good in the highest degree; for the better man always deserves more, and the best man most. Therefore the truly proud man must be good. And greatness in every virtue would seem to be characteristic of a proud man. And it would be most unbecoming for a proud man to fly from danger, swinging his arms by his sides, or to wrong another; for to what end should he do disgraceful acts, he to whom nothing is great? If we consider him point by point we shall see the utter absurdity of a proud man who is not good. Nor, again, would he be worthy of honour if he were bad; for honour is the prize of virtue, and it is to the good that it is rendered. Pride, then, seems to be a sort of crown of the virtues; for it makes them greater, and it is not found without them. Therefore it is hard to be truly proud; for it is impossible without nobility and goodness of character. It is chiefly with honours and dishonours, then, that the proud man is concerned; and at honours that are great and conferred by good men he will be moderately Pleased, thinking that he is coming by his own or even less than his own; for there can be no honour that is worthy of perfect virtue, yet he will at any rate accept it since they have nothing greater to bestow on him; but honour from casual people and on trifling grounds he will utterly despise, since it is not this that he deserves, and dishonour too, since in his case it cannot be just. In the first place, then, as has been said, the proud man is concerned with honours; yet he will also bear himself with moderation towards wealth and power and all good or evil fortune, whatever may befall him, and will be neither over-joyed by good fortune nor over-pained by evil. For not even towards honour does he bear himself as if it were a very great thing. Power and wealth are desirable for the sake of honour (at least those who have them wish to get honour by means of them); and for him to whom even honour is a little thing the others must be so too. Hence proud men are thought to be disdainful.

The goods of fortune also are thought to contribute towards pride. For men who are well-born are thought worthy of honour, and so are those who enjoy power or wealth; for they are in a superior position, and everything that has a superiority in something good is held in greater honour. Hence even such things make men prouder; for they are honoured by some for having them; but in truth the good man alone is to be honoured; he, however, who has both advantages is thought the more worthy of honour. But those who without virtue have such goods are neither justified in making great claims nor entitled to the name of 'proud'; for these things imply perfect virtue. Disdainful and insolent, however, even those who have such goods become. For without virtue it is not easy to bear gracefully the goods of fortune; and, being unable to bear them, and thinking themselves superior to others, they despise others and themselves do what they please. They imitate the proud man without being like him, and this they do where they can; so they do not act virtuously, but they do despise others. For the proud man despises justly (since he thinks truly), but the many do so at random.

He does not run into trifling dangers, nor is he fond of danger, because he honours few things; but he will face great dangers, and when he is in danger he is unsparing of his life, knowing that there are conditions on which life is not worth having. And he is the sort of man to confer benefits, but he is ashamed of receiving them; for the one is the mark of a superior, the other of an inferior. And he is apt to confer greater benefits in return; for thus the original benefactor besides being paid will incur a debt to him, and will be the gainer by the transaction. They seem also to remember any service they have done, but not those they have received (for he who receives a service is inferior to him who has done it, but the proud man wishes to be superior), and to hear of the former with pleasure, of the latter with displeasure; this, it seems, is why Thetis did not mention to Zeus the services she had done him, and why the Spartans did not recount their services to the Athenians, but those they had received. It is a mark of the proud man also to ask for nothing or scarcely anything, but to give help readily, and to be dignified towards people who enjoy high position and good fortune, but unassuming towards those of the middle class; for it is a difficult and lofty thing to be superior to the former, but easy to be so to the latter, and a lofty bearing over the former is no mark of ill-breeding, but among humble people it is as vulgar as a display of strength against the weak. Again, it is characteristic of the proud man not to aim at the things commonly held in honour, or the things in which others excel; to be sluggish and to hold back except where great honour or a great work is at stake, and to be a man of few deeds, but of great and notable ones. He must also be open in his hate and in his love (for to conceal one's feelings, i.e. to care less for truth than for what people will think, is a coward's part), and must speak and act openly; for he is free of speech because he is contemptuous, and he is given to telling the truth, except when he speaks in irony to the vulgar. He must be unable to make his life revolve round another, unless it be a friend; for this is slavish, and for this reason all flatterers are servile and people lacking in self-respect are flatterers. Nor is he given to admiration; for nothing to him is great. Nor is he mindful of wrongs; for it is not the part of a proud man to have a long memory, especially for wrongs, but rather to overlook them. Nor is he a gossip; for he will speak neither about himself nor about another, since he cares not to be praised nor for others to be blamed; nor again is he given to praise; and for the same reason he is not an evil-speaker, even about his enemies, except from haughtiness. With regard to necessary or small matters he is least of all me given to lamentation or the asking of favours; for it is the part of one who takes such matters seriously to behave so with respect to them. He is one who will possess beautiful and profitless things rather than profitable and useful ones; for this is more proper to a character that suffices to itself.

Further, a slow step is thought proper to the proud man, a deep voice, and a level utterance; for the man who takes few things seriously is not likely to be hurried, nor the man who thinks nothing great to be excited, while a shrill voice and a rapid gait are the results of hurry and excitement.

Such, then, is the proud man; the man who falls short of him is unduly humble, and the man who goes beyond him is vain. Now even these are not thought to be bad (for they are not malicious), but only mistaken. For the unduly humble man, being worthy of good things, robs himself of what he deserves, and to have something bad about him from the fact that he does not think himself worthy of good things, and seems also not to know himself; else he would have desired the things he was worthy of, since these were good. Yet such people are not thought to be fools, but rather unduly retiring. Such a reputation, however, seems actually to make them worse; for each class of people aims at what corresponds to its worth, and these people stand back even from noble actions and undertakings, deeming themselves unworthy, and from external goods no less. Vain people, on the other hand, are fools and ignorant of themselves, and that manifestly; for, not being worthy of them, they attempt honourable undertakings, and then are found out; and tetadorn themselves with clothing and outward show and such things, and wish their strokes of good fortune to be made public, and speak about them as if they would be honoured for them. But undue humility is more opposed to pride than vanity is; for it is both commoner and worse.

Pride, then, is concerned with honour on the grand scale, as has been said.

4

There seems to be in the sphere of honour also, as was said in our first remarks on the subject, a virtue which would appear to be related to pride as liberality is to magnificence. For neither of these has anything to do with the grand scale, but both dispose us as is right with regard to middling and unimportant objects; as in getting and giving of wealth there is a mean and an excess and defect, so too honour may be desired more than is right, or less, or from the right sources and in the right way. We blame both the ambitious man as am at honour more than is right and from wrong sources, and the unambitious man as not willing to be honoured even for noble reasons. But sometimes we praise the ambitious man as being manly and a lover of what is noble, and the unambitious man as being moderate and self-controlled, as we said in our first treatment of the subject. Evidently, since 'fond of such and such an object' has more than one meaning, we do not assign the term 'ambition' or 'love of honour' always to the same thing, but when we praise the quality we think of the man who loves honour more than most people, and when we blame it we think of him who loves it more than is right. The mean being without a name, the extremes seem to dispute for its place as though that were vacant by default. But where there is excess and defect, there is also an intermediate; now men desire honour both more than they should and less; therefore it is possible also to do so as one should; at all events this is the state of character that is praised, being an unnamed mean in respect of honour. Relatively to ambition it seems to be unambitiousness, and relatively to unambitiousness it seems to be ambition, while relatively to both severally it seems in a sense to be both together. This appears to be true of the other virtues also. But in this case the extremes seem to be contradictories because the mean has not received a name.

5

Good temper is a mean with respect to anger; the middle state being unnamed, and the extremes almost without a name as well, we place good temper in the middle position, though it inclines towards the deficiency, which is without a name. The excess might called a sort of 'irascibility'. For the passion is anger, while its causes are many and diverse.

The man who is angry at the right things and with the right people, and, further, as he ought, when he ought, and as long as he ought, is praised. This will be the good-tempered man, then, since good temper is praised. For the good-tempered man tends to be unperturbed and not to be led by passion, but to be angry in the manner, at the things, and for the length of time, that the rule dictates; but he is thought to err rather in the direction of deficiency; for the good-tempered man is not revengeful, but rather tends to make allowances.

The deficiency, whether it is a sort of 'inirascibility' or whatever it is, is blamed. For those who are not angry at the things they should be angry at are thought to be fools, and so are those who are not angry in the right way, at the right time, or with the right persons; for such a man is thought not to feel things nor to be pained by them, and, since he does not get angry, he is thought unlikely to defend himself; and to endure being insulted and put up with insult to one's friends is slavish.

The excess can be manifested in all the points that have been named (for one can be angry with the wrong persons, at the wrong things, more than is right, too quickly, or too long);

yet all are not found in the same person. Indeed they could not; for evil destroys even itself, and if it is complete becomes unbearable. Now hot-tempered people get angry quickly and with the wrong persons and at the wrong things and more than is right, but their anger ceases quickly-which is the best point about them. This happens to them because they do not restrain their anger but retaliate openly owing to their quickness of temper, and then their anger ceases. By reason of excess choleric people are quick-tempered and ready to be angry with everything and on every occasion; whence their name. Sulky people are hard to appease, and retain their anger long; for they repress their passion. But it ceases when they retaliate; for revenge relieves them of their anger, producing in them pleasure instead of pain. If this does not happen they retain their burden; for owing to its not being obvious no one even reasons with them, and to digest one's anger in oneself takes time. Such people are most troublesome to themselves and to their dearest friends. We call had-tempered those who are angry at the wrong things, more than is right, and longer, and cannot be appeased until they inflict vengeance or punishment.

To good temper we oppose the excess rather than the defect; for not only is it commoner since revenge is the more human), but bad-tempered people are worse to live with.

What we have said in our earlier treatment of the subject is plain also from what we are now saying; viz. that it is not easy to define how, with whom, at what, and how long one should be angry, and at what point right action ceases and wrong begins. For the man who strays a little from the path, either towards the more or towards the less, is not blamed; since sometimes we praise those who exhibit the deficiency, and call them good-tempered, and sometimes we call angry people manly, as being capable of ruling. How far, therefore, and how a man must stray before he becomes blameworthy, it is not easy to state in words; for the decision depends on the particular facts and on perception. But so much at least is plain, that the middle state is praiseworthy- that in virtue of which we are angry with the right people, at the right things, in the right way, and so on, while the excesses and defects are blameworthy- slightly so if they are present in a low degree, more if in a higher degree, and very much if in a high degree. Evidently, then, we must cling to the middle state.- Enough of the states relative to anger.

6

In gatherings of men, in social life and the interchange of words and deeds, some men are thought to be obsequious, viz. those who to give pleasure praise everything and never oppose, but think it their duty 'to give no pain to the people they meet'; while those who, on the contrary, oppose everything and care not a whit about giving pain are called churlish and contentious. That the states we have named are culpable is plain enough, and that the middle state is laudable- that in virtue of which a man will put up with, and will resent, the right things and in the right way; but no name has been assigned to it, though it most resembles friendship. For the man who corresponds to this middle state is very much what, with affection added, we call a good friend. But the state in question differs from friendship in that it implies no passion or affection for one's associates; since it is not by reason of loving or hating that such a man takes everything in the right way, but by being a man of a certain kind. For he will behave so alike towards those he knows and those he does not know, towards intimates and those who are not so, except that in each of these cases he will behave as is befitting; for it is not proper to have the same care for intimates and for strangers, nor again is it the same conditions that make it right to give pain to them. Now we have said generally that he will associate with people in the right way; but it is by reference to what is honourable and expedient that he will aim at not giving pain or at contributing pleasure. For he seems to be concerned with the pleasures and pains of social life; and wherever it is not honourable, or is harmful, for him to contribute pleasure, he will refuse, and will choose rather to give pain; also if his acquiescence in another's action would bring disgrace, and that in a high degree, or injury, on that other, while his opposition brings a little pain, he will not acquiesce but will decline. He will associate differently with people in high station and with ordinary people, with closer and more distant acquaintances, and so too with regard to all other differences, rendering to each class what is befitting, and while for its own sake he chooses to contribute pleasure, and avoids the giving of pain, he will be guided by the consequences, if these are greater, i.e. honour and expediency. For the sake of a great future pleasure, too, he will inflict small pains.

The man who attains the mean, then, is such as we have described, but has not received a name; of those who contribute pleasure, the man who aims at being pleasant with no ulterior object is obsequious, but the man who does so in order that he may get some advantage in the direction of money or the things that money buys is a flatterer; while the man who quarrels with everything is, as has been said, churlish and contentious. And the extremes seem to be contradictory to each other because the mean is without a name.

7

The mean opposed to boastfulness is found in almost the same sphere; and this also is without a name. It will be no bad plan to describe these states as well; for we shall both know the facts about character better if we go through them in detail, and we shall be convinced that the virtues are means if we see this to be so in all cases. In the field of social life those who make the giving of pleasure or pain their object in associating with others have been described; let us now describe those who pursue truth or falsehood alike in words and deeds and in the claims they put forward. The boastful man, then, is thought to be apt to claim the things that bring glory, when he has not got them, or to claim more of them than he has, and the mock-modest man on the other hand to disclaim what he has or belittle it, while the man who observes the mean is one who calls a thing by its own name, being truthful both in life and in word, owning to what he has, and neither more nor less. Now each of these courses may be adopted either with or without an object. But each man speaks and acts and lives in accordance with his character, if he is not acting for some ulterior object. And falsehood is in itself mean and culpable, and truth noble and worthy of praise. Thus the truthful man is another case of a man who, being in the mean, is worthy of praise, and both forms of untruthful man are culpable, and particularly the boastful man.

Let us discuss them both, but first of all the truthful man. We are not speaking of the man who keeps faith in his agreements, i.e. in the things that pertain to justice or injustice (for this would belong to another virtue), but the man who in the matters in which nothing of this sort is at stake is true both in word and in life because his character is such. But such a man would seem to be as a matter of fact equitable. For the man who loves truth, and is truthful where nothing is at stake, will still more be truthful where something is at stake; he will avoid falsehood as something base, seeing that he avoided it even for its own sake; and such a man is worthy of praise. He inclines rather to understate the truth; for this seems in better taste because exaggerations are wearisome.

He who claims more than he has with no ulterior object is a contemptible sort of fellow (otherwise he would not have delighted in falsehood), but seems futile rather than bad; but if he does it for an object, he who does it for the sake of reputation or honour is (for a boaster) not very much to be blamed, but he who does it for money, or the things that lead to money, is an uglier character (it is not the capacity that makes the boaster, but the purpose; for it is in virtue of his state of character and by being a man of a certain kind that he is boaster); as one man is a liar because he enjoys the lie itself, and another because he desires reputation or gain. Now those who boast for the sake of reputation claim such qualities as will praise or congratulation, but those whose object is gain claim qualities which are of value to one's neighbours and one's lack of which is not easily detected, e.g. the powers of a seer, a sage, or a physician. For this reason it is such things as these that most people claim and boast about; for in them the above-mentioned qualities are found.

Mock-modest people, who understate things, seem more attractive in character; for they are thought to speak not for gain but to avoid parade; and here too it is qualities which bring reputation that they disclaim, as Socrates used to do. Those who disclaim trifling and obvious qualities are called humbugs and are more contemptible; and sometimes this seems to be boastfulness, like the Spartan dress; for both excess and great deficiency are boastful. But those who use understatement with moderation and understate about matters that do not very much force themselves on our notice seem attractive. And it is the boaster that seems to be opposed to the truthful man; for he is the worse character.

8

Since life includes rest as well as activity, and in this is included leisure and amusement, there seems here also to be a kind of intercourse which is tasteful; there is such a thing as saying- and again listening to- what one should and as one should. The kind of people one is speaking or listening to will also make a difference. Evidently here also there is both an excess and a deficiency as compared with the mean. Those who carry humour to excess are thought to be vulgar buffoons, striving after humour at all costs, and aiming rather at raising a laugh than at saying what is becoming and at avoiding pain to the object of their fun; while those who can neither make a joke themselves nor put up with those who do are thought to be boorish and unpolished. But those who joke in a tasteful way are called ready-witted, which implies a sort of readiness to turn this way and that; for such sallies are thought to be movements of the character, and as bodies are discriminated by their movements, so too are characters. The ridiculous side of things is not far to seek, however, and most people delight more than they should in amusement and in jestinly. and so even buffoons are called ready-witted because they are found attractive; but that they differ from the ready-witted man, and to no small extent, is clear from what has been said.

To the middle state belongs also tact; it is the mark of a tactful man to say and listen to such things as befit a good and well-bred man; for there are some things that it befits such a man to say and to hear by way of jest, and the well-bred man's jesting differs from that of a vulgar man, and the joking of an educated man from that of an uneducated. One may see this even from the old and the new comedies; to the authors of the former indecency of language was amusing, to those of the latter innuendo is more so; and these differ in no small degree in respect of propriety. Now should we define the man who jokes well by his saying what is not unbecoming to a well-bred man, or by his not giving pain, or even giving delight, to the hearer? Or is the latter definition, at any rate, itself indefinite, since different things are hateful or pleasant to different people? The kind of jokes he will listen to will be the same; for the kind he can put up with are also the kind he seems to make. There are, then, jokes he will not make; for the jest is a sort of abuse, and there are things that lawgivers forbid us to abuse; and they should, perhaps, have forbidden us even to make a jest of such. The refined and well-bred man, therefore, will be as we have described, being as it were a law to himself.

Such, then, is the man who observes the mean, whether he be called tactful or ready-witted. The buffoon, on the other hand, is the slave of his sense of humour, and spares neither himself nor others if he can raise a laugh, and says things none of which a man of refinement would say, and to some of which he would not even listen. The boor, again, is useless for such social intercourse; for he contributes nothing and finds fault with everything. But relaxation and amusement are thought to be a necessary element in life.

The means in life that have been described, then, are three in number, and are all concerned with an interchange of words and deeds of some kind. They differ, however, in that one is concerned with truth; and the other two with pleasantness. Of those concerned with pleasure, one is displayed in jests, the other in the general social intercourse of life.

9

Shame should not be described as a virtue; for it is more like a feeling than a state of character. It is defined, at any rate, as a kind of fear of dishonour, and produces an effect similar to that produced by fear of danger; for people who feel disgraced blush, and those who fear death turn pale. Both, therefore, seem to be in a sense bodily conditions, which is thought to be characteristic of feeling rather than of a state of character.

The feeling is not becoming to every age, but only to youth. For we think young people should be prone to the feeling of shame because they live by feeling and therefore commit many errors, but are restrained by shame; and we praise young people who are prone to this feeling, but an older person no one would praise for being prone to the sense of disgrace, since we think he should not do anything that need cause this sense. For the sense of disgrace is not even characteristic of a good man, since it is consequent on bad actions (for such actions should not be done; and if some actions are disgraceful in very truth and others only according to common opinion, this makes no difference; for neither class of actions should be done, so that no disgrace should be felt); and it is a mark of a bad man even to be such as to do any disgraceful action. To be so constituted as to feel disgraced if one does such an action, and for this reason to think oneself good, is absurd; for it is for voluntary actions that shame is felt, and the good man will never voluntarily do bad actions. But shame may be said to be conditionally a good thing; if a good man does such actions, he will feel disgraced; but the virtues are not subject to such a qualification. And if shamelessness-not to be ashamed of doing base actions-is bad, that does not make it good to be ashamed of doing such actions. Continence too is not virtue, but a mixed sort of state; this will be shown later. Now, however, let us discuss justice.

Book Five

1

With regards to justice and injustice we must (1) consider what kind of actions they are concerned with, (2) what sort of mean justice is, and (3) between what extremes the just act is intermediate. Our investigation shall follow the same course as the preceding discussions.

We see that all men mean by justice that kind of state of character which makes people disposed to do what is just and makes them act justly and wish for what is just; and similarly by injustice that state which makes them act unjustly and wish for what is unjust. Let us too, then, lay this down as a general basis. For the same is not true of the sciences and the faculties as of states of character. A faculty or a science which is one and the same is held to relate to contrary objects, but a state of character which is one of two contraries does not produce the contrary results; e.g. as a result of health we do not do what is the opposite of healthy, but only what is healthy; for we say a man walks healthily, when he walks as a healthy man would.

Now often one contrary state is recognized from its contrary, and often states are recognized from the subjects that exhibit them; for (A) if good condition is known, bad condition also becomes known, and (B) good condition is known from the things that are in good condition, and they from it. If good condition is firmness of flesh, it is necessary both that bad condition should be flabbiness of flesh and that the wholesome should be that which causes firmness in flesh. And it follows for the most part that if one contrary is ambiguous the other also will be ambiguous; e.g. if 'just' is so, that 'unjust' will be so too.

Now 'justice' and 'injustice' seem to be ambiguous, but because their different meanings approach near to one another the ambiguity escapes notice and is not obvious as it is, comparatively, when the meanings are far apart, e.g. (for here the difference in outward form is great) as the ambiguity in the use of kleis for the collar-bone of an animal and for that with which we lock a door. Let us take as a starting-point, then, the various meanings of 'an unjust man'. Both the lawless man and the grasping and unfair man are thought to be unjust, so that evidently both the law-abiding and the fair man will be just. The just, then, is the lawful and the fair, the unjust the unlawful and the unfair.

Since the unjust man is grasping, he must be concerned with goods-not all goods, but those with which prosperity and adversity have to do, which taken absolutely are always good, but for a particular person are not always good. Now men pray for and pursue these things; but they should not, but should pray that the things that are good absolutely may also be good for them, and should choose the things that are good for them. The unjust man does not always choose the greater, but also the less-in the case of things bad absolutely; but because the lesser evil is itself thought to be in a sense good, and graspingness is directed at the good, therefore he is thought to be grasping. And he is unfair; for this contains and is common to both.

Since the lawless man was seen to be unjust and the law-abiding man just, evidently all lawful acts are in a sense just acts; for the acts laid down by the legislative art are lawful, and each of these, we say, is just. Now the laws in their enactments on all subjects aim at the common advantage either of all or of the best or of those who hold power, or something of the sort; so that in one sense we call those acts just that tend to produce and preserve happiness and its components for the political society. And the law bids us do both the acts of a brave man (e.g. not to desert our post nor take to flight nor throw away our arms), and those of a temperate man (e.g. not to commit adultery nor to gratify one's lust), and those of a good-tempered man (e.g. not to strike another nor to speak evil), and similarly with regard to the other virtues and forms of wickedness, commanding some acts and forbidding others; and the rightly-framed law does this rightly, and the hastily conceived one less well. This form of justice, then, is complete virtue, but not absolutely, but in relation to our neighbour. And therefore justice is often thought to be the greatest of virtues, and 'neither evening nor morning star' is so wonderful; and proverbially 'in justice is every virtue comprehended'. And it is complete virtue in its fullest sense, because it is the actual exercise of complete virtue. It is complete because he who possesses it can exercise his virtue not only in himself but towards his neighbour also; for many men can exercise virtue in their own affairs, but not in their relations to their neighbour. This is why the saying of Bias is thought to be true, that 'rule will show the man'; for a ruler is necessarily in relation to other men and a member of a society. For this same reason justice, alone of the virtues, is thought to be 'another's good', because it is related to our neighbour; for it does what is advantageous to another, either a ruler or a copartner. Now the worst man is he who exercises his wickedness both towards himself and towards his friends, and the best man is not he who exercises his virtue towards himself but he who exercises it towards another; for this is a difficult task. Justice in this sense, then, is not part of virtue but virtue entire, nor is the contrary injustice a part of vice but vice entire. What the difference is between virtue and justice in this sense is plain from what we have said; they are the same but their essence is not the same; what, as a relation to one's neighbour, is justice is, as a certain kind of state without qualification, virtue.

2

But at all events what we are investigating is the justice which is a part of virtue; for there is a justice of this kind, as we maintain. Similarly it is with injustice in the particular sense that we are concerned.

That there is such a thing is indicated by the fact that while the man who exhibits in action the other forms of wickedness acts wrongly indeed, but not graspingly (e.g. the man who throws away his shield through cowardice or speaks harshly through bad temper or fails to help a friend with money through meanness), when a man acts graspingly he often exhibits none of these vices,-no, nor all together, but certainly wickedness of some kind (for we blame him) and injustice. There is, then, another kind of injustice which is a part of injustice in the wide sense, and a use of the word 'unjust' which answers to a part of what is unjust in the wide sense of 'contrary to the law'. Again if one man commits adultery for the sake of gain and makes money by it, while another does so at the bidding of appetite though he loses money and is penalized for it, the latter would be held to be self-indulgent rather than grasping, but the former is unjust, but not self-indulgent; evidently, therefore, he is unjust by reason of his making gain by his act. Again, all other unjust acts are ascribed invariably to some particular kind of wickedness, e.g. adultery to self-indulgence, the desertion of a comrade in battle to cowardice, physical violence to anger; but if a man makes gain, his action is ascribed to no form of wickedness but injustice. Evidently, therefore, there is apart from injustice in the wide sense another, 'particular', injustice which shares the name and nature of the first, because its definition falls within the same genus; for the significance of both consists in a relation to one's neighbour, but the one is concerned with honour or money or safety-or that which includes all these, if we had a single name for it-and its motive is the pleasure that arises from gain; while the other is concerned with all the objects with which the good man is concerned.

It is clear, then, that there is more than one kind of justice, and that there is one which is distinct from virtue entire; we must try to grasp its genus and differentia.

The unjust has been divided into the unlawful and the unfair, and the just into the lawful and the fair. To the unlawful answers the afore-mentioned sense of injustice. But since unfair and the unlawful are not the same, but are different as a part is from its whole (for all that is unfair is unlawful, but not all that is unlawful is unfair), the unjust and injustice in the sense of the unfair are not the same as but different from the former kind, as part from whole; for injustice in this sense is a part of injustice in the wide sense, and similarly justice in the one sense of justice in the other. Therefore we must speak also about particular justice and particular and similarly about the just and the unjust. The justice, then, which answers to the whole of virtue, and the corresponding injustice, one being the exercise of virtue as a whole, and the other that of vice as a whole, towards one's neighbour, we may leave on one side. And how the meanings of 'just' and 'unjust' which answer to these are to be distinguished is evident; for practically the majority of the acts commanded by the law are those which are prescribed from the point of view of virtue taken as a whole; for the law bids us practise every virtue and forbids us to practise any vice. And the things that tend to produce virtue taken as a whole are those of the acts prescribed by the law which have been prescribed with a view to education for the common good. But with regard to the education of the individual as such, which makes him without qualification a good man, we must determine later whether this is the function of the political art or of another; for perhaps it is not the same to be a good man and a good citizen of any state taken at random.

Of particular justice and that which is just in the corresponding sense, (A) one kind is that which is manifested in distributions of honour or money or the other things that fall to be divided among those who have a share in the constitution (for in these it is possible for one man to have a share either unequal or equal to that of another), and (B) one is that which plays a rectifying part in transactions between man and man. Of this there are two divisions; of transactions (1) some are voluntary and (2) others involuntary- voluntary such transactions as sale, purchase, loan for consumption, pledging, loan for use, depositing, letting (they are called voluntary because the origin of these transactions is voluntary), while of the involuntary (a) some are clandestine, such as theft, adultery, poisoning, procuring, enticement of slaves, assassination, false witness, and (b) others are violent, such as assault, imprisonment, murder, robbery with violence, mutilation, abuse, insult.

3

(A) We have shown that both the unjust man and the unjust act are unfair or unequal; now it is clear that there is also an intermediate between the two unequals involved in either case. And this is the equal; for in any kind of action in which there's a more and a less there is also what is equal. If, then, the unjust is unequal, just is equal, as all men suppose it to be, even apart from argument. And since the equal is intermediate, the just will be an intermediate. Now equality implies at least two things. The just, then, must be both intermediate and equal and relative (i.e. for certain persons). And since the equall intermediate it must be between certain things (which are respectively greater and less); equal, it involves two things; qua just, it is for certain people. The just, therefore, involves at least four terms; for the persons for whom it is in fact just are two, and the things in which it is manifested, the objects distributed, are two. And the same equality will exist between the persons and between the things concerned; for as the latter the things concerned-are related, so are the former; if they are not equal, they will not have what is equal, but this is the origin of quarrels and complaints-when either equals have and are awarded unequal shares, or unequals equal shares. Further, this is plain from the fact that awards should be 'according to merit'; for all men agree that what is just in distribution must be according to merit in some sense, though they do not all specify the same sort of merit, but democrats identify it with the status of freeman, supporters of oligarchy with wealth (or with noble birth), and supporters of aristocracy with excellence.

The just, then, is a species of the proportionate (proportion being not a property only of the kind of number which consists of abstract units, but of number in general). For proportion is equality of ratios, and involves four terms at least (that discrete proportion involves four terms is plain, but so does continuous proportion, for it uses one term as two and mentions it twice; e.g. 'as the line A is to the line B, so is the line B to the line C'; the line B, then, has been mentioned twice, so that if the line B be assumed twice, the proportional terms will be four); and the just, too, involves at least four terms, and the ratio between one pair is the same as that between the other pair; for there is a similar distinction between the persons and between the things. As the term A, then, is to B, so will C be to D, and therefore, alternando, as A is to C, B will be to D. Therefore also the whole is in the same ratio to the whole; and this coupling the distribution effects, and, if the terms are so combined, effects justly. The conjunction, then, of the term A with C and of B with D is what is just in distribution, and this species of the just is intermediate, and the unjust is what violates the proportion; for the proportional is intermediate, and the just is proportional. (Mathematicians call this kind of proportion geometrical; for it is in geometrical proportion that it follows that the whole is to the whole as either part is to the corresponding part.) This proportion is not continuous; for we cannot get a single term standing for a person and a thing.

This, then, is what the just is-the proportional; the unjust is what violates the proportion. Hence one term becomes too great, the other too small, as indeed happens in practice; for the man who acts unjustly has too much, and the man who is unjustly treated too little, of what is good. In the case of evil the reverse is true; for the lesser evil is reckoned a good in comparison with the greater evil, since the lesser evil is rather to be chosen than the greater, and what is worthy of choice is good, and what is worthier of choice a greater good.

This, then, is one species of the just.

4

(B) The remaining one is the rectificatory, which arises in connexion with transactions both voluntary and involuntary. This form of the just has a different specific character from the former. For the justice which distributes common possessions is always in accordance with the kind of proportion mentioned above (for in the case also in which the distribution is made from the common funds of a partnership it will be according to the same ratio which the funds put into the business by the partners bear to one another); and the injustice opposed to this kind of justice is that which violates the proportion. But the justice in transactions between man and man is a sort of equality indeed, and the injustice a sort of inequality; not according to that kind of proportion, however, but according to arithmetical proportion. For it makes no difference whether a good man has defrauded a bad man or a bad man a good one, nor whether it is a good or a bad man that has committed adultery; the law looks only to the distinctive character of the injury, and treats the parties as equal, if one is in the wrong and the other is being wronged, and if one inflicted injury and the other has received it. Therefore, this kind of injustice being an inequality, the judge tries to equalize it; for in the case also in which one has received and the other has inflicted a wound, or one has slain and the other been slain, the suffering and the action have been unequally distributed; but the judge tries to equalize by means of the penalty, taking away from the gain of the assailant. For the term 'gain' is applied generally to such cases, even if it be not a term appropriate to certain cases, e.g. to the person who inflicts a woundand 'loss' to the sufferer; at all events when the suffering has been estimated, the one is called loss and the other gain. Therefore the equal is intermediate between the greater and the less, but the gain and the loss are respectively greater and less in contrary ways; more of the good and less of the evil are gain, and the contrary is loss; intermediate between them is, as we saw, equal, which we say is just; therefore corrective justice will be the intermediate between loss and gain. This is why, when people dispute, they take refuge in the judge; and to go to the judge is to go to justice; for the nature of the judge is to be a sort of animate justice; and they seek the judge as an intermediate, and in some states they call judges mediators, on the assumption that if they get what is intermediate they will get what is just. The just, then, is an intermediate, since the judge is so. Now the judge restores equality; it is as though there were a line divided into unequal parts, and he took away that by which the greater segment exceeds the half, and added it to the smaller segment. And when the whole has been equally divided, then they say they have 'their own'-i.e. when they have got what is equal. The equal is intermediate between the greater and the lesser line according to arithmetical proportion. It is for this reason also that it is called just (sikaion), because it is a division into two equal parts (sicha), just as if one were to call it sichaion; and the judge (sikastes) is one who bisects (sichastes). For when something is subtracted from one of two equals and added to the other, the other is in excess by these two; since if what was taken from the one had not been added to the other, the latter would have been in excess by one only. It therefore exceeds the intermediate by one, and the intermediate exceeds by one that from which something was taken. By this, then, we shall recognize both what we must subtract from that which has more, and what we must add to that which has less; we must add to the latter that by which the intermediate exceeds it, and subtract from the greatest that by which it exceeds the intermediate. Let the lines AA', BB', CC' be equal to one another; from the line AA' let the segment AE have been subtracted, and to the line CC' let the segment Cd have been added, so that the whole line DCC' exceeds the line EA' by the segment CD and the segment CF; therefore it exceeds the line Bb' by the segment CD. (See diagram.)

These names, both loss and gain, have come from voluntary exchange; for to have more than one's own is called gaining, and to have less than one's original share is called losing, e.g. in buying and selling and in all other matters in which the law has left people free to make their own terms; but when they get neither more nor less but just what belongs to themselves, they say that they have their own and that they neither lose nor gain.

Therefore the just is intermediate between a sort of gain and a sort of loss, viz. those which are involuntary; it consists in having an equal amount before and after the transaction.

5

Some think that reciprocity is without qualification just, as the Pythagoreans said; for they defined justice without qualification as reciprocity. Now 'reciprocity' fits neither distributive nor rectificatory justice-yet people want even the justice of Rhadamanthus to mean this:

Should a man suffer what he did, right justice would be done -for in many cases reciprocity and rectificatory justice are not in accord; e.g. (1) if an official has inflicted a wound, he should not be wounded in return, and if some one has wounded an official, he ought not to be wounded only but punished in addition. Further (2) there is a great difference between a voluntary and an involuntary act. But in associations for exchange this sort of justice does hold men together-reciprocity in accordance with a proportion and not on the basis of precisely equal return. For it is by proportionate requital that the city holds together. Men seek to return either evil for evil-and if they cana not do so, think their position mere slavery-or good for good-and if they cannot do so there is no exchange, but it is by exchange that they hold together. This is why they give a prominent place to the temple of the Graces-to promote the requital of services; for this is characteristic of grace-we should serve in return one who has shown grace to us, and should another time take the initiative in showing it.

Now proportionate return is secured by cross-conjunction. Let A be a builder, B a shoemaker, C a house, D a shoe. The builder, then, must get from the shoemaker the latter's work, and must himself give him in return his own. If, then, first there is proportionate equality of goods, and then reciprocal action takes place, the result we mention will be effected. If not, the bargain is not equal, and does not hold; for there is nothing to prevent the work of the one being better than that of the other; they must therefore be equated. (And this is true of the other arts also; for they would have been destroyed if what the patient suffered had not been just what the agent did, and of the same amount and kind.) For it is not two doctors that associate for exchange, but a doctor and a farmer, or in general people who are different and unequal; but these must be equated. This is why all things that are exchanged must be somehow comparable. It is for this end that money has been introduced, and it becomes in a sense an intermediate; for it measures all things, and therefore the excess and the defect-how many shoes are equal to a house or to a given amount of food. The number of shoes exchanged for a house (or for a given amount of food) must therefore correspond to the ratio of builder to shoemaker. For if this be not so, there will be no exchange and no intercourse. And this proportion will not be effected unless the goods are somehow equal. All goods must therefore be measured by some one thing, as we said before. Now this unit is in truth demand, which holds all things together (for if men did not need one another's goods at all, or did not need them equally, there would be either no exchange or not the same exchange); but money has become by convention a sort of representative of demand; and this is why it has the name 'money' (nomisma)-because it exists not by nature but by law (nomos) and it is in our power to change it and make it useless. There will, then, be reciprocity when the terms have been equated so that as farmer is to shoemaker, the amount of the shoemaker's work is to that of the farmer's work for which it exchanges. But we must not bring them into a figure of proportion when they have already exchanged (otherwise one extreme will have both excesses), but when they still have their own goods. Thus they are equals and associates just because this equality can be effected in their case. Let A be a farmer, C food, B a shoemaker, D his product equated to C. If it had not been possible for reciprocity to be thus effected, there would have been no association of the parties. That demand holds things together as a single unit is shown by the fact that when men do not need one another, i.e. when neither needs the other or one does not need the other, they do not exchange, as we do when some one wants what one has oneself, e.g. when people permit the exportation of corn in exchange for wine. This equation therefore must be established. And for the future exchange-that if we do not need a thing now we shall have it if ever we do need it-money is as it were our surety; for it must be possible for us to get what we want by bringing the money. Now the same thing happens to money itself as to goods-it is not always worth the same; yet it tends to be steadier. This is why all goods must have a price set on them; for then there will always be exchange, and if so, association of man with man. Money, then, acting as a measure, makes goods commensurate and equates them; for neither would there have been association if there were not exchange, nor exchange if there were not equality, nor equality if there were not commensurability. Now in truth it is impossible that things differing so much should become commensurate, but with reference to demand they may become so sufficiently. There must, then, be a unit, and that fixed by agreement (for which reason it is called money); for it is this that makes all things commensurate, since all things are measured by money. Let A be a house, B ten minae, C a bed. A is half of B, if the house is worth five minae or equal to them; the bed, C, is a tenth of B; it is plain, then, how many beds are equal to a house, viz. five. That exchange took place thus before there was money is plain; for it makes no difference whether it is five beds that exchange for a house, or the money value of five beds.

We have now defined the unjust and the just. These having been marked off from each other, it is plain that just action is intermediate between acting unjustly and being unjustly treated; for the one is to have too much and the other to have too little. Justice is a kind of mean, but not in the same way as the other virtues, but because it relates to an intermediate amount, while injustice relates to the extremes. And justice is that in virtue of which the just man is said to be a doer, by choice, of that which is just, and one who will distribute either between himself and another or between two others not so as to give more of what is desirable to himself and less to his neighbour (and conversely with what is harmful), but so as to give what is equal in accordance with proportion; and similarly in distributing between two other persons. Injustice on the other hand is similarly related to the unjust, which is excess and defect, contrary to proportion, of the useful or hurtful. For which reason injustice is excess and defect, viz. because it is productive of excess and defect-in one's own case excess of what is in its own nature useful and defect of what is hurtful, while in the case of others it is as a whole like what it is in one's own case, but proportion may be violated in either direction. In the unjust act to have too little is to be unjustly treated; to have too much is to act unjustly.

Let this be taken as our account of the nature of justice and injustice, and similarly of the just and the unjust in general.

6

Since acting unjustly does not necessarily imply being unjust, we must ask what sort of unjust acts imply that the doer is unjust with respect to each type of injustice, e.g. a thief, an adulterer, or a brigand. Surely the answer does not turn on the difference between these types. For a man might even lie with a woman knowing who she was, but the origin of his might be not deliberate choice but passion. He acts unjustly, then, but is not unjust; e.g. a man is not a thief, yet he stole, nor an adulterer, yet he committed adultery; and similarly in all other cases.

Now we have previously stated how the reciprocal is related to the just; but we must not forget that what we are looking for is not only what is just without qualification but also political justice. This is found among men who share their life with a view to selfsufficiency, men who are free and either proportionately or arithmetically equal, so that between those who do not fulfil this condition there is no political justice but justice in a special sense and by analogy. For justice exists only between men whose mutual relations are governed by law; and law exists for men between whom there is injustice; for legal justice is the discrimination of the just and the unjust. And between men between whom there is injustice there is also unjust action (though there is not injustice between all between whom there is unjust action), and this is assigning too much to oneself of things good in themselves and too little of things evil in themselves. This is why we do not allow a man to rule, but rational principle, because a man behaves thus in his own interests and becomes a tyrant. The magistrate on the other hand is the guardian of justice, and, if of justice, then of equality also. And since he is assumed to have no more than his share, if he is just (for he does not assign to himself more of what is good in itself, unless such a share is proportional to his merits-so that it is for others that he labours, and it is for this reason that men, as we stated previously, say that justice is 'another's good'), therefore a reward must be given him, and this is honour and privilege; but those for whom such things are not enough become tyrants.

The justice of a master and that of a father are not the same as the justice of citizens, though they are like it; for there can be no injustice in the unqualified sense towards thing that are one's own, but a man's chattel, and his child until it reaches a certain age and sets up for itself, are as it were part of himself, and no one chooses to hurt himself (for which reason there can be no injustice towards oneself). Therefore the justice or injustice of citizens is not manifested in these relations; for it was as we saw according to law, and between people naturally subject to law, and these as we saw' are people who have an equal share in ruling and being ruled. Hence justice can more truly be manifested towards a wife than towards children and chattels, for the former is household justice; but even this is different from political justice.

7

Of political justice part is natural, part legal, natural, that which everywhere has the same force and does not exist by people's thinking this or that; legal, that which is originally indifferent, but when it has been laid down is not indifferent, e.g. that a prisoner's ransom shall be a mina, or that a goat and not two sheep shall be sacrificed, and again all the laws that are passed for particular cases, e.g. that sacrifice shall be made in honour of Brasidas, and the provisions of decrees. Now some think that all justice is of this sort, because that which is by nature is unchangeable and has everywhere the same force (as fire burns both here and in Persia), while they see change in the things recognized as just. This, however, is not true in this unqualified way, but is true in a sense; or rather, with the gods it is perhaps not true at all, while with us there is something that is just even by nature, yet all of it is changeable; but still some is by nature, some not by nature. It is evident which sort of thing, among things capable of being otherwise, is by nature, and which is not but is legal and conventional, assuming that both are equally changeable. And in all other things the same distinction will apply; by nature the right hand is stronger, yet it is possible that all men should come to be ambidextrous. The things which are just by virtue of convention and expediency are like measures; for wine and corn measures are not everywhere equal, but larger in wholesale and smaller in retail markets. Similarly, the things which are just not by nature but by human enactment are not everywhere the same, since constitutions also are not the same, though there is but one which is everywhere by nature the best. Of things just and lawful each is related as the universal to its particulars; for the things that are done are many, but of them each is one, since it is universal.

There is a difference between the act of injustice and what is unjust, and between the act of justice and what is just; for a thing is unjust by nature or by enactment; and this very thing, when it has been done, is an act of injustice, but before it is done is not yet that but is unjust. So, too, with an act of justice (though the general term is rather 'just action', and 'act of justice' is applied to the correction of the act of injustice).

Each of these must later be examined separately with regard to the nature and number of its species and the nature of the things with which it is concerned.

8

Acts just and unjust being as we have described them, a man acts unjustly or justly whenever he does such acts voluntarily; when involuntarily, he acts neither unjustly nor justly except in an incidental way; for he does things which happen to be just or unjust. Whether an act is or is not one of injustice (or of justice) is determined by its voluntariness or involuntariness; for when it is voluntary it is blamed, and at the same time is then an act of injustice; so that there will be things that are unjust but not yet acts of injustice, if voluntariness be not present as well. By the voluntary I mean, as has been said before, any of the things in a man's own power which he does with knowledge, i.e. not in ignorance either of the person acted on or of the instrument used or of the end that will be attained (e.g. whom he is striking, with what, and to what end), each such act being done not incidentally nor under compulsion (e.g. if A takes B's hand and therewith strikes C, B does not act voluntarily; for the act was not in his own power). The person struck may be the striker's father, and the striker may know that it is a man or one of the persons present, but not know that it is his father; a similar distinction may be made in the case of the end, and with regard to the whole action. Therefore that which is done in ignorance, or though not done in ignorance is not in the agent's power, or is done under compulsion, is involuntary (for many natural processes, even, we knowingly both perform and experience, none of which is either voluntary or involuntary; e.g. growing old or dying). But in the case of unjust and just acts alike the injustice or justice may be only incidental; for a man might return a deposit unwillingly and from fear, and then he must not be said either to do what is just or to act justly, except in an incidental way. Similarly the man who under compulsion and unwillingly fails to return the deposit must be said to act unjustly, and to do what is unjust, only incidentally. Of voluntary acts we do some by choice, others not by choice; by choice those which we do after deliberation, not by choice those which we do without previous deliberation. Thus there are three kinds of injury in transactions between man and man; those done in ignorance are mistakes when the person acted on, the act, the instrument, or the end that will be attained is other than the agent supposed; the agent thought either that he was not hiting any one or that he was not hitting with this missile or not hitting this person or to this end, but a result followed other than that which he thought likely (e.g. he threw not with intent to wound but only to prick), or the person hit or the missile was other than he supposed. Now when (1) the injury takes place contrary to reasonable expectation, it is a misadventure. When (2) it is not contrary to reasonable expectation, but does not imply vice, it is a mistake (for a man makes a mistake when the fault originates in him, but is the victim of accident when the origin lies outside him). When (3) he acts with knowledge but not after deliberation, it is an act of injustice-e.g. the acts due to anger or to other passions necessary or natural to man; for when men do such harmful and mistaken acts they act unjustly, and the acts are acts of injustice, but this does not imply that the doers are unjust or wicked; for the injury is not due to vice. But when (4) a man acts from choice, he is an unjust man and a vicious man.

Hence acts proceeding from anger are rightly judged not to be done of malice aforethought; for it is not the man who acts in anger but he who enraged him that starts the mischief. Again, the matter in dispute is not whether the thing happened or not, but its justice; for it is apparent injustice that occasions rage. For they do not dispute about the occurrence of the act-as in commercial transactions where one of the two parties must be vicious-unless they do so owing to forgetfulness; but, agreeing about the fact, they dispute on which side justice lies (whereas a man who has deliberately injured another cannot help knowing that he has done so), so that the one thinks he is being treated unjustly and the other disagrees.

But if a man harms another by choice, he acts unjustly; and these are the acts of injustice which imply that the doer is an unjust man, provided that the act violates proportion or equality. Similarly, a man is just when he acts justly by choice; but he acts justly if he merely acts voluntarily.

Of involuntary acts some are excusable, others not. For the mistakes which men make not only in ignorance but also from ignorance are excusable, while those which men do not from ignorance but (though they do them in ignorance) owing to a passion which is neither natural nor such as man is liable to, are not excusable.

9

Assuming that we have sufficiently defined the suffering and doing of injustice, it may be asked (1) whether the truth in expressed in Euripides' paradoxical words:

I slew my mother, that's my tale in brief. Were you both willing, or unwilling both?

Is it truly possible to be willingly treated unjustly, or is all suffering of injustice the contrary involuntary, as all unjust action is voluntary? And is all suffering of injustice of the latter kind or else all of the former, or is it sometimes voluntary, sometimes involuntary? So, too, with the case of being justly treated; all just action is voluntary, so that it is reasonable that there should be a similar opposition in either case-that both being unjustly and being justly treated should be either alike voluntary or alike involuntary. But it would be thought paradoxical even in the case of being justly treated, if it were always voluntary; for some are unwillingly treated justly. (2) One might raise this question also, whether every one who has suffered what is unjust is being unjustly treated, or on the other hand it is with suffering as with acting. In action and in passivity alike it is possible to partake of justice incidentally, and similarly (it is plain) of injustice; for to do what is unjust is not the same as to act unjustly, nor to suffer what is unjust as to be treated unjustly, and similarly in the case of acting justly and being justly treated; for it is impossible to be unjustly treated if the other does not act unjustly, or justly treated unless he acts justly. Now if to act unjustly is simply to harm some one voluntarily, and 'voluntarily' means 'knowing the person acted on, the instrument, and the manner of one's acting', and the incontinent man voluntarily harms himself, not only will he voluntarily be unjustly treated but it will be possible to treat oneself unjustly. (This also is one of the questions in doubt, whether a man can treat himself unjustly.) Again, a man may voluntarily, owing to incontinence, be harmed by another who acts voluntarily, so that it would be possible to be voluntarily treated unjustly. Or is our definition incorrect; must we to 'harming another, with knowledge both of the person acted on, of the instrument, and of the manner' add 'contrary to the wish of the person acted on'? Then a man may be voluntarily harmed and voluntarily suffer what is unjust, but no one is voluntarily treated unjustly; for no one wishes to be unjustly treated, not even the incontinent man. He acts contrary to his wish; for no one wishes for what he does not think to be good, but the incontinent man does do things that he does not think he ought to do. Again, one who gives what is his own, as Homer says Glaucus gave Diomede

Armour of gold for brazen, the price of a hundred beeves for nine, is not unjustly treated; for though to give is in his power, to be unjustly treated is not, but there must be some one to treat him unjustly. It is plain, then, that being unjustly treated is not voluntary.

Of the questions we intended to discuss two still remain for discussion; (3) whether it is the man who has assigned to another more than his share that acts unjustly, or he who has the excessive share, and (4) whether it is possible to treat oneself unjustly. The questions are connected; for if the former alternative is possible and the distributor acts unjustly and not the man who has the excessive share, then if a man assigns more to another than to himself, knowingly and voluntarily, he treats himself unjustly; which is what modest people seem to do, since the virtuous man tends to take less than his share. Or does this statement too need qualification? For (a) he perhaps gets more than his share of some other good, e.g. of honour or of intrinsic nobility. (b) The question is solved by applying the distinction we applied to unjust action; for he suffers nothing contrary to his own wish, so that he is not unjustly treated as far as this goes, but at most only suffers harm.

It is plain too that the distributor acts unjustly, but not always the man who has the excessive share; for it is not he to whom what is unjust appertains that acts unjustly, but he to whom it appertains to do the unjust act voluntarily, i.e. the person in whom lies the origin of the action, and this lies in the distributor, not in the receiver. Again, since the word 'do' is ambiguous, and there is a sense in which lifeless things, or a hand, or a servant who obeys an order, may be said to slay, he who gets an excessive share does not act unjustly, though he 'does' what is unjust.

Again, if the distributor gave his judgement in ignorance, he does not act unjustly in respect of legal justice, and his judgement is not unjust in this sense, but in a sense it is unjust (for legal justice and primordial justice are different); but if with knowledge he judged unjustly, he is himself aiming at an excessive share either of gratitude or of revenge. As much, then, as if he were to share in the plunder, the man who has judged unjustly for these reasons has got too much; the fact that what he gets is different from what he distributes makes no difference, for even if he awards land with a view to sharing in the plunder he gets not land but money.

Men think that acting unjustly is in their power, and therefore that being just is easy. But it is not; to lie with one's neighbour's wife, to wound another, to deliver a bribe, is easy and in our power, but to do these things as a result of a certain state of character is neither easy nor in our power. Similarly to know what is just and what is unjust requires, men think, no great wisdom, because it is not hard to understand the matters dealt with by the laws (though these are not the things that are just, except incidentally); but how actions must be done and distributions effected in order to be just, to know this is a greater achievement than knowing what is good for the health; though even there, while it is easy to know that honey, wine, hellebore, cautery, and the use of the knife are so, to know how, to whom, and when these should be applied with a view to producing health, is no less an achievement than that of being a physician. Again, for this very reason men think that acting unjustly is characteristic of the just man no less than of the unjust, because he would be not less but even more capable of doing each of these unjust acts; for he could lie with a woman or wound a neighbour; and the brave man could throw away his shield and turn to flight in this direction or in that. But to play the coward or to act unjustly consists not in doing these things, except incidentally, but in doing them as the result of a certain state of character, just as to practise medicine and healing consists not in applying or not applying the knife, in using or not using medicines, but in doing so in a certain way.

Just acts occur between people who participate in things good in themselves and can have too much or too little of them; for some beings (e.g. presumably the gods) cannot have too much of them, and to others, those who are incurably bad, not even the smallest share in them is beneficial but all such goods are harmful, while to others they are beneficial up to a point; therefore justice is essentially something human.

10

Our next subject is equity and the equitable (to epiekes), and their respective relations to justice and the just. For on examination they appear to be neither absolutely the same nor generically different; and while we sometime praise what is equitable and the equitable man (so that we apply the name by way of praise even to instances of the other virtues, instead of 'good' meaning by epieikestebon that a thing is better), at other times, when we reason it out, it seems strange if the equitable, being something different from the just, is yet praiseworthy; for either the just or the equitable is not good, if they are different; or, if both are good, they are the same.

These, then, are pretty much the considerations that give rise to the problem about the equitable; they are all in a sense correct and not opposed to one another; for the equitable, though it is better than one kind of justice, yet is just, and it is not as being a different class of thing that it is better than the just. The same thing, then, is just and equitable, and while both are good the equitable is superior. What creates the problem is that the equitable is just, but not the legally just but a correction of legal justice. The reason is that all law is universal but about some things it is not possible to make a universal statement which shall be correct. In those cases, then, in which it is necessary to speak universally, but not possible to do so correctly, the law takes the usual case, though it is not ignorant of the possibility of error. And it is none the less correct; for the error is in the law nor in the legislator but in the nature of the thing, since the matter of practical affairs is of this kind from the start. When the law speaks universally, then, and a case arises on it which is not covered by the universal statement, then it is right, where the legislator fails us and has erred by oversimplicity, to correct the omission-to say what the legislator himself would have said had he been present, and would have put into his law if he had known. Hence the equitable is just, and better than one kind of justice-not better than absolute justice but better than the error that arises from the absoluteness of the statement. And this is the nature of the equitable, a correction of law where it is defective owing to its universality. In fact this is the reason why all things are not determined by law, that about some things it is impossible to lay down a law, so that a decree is needed. For when the thing is indefinite the rule also is indefinite, like the leaden rule used in making the Lesbian moulding; the rule adapts itself to the shape of the stone and is not rigid, and so too the decree is adapted to the facts.

It is plain, then, what the equitable is, and that it is just and is better than one kind of justice. It is evident also from this who the equitable man is; the man who chooses and does such acts, and is no stickler for his rights in a bad sense but tends to take less than his share though he has the law oft his side, is equitable, and this state of character is equity, which is a sort of justice and not a different state of character.

11

Whether a man can treat himself unjustly or not, is evident from what has been said. For (a) one class of just acts are those acts in accordance with any virtue which are prescribed by the law; e.g. the law does not expressly permit suicide, and what it does not expressly permit it forbids. Again, when a man in violation of the law harms another (otherwise than in retaliation) voluntarily, he acts unjustly, and a voluntary agent is one who knows both the person he is affecting by his action and the instrument he is using; and he who through anger voluntarily stabs himself does this contrary to the right rule of life, and this the law does not allow; therefore he is acting unjustly. But towards whom? Surely towards the state, not towards himself. For he suffers voluntarily, but no one is voluntarily treated unjustly. This is also the reason why the state punishes; a certain loss of civil rights attaches to the man who destroys himself, on the ground that he is treating the state unjustly.

Further (b) in that sense of 'acting unjustly' in which the man who 'acts unjustly' is unjust only and not bad all round, it is not possible to treat oneself unjustly (this is different from the former sense; the unjust man in one sense of the term is wicked in a particularized way just as the coward is, not in the sense of being wicked all round, so that his 'unjust act' does not manifest wickedness in general). For (i) that would imply the possibility of the same thing's having been subtracted from and added to the same thing at the same time; but this is impossible-the just and the unjust always involve more than one person. Further, (ii) unjust action is voluntary and done by choice, and takes the initiative (for the man who because he has suffered does the same in return is not thought to act unjustly); but if a man harms himself he suffers and does the same things at the same time. Further, (iii) if a man could treat himself unjustly, he could be voluntarily treated unjustly. Besides, (iv) no one acts unjustly without committing particular acts of injustice; but no one can commit adultery with his own wife or housebreaking on his own house or theft on his own property,

In general, the question 'can a man treat himself unjustly?' is solved also by the distinction we applied to the question 'can a man be voluntarily treated unjustly?'

(It is evident too that both are bad, being unjustly treated and acting unjustly; for the one means having less and the other having more than the intermediate amount, which plays the part here that the healthy does in the medical art, and that good condition does in the art of bodily training. But still acting unjustly is the worse, for it involves vice and is blameworthy-involves vice which is either of the complete and unqualified kind or almost so (we must admit the latter alternative, because not all voluntary unjust action implies injustice as a state of character), while being unjustly treated does not involve vice and injustice in oneself. In itself, then, being unjustly treated is less bad, but there is nothing to prevent its being incidentally a greater evil. But theory cares nothing for this; it calls pleurisy a more serious mischief than a stumble; yet the latter may become incidentally the more serious, if the fall due to it leads to your being taken prisoner or put to death the enemy.)

Metaphorically and in virtue of a certain resemblance there is a justice, not indeed between a man and himself, but between certain parts of him; yet not every kind of justice but that of master and servant or that of husband and wife. For these are the ratios in which the part of the soul that has a rational principle stands to the irrational part; and it is with a view to these parts that people also think a man can be unjust to himself, viz. because these parts are liable to suffer something contrary to their respective desires; there is therefore thought to be a mutual justice between them as between ruler and ruled.

Let this be taken as our account of justice and the other, i.e. the other moral, virtues.

Book Six

1

Since we have previously said that one ought to choose that which is intermediate, not the excess nor the defect, and that the intermediate is determined by the dictates of the right rule, let us discuss the nature of these dictates. In all the states of character we have mentioned, as in all other matters, there is a mark to which the man who has the rule looks, and heightens or relaxes his activity accordingly, and there is a standard which determines the mean states which we say are intermediate between excess and defect, being in accordance with the right rule. But such a statement, though true, is by no means clear; for not only here but in all other pursuits which are objects of knowledge it is indeed true to say that we must not exert ourselves nor relax our efforts too much nor too little, but to an intermediate extent and as the right rule dictates; but if a man had only this knowledge he would be none the wiser e.g. we should not know what sort of medicines to apply to our body if some one were to say 'all those which the medical art prescribes, and which agree with the practice of one who possesses the art'. Hence it is necessary with regard to the states of the soul also not only that this true statement should be made, but also that it should be determined what is the right rule and what is the standard that fixes it.

We divided the virtues of the soul and a said that some are virtues of character and others of intellect. Now we have discussed in detail the moral virtues; with regard to the others let us express our view as follows, beginning with some remarks about the soul. We said before that there are two parts of the soul-that which grasps a rule or rational principle, and the irrational; let us now draw a similar distinction within the part which grasps a rational principle. And let it be assumed that there are two parts which grasp a rational principle-one by which we contemplate the kind of things whose originative causes are invariable, and one by which we contemplate variable things; for where objects differ in kind the part of the soul answering to each of the two is different in kind, since it is in virtue of a certain likeness and kinship with their objects that they have the knowledge they have. Let one of these parts be called the scientific and the other the calculative; for to deliberate and to calculate are the same thing, but no one deliberates about the invariable. Therefore the calculative is one part of the faculty which grasps a rational principle. We must, then, learn what is the best state of each of these two parts; for this is the virtue of each.

2

The virtue of a thing is relative to its proper work. Now there are three things in the soul which control action and truth-sensation, reason, desire.

Of these sensation originates no action; this is plain from the fact that the lower animals have sensation but no share in action.

What affirmation and negation are in thinking, pursuit and avoidance are in desire; so that since moral virtue is a state of character concerned with choice, and choice is deliberate desire, therefore both the reasoning must be true and the desire right, if the choice is to be good, and the latter must pursue just what the former asserts. Now this kind of intellect and of truth is practical; of the intellect which is contemplative, not practical nor productive, the good and the bad state are truth and falsity respectively (for this is the work of everything intellectual); while of the part which is practical and intellectual the good state is truth in agreement with right desire.

The origin of action-its efficient, not its final cause-is choice, and that of choice is desire and reasoning with a view to an end. This is why choice cannot exist either without reason and intellect or without a moral state; for good action and its opposite cannot exist without a combination of intellect and character. Intellect itself, however, moves nothing, but only the intellect which aims at an end and is practical; for this rules the productive intellect, as well, since every one who makes makes for an end, and that which is made is not an end in the unqualified sense (but only an end in a particular relation, and the end of a particular operation)-only that which is done is that; for good action is an end, and desire aims at this. Hence choice is either desiderative reason or ratiocinative desire, and such an origin of action is a man. (It is to be noted that nothing that is past is an object of choice, e.g. no one chooses to have sacked Troy; for no one deliberates about the past, but about what is future and capable of being otherwise, while what is past is not capable of not having taken place; hence Agathon is right in saying

For this alone is lacking even to God, To make undone things thathave once been done.)

The work of both the intellectual parts, then, is truth. Therefore the states that are most strictly those in respect of which each of these parts will reach truth are the virtues of the two parts.

3

Let us begin, then, from the beginning, and discuss these states once more. Let it be assumed that the states by virtue of which the soul possesses truth by way of affirmation or denial are five in number, i.e. art, scientific knowledge, practical wisdom, philosophic wisdom, intuitive reason; we do not include judgement and opinion because in these we may be mistaken.

Now what scientific knowledge is, if we are to speak exactly and not follow mere similarities, is plain from what follows. We all suppose that what we know is not even capable of being otherwise; of things capable of being otherwise we do not know, when they have passed outside our observation, whether they exist or not. Therefore the object of scientific knowledge is of necessity. Therefore it is eternal; for things that are of necessity in the unqualified sense are all eternal; and things that are eternal are ungenerated and imperishable. Again, every science is thought to be capable of being taught, and its object of being learned. And all teaching starts from what is already known, as we maintain in the Analytics also; for it proceeds sometimes through induction and sometimes by syllogism. Now induction is the starting-point which knowledge even of the universal presupposes, while syllogism proceeds from universals. There are therefore starting-points from which syllogism proceeds, which are not reached by syllogism; it is therefore by induction that they are acquired. Scientific knowledge is, then, a state of capacity to demonstrate, and has the other limiting characteristics which we specify in the Analytics, for it is when a man believes in a certain way and the starting-points are known to him that he has scientific knowledge, since if they are not better known to him than the conclusion, he will have his knowledge only incidentally.

Let this, then, be taken as our account of scientific knowledge.

4

In the variable are included both things made and things done; making and acting are different (for their nature we treat even the discussions outside our school as reliable); so that the reasoned state of capacity to act is different from the reasoned state of capacity to make. Hence too they are not included one in the other; for neither is acting making nor is making acting. Now since architecture is an art and is essentially a reasoned state of capacity to make, and there is neither any art that is not such a state nor any such state that is not an art, art is identical with a state of capacity to make, involving a true course of reasoning. All art is concerned with coming into being, i.e. with contriving and considering how something may come into being which is capable of either being or not being, and whose origin is in the maker and not in the thing made; for art is concerned neither with things that are, or come into being, by necessity, nor with things that do so in accordance with nature (since these have their origin in themselves). Making and acting being different, art must be a matter of making, not of acting. And in a sense chance and art are concerned with the same objects; as Agathon says, 'art loves chance and chance loves art'. Art, then, as has been is a state concerned with making, involving a true course of reasoning, and lack of art on the contrary is a state concerned with making, involving a false course of reasoning; both are concerned with the variable.

5

Regarding practical wisdom we shall get at the truth by considering who are the persons we credit with it. Now it is thought to be the mark of a man of practical wisdom to be able to deliberate well about what is good and expedient for himself, not in some particular respect, e.g. about what sorts of thing conduce to health or to strength, but about what sorts of thing conduce to the good life in general. This is shown by the fact that we credit men with practical wisdom in some particular respect when they have calculated well with a view to some good end which is one of those that are not the object of any art. It follows that in the general sense also the man who is capable of deliberating has practical wisdom. Now no one deliberates about things that are invariable, nor about things that it is impossible for him to do. Therefore, since scientific knowledge involves demonstration, but there is no demonstration of things whose first principles are variable (for all such things might actually be otherwise), and since it is impossible to deliberate about things that are of necessity, practical wisdom cannot be scientific knowledge nor art; not science because that which can be done is capable of being otherwise, not art because action and making are different kinds of thing. The remaining alternative, then, is that it is a true and reasoned state of capacity to act with regard to the things that are good or bad for man. For while making has an end other than itself, action cannot; for good action itself is its end. It is for this reason that we think Pericles and men like him have practical wisdom, viz. because they can see what is good for themselves and what is good for men in general; we consider that those can do this who are good at managing households or states. (This is why we call temperance (sophrosune) by this name; we imply that it preserves one's practical wisdom (sozousa tan phronsin). Now what it preserves is a judgement of the kind we have described. For it is not any and every judgement that pleasant and painful objects destroy and pervert, e.g. the judgement that the triangle has or has not its angles equal to two right angles, but only judgements about what is to be done. For the originating causes of the things that are done consist in the end at which they are aimed; but the man who has been ruined by pleasure or pain forthwith fails to see any such originating cause-to see that for the sake of this or because of this he ought to choose and do whatever he chooses and does; for vice is destructive of the originating cause of action.) Practical wisdom, then, must be a reasoned and true state of capacity to act with regard to human goods. But further, while there is such a thing as excellence in art, there is no such thing as excellence in practical wisdom; and in art he who errs willingly is preferable, but in practical wisdom, as in the virtues, he is the reverse. Plainly, then, practical wisdom is a virtue and not an art. There being two parts of the soul that can follow a course of reasoning, it must be the virtue of one of the two, i.e. of that part which forms opinions; for opinion is about the variable and so is practical wisdom. But yet it is not only a reasoned state; this is shown by the fact that a state of that sort may forgotten but practical wisdom cannot.

6

Scientific knowledge is judgement about things that are universal and necessary, and the conclusions of demonstration, and all scientific knowledge, follow from first principles (for scientific knowledge involves apprehension of a rational ground). This being so, the first principle from which what is scientifically known follows cannot be an object of scientific knowledge, of art, or of practical wisdom; for that which can be scientifically known can be demonstrated, and art and practical wisdom deal with things that are variable. Nor are these first principles the objects of philosophic wisdom, for it is a mark of the philosopher to have demonstration about some things. If, then, the states of mind by which we have truth and are never deceived about things invariable or even variable are scientific knowlededge, practical wisdom, philosophic wisdom, and intuitive reason, and it cannot be any of the three (i.e. practical wisdom, scientific knowledge, or philosophic wisdom), the remaining alternative is that it is intuitive reason that grasps the first principles.

7

Wisdom (1) in the arts we ascribe to their most finished exponents, e.g. to Phidias as a sculptor and to Polyclitus as a maker of portrait-statues, and here we mean nothing by wisdom except excellence in art; but (2) we think that some people are wise in general, not in some particular field or in any other limited respect, as Homer says in the Margites,

Him did the gods make neither a digger nor yet a ploughman Nor wise in anything else. Therefore wisdom must plainly be the most finished of the forms of knowledge. It follows that the wise man must not only know what follows from the first principles, but must also possess truth about the first principles. Therefore wisdom must be intuitive reason combined with scientific knowledge-scientific knowledge of the highest objects which has received as it were its proper completion.

Of the highest objects, we say; for it would be strange to think that the art of politics, or practical wisdom, is the best knowledge, since man is not the best thing in the world. Now if what is healthy or good is different for men and for fishes, but what is white or straight is always the same, any one would say that what is wise is the same but what is practically wise is different; for it is to that which observes well the various matters concerning itself that one ascribes practical wisdom, and it is to this that one will entrust such matters. This is why we say that some even of the lower animals have practical wisdom, viz. those which are found to have a power of foresight with regard to their own life. It is evident also that philosophic wisdom and the art of politics cannot be the same; for if the state of mind concerned with a man's own interests is to be called philosophic wisdom, there will be many philosophic wisdoms; there will not be one concerned with the good of all animals (any more than there is one art of medicine for all existing things), but a different philosophic wisdom about the good of each species.

But if the argument be that man is the best of the animals, this makes no difference; for there are other things much more divine in their nature even than man, e.g., most conspicuously, the bodies of which the heavens are framed. From what has been said it is plain, then, that philosophic wisdom is scientific knowledge, combined with intuitive reason, of the things that are highest by nature. This is why we say Anaxagoras, Thales, and men like them have philosophic but not practical wisdom, when we see them ignorant of what is to their own advantage, and why we say that they know things that are remarkable, admirable, difficult, and divine, but useless; viz. because it is not human goods that they seek.

Practical wisdom on the other hand is concerned with things human and things about which it is possible to deliberate; for we say this is above all the work of the man of practical wisdom, to deliberate well, but no one deliberates about things invariable, nor about things which have not an end, and that a good that can be brought about by action. The man who is without qualification good at deliberating is the man who is capable of aiming in accordance with calculation at the best for man of things attainable by action. Nor is practical wisdom concerned with universals only-it must also recognize the particulars; for it is practical, and practice is concerned with particulars. This is why some who do not know, and especially those who have experience, are more practical than others who know; for if a man knew that light meats are digestible and wholesome, but did not know which sorts of meat are light, he would not produce health, but the man who knows that chicken is wholesome is more likely to produce health.

Now practical wisdom is concerned with action; therefore one should have both forms of it, or the latter in preference to the former. But of practical as of philosophic wisdom there must be a controlling kind.

8

Political wisdom and practical wisdom are the same state of mind, but their essence is not the same. Of the wisdom concerned with the city, the practical wisdom which plays a controlling part is legislative wisdom, while that which is related to this as particulars to their universal is known by the general name 'political wisdom'; this has to do with action and deliberation, for a decree is a thing to be carried out in the form of an individual act. This is why the exponents of this art are alone said to 'take part in politics'; for these alone 'do things' as manual labourers 'do things'.

Practical wisdom also is identified especially with that form of it which is concerned with a man himself-with the individual; and this is known by the general name 'practical wisdom'; of the other kinds one is called household management, another legislation, the third politics, and of the latter one part is called deliberative and the other judicial. Now knowing what is good for oneself will be one kind of knowledge, but it is very different from the other kinds; and the man who knows and concerns himself with his own interests is thought to have practical wisdom, while politicians are thought to be busybodies; hence the word of Euripides,

But how could I be wise, who might at ease, Numbered among the army's multitude, Have had an equal share? For those who aim too high and do too much. Those who think thus seek their own good, and consider that one ought to do so. From this opinion, then, has come the view that such men have practical wisdom; yet perhaps one's own good cannot exist without household management, nor without a form of government. Further, how one should order one's own affairs is not clear and needs inquiry.

What has been said is confirmed by the fact that while young men become geometricians and mathematicians and wise in matters like these, it is thought that a young man of practical wisdom cannot be found. The cause is that such wisdom is concerned not only with universals but with particulars, which become familiar from experience, but a young man has no experience, for it is length of time that gives experience; indeed one might ask this question too, why a boy may become a mathematician, but not a philosopher or a physicist. It is because the objects of mathematics exist by abstraction, while the first principles of these other subjects come from experience, and because young men have no conviction about the latter but merely use the proper language, while the essence of mathematical objects is plain enough to them?

Further, error in deliberation may be either about the universal or about the particular; we may fall to know either that all water that weighs heavy is bad, or that this particular water weighs heavy.

That practical wisdom is not scientific knowledge is evident; for it is, as has been said, concerned with the ultimate particular fact, since the thing to be done is of this nature. It is opposed, then, to intuitive reason; for intuitive reason is of the limiting premisses, for which no reason can be given, while practical wisdom is concerned with the ultimate particular, which is the object not of scientific knowledge but of perception-not the perception of qualities peculiar to one sense but a perception akin to that by which we perceive that the particular figure before us is a triangle; for in that direction as well as in that of the major premiss there will be a limit. But this is rather perception than practical wisdom, though it is another kind of perception than that of the qualities peculiar to each sense.

9

There is a difference between inquiry and deliberation; for deliberation is inquiry into a particular kind of thing. We must grasp the nature of excellence in deliberation as well whether it is a form of scientific knowledge, or opinion, or skill in conjecture, or some other kind of thing. Scientific knowledge it is not; for men do not inquire about the things they know about, but good deliberation is a kind of deliberation, and he who deliberates inquires and calculates. Nor is it skill in conjecture; for this both involves no reasoning and is something that is quick in its operation, while men deliberate a long time, and they say that one should carry out quickly the conclusions of one's deliberation, but should deliberate slowly. Again, readiness of mind is different from excellence in deliberation; it is a sort of skill in conjecture. Nor again is excellence in deliberation opinion of any sort. But since the man who deliberates badly makes a mistake, while he who deliberates well does so correctly, excellence in deliberation is clearly a kind of correctness, but neither of knowledge nor of opinion; for there is no such thing as correctness of knowledge (since there is no such thing as error of knowledge), and correctness of opinion is truth; and at the same time everything that is an object of opinion is already determined. But again excellence in deliberation involves reasoning. The remaining alternative, then, is that it is correctness of thinking; for this is not yet assertion, since, while even opinion is not inquiry but has reached the stage of assertion, the man who is deliberating, whether he does so well or ill, is searching for something and calculating.

But excellence in deliberation is a certain correctness of deliberation; hence we must first inquire what deliberation is and what it is about. And, there being more than one kind of correctness, plainly excellence in deliberation is not any and every kind; for (1) the incontinent man and the bad man, if he is clever, will reach as a result of his calculation what he sets before himself, so that he will have deliberated correctly, but he will have got for himself a great evil. Now to have deliberated well is thought to be a good thing; for it is this kind of correctness of deliberation that is excellence in deliberation, viz. that which tends to attain what is good. But (2) it is possible to attain even good by a false syllogism, and to attain what one ought to do but not by the right means, the middle term being false; so that this too is not yet excellence in deliberation this state in virtue of which one attains what one ought but not by the right means. Again (3) it is possible to attain it by long deliberation while another man attains it quickly. Therefore in the former case we have not yet got excellence in deliberation, which is rightness with regard to the expedient-rightness in respect both of the end, the manner, and the time. (4) Further it is possible to have deliberated well either in the unqualified sense or with reference to a particular end. Excellence in deliberation in the unqualified sense, then, is that which succeeds with reference to what is the end in the unqualified sense, and excellence in deliberation in a particular sense is that which succeeds relatively to a particular end. If, then, it is characteristic of men of practical wisdom to have deliberated well, excellence in deliberation will be correctness with regard to what conduces to the end of which practical wisdom is the true apprehension.

10

Understanding, also, and goodness of understanding, in virtue of which men are said to be men of understanding or of good understanding, are neither entirely the same as opinion or scientific knowledge (for at that rate all men would have been men of understanding), nor are they one of the particular sciences, such as medicine, the science of things connected with health, or geometry, the science of spatial magnitudes. For understanding is neither about things that are always and are unchangeable, nor about any and every one of the things that come into being, but about things which may become subjects of questioning and deliberation. Hence it is about the same objects as practical wisdom; but understanding and practical wisdom are not the same. For practical wisdom issues commands, since its end is what ought to be done or not to be done; but understanding only judges. (Understanding is identical with goodness of understanding, men of understanding with men of good understanding.) Now understanding is neither the having nor the acquiring of practical wisdom; but as learning is called understanding when it means the exercise of the faculty of knowledge, so 'understanding' is applicable to the exercise of the faculty of opinion for the purpose of judging of what some one else says about matters with which practical wisdom is concerned-and of judging soundly; for 'well' and 'soundly' are the same thing. And from this has come the use of the name 'understanding' in virtue of which men are said to be 'of good understanding', viz. from the application of the word to the grasping of scientific truth; for we often call such grasping understanding.

11

What is called judgement, in virtue of which men are said to 'be sympathetic judges' and to 'have judgement', is the right discrimination of the equitable. This is shown by the fact that we say the equitable man is above all others a man of sympathetic judgement, and identify equity with sympathetic judgement about certain facts. And sympathetic judgement is judgement which discriminates what is equitable and does so correctly; and correct judgement is that which judges what is true.

Now all the states we have considered converge, as might be expected, to the same point; for when we speak of judgement and understanding and practical wisdom and intuitive reason we credit the same people with possessing judgement and having reached years of reason and with having practical wisdom and understanding. For all these faculties deal with ultimates, i.e. with particulars; and being a man of understanding and of good or sympathetic judgement consists in being able judge about the things with which practical wisdom is concerned; for the equities are common to all good men in relation to other men. Now all things which have to be done are included among particulars or ultimates; for not only must the man of practical wisdom know particular facts, but understanding and judgement are also concerned with things to be done, and these are ultimates. And intuitive reason is concerned with the ultimates in both directions; for both the first terms and the last are objects of intuitive reason and not of argument, and the intuitive reason which is presupposed by demonstrations grasps the unchangeable and first terms, while the intuitive reason involved in practical reasonings grasps the last and variable fact, i.e. the minor premiss. For these variable facts are the starting-points for the apprehension of the end, since the universals are reached from the particulars; of these therefore we must have perception, and this perception is intuitive reason.

This is why these states are thought to be natural endowments-why, while no one is thought to be a philosopher by nature, people are thought to have by nature judgement, understanding, and intuitive reason. This is shown by the fact that we think our powers correspond to our time of life, and that a particular age brings with it intuitive reason and judgement; this implies that nature is the cause. (Hence intuitive reason is both beginning and end; for demonstrations are from these and about these.) Therefore we ought to attend to the undemonstrated sayings and opinions of experienced and older people or of people of practical wisdom not less than to demonstrations; for because experience has given them an eye they see aright.

We have stated, then, what practical and philosophic wisdom are, and with what each of them is concerned, and we have said that each is the virtue of a different part of the soul.

12

Difficulties might be raised as to the utility of these qualities of mind. For (1) philosophic wisdom will contemplate none of the things that will make a man happy (for it is not concerned with any coming into being), and though practical wisdom has this merit, for what purpose do we need it? Practical wisdom is the quality of mind concerned with things just and noble and good for man, but these are the things which it is the mark of a good man to do, and we are none the more able to act for knowing them if the virtues are states of character, just as we are none the better able to act for knowing the things that are healthy and sound, in the sense not of producing but of issuing from the state of health; for we are none the more able to act for having the art of medicine or of gymnastics. But (2) if we are to say that a man should have practical wisdom not for the sake of knowing moral truths but for the sake of becoming good, practical wisdom will be of no use to those who are good; again it is of no use to those who have not virtue; for it will make no difference whether they have practical wisdom themselves or obey others who have it, and it would be enough for us to do what we do in the case of health; though we wish to become healthy, yet we do not learn the art of medicine. (3) Besides this, it would be thought strange if practical wisdom, being inferior to philosophic wisdom, is to be put in authority over it, as seems to be implied by the fact that the art which produces anything rules and issues commands about that thing.

These, then, are the questions we must discuss; so far we have only stated the difficulties.

(1) Now first let us say that in themselves these states must be worthy of choice because they are the virtues of the two parts of the soul respectively, even if neither of them produce anything.

(2) Secondly, they do produce something, not as the art of medicine produces health, however, but as health produces health; so does philosophic wisdom produce happiness; for, being a part of virtue entire, by being possessed and by actualizing itself it makes a man happy.

(3) Again, the work of man is achieved only in accordance with practical wisdom as well as with moral virtue; for virtue makes us aim at the right mark, and practical wisdom makes us take the right means. (Of the fourth part of the soul-the nutritive-there is no such virtue; for there is nothing which it is in its power to do or not to do.)

(4) With regard to our being none the more able to do because of our practical wisdom what is noble and just, let us begin a little further back, starting with the following principle. As we say that some people who do just acts are not necessarily just, i.e. those who do the acts ordained by the laws either unwillingly or owing to ignorance or for some other reason and not for the sake of the acts themselves (though, to be sure, they do what they should and all the things that the good man ought), so is it, it seems, that in order to be good one must be in a certain state when one does the several acts, i.e. one must do them as a result of choice and for the sake of the acts themselves. Now virtue makes the choice right, but the question of the things which should naturally be done to carry out our choice belongs not to virtue but to another faculty. We must devote our attention to these matters and give a clearer statement about them. There is a faculty which is called cleverness; and this is such as to be able to do the things that tend towards the mark we have set before ourselves, and to hit it. Now if the mark be noble, the cleverness is laudable, but if the mark be bad, the cleverness is mere smartness; hence we call even men of practical wisdom clever or smart. Practical wisdom is not the faculty, but it does not exist without this faculty. And this eye of the soul acquires its formed state not without the aid of virtue, as has been said and is plain; for the syllogisms which deal with acts to be done are things which involve a starting-point, viz. 'since the end, i.e. what is best, is of such and such a nature', whatever it may be (let it for the sake of argument be what we please); and this is not evident except to the good man; for wickedness perverts us and causes us to be deceived about the starting-points of action. Therefore it is evident that it is impossible to be practically wise without being good.

13

We must therefore consider virtue also once more; for virtue too is similarly related; as practical wisdom is to cleverness-not the same, but like it-so is natural virtue to virtue in the strict sense. For all men think that each type of character belongs to its possessors in some sense by nature; for from the very moment of birth we are just or fitted for selfcontrol or brave or have the other moral qualities; but yet we seek something else as that which is good in the strict sense-we seek for the presence of such qualities in another way. For both children and brutes have the natural dispositions to these qualities, but without reason these are evidently hurtful. Only we seem to see this much, that, while one may be led astray by them, as a strong body which moves without sight may stumble badly because of its lack of sight, still, if a man once acquires reason, that makes a difference in action; and his state, while still like what it was, will then be virtue in the strict sense. Therefore, as in the part of us which forms opinions there are two types, cleverness and practical wisdom, so too in the moral part there are two types, natural virtue and virtue in the strict sense, and of these the latter involves practical wisdom. This is why some say that all the virtues are forms of practical wisdom, and why Socrates in one respect was on the right track while in another he went astray; in thinking that all the virtues were forms of practical wisdom he was wrong, but in saying they implied practical wisdom he was right. This is confirmed by the fact that even now all men, when they define virtue, after naming the state of character and its objects add 'that (state) which is in accordance with the right rule'; now the right rule is that which is in accordance with practical wisdom. All men, then, seem somehow to divine that this kind of state is virtue, viz. that which is in accordance with practical wisdom. But we must go a little further. For it is not merely the state in accordance with the right rule, but the state that implies the presence of the right rule, that is virtue; and practical wisdom is a right rule about such matters. Socrates, then, thought the virtues were rules or rational principles (for he thought they were, all of them, forms of scientific knowledge), while we think they involve a rational principle.

It is clear, then, from what has been said, that it is not possible to be good in the strict sense without practical wisdom, nor practically wise without moral virtue. But in this way we may also refute the dialectical argument whereby it might be contended that the virtues exist in separation from each other; the same man, it might be said, is not best equipped by nature for all the virtues, so that he will have already acquired one when he has not yet acquired another. This is possible in respect of the natural virtues, but not in respect of those in respect of which a man is called without qualification good; for with the presence of the one quality, practical wisdom, will be given all the virtues. And it is plain that, even if it were of no practical value, we should have needed it because it is the virtue of the part of us in question; plain too that the choice will not be right without practical wisdom any more than without virtue; for the one deter, mines the end and the other makes us do the things that lead to the end.

But again it is not supreme over philosophic wisdom, i.e. over the superior part of us, any more than the art of medicine is over health; for it does not use it but provides for its coming into being; it issues orders, then, for its sake, but not to it. Further, to maintain its supremacy would be like saying that the art of politics rules the gods because it issues orders about all the affairs of the state.

Book Seven

1

Let us now make a fresh beginning and point out that of moral states to be avoided there are three kinds-vice, incontinence, brutishness. The contraries of two of these are evident,-one we call virtue, the other continence; to brutishness it would be most fitting to oppose superhuman virtue, a heroic and divine kind of virtue, as Homer has represented Priam saying of Hector that he was very good,

For he seemed not, he, The child of a mortal man, but as one that of God's seed came.

Therefore if, as they say, men become gods by excess of virtue, of this kind must evidently be the state opposed to the brutish state; for as a brute has no vice or virtue, so neither has a god; his state is higher than virtue, and that of a brute is a different kind of state from vice.

Now, since it is rarely that a godlike man is found-to use the epithet of the Spartans, who when they admire any one highly call him a 'godlike man'-so too the brutish type is rarely found among men; it is found chiefly among barbarians, but some brutish qualities are also produced by disease or deformity; and we also call by this evil name those men who go beyond all ordinary standards by reason of vice. Of this kind of disposition, however, we must later make some mention, while we have discussed vice before we must now discuss incontinence and softness (or effeminacy), and continence and endurance; for we must treat each of the two neither as identical with virtue or wickedness, nor as a different genus. We must, as in all other cases, set the observed facts before us and, after first discussing the difficulties, go on to prove, if possible, the truth of all the common opinions about these affections of the mind, or, failing this, of the greater number and the most authoritative; for if we both refute the objections and leave the common opinions undisturbed, we shall have proved the case sufficiently.

Now (1) both continence and endurance are thought to be included among things good and praiseworthy, and both incontinence and soft, ness among things bad and blameworthy; and the same man is thought to be continent and ready to abide by the result of his calculations, or incontinent and ready to abandon them. And (2) the incontinent man, knowing that what he does is bad, does it as a result of passion, while the continent man, knowing that his appetites are bad, refuses on account of his rational principle to follow them (3) The temperate man all men call continent and disposed to endurance, while the continent man some maintain to be always temperate but others do not; and some call the self-indulgent man incontinent and the incontinent man selfindulgent indiscriminately, while others distinguish them. (4) The man of practical wisdom, they sometimes say, cannot be incontinent, while sometimes they say that some who are practically wise and clever are incontinent. Again (5) men are said to be incontinent even with respect to anger, honour, and gain.-These, then, are the things that are said.

2

Now we may ask (1) how a man who judges rightly can behave incontinently. That he should behave so when he has knowledge, some say is impossible; for it would be strange-so Socrates thought-if when knowledge was in a man something else could master it and drag it about like a slave. For Socrates was entirely opposed to the view in question, holding that there is no such thing as incontinence; no one, he said, when he judges acts against what he judges best-people act so only by reason of ignorance. Now this view plainly contradicts the observed facts, and we must inquire about what happens to such a man; if he acts by reason of ignorance, what is the manner of his ignorance? For that the man who behaves incontinently does not, before he gets into this state, think he ought to act so, is evident. But there are some who concede certain of Socrates' contentions but not others; that nothing is stronger than knowledge they admit, but not that on one acts contrary to what has seemed to him the better course, and therefore they say that the incontinent man has not knowledge when he is mastered by his pleasures, but opinion. But if it is opinion and not knowledge, if it is not a strong conviction that resists but a weak one, as in men who hesitate, we sympathize with their failure to stand by such convictions against strong appetites; but we do not sympathize with wickedness, nor with any of the other blameworthy states. Is it then practical wisdom whose resistance is mastered? That is the strongest of all states. But this is absurd; the same man will be at once practically wise and incontinent, but no one would say that it is the part of a practically wise man to do willingly the basest acts. Besides, it has been shown before that the man of practical wisdom is one who will act (for he is a man concerned with the individual facts) and who has the other virtues.

(2) Further, if continence involves having strong and bad appetites, the temperate man will not be continent nor the continent man temperate; for a temperate man will have neither excessive nor bad appetites. But the continent man must; for if the appetites are good, the state of character that restrains us from following them is bad, so that not all continence will be good; while if they are weak and not bad, there is nothing admirable in resisting them, and if they are weak and bad, there is nothing great in resisting these either.

(3) Further, if continence makes a man ready to stand by any and every opinion, it is bad, i.e. if it makes him stand even by a false opinion; and if incontinence makes a man apt to abandon any and every opinion, there will be a good incontinence, of which Sophocles' Neoptolemus in the Philoctetes will be an instance; for he is to be praised for not standing by what Odysseus persuaded him to do, because he is pained at telling a lie.

(4) Further, the sophistic argument presents a difficulty; the syllogism arising from men's wish to expose paradoxical results arising from an opponent's view, in order that they may be admired when they succeed, is one that puts us in a difficulty (for thought is bound fast when it will not rest because the conclusion does not satisfy it, and cannot advance because it cannot refute the argument). There is an argument from which it follows that folly coupled with incontinence is virtue; for a man does the opposite of what he judges, owing to incontinence, but judges what is good to be evil and something that he should not do, and consequence he will do what is good and not what is evil.

(5) Further, he who on conviction does and pursues and chooses what is pleasant would be thought to be better than one who does so as a result not of calculation but of incontinence; for

he is easier to cure since he may be persuaded to change his mind. But to the incontinent man may be applied the proverb 'when water chokes, what is one to wash it down with?' If he had been persuaded of the rightness of what he does, he would have desisted when he was persuaded to change his mind; but now he acts in spite of his being persuaded of something quite different.

(6) Further, if incontinence and continence are concerned with any and every kind of object, who is it that is incontinent in the unqualified sense? No one has all the forms of incontinence, but we say some people are incontinent without qualification.

3

Of some such kind are the difficulties that arise; some of these points must be refuted and the others left in possession of the field; for the solution of the difficulty is the discovery of the truth. (1) We must consider first, then, whether incontinent people act knowingly or not, and in what sense knowingly; then (2) with what sorts of object the incontinent and the continent man may be said to be concerned (i.e. whether with any and every pleasure and pain or with certain determinate kinds), and whether the continent man and the man of endurance are the same or different; and similarly with regard to the other matters germane to this inquiry. The starting-point of our investigation is (a) the question whether the continent man and the incontinent are differentiated by their objects or by their attitude, i.e. whether the incontinent man is incontinent simply by being concerned with such and such objects, or, instead, by his attitude, or, instead of that, by both these things; (b) the second question is whether incontinence and continence are concerned with any and every object or not. The man who is incontinent in the unqualified sense is neither concerned with any and every object, but with precisely those with which the self-indulgent man is concerned, nor is he characterized by being simply related to these (for then his state would be the same as self-indulgence), but by being related to them in a certain way. For the one is led on in accordance with his own choice, thinking that he ought always to pursue the present pleasure; while the other does not think so, but yet pursues it.

(1) As for the suggestion that it is true opinion and not knowledge against which we act incontinently, that makes no difference to the argument; for some people when in a state of opinion do not hesitate, but think they know exactly. If, then, the notion is that owing to their weak conviction those who have opinion are more likely to act against their judgement than those who know, we answer that there need be no difference between knowledge and opinion in this respect; for some men are no less convinced of what they think than others of what they know; as is shown by the of Heraclitus. But (a), since we use the word 'know' in two senses (for both the man who has knowledge but is not using it and he who is using it are said to know), it will make a difference whether, when a man does what he should not, he has the knowledge but is not exercising it, or is exercising it; for the latter seems strange, but not the former.

(b) Further, since there are two kinds of premisses, there is nothing to prevent a man's having both premisses and acting against his knowledge, provided that he is using only the universal premiss and not the particular; for it is particular acts that have to be done. And there are also two kinds of universal term; one is predicable of the agent, the other of the object; e.g. 'dry food is good for every man', and 'I am a man', or 'such and such food is dry'; but whether 'this food is such and such', of this the incontinent man either has not or is not exercising the knowledge. There will, then, be, firstly, an enormous difference between these manners of knowing, so that to know in one way when we act incontinently would not seem anything strange, while to know in the other way would be extraordinary.

And further (c) the possession of knowledge in another sense than those just named is something that happens to men; for within the case of having knowledge but not using it we see a difference of state, admitting of the possibility of having knowledge in a sense and yet not having it, as in the instance of a man asleep, mad, or drunk. But now this is just the condition of men under the influence of passions; for outbursts of anger and sexual appetites and some other such passions, it is evident, actually alter our bodily condition, and in some men even produce fits of madness. It is plain, then, that incontinent people must be said to be in a similar condition to men asleep, mad, or drunk. The fact that men use the language that flows from knowledge proves nothing; for even men under the influence of these passions utter scientific proofs and verses of Empedocles, and those who have just begun to learn a science can string together its phrases, but do not yet know it; for it has to become part of themselves, and that takes time; so that we must suppose that the use of language by men in an incontinent state means no more than its utterance by actors on the stage. (d) Again, we may also view the cause as follows with reference to the facts of human nature. The one opinion is universal, the other is concerned with the particular facts, and here we come to something within the sphere of perception; when a single opinion results from the two, the soul must in one type of case affirm the conclusion, while in the case of opinions concerned with production it must immediately act (e.g. if 'everything sweet ought to be tasted', and 'this is sweet', in the sense of being one of the particular sweet things, the man who can act and is not prevented must at the same time actually act accordingly). When, then, the universal opinion is present in us forbidding us to taste, and there is also the opinion that 'everything sweet is pleasant', and that 'this is sweet' (now this is the opinion that is active), and when appetite happens to be present in us, the one opinion bids us avoid the object, but appetite leads us towards it (for it can move each of our bodily parts); so that it turns out that a man behaves incontinently under the influence (in a sense) of a rule and an opinion, and of one not contrary in itself, but only incidentally-for the appetite is contrary, not the opinion-to the right rule. It also follows that this is the reason why the lower animals are not incontinent, viz. because they have no universal judgement but only imagination and memory of particulars.

The explanation of how the ignorance is dissolved and the incontinent man regains his knowledge, is the same as in the case of the man drunk or asleep and is not peculiar to this condition; we must go to the students of natural science for it. Now, the last premiss both being an opinion about a perceptible object, and being what determines our actions this a man either has not when he is in the state of passion, or has it in the sense in which having knowledge did not mean knowing but only talking, as a drunken man may utter the verses of Empedocles. And because the last term is not universal nor equally an object of scientific knowledge with the universal term, the position that Socrates sought to establish actually seems to result; for it is not in the presence of what is thought to be knowledge proper that the affection of incontinence arises (nor is it this that is 'dragged about' as a result of the state of passion), but in that of perceptual knowledge.

This must suffice as our answer to the question of action with and without knowledge, and how it is possible to behave incontinently with knowledge.

4

(2) We must next discuss whether there is any one who is incontinent without qualification, or all men who are incontinent are so in a particular sense, and if there is, with what sort of objects he is concerned. That both continent persons and persons of endurance, and incontinent and soft persons, are concerned with pleasures and pains, is evident.

Now of the things that produce pleasure some are necessary, while others are worthy of choice in themselves but admit of excess, the bodily causes of pleasure being necessary (by such I mean both those concerned with food and those concerned with sexual intercourse, i.e. the bodily matters with which we defined self-indulgence and temperance as being concerned), while the others are not necessary but worthy of choice in themselves (e.g. victory, honour, wealth, and good and pleasant things of this sort). This being so, (a) those who go to excess with reference to the latter, contrary to the right rule which is in themselves, are not called incontinent simply, but incontinent with the qualification 'in respect of money, gain, honour, or anger',-not simply incontinent, on the ground that they are different from incontinent people and are called incontinent by reason of a resemblance. (Compare the case of Anthropos (Man), who won a contest at the Olympic games; in his case the general definition of man differed little from the definition peculiar to him, but yet it was different.) This is shown by the fact that incontinence either without qualification or in respect of some particular bodily pleasure is blamed not only as a fault but as a kind of vice, while none of the people who are incontinent in these other respects is so blamed.

But (b) of the people who are incontinent with respect to bodily enjoyments, with which we say the temperate and the self-indulgent man are concerned, he who pursues the excesses of things pleasant-and shuns those of things painful, of hunger and thirst and heat and cold and all the objects of touch and taste-not by choice but contrary to his choice and his judgement, is called incontinent, not with the qualification 'in respect of this or that', e.g. of anger, but just simply. This is confirmed by the fact that men are called 'soft' with regard to these pleasures, but not with regard to any of the others. And for this reason we group together the incontinent and the self-indulgent, the continent and the temperate man-but not any of these other types-because they are concerned somehow with the same pleasures and pains; but though these are concerned with the same objects, they are not similarly related to them, but some of them make a deliberate choice while the others do not.

This is why we should describe as self-indulgent rather the man who without appetite or with but a slight appetite pursues the excesses of pleasure and avoids moderate pains, than the man who does so because of his strong appetites; for what would the former do, if he had in addition a vigorous appetite, and a violent pain at the lack of the 'necessary' objects?

Now of appetites and pleasures some belong to the class of things generically noble and good-for some pleasant things are by nature worthy of choice, while others are contrary to these, and others are intermediate, to adopt our previous distinction-e.g. wealth, gain, victory, honour. And with reference to all objects whether of this or of the intermediate kind men are not blamed for being affected by them, for desiring and loving them, but for doing so in a certain way, i.e. for going to excess. (This is why all those who contrary to the rule either are mastered by or pursue one of the objects which are naturally noble and good, e.g. those who busy themselves more than they ought about honour or about children and parents, (are not wicked); for these too are good, and those who busy themselves about them are praised; but yet there is an excess even in them-if like Niobe one were to fight even against the gods, or were to be as much devoted to one's father as Satyrus nicknamed 'the filial', who was thought to be very silly on this point.) There is no wickedness, then, with regard to these objects, for the reason named, viz. because each of them is by nature a thing worthy of choice for its own sake; yet excesses in respect of them are bad and to be avoided. Similarly there is no incontinence with regard to them; for incontinence is not only to be avoided but is also a thing worthy of blame; but owing to a similarity in the state of feeling people apply the name incontinence, adding in each case what it is in respect of, as we may describe as a bad doctor or a bad actor one whom we should not call bad, simply. As, then, in this case we do not apply the term without qualification because each of these conditions is no shadness but only analogous to it, so it is clear that in the other case also that alone must be taken to be incontinence and continence which is concerned with the same objects as temperance and self-indulgence, but we apply the term to anger by virtue of a resemblance; and this is why we say with a qualification 'incontinent in respect of anger' as we say 'incontinent in respect of honour, or of gain'.

5

(1) Some things are pleasant by nature, and of these (a) some are so without qualification, and (b) others are so with reference to particular classes either of animals or of men; while (2) others are not pleasant by nature, but (a) some of them become so by reason of injuries to the system,

and (b) others by reason of acquired habits, and (c) others by reason of originally bad natures. This being so, it is possible with regard to each of the latter kinds to discover similar states of character to those recognized with regard to the former; I mean (A) the brutish states, as in the case of the female who, they say, rips open pregnant women and devours the infants, or of the things in which some of the tribes about the Black Sea that have gone savage are said to delight-in raw meat or in human flesh, or in lending their children to one another to feast upon-or of the story told of Phalaris.

These states are brutish, but (B) others arise as a result of disease (or, in some cases, of madness, as with the man who sacrificed and ate his mother, or with the slave who ate the liver of his fellow), and others are morbid states (C) resulting from custom, e.g. the habit of plucking out the hair or of gnawing the nails, or even coals or earth, and in addition to these paederasty; for these arise in some by nature and in others, as in those who have been the victims of lust from childhood, from habit.

Now those in whom nature is the cause of such a state no one would call incontinent, any more than one would apply the epithet to women because of the passive part they play in copulation; nor would one apply it to those who are in a morbid condition as a result of habit. To have these various types of habit is beyond the limits of vice, as brutishness is too; for a man who has them to master or be mastered by them is not simple (continence or) incontinence but that which is so by analogy, as the man who is in this condition in respect of fits of anger is to be called incontinent in respect of that feeling but not incontinent simply. For every excessive state whether of folly, of cowardice, of self-indulgence, or of bad temper, is either brutish or morbid; the man who is by nature apt to fear everything, even the squeak of a mouse, is cowardly with a brutish cowardice, while the man who feared a weasel did so in consequence of disease; and of foolish people those who by nature are thoughtless and live by their senses alone are brutish, like some races of the distant barbarians, while those who are so as a result of disease (e.g. of epilepsy) or of madness are morbid. Of these characteristics it is possible to have some only at times, and not to be mastered by them. e.g. Phalaris may have restrained a desire to eat the flesh of a child or an appetite for unnatural sexual pleasure; but it is also possible to be mastered, not merely to have the feelings. Thus, as the wickedness which is on the human level is called wickedness simply, while that which is not is called wickedness not simply but with the qualification 'brutish' or 'morbid', in the same way it is plain that some incontinence is brutish and some morbid, while only that which corresponds to human self-indulgence is incontinence simply.

That incontinence and continence, then, are concerned only with the same objects as selfindulgence and temperance and that what is concerned with other objects is a type distinct from incontinence, and called incontinence by a metaphor and not simply, is plain.

6

That incontinence in respect of anger is less disgraceful than that in respect of the appetites is what we will now proceed to see. (1) Anger seems to listen to argument to some extent, but to mishear it, as do hasty servants who run out before they have heard the whole of what one says, and then muddle the order, or as dogs bark if there is but a knock at the door, before looking to see if it is a friend; so anger by reason of the warmth and hastiness of its nature, though it hears, does not hear an order, and springs to take revenge. For argument or imagination informs us that we have been insulted or slighted, and anger, reasoning as it were that anything like this must be fought against, boils up straightway; while appetite, if argument or perception merely says that an object is pleasant, springs to the enjoyment of it. Therefore anger obeys the argument in a sense, but appetite does not. It is therefore more disgraceful; for the man who is incontinent in respect of anger is in a sense conquered by argument, while the other is conquered by appetite and not by argument.

(2) Further, we pardon people more easily for following natural desires, since we pardon them more easily for following such appetites as are common to all men, and in so far as they are common; now anger and bad temper are more natural than the appetites for excess, i.e. for unnecessary objects. Take for instance the man who defended himself on the charge of striking his father by saying 'yes, but he struck his father, and he struck his, and' (pointing to his child) 'this boy will strike me when he is a man; it runs in the family'; or the man who when he was being dragged along by his son bade him stop at the doorway, since he himself had dragged his father only as far as that.

(2) Further, those who are more given to plotting against others are more criminal. Now a passionate man is not given to plotting, nor is anger itself-it is open; but the nature of appetite is illustrated by what the poets call Aphrodite, 'guile-weaving daughter of Cyprus', and by Homer's words about her 'embroidered girdle':

And the whisper of wooing is there, Whose subtlety stealeth the wits of the wise, how prudent soe'er. Therefore if this form of incontinence is more criminal and disgraceful than that in respect of anger, it is both incontinence without qualification and in a sense vice.

(4) Further, no one commits wanton outrage with a feeling of pain, but every one who acts in anger acts with pain, while the man who commits outrage acts with pleasure. If, then, those acts at which it is most just to be angry are more criminal than others, the incontinence which is due to appetite is the more criminal; for there is no wanton outrage involved in anger.

Plainly, then, the incontinence concerned with appetite is more disgraceful than that concerned with anger, and continence and incontinence are concerned with bodily appetites and pleasures; but we must grasp the differences among the latter themselves. For, as has been said at the beginning, some are human and natural both in kind and in magnitude, others are brutish, and others are due to organic injuries and diseases. Only with the first of these are temperance and self-indulgence concerned; this is why we call the lower animals neither temperate nor self-indulgent except by a metaphor, and only if some one race of animals exceeds another as a whole in wantonness, destructiveness, and omnivorous greed; these have no power of choice or calculation, but they are departures from the natural norm, as, among men, madmen are. Now brutishness is a less evil than vice, though more alarming; for it is not that the better part has been perverted, as in man,-they have no better part. Thus it is like comparing a lifeless thing with a living in respect of badness; for the badness of that which has no originative source of movement is always less hurtful, and reason is an originative source. Thus it is like comparing injustice in the abstract with an unjust man. Each is in some sense worse; for a bad man will do ten thousand times as much evil as a brute.

7

With regard to the pleasures and pains and appetites and aversions arising through touch and taste, to which both self-indulgence and temperance were formerly narrowed down, it possible to be in such a state as to be defeated even by those of them which most people master, or to master even those by which most people are defeated; among these possibilities, those relating to pleasures are incontinence and continence, those relating to pains softness and endurance. The state of most people is intermediate, even if they lean more towards the worse states.

Now, since some pleasures are necessary while others are not, and are necessary up to a point while the excesses of them are not, nor the deficiencies, and this is equally true of appetites and pains, the man who pursues the excesses of things pleasant, or pursues to excess necessary objects, and does so by choice, for their own sake and not at all for the sake of any result distinct from them, is self-indulgent; for such a man is of necessity unlikely to repent, and therefore incurable, since a man who cannot repent cannot be cured. The man who is deficient in his pursuit of them is the opposite of self-indulgent; the man who is intermediate is temperate. Similarly, there is the man who avoids bodily pains not because he is defeated by them but by choice. (Of those who do not choose such acts, one kind of man is led to them as a result of the pleasure involved, another because he avoids the pain arising from the appetite, so that these types differ from one another. Now any one would think worse of a man with no appetite or with weak appetite were he to do something disgraceful, than if he did it under the influence of powerful appetite, and worse of him if he struck a blow not in anger than if he did it in anger; for what would he have done if he had been strongly affected? This is why the self-indulgent man is worse than the incontinent.) of the states named, then, the latter is rather a kind of softness; the former is self-indulgence. While to the incontinent man is opposed the continent, to the soft is opposed the man of endurance; for endurance consists in resisting, while continence consists in conquering, and resisting and conquering are different, as not being beaten is different from winning; this is why continence is also more worthy of choice than endurance. Now the man who is defective in respect of resistance to the things which most men both resist and resist successfully is soft and effeminate; for effeminacy too is a kind of softness; such a man trails his cloak to avoid the pain of lifting it, and plays the invalid without thinking himself wretched, though the man he imitates is a wretched man.

The case is similar with regard to continence and incontinence. For if a man is defeated by violent and excessive pleasures or pains, there is nothing wonderful in that; indeed we are ready to pardon him if he has resisted, as Theodectes' Philoctetes does when bitten by the snake, or Carcinus' Cercyon in the Alope, and as people who try to restrain their laughter burst out into a guffaw, as happened to Xenophantus. But it is surprising if a man is defeated by and cannot resist pleasures or pains which most men can hold out against, when this is not due to heredity or disease, like the softness that is hereditary with the kings of the Scythians, or that which distinguishes the female sex from the male.

The lover of amusement, too, is thought to be self-indulgent, but is really soft. For amusement is a relaxation, since it is a rest from work; and the lover of amusement is one of the people who go to excess in this.

Of incontinence one kind is impetuosity, another weakness. For some men after deliberating fail, owing to their emotion, to stand by the conclusions of their deliberation, others because they have not deliberated are led by their emotion; since some men (just as people who first tickle others are not tickled themselves), if they have first perceived and seen what is coming and have first roused themselves and their calculative faculty, are not defeated by their emotion, whether it be pleasant or painful. It is keen and excitable people that suffer especially from the impetuous form of incontinence; for the former by reason of their quickness and the latter by reason of the violence of their passions do not await the argument, because they are apt to follow their imagination.

8

The self-indulgent man, as was said, is not apt to repent; for he stands by his choice; but incontinent man is likely to repent. This is why the position is not as it was expressed in the formulation of the problem, but the selfindulgent man is incurable and the incontinent man curable; for wickedness is like a disease such as dropsy or consumption, while incontinence is like epilepsy; the former is a permanent, the latter an intermittent badness. And generally incontinence and vice are different in kind; vice is unconscious of itself, incontinence is not (of incontinent men themselves, those who become temporarily beside themselves are better than those who have the rational principle but do not abide by it, since the latter are defeated by a weaker passion, and do not act without previous deliberation like the others); for the incontinent man is like the people who get drunk quickly and on little wine, i.e. on less than most people.

Evidently, then, incontinence is not vice (though perhaps it is so in a qualified sense); for incontinence is contrary to choice while vice is in accordance with choice; not but what they are similar in respect of the actions they lead to; as in the saying of Demodocus about the

Milesians, 'the Milesians are not without sense, but they do the things that senseless people do', so too incontinent people are not criminal, but they will do criminal acts.

Now, since the incontinent man is apt to pursue, not on conviction, bodily pleasures that are excessive and contrary to the right rule, while the self-indulgent man is convinced because he is the sort of man to pursue them, it is on the contrary the former that is easily persuaded to change his mind, while the latter is not. For virtue and vice respectively preserve and destroy the first principle, and in actions the final cause is the first principle, as the hypotheses are in mathematics; neither in that case is it argument that teaches the first principles, nor is it so here-virtue either natural or produced by habituation is what teaches right opinion about the first principle. Such a man as this, then, is temperate; his contrary is the self-indulgent.

But there is a sort of man who is carried away as a result of passion and contrary to the right rule-a man whom passion masters so that he does not act according to the right rule, but does not master to the extent of making him ready to believe that he ought to pursue such pleasures without reserve; this is the incontinent man, who is better than the self-indulgent man, and not bad without qualification; for the best thing in him, the first principle, is preserved. And contrary to him is another kind of man, he who abides by his convictions and is not carried away, at least as a result of passion. It is evident from these considerations that the latter is a good state and the former a bad one.

9

Is the man continent who abides by any and every rule and any and every choice, or the man who abides by the right choice, and is he incontinent who abandons any and every choice and any and every rule, or he who abandons the rule that is not false and the choice that is right; this is how we put it before in our statement of the problem. Or is it incidentally any and every choice but per se the true rule and the right choice by which the one abides and the other does not? If any one chooses or pursues this for the sake of that, per se he pursues and chooses the latter, but incidentally the former. But when we speak without qualification we mean what is per se. Therefore in a sense the one abides by, and the other abandons, any and every opinion; but without qualification, the true opinion.

There are some who are apt to abide by their opinion, who are called strong-headed, viz. those who are hard to persuade in the first instance and are not easily persuaded to change; these have in them something like the continent man, as the prodigal is in a way like the liberal man and the rash man like the confident man; but they are different in many respects. For it is to passion and appetite that the one will not yield, since on occasion the continent man will be easy to persuade; but it is to argument that the others refuse to yield, for they do form appetites and many of them are led by their pleasures. Now the people who are strong-headed are the opinionated, the ignorant, and the boorish-the opinionated being influenced by pleasure and pain; for they delight in the victory they gain if they are not persuaded to change, and are pained if their decisions become null and void as decrees sometimes do; so that they are liker the incontinent than the continent man.

But there are some who fail to abide by their resolutions, not as a result of incontinence, e.g. Neoptolemus in Sophocles' Philoctetes; yet it was for the sake of pleasure that he did not stand fast-but a noble pleasure; for telling the truth was noble to him, but he had been persuaded by Odysseus to tell the lie. For not every one who does anything for the sake of pleasure is either self-indulgent or bad or incontinent, but he who does it for a disgraceful pleasure.

Since there is also a sort of man who takes less delight than he should in bodily things, and does not abide by the rule, he who is intermediate between him and the incontinent man is the continent man; for the incontinent man fails to abide by the rule because he delights too much in them, and this man because he delights in them too little; while the continent man abides by the rule and does not change on either account. Now if continence is good, both the contrary states must be bad, as they actually appear to be; but because the other extreme is seen in few people and seldom, as temperance is thought to be contrary only to self-indulgence, so is continence to incontinence.

Since many names are applied analogically, it is by analogy that we have come to speak of the 'continence' the temperate man; for both the continent man and the temperate man are such as to do nothing contrary to the rule for the sake of the bodily pleasures, but the former has and the latter has not bad appetites, and the latter is such as not to feel pleasure contrary to the rule, while the former is such as to feel pleasure but not to be led by it. And the incontinent and the self-indulgent man are also like another; they are different, but both pursue bodily pleasures- the latter, however, also thinking that he ought to do so, while the former does not think this.

10

Nor can the same man have practical wisdom and be incontinent; for it has been shown' that a man is at the same time practically wise, and good in respect of character. Further, a man has practical wisdom not by knowing only but by being able to act; but the incontinent man is unable to act-there is, however, nothing to prevent a clever man from being incontinent; this is why it is sometimes actually thought that some people have practical wisdom but are incontinent, viz. because cleverness and practical wisdom differ in the way we have described in our first discussions, and are near together in respect of their reasoning, but differ in respect of their purpose-nor yet is the incontinent man like the man who knows and is contemplating a truth, but like the man who is asleep or drunk. And he acts willingly (for he acts in a sense with knowledge both of what he does and of the end to which he does it), but is not wicked, since his purpose is good; so that he is half-wicked. And he is not a criminal; for he does not act of malice aforethought; of the two types of incontinent man the one does not abide by the conclusions of his deliberation, while the excitable man does not deliberate at all. And thus the incontinent man like a city which passes all the right decrees and has good laws, but makes no use of them, as in Anaxandrides' jesting remark,

The city willed it, that cares nought for laws; but the wicked man is like a city that uses its laws, but has wicked laws to use.

Now incontinence and continence are concerned with that which is in excess of the state characteristic of most men; for the continent man abides by his resolutions more and the incontinent man less than most men can.

Of the forms of incontinence, that of excitable people is more curable than that of those who deliberate but do not abide by their decisions, and those who are incontinent through habituation are more curable than those in whom incontinence is innate; for it is easier to change a habit than to change one's nature; even habit is hard to change just because it is like nature, as Evenus says:

I say that habit's but a long practice, friend, And this becomes men's nature in the end.

We have now stated what continence, incontinence, endurance, and softness are, and how these states are related to each other.

11

The study of pleasure and pain belongs to the province of the political philosopher; for he is the architect of the end, with a view to which we call one thing bad and another good without qualification. Further, it is one of our necessary tasks to consider them; for not only did we lay it down that moral virtue and vice are concerned with pains and pleasures, but most people say that happiness involves pleasure; this is why the blessed man is called by a name derived from a word meaning enjoyment.

Now (1) some people think that no pleasure is a good, either in itself or incidentally, since the good and pleasure are not the same; (2) others think that some pleasures are good but that most are bad. (3) Again there is a third view, that even if all pleasures are good, yet the best thing in the world cannot be pleasure. (1) The reasons given for the view that pleasure is not a good at all are (a) that every pleasure is a perceptible process to a natural state, and that no process is of the same kind as its end, e.g. no process of building of the same kind as a house. (b) A temperate man avoids pleasures. (c) A man of practical wisdom pursues what is free from pain, not what is pleasant. (d) The pleasures are a hindrance to thought, and the more so the more one delights in them, e.g. in sexual pleasure; for no one could think of anything while absorbed in this. (e) There is no art of pleasure; but every good is the product of some art. (f) Children and the brutes pursue pleasures. (2) The reasons for the view that not all pleasures are good are that (a) there are pleasures that are actually base and objects of reproach, and (b) there are harmful pleasures; for some pleasant things are unhealthy. (3) The reason for the view that the best thing in the world is not pleasure is that pleasure is not an end but a process.

12

These are pretty much the things that are said. That it does not follow from these grounds that pleasure is not a good, or even the chief good, is plain from the following considerations. (A) (a) First, since that which is good may be so in either of two senses (one thing good simply and another good for a particular person), natural constitutions and states of being, and therefore also the corresponding movements and processes, will be correspondingly divisible. Of those which are thought to be bad some will be bad if taken without qualification but not bad for a particular person, but worthy of his choice, and some will not be worthy of choice even for a particular person, but only at a particular time and for a short period, though not without qualification; while others are not even pleasures, but seem to be so, viz. all those which involve pain and whose end is curative, e.g. the processes that go on in sick persons.

(b) Further, one kind of good being activity and another being state, the processes that restore us to our natural state are only incidentally pleasant; for that matter the activity at work in the appetites for them is the activity of so much of our state and nature as has remained unimpaired; for there are actually pleasures that involve no pain or appetite (e.g. those of contemplation), the nature in such a case not being defective at all. That the others are incidental is indicated by the fact that men do not enjoy the same pleasant objects when their nature is in its settled state as they do when it is being replenished, but in the former case they enjoy the things that are pleasant without qualification, in the latter the contraries of these as well; for then they enjoy even sharp and bitter things, none of which is pleasant either by nature or without qualification. The states they produce, therefore, are not pleasures naturally or without qualification; for as pleasant things differ, so do the pleasures arising from them.

(c) Again, it is not necessary that there should be something else better than pleasure, as some say the end is better than the process; for leasures are not processes nor do they all involve process-they are activities and ends; nor do they arise when we are becoming something, but when we are exercising some faculty; and not all pleasures have an end different from themselves, but only the pleasures of persons who are being led to the perfecting of their nature. This is why it is not right to say that pleasure is perceptible process, but it should rather be called activity of the natural state, and instead of 'perceptible' 'unimpeded'. It is thought by some people to be process just because they think it is in the strict sense good; for they think that activity is process, which it is not.

(B) The view that pleasures are bad because some pleasant things are unhealthy is like saying that healthy things are bad because some healthy things are bad for money-making; both are bad in the respect mentioned, but they are not bad for that reason-indeed, thinking itself is sometimes injurious to health.

Neither practical wisdom nor any state of being is impeded by the pleasure arising from it; it is foreign pleasures that impede, for the pleasures arising from thinking and learning will make us think and learn all the more.

(C) The fact that no pleasure is the product of any art arises naturally enough; there is no art of any other activity either, but only of the corresponding faculty; though for that matter the arts of the perfumer and the cook are thought to be arts of pleasure.

(D) The arguments based on the grounds that the temperate man avoids pleasure and that the man of practical wisdom pursues the painless life, and that children and the brutes pursue pleasure, are all refuted by the same consideration. We have pointed out in what sense pleasures are good without qualification and in what sense some are not good; now both the brutes and children pursue pleasures of the latter kind (and the man of practical wisdom pursues tranquil freedom from that kind), viz. those which imply appetite and pain, i.e. the bodily pleasures (for it is these that are of this nature) and the excesses of them, in respect of which the self-indulgent man is self-indulent. This is why the temperate man avoids these pleasures; for even he has pleasures of his own.

13

But further (E) it is agreed that pain is bad and to be avoided; for some pain is without qualification bad, and other pain is bad because it is in some respect an impediment to us. Now the contrary of that which is to be avoided, qua something to be avoided and bad, is good. Pleasure, then, is necessarily a good. For the answer of Speusippus, that pleasure is contrary both to pain and to good, as the greater is contrary both to the less and to the equal, is not successful; since he would not say that pleasure is essentially just a species of evil.

And (F) if certain pleasures are bad, that does not prevent the chief good from being some pleasure, just as the chief good may be some form of knowledge though certain kinds of knowledge are bad. Perhaps it is even necessary, if each disposition has unimpeded activities, that, whether the activity (if unimpeded) of all our dispositions or that of some one of them is happiness, this should be the thing most worthy of our choice; and this activity is pleasure. Thus the chief good would be some pleasure, though most pleasures might perhaps be bad without qualification. And for this reason all men think that the happy life is pleasant and weave pleasure into their ideal of happiness-and reasonably too; for no activity is perfect when it is impeded, and happiness is a perfect thing; this is why the happy man needs the goods of the body and external goods, i.e. those of fortune, viz. in order that he may not be impeded in these ways. Those who say that the victim on the rack or the man who falls into great misfortunes is happy if he is good, are, whether they mean to or not, talking nonsense. Now because we need fortune as well as other things, some people think good fortune the same thing as happiness; but it is not that, for even good fortune itself when in excess is an impediment, and perhaps should then be no longer called good fortune; for its limit is fixed by reference to happiness.

And indeed the fact that all things, both brutes and men, pursue pleasure is an indication of its being somehow the chief good:

No voice is wholly lost that many peoples... But since no one nature or state either is or is thought the best for all, neither do all pursue the same pleasure; yet all pursue pleasure. And perhaps they actually pursue not the pleasure they think they pursue nor that which they would say they pursue, but the same pleasure; for all things have by nature something divine in them. But the bodily pleasures have appropriated the name both because we oftenest steer our course for them and because all men share in them; thus because they alone are familiar, men think there are no others.

It is evident also that if pleasure, i.e. the activity of our faculties, is not a good, it will not be the case that the happy man lives a pleasant life; for to what end should he need pleasure, if it is not a good but the happy man may even live a painful life? For pain is neither an evil nor a good, if pleasure is not; why then should he avoid it? Therefore, too, the life of the good man will not be pleasanter than that of any one else, if his activities are not more pleasant.

14

(G) With regard to the bodily pleasures, those who say that some pleasures are very much to be chosen, viz. the noble pleasures, but not the bodily pleasures, i.e. those with which the self-indulgent man is concerned, must consider why, then, the contrary pains are bad. For the contrary of bad is good. Are the necessary pleasures good in the sense in which even that which is not bad is good? Or are they good up to a point? Is it that where you have states and processes of which there cannot be too much, there cannot be too much of the corresponding pleasure, and that where there can be too much of the one there can be too much of the other also? Now there can be too much of bodily goods, and the bad man is bad by virtue of pursuing the excess, not by virtue of pursuing the necessary pleasures (for all men enjoy in some way or other both dainty foods and wines and sexual intercourse, but not all men do so as they ought). The contrary is the case with pain; for he does not avoid the excess of it, he avoids it altogether; and this is peculiar to him, for the alternative to excess of pleasure is not pain, except to the man who pursues this excess.

Since we should state not only the truth, but also the cause of error-for this contributes towards producing conviction, since when a reasonable explanation is given of why the false view appears true, this tends to produce belief in the true view-therefore we must state why the bodily pleasures appear the more worthy of choice. (a) Firstly, then, it is because they expel pain; owing to the excesses of pain that men experience, they pursue excessive and in general bodily pleasure as being a cure for the pain. Now curative agencies produce intense feeling-which is the reason why they are pursued-because they show up against the contrary pain. (Indeed pleasure is thought not to be good for these two reasons, as has been said, viz. that (a) some of them are activities belonging to a bad nature-either congenital, as in the case of a brute, or due to habit, i.e. those of bad men; while (b) others are meant to cure a defective nature, and it is better to be in a healthy state than to be getting into it, but these arise during the process of being made perfect and are therefore only incidentally good.) (b) Further, they are pursued because of their violence by those who cannot enjoy other pleasures. (At all events they go out of their way to manufacture thirsts somehow for themselves. When these are harmless, the practice is irreproachable; when they are hurtful, it is bad.) For they have nothing else to enjoy, and, besides, a neutral state is painful to many people because of their nature. For the animal nature is always in travail, as the students of natural science also testify, saying that sight and hearing are painful; but we have become used to this, as they maintain. Similarly, while, in youth, people are, owing to the growth that is going on, in a situation like that of drunken men, and youth is pleasant, on the other hand people of excitable nature always need relief; for even their body is ever in torment owing to its special composition, and they are always under the influence of violent desire; but pain is driven out both by the contrary pleasure, and by any chance pleasure if it be strong; and for these reasons they become self-indulgent and bad. But the pleasures that do not involve pains do not admit of excess; and these are among the things pleasant by nature and not incidentally. By things pleasant incidentally I mean those that act as cures (for because as a result people are cured, through some action of the part that remains healthy, for this reason the process is thought pleasant); by things naturally pleasant I mean those that stimulate the action of the healthy nature.

There is no one thing that is always pleasant, because our nature is not simple but there is another element in us as well, inasmuch as we are perishable creatures, so that if the one element does something, this is unnatural to the other nature, and when the two elements are evenly balanced, what is done seems neither painful nor pleasant; for if the nature of anything were simple, the same action would always be most pleasant to it. This is why God always enjoys a single and simple pleasure; for there is not only an activity of movement but an activity of immobility, and pleasure is found more in rest than in movement. But 'change in all things is sweet', as the poet says, because of some vice; for as it is the vicious man that is changeable, so the nature that needs change is vicious; for it is not simple nor good.

We have now discussed continence and incontinence, and pleasure and pain, both what each is and in what sense some of them are good and others bad; it remains to speak of friendship.

Book Eight

1

After what we have said, a discussion of friendship would naturally follow, since it is a virtue or implies virtue, and is besides most necessary with a view to living. For without friends no one would choose to live, though he had all other goods; even rich men and those in possession of office and of dominating power are thought to need friends most of all; for what is the use of such prosperity without the opportunity of beneficence, which is exercised chiefly and in its most laudable form towards friends? Or how can prosperity be guarded and preserved without friends? The greater it is, the more exposed is it to risk. And in poverty and in other misfortunes men think friends are the only refuge. It helps the young, too, to keep from error; it aids older people by ministering to their needs and supplementing the activities that are failing from weakness; those in the prime of life it stimulates to noble actions-'two going together'-for with friends men are more able both to think and to act. Again, parent seems by nature to feel it for offspring and offspring for parent, not only among men but among birds and among most animals; it is felt mutually by members of the same race, and especially by men, whence we praise lovers of their fellowmen. We may even in our travels how near and dear every man is to every other. Friendship seems too to hold states together, and lawgivers to care more for it than for justice; for unanimity seems to be something like friendship, and this they aim at most of all, and expel faction as their worst enemy; and when men are friends they have no need of justice, while when they are just they need friendship as well, and the truest form of justice is thought to be a friendly quality.

But it is not only necessary but also noble; for we praise those who love their friends, and it is thought to be a fine thing to have many friends; and again we think it is the same people that are good men and are friends.

Not a few things about friendship are matters of debate. Some define it as a kind of likeness and say like people are friends, whence come the sayings 'like to like', 'birds of a feather flock together', and so on; others on the contrary say 'two of a trade never agree'. On this very question they inquire for deeper and more physical causes, Euripides saying that 'parched earth loves the rain, and stately heaven when filled with rain loves to fall to earth', and Heraclitus that 'it is what opposes that helps' and 'from different tones comes the fairest tune' and 'all things are produced through strife'; while Empedocles, as well as others, expresses the opposite view that like aims at like. The physical problems we may leave alone (for they do not belong to the present inquiry); let us examine those which are human and involve character and feeling, e.g. whether friendship can arise between any two people or people cannot be friends if they are wicked, and whether there is one species of friendship or more than one. Those who think there is only one because it admits of degrees have relied on an inadequate indication; for even things different in species admit of degree. We have discussed this matter previously.

2

The kinds of friendship may perhaps be cleared up if we first come to know the object of love. For not everything seems to be loved but only the lovable, and this is good, pleasant, or useful; but it would seem to be that by which some good or pleasure is produced that is useful, so that it is the good and the useful that are lovable as ends. Do men love, then, the good, or what is good for them? These sometimes clash. So too with regard to the pleasant. Now it is thought that each loves what is good for himself, and that the good is without qualification lovable, and what is good for each man is lovable for him; but each man loves not what is good for him but what seems good. This however will make no difference; we shall just have to say that this is 'that which seems lovable'. Now there are three grounds on which people love; of the love of lifeless objects we do not use the word 'friendship'; for it is not mutual love, nor is there a wishing of good to the other (for it would surely be ridiculous to wish wine well; if one wishes anything for it, it is that it may keep, so that one may have it oneself); but to a friend we say we ought to wish what is good for his sake. But to those who thus wish good we ascribe only goodwill, if the wish is not reciprocated; goodwill when it is reciprocal being friendship. Or must we add 'when it is recognized'? For many people have goodwill to those whom they have not seen but judge to be good or useful; and one of these might return this feeling. These people seem to bear goodwill to each other; but how could one call them friends when they do not know their mutual feelings? To be friends, then, the must be mutually recognized as bearing goodwill and wishing well to each other for one of the aforesaid reasons.

3

Now these reasons differ from each other in kind; so, therefore, do the corresponding forms of love and friendship. There are therefore three kinds of friendship, equal in number to the things that are lovable; for with respect to each there is a mutual and recognized love, and those who love each other wish well to each other in that respect in which they love one another. Now those who love each other for their utility do not love each other for themselves but in virtue of some good which they get from each other. So too with those who love for the sake of pleasure; it is not for their character that men love ready-witted people, but because they find them pleasant. Therefore those who love for the sake of utility love for the sake of what is good for themselves, and those who love for the sake of pleasure do so for the sake of what is pleasant to themselves, and not in so far as the other is the person loved but in so far as he is useful or pleasant. And thus these friendships are only incidental; for it is not as being the man he is that the loved person is loved, but as providing some good or pleasure. Such friendships, then, are easily dissolved, if the parties do not remain like themselves; for if the one party is no longer pleasant or useful the other ceases to love him.

Now the useful is not permanent but is always changing. Thus when the motive of the friendship is done away, the friendship is dissolved, inasmuch as it existed only for the ends in question. This kind of friendship seems to exist chiefly between old people (for at that age people pursue not the pleasant but the useful) and, of those who are in their prime or young, between those who pursue utility. And such people do not live much with each other either; for sometimes they do not even find each other pleasant; therefore they do not need such companionship unless they are useful to each other; for they are pleasant to each other only in so far as they rouse in each other hopes of something good to come. Among such friendships people also class the friendship of a host and guest. On the other hand the friendship of young people seems to aim at pleasure; for they live under the guidance of emotion, and pursue above all what is pleasant to themselves and what is immediately before them; but with increasing age their pleasures become different. This is why they quickly become friends and quickly cease to be so; their friendship changes with the object that is found pleasant, and such pleasure alters quickly. Young people are amorous too; for the greater part of the friendship of love depends on emotion and aims at pleasure; this is why they fall in love and quickly fall out of love, changing often within a single day. But these people do wish to spend their days and lives together; for it is thus that they attain the purpose of their friendship.

Perfect friendship is the friendship of men who are good, and alike in virtue; for these wish well alike to each other qua good, and they are good themselves. Now those who wish well to their friends for their sake are most truly friends; for they do this by reason of own nature and not incidentally; therefore their friendship lasts as long as they are good-and goodness is an enduring thing. And each is good without qualification and to his friend, for the good are both good without qualification and useful to each other. So too they are pleasant; for the good are pleasant both without qualification and to each other, since to each his own activities and others like them are pleasurable, and the actions of the good are the same or like. And such a friendship is as might be expected permanent, since there meet in it all the qualities that friends should have. For all friendship is for the sake of good or of pleasure-good or pleasure either in the abstract or such as will be enjoyed by him who has the friendly feeling-and is based on a certain resemblance; and to a friendship of good men all the qualities we have named belong in virtue of the nature of the friends themselves; for in the case of this kind of friendship the other qualities also are alike in both friends, and that which is good without qualification is also without qualification pleasant, and these are the most lovable qualities. Love and friendship therefore are found most and in their best form between such men.

But it is natural that such friendships should be infrequent; for such men are rare. Further, such friendship requires time and familiarity; as the proverb says, men cannot know each other till they have 'eaten salt together'; nor can they admit each other to friendship or be friends till each has been found lovable and been trusted by each. Those who quickly show the marks of friendship to each other wish to be friends, but are not friends unless they both are lovable and know the fact; for a wish for friendship may arise quickly, but friendship does not.

4

This kind of friendship, then, is perfect both in respect of duration and in all other respects, and in it each gets from each in all respects the same as, or something like what, he gives; which is what ought to happen between friends. Friendship for the sake of pleasure bears a resemblance to this kind; for good people too are pleasant to each other. So too does friendship for the sake of utility; for the good are also useful to each other. Among men of these inferior sorts too, friendships are most permanent when the friends get the same thing from each other (e.g. pleasure), and not only that but also from the same source, as happens between readywitted people, not as happens between lover and beloved. For these do not take pleasure in the same things, but the one in seeing the beloved and the other in receiving attentions from his lover; and when the bloom of youth is passing the friendship sometimes passes too (for the one finds no pleasure in the sight of the other, and the other gets no attentions from the first); but many lovers on the other hand are constant, if familiarity has led them to love each other's characters, these being alike. But those who exchange not pleasure but utility in their amour are both less truly friends and less constant. Those who are friends for the sake of utility part when the advantage is at an end; for they were lovers not of each other but of profit.

For the sake of pleasure or utility, then, even bad men may be friends of each other, or good men of bad, or one who is neither good nor bad may be a friend to any sort of person, but for their own sake clearly only good men can be friends; for bad men do not delight in each other unless some advantage come of the relation.

The friendship of the good too and this alone is proof against slander; for it is not easy to trust any one talk about a man who has long been tested by oneself; and it is among good men that trust and the feeling that 'he would never wrong me' and all the other things that are demanded in true friendship are found. In the other kinds of friendship, however, there is nothing to prevent these evils arising. For men apply the name of friends even to those whose motive is utility, in which sense states are said to be friendly (for the alliances of states seem to aim at advantage), and to those who love each other for the sake of pleasure, in which sense children are called friends. Therefore we too ought perhaps to call such people friends, and say that there are several kinds of friendship-firstly and in the proper sense that of good men qua good, and by analogy the other kinds; for it is in virtue of something good and something akin to what is found in true friendship that they are friends, since even the pleasant is good for the lovers of pleasure. But these two kinds of friendship are not often united, nor do the same people become friends for the sake of utility and of pleasure; for things that are only incidentally connected are not often coupled together.

Friendship being divided into these kinds, bad men will be friends for the sake of pleasure or of utility, being in this respect like each other, but good men will be friends for their own sake, i.e. in virtue of their goodness. These, then, are friends without qualification; the others are friends incidentally and through a resemblance to these.

5

As in regard to the virtues some men are called good in respect of a state of character, others in respect of an activity, so too in the case of friendship; for those who live together delight in each other and confer benefits on each other, but those who are asleep or locally separated are not performing, but are disposed to perform, the activities of friendship; distance does not break off the friendship absolutely, but only the activity of it. But if the absence is lasting, it seems actually to make men forget their friendship; hence the saying 'out of sight, out of mind'. Neither old people nor sour people seem to make friends easily; for there is little that is pleasant in them, and no one can spend his days with one whose company is painful, or not pleasant, since nature seems above all to avoid the painful and to aim at the pleasant. Those, however, who approve of each other but do not live together seem to be well-disposed rather than actual friends. For there is nothing so characteristic of friends as living together (since while it people who are in need that desire benefits, even those who are supremely happy desire to spend their days together; for solitude suits such people least of all); but people cannot live together if they are not pleasant and do not enjoy the same things, as friends who are companions seem to do.

The truest friendship, then, is that of the good, as we have frequently said; for that which is without qualification good or pleasant seems to be lovable and desirable, and for each person that which is good or pleasant to him; and the good man is lovable and desirable to the good man for both these reasons. Now it looks as if love were a feeling, friendship a state of character; for love may be felt just as much towards lifeless things, but mutual love involves choice and choice springs from a state of character; and men wish well to those whom they love, for their sake, not as a result of feeling but as a result of a state of character. And in loving a friend men love what is good for themselves; for the good man in becoming a friend becomes a good to his friend. Each, then, both loves what is good for himself, and makes an equal return in goodwill and in pleasantness; for friendship is said to be equality, and both of these are found most in the friendship of the good.

6

Between sour and elderly people friendship arises less readily, inasmuch as they are less good-tempered and enjoy companionship less; for these are thou to be the greatest marks of friendship productive of it. This is why, while men become friends quickly, old men do not; it is because men do not become friends with those in whom they do not delight; and similarly sour people do not quickly make friends either. But such men may bear goodwill to each other; for they wish one another well and aid one another in need; but they are hardly friends because they do not spend their days together nor delight in each other, and these are thought the greatest marks of friendship.

One cannot be a friend to many people in the sense of having friendship of the perfect type with them, just as one cannot be in love with many people at once (for love is a sort of excess of feeling, and it is the nature of such only to be felt towards one person); and it is not easy for many people at the same time to please the same person very greatly, or perhaps even to be good in his eyes. One must, too, acquire some experience of the other person and become familiar with him, and that is very hard. But with a view to utility or pleasure it is possible that many people should please one; for many people are useful or pleasant, and these services take little time.

Of these two kinds that which is for the sake of pleasure is the more like friendship, when both parties get the same things from each other and delight in each other or in the things, as in the friendships of the young; for generosity is more found in such friendships. Friendship based on utility is for the commercially minded. People who are supremely happy, too, have no need of useful friends, but do need pleasant friends; for they wish to live with some one and, though they can endure for a short time what is painful, no one could put up with it continuously, nor even with the Good itself if it were painful to him; this is why they look out for friends who are pleasant. Perhaps they should look out for friends who, being pleasant, are also good, and good for them too; for so they will have all the characteristics that friends should have.

People in positions of authority seem to have friends who fall into distinct classes; some people are useful to them and others are pleasant, but the same people are rarely both; for they seek neither those whose pleasantness is accompanied by virtue nor those whose utility is with a view to noble objects, but in their desire for pleasure they seek for ready-witted people, and their other friends they choose as being clever at doing what they are told, and these characteristics are rarely combined. Now we have said that the good man is at the same time pleasant and useful; but such a man does not become the friend of one who surpasses him in station, unless he is surpassed also in virtue; if this is not so, he does not establish equality by being proportionally exceeded in both respects. But people who surpass him in both respects are not so easy to find.

However that may be, the aforesaid friendships involve equality; for the friends get the same things from one another and wish the same things for one another, or exchange one thing for another, e.g. pleasure for utility; we have said, however, that they are both less truly friendships and less permanent.

But it is from their likeness and their unlikeness to the same thing that they are thought both to be and not to be friendships. It is by their likeness to the friendship of virtue that they seem to be friendships (for one of them involves pleasure and the other utility, and these characteristics belong to the friendship of virtue as well); while it is because the friendship of virtue is proof against slander and permanent, while these quickly change (besides differing from the former in many other respects), that they appear not to be friendships; i.e. it is because of their unlikeness to the friendship of virtue.

7

But there is another kind of friendship, viz. that which involves an inequality between the parties, e.g. that of father to son and in general of elder to younger, that of man to wife and in general that of ruler to subject. And these friendships differ also from each other; for it is not the same that exists between parents and children and between rulers and subjects, nor is even that of father to son the same as that of son to father, nor that of husband to wife the same as that of wife to husband. For the virtue and the function of each of these is different, and so are the reasons for which they love; the love and the friendship are therefore different also. Each party, then, neither gets the same from the other, nor ought to seek it; but when children render to parents what they ought to render to those who brought them into the world, and parents render what they should to their children, the friendship of such persons will be abiding and excellent. In all friendships implying inequality the love also should be proportional, i.e. the better should be more loved than he loves, and so should the more useful, and similarly in each of the other cases; for when the love is in proportion to the merit of the parties, then in a sense arises equality, which is certainly held to be characteristic of friendship.

But equality does not seem to take the same form in acts of justice and in friendship; for in acts of justice what is equal in the primary sense is that which is in proportion to merit, while quantitative equality is secondary, but in friendship quantitative equality is primary and proportion to merit secondary. This becomes clear if there is a great interval in respect of virtue or vice or wealth or anything else between the parties; for then they are no longer friends, and do not even expect to be so. And this is most manifest in the case of the gods; for they surpass us most decisively in all good things. But it is clear also in the case of kings; for with them, too, men who are much their inferiors do not expect to be friends; nor do men of no account expect to be friends with the best or wisest men. In such cases it is not possible to define exactly up to what point friends can remain friends; for much can be taken away and friendship remain, but when one party is removed to a great distance, as God is, the possibility of friendship ceases. This is in fact the origin of the question whether friends really wish for their friends the greatest goods, e.g. that of being gods; since in that case their friends will no longer be friends to them, and therefore will not be good things for them (for friends are good things). The answer is that if we were right in saying that friend wishes good to friend for his sake, his friend must remain the sort of being he is, whatever that may be; therefore it is for him only so long as he remains a man that he will wish the greatest goods. But perhaps not all the greatest goods; for it is for himself most of all that each man wishes what is good.

8

Most people seem, owing to ambition, to wish to be loved rather than to love; which is why most men love flattery; for the flatterer is a friend in an inferior position, or pretends to be such and to love more than he is loved; and being loved seems to be akin to being honoured, and this is what most people aim at. But it seems to be not for its own sake that people choose honour, but incidentally. For most people enjoy being honoured by those in positions of authority because of their hopes (for they think that if they want anything they will get it from them; and therefore they delight in honour as a token of favour to come); while those who desire honour from good men, and men who know, are aiming at confirming their own opinion of themselves; they delight in honour, therefore, because they believe in their own goodness on the strength of the judgement of those who speak about them. In being loved, on the other hand, people delight for its own sake; whence it would seem to be better than being honoured, and friendship to be desirable in itself. But it seems to lie in loving rather than in being loved, as is indicated by the delight mothers take in loving; for some mothers hand over their children to be brought up, and so long as they know their fate they love them and do not seek to be loved in return (if they cannot have both), but seem to be satisfied if they see them prospering; and they themselves love their children even if these owing to their ignorance give them nothing of a mother's due. Now since friendship depends more on loving, and it is those who love their friends that are praised, loving seems to be the characteristic virtue of friends, so that it is only those in whom this is found in due measure that are lasting friends, and only their friendship that endures.

It is in this way more than any other that even unequals can be friends; they can be equalized. Now equality and likeness are friendship, and especially the likeness of those who are like in virtue; for being steadfast in themselves they hold fast to each other, and neither ask nor give base services, but (one may say) even prevent them; for it is characteristic of good men neither to go wrong themselves nor to let their friends do so. But wicked men have no steadfastness (for they do not remain even like to themselves), but become friends for a short time because they delight in each other's wickedness. Friends who are useful or pleasant last longer; i.e. as long as they provide each other with enjoyments or advantages. Friendship for utility's sake seems to be that which most easily exists between contraries, e.g. between poor and rich, between ignorant and learned; for what a man actually lacks he aims at, and one gives something else in return. But under this head, too, might bring lover and beloved, beautiful and ugly. This is why lovers sometimes seem ridiculous, when they demand to be loved as they love; if they are equally lovable their claim can perhaps be justified, but when they have nothing lovable about them it is ridiculous. Perhaps, however, contrary does not even aim at contrary by its own nature, but only incidentally, the desire being for what is intermediate; for that is what is good, e.g. it is good for the dry not to become wet but to come to the intermediate state, and similarly with the hot and in all other cases. These subjects we may dismiss; for they are indeed somewhat foreign to our inquiry.

9

Friendship and justice seem, as we have said at the outset of our discussion, to be concerned with the same objects and exhibited between the same persons. For in every community there is thought to be some form of justice, and friendship too; at least men address as friends their fellow-voyagers and fellowsoldiers, and so too those associated with them in any other kind of community. And the extent of their association is the extent of their friendship, as it is the extent to which justice exists between them. And the proverb 'what friends have is common property' expresses the truth; for friendship depends on community. Now brothers and comrades have all things in common, but the others to whom we have referred have definite things in common-some more things, others fewer; for of friendships, too, some are more and others less truly friendships. And the claims of justice differ too; the duties of parents to children, and those of brothers to each other are not the same, nor those of comrades and those of fellow-citizens, and so, too, with the other kinds of friendship. There is a difference, therefore, also between the acts that are unjust towards each of these classes of associates, and the injustice increases by being exhibited towards those who are friends in a fuller sense; e.g. it is a more terrible thing to defraud a comrade than a fellow-citizen, more terrible not to help a brother than a stranger, and more terrible to wound a father than any one else. And the demands of justice also seem to increase with the intensity of the friendship, which implies that friendship and justice exist between the same persons and have an equal extension.

Now all forms of community are like parts of the political community; for men journey together with a view to some particular advantage, and to provide something that they need for the purposes of life; and it is for the sake of advantage that the political community too seems both to have come together originally and to endure, for this is what legislators aim at, and they call just that which is to the common advantage. Now the other communities aim at advantage bit by bit, e.g. sailors at what is advantageous on a voyage with a view to making money or something of the kind, fellow-soldiers at what is advantageous in war, whether it is wealth or victory or the taking of a city that they seek, and members of tribes and demes act similarly (Some communities seem to arise for the sake or pleasure, viz. religious guilds and social clubs; for these exist respectively for the sake of offering sacrifice and of companionship. But all these seem to fall under the political community; for it aims not at present advantage but at what is advantageous for life as a whole), offering sacrifices and arranging gatherings for the purpose, and assigning honours to the gods, and providing pleasant relaxations for themselves. For the ancient sacrifices and gatherings seem to take place after the harvest as a sort of firstfruits, because it was at these seasons that people had most leisure. All the communities, then, seem to be parts of the political community; and the particular kinds friendship will correspond to the particular kinds of community.

10

There are three kinds of constitution, and an equal number of deviation-forms--perversions, as it were, of them. The constitutions are monarchy, aristocracy, and thirdly that which is based on a property qualification, which it seems appropriate to call timocratic, though most people are wont to call it polity. The best of these is monarchy, the worst timocracy. The deviation from monarchy is tyrany; for both are forms of one-man rule, but there is the greatest difference between them; the tyrant looks to his own advantage, the king to that of his subjects. For a man is not a king unless he is sufficient to himself and excels his subjects in all good things; and such a man needs nothing further; therefore he will not look to his own interests but to those of his subjects; for a king who is not like that would be a mere titular king. Now tyranny is the very contrary of this; the tyrant pursues his own good. And it is clearer in the case of tyranny that it is the worst deviation-form; but it is the contrary of the best that is worst. Monarchy passes over into tyranny; for tyranny is the evil form of one-man rule and the bad king becomes a tyrant. Aristocracy passes over into oligarchy by the badness of the rulers, who distribute contrary to equity what belongs to the city-all or most of the good things to themselves, and office always to the same people, paying most regard to wealth; thus the rulers are few and are bad men instead of the most worthy. Timocracy passes over into democracy; for these are coterminous, since it is the ideal even of timocracy to be the rule of the majority, and all who have the property qualification count as equal. Democracy is the least bad of the deviations; for in its case the form of constitution is but a slight deviation. These then are the changes to which constitutions are most subject; for these are the smallest and easiest transitions.

One may find resemblances to the constitutions and, as it were, patterns of them even in households. For the association of a father with his sons bears the form of monarchy, since the father cares for his children; and this is why Homer calls Zeus 'father'; it is the ideal of monarchy to be paternal rule. But among the Persians the rule of the father is tyrannical; they use their sons as slaves. Tyrannical too is the rule of a master over slaves; for it is the advantage of the master that is brought about in it. Now this seems to be a correct form of government, but the Persian type is perverted; for the modes of rule appropriate to different relations are diverse. The association of man and wife seems to be aristocratic; for the man rules in accordance with his worth, and in those matters in which a man should rule, but the matters that befit a woman he hands over to her. If the man rules in everything the relation passes over into oligarchy; for in doing so he is not acting in accordance with their respective worth, and not ruling in virtue of his superiority. Sometimes, however, women rule, because they are heiresses; so their rule is not in virtue of excellence but due to wealth and power, as in oligarchies. The association of brothers is like timocracy; for they are equal, except in so far as they differ in age; hence if they differ much in age, the friendship is no longer of the fraternal type. Democracy is found chiefly in masterless dwellings (for here every one is on an equality), and in those in which the ruler is weak and every one has licence to do as he pleases.

11

Each of the constitutions may be seen to involve friendship just in so far as it involves justice. The friendship between a king and his subjects depends on an excess of benefits conferred; for he confers benefits on his subjects if being a good man he cares for them with a view to their well-being, as a shepherd does for his sheep (whence Homer called Agamemnon 'shepherd of the peoples'). Such too is the friendship of a father, though this exceeds the other in the greatness of the benefits conferred; for he is responsible for the existence of his children, which is thought the greatest good, and for their nurture and upbringing.

These things are ascribed to ancestors as well. Further, by nature a father tends to rule over his sons, ancestors over descendants, a king over his subjects. These friendships imply superiority of one party over the other, which is why ancestors are honoured. The justice therefore that exists between persons so related is not the same on both sides but is in every case proportioned to merit; for that is true of the friendship as well. The friendship of man and wife, again, is the same that is found in an aristocracy; for it is in accordance with virtue the better gets more of what is good, and each gets what befits him; and so, too, with the justice in these relations. The friendship of brothers is like that of comrades; for they are equal and of like age, and such persons are for the most part like in their feelings and their character. Like this, too, is the friendship appropriate to timocratic government; for in such a constitution the ideal is for the citizens to be equal and fair; therefore rule is taken in turn, and on equal terms; and the friendship appropriate here will correspond.

But in the deviation-forms, as justice hardly exists, so too does friendship. It exists least in the worst form; in tyranny there is little or no friendship. For where there is nothing common to ruler and ruled, there is not friendship either, since there is not justice; e.g. between craftsman and tool, soul and body, master and slave; the latter in each case is benefited by that which uses it, but there is no friendship nor justice towards lifeless things. But neither is there friendship towards a horse or an ox, nor to a slave qua slave. For there is nothing common to the two parties; the slave is a living tool and the tool a lifeless slave. Qua slave then, one cannot be friends with him. But qua man one can; for there seems to be some justice between any man and any other who can share in a system of law or be a party to an agreement; therefore there can also be friendship with him in so far as he is a man. Therefore while in tyrannies friendship and justice hardly exist, in democracies they exist more fully; for where the citizens are equal they have much in common.

12

Every form of friendship, then, involves association, as has been said. One might, however, mark off from the rest both the friendship of kindred and that of comrades. Those of fellow-citizens, fellow-tribesmen, fellow-voyagers, and the like are more like mere friendships of association; for they seem to rest on a sort of compact. With them we might class the friendship of host and guest. The friendship of kinsmen itself, while it seems to be of many kinds, appears to depend in every case on parental friendship; for parents love their children as being a part of themselves, and children their parents as being something originating from them. Now (1) parents know their offspring better than there children know that they are their children, and (2) the originator feels his offspring to be his own more than the offspring do their begetter; for the product belongs to the producer (e.g. a tooth or hair or anything else to him whose it is), but the producer does not belong to the product, or belongs in a less degree. And (3) the length of time produces the same result; parents love their children as soon as these are born, but children love their parents only after time has elapsed and they have acquired understanding or the power of discrimination by the senses. From these considerations it is also plain why mothers love more than fathers do. Parents, then, love their children as themselves (for their issue are by virtue of their separate existence a sort of other selves), while children love their parents as being born of them, and brothers love each other as being born of the same parents; for their identity with them makes them identical with each other (which is the reason why people talk of 'the same blood', 'the same stock', and so on). They are, therefore, in a sense the same thing, though in separate individuals. Two things that contribute greatly to friendship are a common upbringing and similarity of age; for 'two of an age take to each other', and people brought up together tend to be comrades; whence the friendship of brothers is akin to that of comrades. And cousins and other kinsmen are bound up together by derivation from brothers, viz. by being derived from the same parents. They come to be closer together or farther apart by virtue of the nearness or distance of the original ancestor.

The friendship of children to parents, and of men to gods, is a relation to them as to something good and superior; for they have conferred the greatest benefits, since they are the causes of their being and of their nourishment, and of their education from their birth; and this kind of friendship possesses pleasantness and utility also, more than that of strangers, inasmuch as their life is lived more in common. The friendship of brothers has the characteristics found in that of comrades (and especially when these are good), and in general between people who are like each other, inasmuch as they belong more to each other and start with a love for each other from their very birth, and inasmuch as those born of the same parents and brought up together and similarly educated are more akin in character; and the test of time has been applied most fully and convincingly in their case.

Between other kinsmen friendly relations are found in due proportion. Between man and wife friendship seems to exist by nature; for man is naturally inclined to form couples-even more than to form cities, inasmuch as the household is earlier and more necessary than the city, and reproduction is more common to man with the animals. With the other animals the union extends only to this point, but human beings live together not only for the sake of reproduction but also for the various purposes of life; for from the start the functions are divided, and those of man and woman are different; so they help each other by throwing their peculiar gifts into the common stock. It is for these reasons that both utility and pleasure seem to be found in this kind of friendship. But this friendship may be based also on virtue, if the parties are good; for each has its own virtue and they will delight in the fact. And children seem to be a bond of union (which is the reason why childless people part more easily); for children are a good common to both and what is common holds them together.

How man and wife and in general friend and friend ought mutually to behave seems to be the same question as how it is just for them to behave; for a man does not seem to have the same duties to a friend, a stranger, a comrade, and a schoolfellow.

13

There are three kinds of friendship, as we said at the outset of our inquiry, and in respect of each some are friends on an equality and others by virtue of a superiority (for not only can equally good men become friends but a better man can make friends with a worse, and similarly in friendships of pleasure or utility the friends may be equal or unequal in the benefits they confer). This being so, equals must effect the required equalization on a basis of equality in love and in all other respects, while unequals must render what is in proportion to their superiority or inferiority. Complaints and reproaches arise either only or chiefly in the friendship of utility, and this is only to be expected. For those who are friends on the ground of virtue are anxious to do well by each other (since that is a mark of virtue and of friendship), and between men who are emulating each other in this there cannot be complaints or quarrels; no one is offended by a man who loves him and does well by him-if he is a person of nice feeling he takes his revenge by doing well by the other. And the man who excels the other in the services he renders will not complain of his friend, since he gets what he aims at; for each man desires what is good. Nor do complaints arise much even in friendships of pleasure; for both get at the same time what they desire, if they enjoy spending their time together; and even a man who complained of another for not affording him pleasure would seem ridiculous, since it is in his power not to spend his days with him.

But the friendship of utility is full of complaints; for as they use each other for their own interests they always want to get the better of the bargain, and think they have got less than they should, and blame their partners because they do not get all they 'want and deserve'; and those who do well by others cannot help them as much as those whom they benefit want.

Now it seems that, as justice is of two kinds, one unwritten and the other legal, one kind of friendship of utility is moral and the other legal. And so complaints arise most of all when men do not dissolve the relation in the spirit of the same type of friendship in which they contracted it. The legal type is that which is on fixed terms; its purely commercial variety is on the basis of immediate payment, while the more liberal variety allows time but stipulates for a definite quid pro quo. In this variety the debt is clear and not ambiguous, but in the postponement it contains an element of friendliness; and so some states do not allow suits arising out of such agreements, but think men who have bargained on a basis of credit ought to accept the consequences. The moral type is not on fixed terms; it makes a gift, or does whatever it does, as to a friend; but one expects to receive as much or more, as having not given but lent; and if a man is worse off when the relation is dissolved than he was when it was contracted he will complain. This happens because all or most men, while they wish for what is noble, choose what is advantageous; now it is noble to do well by another without a view to repayment, but it is the receiving of benefits that is advantageous. Therefore if we can we should return the equivalent of what we have received (for we must not make a man our friend against his will; we must recognize that we were mistaken at the first and took a benefit from a person we should not have taken it from-since it was not from a friend, nor from one who did it just for the sake of acting so-and we must settle up just as if we had been benefited on fixed terms). Indeed, one would agree to repay if one could (if one could not, even the giver would not have expected one to do so); therefore if it is possible we must repay. But at the outset we must consider the man by whom we are being benefited and on what terms he is acting, in order that we may accept the benefit on these terms, or else decline it.

It is disputable whether we ought to measure a service by its utility to the receiver and make the return with a view to that, or by the benevolence of the giver. For those who have received say they have received from their benefactors what meant little to the latter and what they might have got from others-minimizing the service; while the givers, on the contrary, say it was the biggest thing they had, and what could not have been got from others, and that it was given in times of danger or similar need. Now if the friendship is one that aims at utility, surely the advantage to the receiver is the measure. For it is he that asks for the service, and the other man helps him on the assumption that he will receive the equivalent; so the assistance has been precisely as great as the advantage to the receiver, and therefore he must return as much as he has received, or even more (for that would be nobler). In friendships based on virtue on the other hand, complaints do not arise, but the purpose of the doer is a sort of measure; for in purpose lies the essential element of virtue and character.

14

Differences arise also in friendships based on superiority; for each expects to get more out of them, but when this happens the friendship is dissolved. Not only does the better man think he ought to get more, since more should be assigned to a good man, but the more useful similarly expects this; they say a useless man should not get as much as they should, since it becomes an act of public service and not a friendship if the proceeds of the friendship do not answer to the worth of the benefits conferred. For they think that, as in a commercial partnership those who put more in get more out, so it should be in friendship. But the man who is in a state of need and inferiority makes the opposite claim; they think it is the part of a good friend to help those who are in need; what, they say, is the use of being the friend of a good man or a powerful man, if one is to get nothing out of it?

At all events it seems that each party is justified in his claim, and that each should get more out of the friendship than the other-not more of the same thing, however, but the superior more honour and the inferior more gain; for honour is the prize of virtue and of beneficence, while gain is the assistance required by inferiority.

It seems to be so in constitutional arrangements also; the man who contributes nothing good to the common stock is not honoured; for what belongs to the public is given to the man who benefits the public, and honour does belong to the public. It is not possible to get wealth from the common stock and at the same time honour. For no one puts up with the smaller share in all things; therefore to the man who loses in wealth they assign honour and to the man who is willing to be paid, wealth, since the proportion to merit equalizes the parties and preserves the friendship, as we have said. This then is also the way in which we should associate with unequals; the man who is benefited in respect of wealth or virtue must give honour in return, repaying what he can. For friendship asks a man to do what he can, not what is proportional to the merits of the case; since that cannot always be done, e.g. in honours paid to the gods or to parents; for no one could ever return to them the equivalent of what he gets, but the man who serves them to the utmost of his power is thought to be a good man. This is why it would not seem open to a man to disown his father (though a father may disown his son); being in debt, he should repay, but there is nothing by doing which a son will have done the equivalent of what he has received, so that he is always in debt. But creditors can remit a debt; and a father can therefore do so too. At the same time it is thought that presumably no one would repudiate a son who was not far gone in wickedness; for apart from the natural friendship of father and son it is human nature not to reject a son's assistance. But the son, if he is wicked, will naturally avoid aiding his father, or not be zealous about it; for most people wish to get benefits, but avoid doing them, as a thing unprofitable.-So much for these questions.

Book Nine

1

In all friendships between dissimilars it is, as we have said, proportion that equalizes the parties and preserves the friendship; e.g. in the political form of friendship the shoemaker gets a return for his shoes in proportion to his worth, and the weaver and all other craftsmen do the same. Now here a common measure has been provided in the form of money, and therefore everything is referred to this and measured by this; but in the friendship of lovers sometimes the lover complains that his excess of love is not met by love in return though perhaps there is nothing lovable about him), while often the beloved complains that the lover who formerly promised everything now performs nothing. Such incidents happen when the lover loves the beloved for the sake of pleasure while the beloved loves the lover for the sake of utility, and they do not both possess the qualities expected of them. If these be the objects of the friendship it is dissolved when they do not get the things that formed the motives of their love; for each did not love the other person himself but the qualities he had, and these were not enduring; that is why the friendships also are transient. But the love of characters, as has been said, endures because it is self-dependent. Differences arise when what they get is something different and not what they desire; for it is like getting nothing at all when we do not get what we aim at; compare the story of the person who made promises to a lyre-player, promising him the more, the better he sang, but in the morning, when the other demanded the fulfilment of his promises, said that he had given pleasure for pleasure. Now if this had been what each wanted, all would have been well; but if the one wanted enjoyment but the other gain, and the one has what he wants while the other has not, the terms of the association will not have been properly fulfilled; for what each in fact wants is what he attends to, and it is for the sake of that that that he will give what he has.

But who is to fix the worth of the service; he who makes the sacrifice or he who has got the advantage? At any rate the other seems to leave it to him. This is what they say Protagoras used to do; whenever he taught anything whatsoever, he bade the learner assess the value of the knowledge, and accepted the amount so fixed. But in such matters some men approve of the saying 'let a man have his fixed reward'. Those who get the money first and then do none of the things they said they would, owing to the extravagance of their promises, naturally find themselves the objects of complaint; for they do not fulfil what they agreed to. The sophists are perhaps compelled to do this because no one would give money for the things they do know. These people then, if they do not do what they have been paid for, are naturally made the objects of complaint.

But where there is no contract of service, those who give up something for the sake of the other party cannot (as we have said) be complained of (for that is the nature of the friendship of virtue), and the return to them must be made on the basis of their purpose (for it is purpose that is the characteristic thing in a friend and in virtue). And so too, it seems, should one make a return to those with whom one has studied philosophy; for their worth cannot be measured against money, and they can get no honour which will balance their services, but still it is perhaps enough, as it is with the gods and with one's parents, to give them what one can.

If the gift was not of this sort, but was made with a view to a return, it is no doubt preferable that the return made should be one that seems fair to both parties, but if this cannot be achieved, it would seem not only necessary that the person who gets the first service should fix the reward, but also just; for if the other gets in return the equivalent of the advantage the beneficiary has received, or the price lie would have paid for the pleasure, he will have got what is fair as from the other.

We see this happening too with things put up for sale, and in some places there are laws providing that no actions shall arise out of voluntary contracts, on the assumption that one should settle with a person to whom one has given credit, in the spirit in which one bargained with him. The law holds that it is more just that the person to whom credit was given should fix the terms than that the person who gave credit should do so. For most things are not assessed at the same value by those who have them and those who want them; each class values highly what is its own and what it is offering; yet the return is made on the terms fixed by the receiver. But no doubt the receiver should assess a thing not at what it seems worth when he has it, but at what he assessed it at before he had it.

2

A further problem is set by such questions as, whether one should in all things give the preference to one's father and obey him, or whether when one is ill one should trust a doctor, and when one has to elect a general should elect a man of military skill; and similarly whether one should render a service by preference to a friend or to a good man, and should show gratitude to a benefactor or oblige a friend, if one cannot do both.

All such questions are hard, are they not, to decide with precision? For they admit of many variations of all sorts in respect both of the magnitude of the service and of its nobility necessity. But that we should not give the preference in all things to the same person is plain enough; and we must for the most part return benefits rather than oblige friends, as we must pay back a loan to a creditor rather than make one to a friend. But perhaps even this is not always true; e.g. should a man who has been ransomed out of the hands of brigands ransom his ransomer in return, whoever he may be (or pay him if he has not been captured but demands payment) or should he ransom his father? It would seem that he should ransom his father in preference even to himself. As we have said, then, generally the debt should be paid, but if the gift is exceedingly noble or exceedingly necessary, one should defer to these considerations. For sometimes it is not even fair to return the equivalent of what one has received, when the one man has done a service to one whom he knows to be good, while the other makes a return to one whom he believes to be bad. For that matter, one should sometimes not lend in return to one who has lent to oneself; for the one person lent to a good man, expecting to recover his loan, while the other has no hope of recovering from one who is believed to be bad. Therefore if the facts really are so, the demand is not fair; and if they are not, but people think they are, they would be held to be doing nothing strange in refusing. As we have often pointed out, then, discussions about feelings and actions have just as much definiteness as their subject-matter.

That we should not make the same return to every one, nor give a father the preference in everything, as one does not sacrifice everything to Zeus, is plain enough; but since we ought to render different things to parents, brothers, comrades, and benefactors, we ought to render to each class what is appropriate and becoming. And this is what people seem in fact to do; to marriages they invite their kinsfolk; for these have a part in the family and therefore in the doings that affect the family; and at funerals also they think that kinsfolk, before all others, should meet, for the same reason. And it would be thought that in the matter of food we should help our parents before all others, since we owe our own nourishment to them, and it is more honourable to help in this respect the authors of our being even before ourselves; and honour too one should give to one's parents as one does to the gods, but not any and every honour; for that matter one should not give the same honour to one's father and one's mother, nor again should one give them the honour due to a philosopher or to a general, but the honour due to a father, or again to a mother. To all older persons, too, one should give honour appropriate to their age, by rising to receive them and finding seats for them and so on; while to comrades and brothers one should allow freedom of speech and common use of all things. To kinsmen, too, and fellow-tribesmen and fellow-citizens and to every other class one should always try to assign what is appropriate, and to compare the claims of each class with respect to nearness of relation and to virtue or usefulness. The comparison is easier when the persons belong to the same class, and more laborious when they are different. Yet we must not on that account shrink from the task, but decide the question as best we can.

3

Another question that arises is whether friendships should or should not be broken off when the other party does not remain the same. Perhaps we may say that there is nothing strange in breaking off a friendship based on utility or pleasure, when our friends no longer have these attributes. For it was of these attributes that we were the friends; and when these have failed it is reasonable to love no longer. But one might complain of another if, when he loved us for our usefulness or pleasantness, he pretended to love us for our character. For, as we said at the outset, most differences arise between friends when they are not friends in the spirit in which they think they are. So when a man has deceived himself and has thought he was being loved for his character, when the other person was doing nothing of the kind, he must blame himself; when he has been deceived by the pretences of the other person, it is just that he should complain against his deceiver; he will complain with more justice than one does against people who counterfeit the currency, inasmuch as the wrongdoing is concerned with something more valuable.

But if one accepts another man as good, and he turns out badly and is seen to do so, must one still love him? Surely it is impossible, since not everything can be loved, but only what is good. What is evil neither can nor should be loved; for it is not one's duty to be a lover of evil, nor to become like what is bad; and we have said that like is dear like. Must the friendship, then, be forthwith broken off? Or is this not so in all cases, but only when one's friends are incurable in their wickedness? If they are capable of being reformed one should rather come to the assistance of their character or their property, inasmuch as this is better and more characteristic of friendship. But a man who breaks off such a friendship would seem to be doing nothing strange; for it was not to a man of this sort that he was a friend; when his friend has changed, therefore, and he is unable to save him, he gives him up.

But if one friend remained the same while the other became better and far outstripped him in virtue, should the latter treat the former as a friend? Surely he cannot. When the interval is great this becomes most plain, e.g. in the case of childish friendships; if one friend remained a child in intellect while the other became a fully developed man, how could they be friends when they neither approved of the same things nor delighted in and were pained by the same things? For not even with regard to each other will their tastes agree, and without this (as we saw) they cannot be friends; for they cannot live together. But we have discussed these matters.

Should he, then, behave no otherwise towards him than he would if he had never been his friend? Surely he should keep a remembrance of their former intimacy, and as we think we ought to oblige friends rather than strangers, so to those who have been our friends we ought to make some allowance for our former friendship, when the breach has not been due to excess of wickedness.

4

Friendly relations with one's neighbours, and the marks by which friendships are defined, seem to have proceeded from a man's relations to himself. For (1) we define a friend as one who wishes and does what is good, or seems so, for the sake of his friend, or (2) as one who wishes his friend to exist and live, for his sake; which mothers do to their children, and friends do who have come into conflict. And (3) others define him as one who lives with and (4) has the same tastes as another, or (5) one who grieves and rejoices with his friend; and this too is found in mothers most of all. It is by some one of these characterstics that friendship too is defined.

Now each of these is true of the good man's relation to himself (and of all other men in so far as they think themselves good; virtue and the good man seem, as has been said, to be the measure of every class of things). For his opinions are harmonious, and he desires the same things with all his soul; and therefore he wishes for himself what is good and what seems so, and does it (for it is characteristic of the good man to work out the good), and does so for his own sake (for he does it for the sake of the intellectual element in him, which is thought to be the man himself); and he wishes himself to live and be preserved, and especially the element by virtue of which he thinks. For existence is good to the virtuous man, and each man wishes himself what is good, while no one chooses to possess the whole world if he has first to become some one else (for that matter, even now God possesses the good); he wishes for this only on condition of being whatever he is; and the element that thinks would seem to be the individual man, or to be so more than any other element in him. And such a man wishes to live with himself; for he does so with pleasure, since the memories of his past acts are delightful and his hopes for the future are good, and therefore pleasant. His mind is well stored too with subjects of contemplation. And he grieves and rejoices, more than any other, with himself; for the same thing is always painful, and the same thing always pleasant, and not one thing at one time and another at another; he has, so to speak, nothing to repent of.

Therefore, since each of these characteristics belongs to the good man in relation to himself, and he is related to his friend as to himself (for his friend is another self), friendship too is thought to be one of these attributes, and those who have these attributes to be friends. Whether there is or is not friendship between a man and himself is a question we may dismiss for the present; there would seem to be friendship in so far as he is two or more, to judge from the afore-mentioned attributes of friendship, and from the fact that the extreme of friendship is likened to one's love for oneself.

But the attributes named seem to belong even to the majority of men, poor creatures though they may be. Are we to say then that in so far as they are satisfied with themselves and think they are good, they share in these attributes? Certainly no one who is thoroughly bad and impious has these attributes, or even seems to do so. They hardly belong even to inferior people; for they are at variance with themselves, and have appetites for some things and rational desires for others. This is true, for instance, of incontinent people; for they choose, instead of the things they themselves think good, things that are pleasant but hurtful; while others again, through cowardice and laziness, shrink from doing what they think best for themselves. And those who have done many terrible deeds and are hated for their wickedness even shrink from life and destroy themselves. And wicked men seek for people with whom to spend their days, and shun themselves; for they remember many a grevious deed, and anticipate others like them, when they are by themselves, but when they are with others they forget. And having nothing lovable in them they have no feeling of love to themselves. Therefore also such men do not rejoice or grieve with themselves; for their soul is rent by faction, and one element in it by reason of its wickedness grieves when it abstains from certain acts, while the other part is pleased, and one draws them this way and the other that, as if they were pulling them in pieces. If a man cannot at the same time be pained and pleased, at all events after a short time he is pained because he was pleased, and he could have wished that these things had not been pleasant to him; for bad men are laden with repentance.

Therefore the bad man does not seem to be amicably disposed even to himself, because there is nothing in him to love; so that if to be thus is the height of wretchedness, we should strain every nerve to avoid wickedness and should endeavour to be good; for so and only so can one be either friendly to oneself or a friend to another.

5

Goodwill is a friendly sort of relation, but is not identical with friendship; for one may have goodwill both towards people whom one does not know, and without their knowing it, but not friendship. This has indeed been said already.' But goodwill is not even friendly feeling. For it does not involve intensity or desire, whereas these accompany friendly feeling; and friendly feeling implies intimacy while goodwill may arise of a sudden, as it does towards competitors in a contest; we come to feel goodwill for them and to share in their wishes, but we would not do anything with them; for, as we said, we feel goodwill suddenly and love them only superficially.

Goodwill seems, then, to be a beginning of friendship, as the pleasure of the eye is the beginning of love. For no one loves if he has not first been delighted by the form of the beloved, but he who delights in the form of another does not, for all that, love him, but only does so when he also longs for him when absent and craves for his presence; so too it is not possible for people to be friends if they have not come to feel goodwill for each other, but those who feel goodwill are not for all that friends; for they only wish well to those for whom they feel goodwill, and would not do anything with them nor take trouble for them. And so one might by an extension of the term friendship say that goodwill is inactive friendship, though when it is prolonged and reaches the point of intimacy it becomes friendship-not the friendship based on utility nor that based on pleasure; for goodwill too does not arise on those terms. The man who has received a benefit bestows goodwill in return for what has been done to him, but in doing so is only doing what is just; while he who wishes some one to prosper because he hopes for enrichment through him seems to have goodwill not to him but rather to himself, just as a man is not a friend to another if he cherishes him for the sake of some use to be made of him. In general, goodwill arises on account of some excellence and worth, when one man seems to another beautiful or brave or something of the sort, as we pointed out in the case of competitors in a contest.

6

Unanimity also seems to be a friendly relation. For this reason it is not identity of opinion; for that might occur even with people who do not know each other; nor do we say that people who have the same views on any and every subject are unanimous, e.g. those who agree about the heavenly bodies (for unanimity about these is not a friendly relation), but we do say that a city is unanimous when men have the same opinion about what is to their interest, and choose the same actions, and do what they have resolved in common. It is about things to be done, therefore, that people are said to be unanimous, and, among these, about matters of consequence and in which it is possible for both or all parties to get what they want; e.g. a city is unanimous when all its citizens think that the offices in it should be elective, or that they should form an alliance with Sparta, or that Pittacus should be their ruler-at a time when he himself was also willing to rule. But when each of two people wishes himself to have the thing in question, like the captains in the Phoenissae, they are in a state of faction; for it is not unanimity when each of two parties thinks of the same thing, whatever that may be, but only when they think of the same thing in the same hands, e.g. when both the common people and those of the better class wish the best men to rule; for thus and thus alone do all get what they aim at. Unanimity seems, then, to be political friendship, as indeed it is commonly said to be; for it is concerned with things that are to our interest and have an influence on our life.

Now such unanimity is found among good men; for they are unanimous both in themselves and with one another, being, so to say, of one mind (for the wishes of such men are constant and not at the mercy of opposing currents like a strait of the sea), and they wish for what is just and what is advantageous, and these are the objects of their common endeavour as well. But bad men cannot be unanimous except to a small extent, any more than they can be friends, since they aim at getting more than their share of advantages, while in labour and public service they fall short of their share; and each man wishing for advantage to himself criticizes his neighbour and stands in his way; for if people do not watch it carefully the common weal is soon destroyed. The result is that they are in a state of faction, putting compulsion on each other but unwilling themselves to do what is just.

7

Benefactors are thought to love those they have benefited, more than those who have been well treated love those that have treated them well, and this is discussed as though it were paradoxical. Most people think it is because the latter are in the position of debtors and the former of creditors; and therefore as, in the case of loans, debtors wish their creditors did not exist, while creditors actually take care of the safety of their debtors, so it is thought that benefactors wish the objects of their action to exist since they will then get their gratitude, while the beneficiaries take no interest in making this return. Epicharmus would perhaps declare that they say this because they 'look at things on their bad side', but it is quite like human nature; for most people are forgetful, and are more anxious to be well treated than to treat others well. But the cause would seem to be more deeply rooted in the nature of things; the case of those who have lent money is not even analogous. For they have no friendly feeling to their debtors, but only a wish that they may kept safe with a view to what is to be got from them; while those who have done a service to others feel friendship and love for those they have served even if these are not of any use to them and never will be. This is what happens with craftsmen too; every man loves his own handiwork better than he would be loved by it if it came alive; and this happens perhaps most of all with poets; for they have an excessive love for their own poems, doting on them as if they were their children. This is what the position of benefactors is like; for that which they have treated well is their handiwork, and therefore they love this more than the handiwork does its maker. The cause of this is that existence is to all men a thing to be chosen and loved, and that we exist by virtue of activity (i.e. by living and acting), and that the handiwork is in a sense, the producer in activity; he loves his handiwork, therefore, because he loves existence. And this is rooted in the nature of things; for what he is in potentiality, his handiwork manifests in activity.

At the same time to the benefactor that is noble which depends on his action, so that he delights in the object of his action, whereas to the patient there is nothing noble in the agent, but at most something advantageous, and this is less pleasant and lovable. What is pleasant is the activity of the present, the hope of the future, the memory of the past; but most pleasant is that which depends on activity, and similarly this is most lovable. Now for a man who has made something his work remains (for the noble is lasting), but for the person acted on the utility passes away. And the memory of noble things is pleasant, but that of useful things is not likely to be pleasant, or is less so; though the reverse seems true of expectation.

Further, love is like activity, being loved like passivity; and loving and its concomitants are attributes of those who are the more active.

Again, all men love more what they have won by labour; e.g. those who have made their money love it more than those who have inherited it; and to be well treated seems to involve no labour, while to treat others well is a laborious task. These are the reasons, too, why mothers are fonder of their children than fathers; bringing them into the world costs them more pains, and they know better that the children are their own. This last point, too, would seem to apply to benefactors.

8

The question is also debated, whether a man should love himself most, or some one else. People criticize those who love themselves most, and call them self-lovers, using this as an epithet of disgrace, and a bad man seems to do everything for his own sake, and the more so the more wicked he is-and so men reproach him, for instance, with doing nothing of his own accord-while the good man acts for honour's sake, and the more so the better he is, and acts for his friend's sake, and sacrifices his own interest.

But the facts clash with these arguments, and this is not surprising. For men say that one ought to love best one's best friend, and man's best friend is one who wishes well to the object of his wish for his sake, even if no one is to know of it; and these attributes are found most of all in a man's attitude towards himself, and so are all the other attributes by which a friend is defined; for, as we have said, it is from this relation that all the characteristics of friendship have extended to our neighbours. All the proverbs, too, agree with this, e.g. 'a single soul', and 'what friends have is common property', and 'friendship is equality', and 'charity begins at home'; for all these marks will be found most in a man's relation to himself; he is his own best friend and therefore ought to love himself best. It is therefore a reasonable question, which of the two views we should follow; for both are plausible.

Perhaps we ought to mark off such arguments from each other and determine how far and in what respects each view is right. Now if we grasp the sense in which each school uses the phrase 'lover of self', the truth may become evident. Those who use the term as one of reproach ascribe self-love to people who assign to themselves the greater share of wealth, honours, and bodily pleasures; for these are what most people desire, and busy themselves about as though they were the best of all things, which is the reason, too, why they become objects of competition. So those who are grasping with regard to these things gratify their appetites and in general their feelings and the irrational element of the soul; and most men are of this nature (which is the reason why the epithet has come to be used as it is-it takes its meaning from the prevailing type of self-love, which is a bad one); it is just, therefore, that men who are lovers of self in this way are reproached for being so. That it is those who give themselves the preference in regard to objects of this sort that most people usually call lovers of self is plain; for if a man were always anxious that he himself, above all things, should act justly, temperately, or in accordance with any other of the virtues, and in general were always to try to secure for himself the honourable course, no one will call such a man a lover of self or blame him.

But such a man would seem more than the other a lover of self; at all events he assigns to himself the things that are noblest and best, and gratifies the most authoritative element in and in all things obeys this; and just as a city or any other systematic whole is most properly identified with the most authoritative element in it, so is a man; and therefore the man who loves this and gratifies it is most of all a lover of self. Besides, a man is said to have or not to have self-control according as his reason has or has not the control, on the assumption that this is the man himself; and the things men have done on a rational principle are thought most properly their own acts and voluntary acts. That this is the man himself, then, or is so more than anything else, is plain, and also that the good man loves most this part of him. Whence it follows that he is most truly a lover of self, of another type than that which is a matter of reproach, and as different from that as living according to a rational principle is from living as passion dictates, and desiring what is noble from desiring what seems advantageous. Those, then, who busy themselves in an exceptional degree with noble actions all men approve and praise; and if all were to strive towards what is noble and strain every nerve to do the noblest deeds, everything would be as it should be for the common weal, and every one would secure for himself the goods that are greatest, since virtue is the greatest of goods.

Therefore the good man should be a lover of self (for he will both himself profit by doing noble acts, and will benefit his fellows), but the wicked man should not; for he will hurt both himself and his neighbours, following as he does evil passions. For the wicked man, what he does clashes with what he ought to do, but what the good man ought to do he does; for reason in each of its possessors chooses what is best for itself, and the good man obeys his reason. It is true of the good man too that he does many acts for the sake of his friends and his country, and if necessary dies for them; for he will throw away both wealth and honours and in general the goods that are objects of competition, gaining for himself nobility; since he would prefer a short period of intense pleasure to a long one of mild enjoyment, a twelvemonth of noble life to many years of humdrum existence, and one great and noble action to many trivial ones. Now those who die for others doubtless attain this result; it is therefore a great prize that they choose for themselves. They will throw away wealth too on condition that their friends will gain more; for while a man's friend gains wealth he himself achieves nobility; he is therefore assigning the greater good to himself. The same too is true of honour and office; all these things he will sacrifice to his friend; for this is noble and laudable for himself. Rightly then is he thought to be good, since he chooses nobility before all else. But he may even give up actions to his friend; it may be nobler to become the cause of his friend's acting than to act himself. In all the actions, therefore, that men are praised for, the good man is seen to assign to himself the greater share in what is noble. In this sense, then, as has been said, a man should be a lover of self; but in the sense in which most men are so, he ought not.

9

It is also disputed whether the happy man will need friends or not. It is said that those who are supremely happy and self-sufficient have no need of friends; for they have the things that are good, and therefore being self-sufficient they need nothing further, while a friend, being another self, furnishes what a man cannot provide by his own effort; whence the saying 'when fortune is kind, what need of friends?' But it seems strange, when one assigns all good things to the happy man, not to assign friends, who are thought the greatest of external goods. And if it is more characteristic of a friend to do well by another than to be well done by, and to confer benefits is characteristic of the good man and of virtue, and it is nobler to do well by friends than by strangers, the good man will need people to do well by. This is why the question is asked whether we need friends more in prosperity or in adversity, on the assumption that not only does a man in adversity need people to confer benefits on him, but also those who are prospering need people to do well by. Surely it is strange, too, to make the supremely happy man a solitary; for no one would choose the whole world on condition of being alone, since man is a political creature and one whose nature is to live with others. Therefore even the happy man lives with others; for he has the things that are by nature good. And plainly it is better to spend his days with friends and good men than with strangers or any chance persons. Therefore the happy man needs friends.

What then is it that the first school means, and in what respect is it right? Is it that most identify friends with useful people? Of such friends indeed the supremely happy man will have no need, since he already has the things that are good; nor will he need those whom one makes one's friends because of their pleasantness, or he will need them only to a small extent (for his life, being pleasant, has no need of adventitious pleasure); and because he does not need such friends he is thought not to need friends.

But that is surely not true. For we have said at the outset that happiness is an activity; and activity plainly comes into being and is not present at the start like a piece of property. If (1) happiness lies in living and being active, and the good man's activity is virtuous and pleasant in itself, as we have said at the outset, and (2) a thing's being one's own is one of the attributes that make it pleasant, and (3) we can contemplate our neighbours better than ourselves and their actions better than our own, and if the actions of virtuous men who are their friends are pleasant to good men (since these have both the attributes that are naturally pleasant),-if this be so, the supremely happy man will need friends of this sort, since his purpose is to contemplate worthy actions and actions that are his own, and the actions of a good man who is his friend have both these qualities.

Further, men think that the happy man ought to live pleasantly. Now if he were a solitary, life would be hard for him; for by oneself it is not easy to be continuously active; but with others and towards others it is easier. With others therefore his activity will be more continuous, and it is in itself pleasant, as it ought to be for the man who is supremely happy; for a good man qua good delights in virtuous actions and is vexed at vicious ones, as a musical man enjoys beautiful tunes but is pained at bad ones. A certain training in virtue arises also from the company of the good, as Theognis has said before us.

If we look deeper into the nature of things, a virtuous friend seems to be naturally desirable for a virtuous man. For that which is good by nature, we have said, is for the virtuous man good and pleasant in itself. Now life is defined in the case of animals by the power of perception in that of man by the power of perception or thought; and a power is defined by reference to the corresponding activity, which is the essential thing; therefore life seems to be essentially the act of perceiving or thinking. And life is among the things that are good and pleasant in themselves, since it is determinate and the determinate is of the nature of the good; and that which is good by nature is also good for the virtuous man (which is the reason why life seems pleasant to all men); but we must not apply this to a wicked and corrupt life nor to a life spent in pain; for such a life is indeterminate, as are its attributes. The nature of pain will become plainer in what follows. But if life itself is good and pleasant (which it seems to be, from the very fact that all men desire it, and particularly those who are good and supremely happy; for to such men life is most desirable, and their existence is the most supremely happy) and if he who sees perceives that he sees, and he who hears, that he hears, and he who walks, that he walks, and in the case of all other activities similarly there is something which perceives that we are active, so that if we perceive, we perceive that we perceive, and if we think, that we think; and if to perceive that we perceive or think is to perceive that we exist (for existence was defined as perceiving or thinking); and if perceiving that one lives is in itself one of the things that are pleasant (for life is by nature good, and to perceive what is good present in oneself is pleasant); and if life is desirable, and particularly so for good men, because to them existence is good and pleasant for they are pleased at the consciousness of the presence in them of what is in itself good); and if as the virtuous man is to himself, he is to his friend also (for his friend is another self):-if all this be true, as his own being is desirable for each man, so, or almost so, is that of his friend. Now his being was seen to be desirable because he perceived his own goodness, and such perception is pleasant in itself. He needs, therefore, to be conscious of the existence of his friend as well, and this will be realized in their living together and sharing in discussion and thought; for this is what living together would seem to mean in the case of man, and not, as in the case of cattle, feeding in the same place.

If, then, being is in itself desirable for the supremely happy man (since it is by its nature good and pleasant), and that of his friend is very much the same, a friend will be one of the things that are desirable. Now that which is desirable for him he must have, or he will be deficient in this respect. The man who is to be happy will therefore need virtuous friends.

10

Should we, then, make as many friends as possible, or-as in the case of hospitality it is thought to be suitable advice, that one should be 'neither a man of many guests nor a man with none'-will that apply to friendship as well; should a man neither be friendless nor have an excessive number of friends?

To friends made with a view to utility this saying would seem thoroughly applicable; for to do services to many people in return is a laborious task and life is not long enough for its performance. Therefore friends in excess of those who are sufficient for our own life are superfluous, and hindrances to the noble life; so that we have no need of them. Of friends made with a view to pleasure, also, few are enough, as a little seasoning in food is enough.

But as regards good friends, should we have as many as possible, or is there a limit to the number of one's friends, as there is to the size of a city? You cannot make a city of ten men, and if there are a hundred thousand it is a city no longer. But the proper number is presumably not a single number, but anything that falls between certain fixed points. So for friends too there is a fixed number perhaps the largest number with whom one can live together (for that, we found, thought to be very characteristic of friendship); and that one cannot live with many people and divide oneself up among them is plain. Further, they too must be friends of one another, if they are all to spend their days together; and it is a hard business for this condition to be fulfilled with a large number. It is found difficult, too, to rejoice and to grieve in an intimate way with many people, for it may likely happen that one has at once to be happy with one friend and to mourn with another. Presumably, then, it is well not to seek to have as many friends as possible, but as many as are enough for the purpose of living together; for it would seem actually impossible to be a great friend to many people. This is why one cannot love several people; love is ideally a sort of excess of friendship, and that can only be felt towards one person; therefore great friendship too can only be felt towards a few people. This seems to be confirmed in practice; for we do not find many people who are friends in the comradely way of friendship, and the famous friendships of this sort are always between two people. Those who have many friends and mix intimately with them all are thought to be no one's friend, except in the way proper to fellow-citizens, and such people are also called obsequious. In the way proper to fellow-citizens, indeed, it is possible to be the friend of many and yet not be obsequious but a genuinely good man; but one cannot have with many people the friendship based on virtue and on the character of our friends themselves, and we must be content if we find even a few such.

11

Do we need friends more in good fortune or in bad? They are sought after in both; for while men in adversity need help, in prosperity they need people to live with and to make the objects of their beneficence; for they wish to do well by others. Friendship, then, is more necessary in bad fortune, and so it is useful friends that one wants in this case; but it is more noble in good fortune, and so we also seek for good men as our friends, since it is more desirable to confer benefits on these and to live with these. For the very presence of friends is pleasant both in good fortune and also in bad, since grief is lightened when friends sorrow with us. Hence one might ask whether they share as it were our burden, or-without that happening-their presence by its pleasantness, and the thought of their grieving with us, make our pain less. Whether it is for these reasons or for some other that our grief is lightened, is a question that may be dismissed; at all events what we have described appears to take place.

But their presence seems to contain a mixture of various factors. The very seeing of one's friends is pleasant, especially if one is in adversity, and becomes a safeguard against grief (for a friend tends to comfort us both by the sight of him and by his words, if he is tactful, since he knows our character and the things that please or pain us); but to see him pained at our misfortunes is painful; for every one shuns being a cause of pain to his friends. For this reason people of a manly nature guard against making their friends grieve with them, and, unless he be exceptionally insensible to pain, such a man cannot stand the pain that ensues for his friends, and in general does not admit fellow-mourners because he is not himself given to mourning; but women and womanly men enjoy sympathisers in their grief, and love them as friends and companions in sorrow. But in all things one obviously ought to imitate the better type of person.

On the other hand, the presence of friends in our prosperity implies both a pleasant passing of our time and the pleasant thought of their pleasure at our own good fortune. For this cause it would seem that we ought to summon our friends readily to share our good fortunes (for the beneficent character is a noble one), but summon them to our bad fortunes with hesitation; for we ought to give them as little a share as possible in our evils whence the saying 'enough is my misfortune'. We should summon friends to us most of all when they are likely by suffering a few inconveniences to do us a great service.

Conversely, it is fitting to go unasked and readily to the aid of those in adversity (for it is characteristic of a friend to render services, and especially to those who are in need and have not demanded them; such action is nobler and pleasanter for both persons); but when our friends are prosperous we should join readily in their activities (for they need friends for these too), but be tardy in coming forward to be the objects of their kindness; for it is not noble to be keen to receive benefits. Still, we must no doubt avoid getting the reputation of kill-joys by repulsing them; for that sometimes happens.

The presence of friends, then, seems desirable in all circumstances.

12

Does it not follow, then, that, as for lovers the sight of the beloved is the thing they love most, and they prefer this sense to the others because on it love depends most for its being and for its origin, so for friends the most desirable thing is living together? For friendship is a partnership, and as a man is to himself, so is he to his friend; now in his own case the consciousness of his being is desirable, and so therefore is the consciousness of his friend's being, and the activity of this consciousness is produced when they live together, so that it is natural that they aim at this. And whatever existence means for each class of men, whatever it is for whose sake they value life, in that they wish to occupy themselves with their friends; and so some drink together, others dice together, others join in athletic exercises and hunting, or in the study of philosophy, each class spending their days together in whatever they love most in life; for since they wish to live with their friends, they do and share in those things which give them the sense of living together. Thus the friendship of bad men turns out an evil thing (for because of their instability they unite in bad pursuits, and besides they become evil by becoming like each other), while the friendship of good men is good, being augmented by their companionship; and they are thought to become better too by their activities and by improving each other; for from each other they take the mould of the characteristics they approve-whence the saying 'noble deeds from noble men'.-So much, then, for friendship; our next task must be to discuss pleasure.

Book Ten

1

After these matters we ought perhaps next to discuss pleasure. For it is thought to be most intimately connected with our human nature, which is the reason why in educating the young we steer them by the rudders of pleasure and pain; it is thought, too, that to enjoy the things we ought and to hate the things we ought has the greatest bearing on virtue of character. For these things extend right through life, with a weight and power of their own in respect both to virtue and to the happy life, since men choose what is pleasant and avoid what is painful; and such things, it will be thought, we should least of all omit to discuss, especially since they admit of much dispute. For some say pleasure is the good, while others, on the contrary, say it is thoroughly bad-some no doubt being persuaded that the facts are so, and others thinking it has a better effect on our life to exhibit pleasure as a bad thing even if it is not; for most people (they think) incline towards it and are the slaves of their pleasures, for which reason they ought to lead them in the opposite direction, since thus they will reach the middle state. But surely this is not correct. For arguments about matters concerned with feelings and actions are less reliable than facts: and so when they clash with the facts of perception they are despised, and discredit the truth as well; if a man who runs down pleasure is once seen to be aiming at it, his inclining towards it is thought to imply that it is all worthy of being aimed at; for most people are not good at drawing distinctions. True arguments seem, then, most useful, not only with a view to knowledge, but with a view to life also; for since they harmonize with the facts they are believed, and so they stimulate those who understand them to live according to them.-Enough of such questions; let us proceed to review the opinions that have been expressed about pleasure.

2

Eudoxus thought pleasure was the good because he saw all things, both rational and irrational, aiming at it, and because in all things that which is the object of choice is what is excellent, and that which is most the object of choice the greatest good; thus the fact that all things moved towards the same object indicated that this was for all things the chief good (for each thing, he argued, finds its own good, as it finds its own nourishment); and that which is good for all things and at which all aim was the good. His arguments were credited more because of the excellence of his character than for their own sake; he was thought to be remarkably self-controlled, and therefore it was thought that he was not saying what he did say as a friend of pleasure, but that the facts really were so. He believed that the same conclusion followed no less plainly from a study of the contrary of pleasure; pain was in itself an object of aversion to all things, and therefore its contrary must be similarly an object of choice. And again that is most an object of choice which we choose not because or for the sake of something else, and pleasure is admittedly of this nature; for no one asks to what end he is pleased, thus implying that pleasure is in itself an object of choice. Further, he argued that pleasure when added to any good, e.g. to just or temperate action, makes it more worthy of choice, and that it is only by itself that the good can be increased.

This argument seems to show it to be one of the goods, and no more a good than any other; for every good is more worthy of choice along with another good than taken alone. And so it is by an argument of this kind that Plato proves the good not to be pleasure; he argues that the pleasant life is more desirable with wisdom than without, and that if the mixture is better, pleasure is not the good; for the good cannot become more desirable by the addition of anything to it. Now it is clear that nothing else, any more than pleasure, can be the good if it is made more desirable by the addition of any of the things that are good in themselves. What, then, is there that satisfies this criterion, which at the same time we can participate in? It is something of this sort that we are looking for. Those who object that that at which all things aim is not necessarily good are, we may surmise, talking nonsense. For we say that that which every one thinks really is so; and the man who attacks this belief will hardly have anything more credible to maintain instead. If it is senseless creatures that desire the things in question, there might be something in what they say; but if intelligent creatures do so as well, what sense can there be in this view? But perhaps even in inferior creatures there is some natural good stronger than themselves which aims at their proper good.

Nor does the argument about the contrary of pleasure seem to be correct. They say that if pain is an evil it does not follow that pleasure is a good; for evil is opposed to evil and at the same time both are opposed to the neutral state-which is correct enough but does not apply to the things in question. For if both pleasure and pain belonged to the class of evils they ought both to be objects of aversion, while if they belonged to the class of neutrals neither should be an object of aversion or they should both be equally so; but in fact people evidently avoid the one as evil and choose the other as good; that then must be the nature of the opposition between them.

3

Nor again, if pleasure is not a quality, does it follow that it is not a good; for the activities of virtue are not qualities either, nor is happiness. They say, however, that the good is determinate, while pleasure is indeterminate, because it admits of degrees. Now if it is from the feeling of pleasure that they judge thus, the same will be true of justice and the other virtues, in respect of which we plainly say that people of a certain character are so more or less, and act more or less in accordance with these virtues; for people may be more just or brave, and it is possible also to act justly or temperately more or less. But if their judgement is based on the various pleasures, surely they are not stating the real cause, if in fact some pleasures are unmixed and others mixed. Again, just as health admits of degrees without being indeterminate, why should not pleasure? The same proportion is not found in all things, nor a single proportion always in the same thing, but it may be relaxed and yet persist up to a point, and it may differ in degree. The case of pleasure also may therefore be of this kind.

Again, they assume that the good is perfect while movements and comings into being are imperfect, and try to exhibit pleasure as being a movement and a coming into being. But they do not seem to be right even in saying that it is a movement. For speed and slowness are thought to be proper to every movement, and if a movement, e.g. that of the heavens, has not speed or slowness in itself, it has it in relation to something else; but of pleasure neither of these things is true. For while we may become pleased quickly as we may become angry quickly, we cannot be pleased quickly, not even in relation to some one else, while we can walk, or grow, or the like, quickly. While, then, we can change quickly or slowly into a state of pleasure, we cannot quickly exhibit the activity of pleasure, i.e. be pleased. Again, how can it be a coming into being? It is not thought that any chance thing can come out of any chance thing, but that a thing is dissolved into that out of which it comes into being; and pain would be the destruction of that of which pleasure is the coming into being.

They say, too, that pain is the lack of that which is according to nature, and pleasure is replenishment. But these experiences are bodily. If then pleasure is replenishment with that which is according to nature, that which feels pleasure will be that in which the replenishment takes place, i.e. the body; but that is not thought to be the case; therefore the replenishment is not pleasure, though one would be pleased when replenishment was taking place, just as one would be pained if one was being operated on. This opinion seems to be based on the pains and pleasures connected with nutrition; on the fact that when people have been short of food and have felt pain beforehand they are pleased by the replenishment. But this does not happen with all pleasures; for the pleasures of learning and, among the sensuous pleasures, those of smell, and also many sounds and sights, and memories and hopes, do not presuppose pain. Of what then will these be the coming into being? There has not been lack of anything of which they could be the supplying anew.

In reply to those who bring forward the disgraceful pleasures one may say that these are not pleasant; if things are pleasant to people of vicious constitution, we must not suppose that they are also pleasant to others than these, just as we do not reason so about the things that are wholesome or sweet or bitter to sick people, or ascribe whiteness to the things that seem white to those suffering from a disease of the eye. Or one might answer thus-that the pleasures are desirable, but not from these sources, as wealth is desirable, but not as the reward of betrayal, and health, but not at the cost of eating anything and everything. Or perhaps pleasures differ in kind; for those derived from noble sources are different from those derived from base sources, and one cannot the pleasure of the just man without being just, nor that of the musical man without being musical, and so on.

The fact, too, that a friend is different from a flatterer seems to make it plain that pleasure is not a good or that pleasures are different in kind; for the one is thought to consort with us with a view to the good, the other with a view to our pleasure, and the one is reproached for his conduct while the other is praised on the ground that he consorts with us for different ends. And no one would choose to live with the intellect of a child throughout his life, however much he were to be pleased at the things that children are pleased at, nor to get enjoyment by doing some most disgraceful deed, though he were never to feel any pain in consequence. And there are many things we should be keen about even if they brought no pleasure, e.g. seeing, remembering, knowing, possessing the virtues. If pleasures necessarily do accompany these, that makes no odds; we should choose these even if no pleasure resulted. It seems to be clear, then, that neither is pleasure the good nor is all pleasure desirable, and that some pleasures are desirable in themselves, differing in kind or in their sources from the others. So much for the things that are said about pleasure and pain.

4

What pleasure is, or what kind of thing it is, will become plainer if we take up the question aga from the beginning. Seeing seems to be at any moment complete, for it does not lack anything which coming into being later will complete its form; and pleasure also seems to be of this nature. For it is a whole, and at no time can one find a pleasure whose form will be completed if the pleasure lasts longer. For this reason, too, it is not a movement. For every movement (e.g. that of building) takes time and is for the sake of an end, and is complete when it has made what it aims at. It is complete, therefore, only in the whole time or at that final moment. In their parts and during the time they occupy, all movements are incomplete, and are different in kind from the whole movement and from each other. For the fitting together of the stones is different from the fluting of the column, and these are both different from the making of the temple; and the making of the temple is complete (for it lacks nothing with a view to the end proposed), but the making of the base or of the triglyph is incomplete; for each is the making of only a part. They differ in kind, then, and it is not possible to find at any and every time a movement complete in form, but if at all, only in the whole time. So, too, in the case of walking and all other movements. For if locomotion is a movement from to there, it, too, has differences in kind-flying, walking, leaping, and so on. And not only so, but in walking itself there are such differences; for the whence and whither are not the same in the whole racecourse and in a part of it, nor in one part and in another, nor is it the same thing to traverse this line and that; for one traverses not only a line but one which is in a place, and this one is in a different place from that. We have discussed movement with precision in another work, but it seems that it is not complete at any and every time, but that the many movements are incomplete and different in kind, since the whence and whither give them their form. But of pleasure the form is complete at any and every time. Plainly, then, pleasure and movement must be different from each other, and pleasure must be one of the things that are whole and complete. This would seem to be the case, too, from the fact that it is not possible to move otherwise than in time, but it is possible to be pleased; for that which takes place in a moment is a whole.

From these considerations it is clear, too, that these thinkers are not right in saying there is a movement or a coming into being of pleasure. For these cannot be ascribed to all things, but only to those that are divisible and not wholes; there is no coming into being of seeing nor of a point nor of a unit, nor is any of these a movement or coming into being; therefore there is no movement or coming into being of pleasure either; for it is a whole.

Since every sense is active in relation to its object, and a sense which is in good condition acts perfectly in relation to the most beautiful of its objects (for perfect activity seems to be ideally of this nature; whether we say that it is active, or the organ in which it resides, may be assumed to be immaterial), it follows that in the case of each sense the best activity is that of the best-conditioned organ in relation to the finest of its objects. And this activity will be the most complete and pleasant. For, while there is pleasure in respect of any sense, and in respect of thought and contemplation no less, the most complete is pleasantest, and that of a well-conditioned organ in relation to the worthiest of its objects is the most complete; and the pleasure completes the activity. But the pleasure does not complete it in the same way as the combination of object and sense, both good, just as health and the doctor are not in the same way the cause of a man's being healthy. (That pleasure is produced in respect to each sense is plain; for we speak of sights and sounds as pleasant. It is also plain that it arises most of all when both the sense is at its best and it is active in reference to an object which corresponds; when both object and perceiver are of the best there will always be pleasure, since the requisite agent and patient are both present.) Pleasure completes the activity not as the corresponding permanent state does, by its immanence, but as an end which supervenes as the bloom of youth does on those in the flower of their age. So long, then, as both the intelligible or sensible object and the discriminating or contemplative faculty are as they should be, the pleasure will be involved in the activity; for when both the passive and the active factor are unchanged and are related to each other in the same way, the same result naturally follows.

How, then, is it that no one is continuously pleased? Is it that we grow weary? Certainly all human beings are incapable of continuous activity. Therefore pleasure also is not continuous; for it accompanies activity. Some things delight us when they are new, but later do so less, for the same reason; for at first the mind is in a state of stimulation and intensely active about them, as people are with respect to their vision when they look hard at a thing, but afterwards our activity is not of this kind, but has grown relaxed; for which reason the pleasure also is dulled.

One might think that all men desire pleasure because they all aim at life; life is an activity, and each man is active about those things and with those faculties that he loves most; e.g. the musician is active with his hearing in reference to tunes, the student with his mind in reference to theoretical questions, and so on in each case; now pleasure completes the activities, and therefore life, which they desire. It is with good reason, then, that they aim at pleasure too, since for every one it completes life, which is desirable. But whether we choose life for the sake of pleasure or pleasure for the sake of life is a question we may dismiss for the present. For they seem to be bound up together and not to admit of separation, since without activity pleasure does not arise, and every activity is completed by the attendant pleasure.

5

For this reason pleasures seem, too, to differ in kind. For things different in kind are, we think, completed by different things (we see this to be true both of natural objects and of things produced by art, e.g. animals, trees, a painting, a sculpture, a house, an implement); and, similarly, we think that activities differing in kind are completed by things differing in kind. Now the activities of thought differ from those of the senses, and both differ among themselves, in kind; so, therefore, do the pleasures that complete them.

This may be seen, too, from the fact that each of the pleasures is bound up with the activity it completes. For an activity is intensified by its proper pleasure, since each class of things is better judged of and brought to precision by those who engage in the activity with pleasure; e.g. it is those who enjoy geometrical thinking that become geometers and grasp the various propositions better, and, similarly, those who are fond of music or of building, and so on, make progress in their proper function by enjoying it; so the pleasures intensify the activities, and what intensifies a thing is proper to it, but things different in kind have properties different in kind.

This will be even more apparent from the fact that activities are hindered by pleasures arising from other sources. For people who are fond of playing the flute are incapable of attending to arguments if they overhear some one playing the flute, since they enjoy flute-playing more than the activity in hand; so the pleasure connected with fluteplaying destroys the activity concerned with argument. This happens, similarly, in all other cases, when one is active about two things at once; the more pleasant activity drives out the other, and if it is much more pleasant does so all the more, so that one even ceases from the other. This is why when we enjoy anything very much we do not throw ourselves into anything else, and do one thing only when we are not much pleased by another; e.g. in the theatre the people who eat sweets do so most when the actors are poor. Now since activities are made precise and more enduring and better by their proper pleasure, and injured by alien pleasures, evidently the two kinds of pleasure are far apart. For alien pleasures do pretty much what proper pains do, since activities are destroyed by their proper pains; e.g. if a man finds writing or doing sums unpleasant and painful, he does not write, or does not do sums, because the activity is painful. So an activity suffers contrary effects from its proper pleasures and pains, i.e. from those that supervene on it in virtue of its own nature. And alien pleasures have been stated to do much the same as pain; they destroy the activity, only not to the same degree.

Now since activities differ in respect of goodness and badness, and some are worthy to be chosen, others to be avoided, and others neutral, so, too, are the pleasures; for to each activity there is a proper pleasure. The pleasure proper to a worthy activity is good and that proper to an unworthy activity bad; just as the appetites for noble objects are laudable, those for base objects culpable. But the pleasures involved in activities are more proper to them than the desires; for the latter are separated both in time and in nature, while the former are close to the activities, and so hard to distinguish from them that it admits of dispute whether the activity is not the same as the pleasure. (Still, pleasure does not seem to be thought or perception-that would be strange; but because they are not found apart they appear to some people the same.) As activities are different, then, so are the corresponding pleasures. Now sight is superior to touch in purity, and hearing and smell to taste; the pleasures, therefore, are similarly superior, and those of thought superior to these, and within each of the two kinds some are superior to others.

Each animal is thought to have a proper pleasure, as it has a proper function; viz. that which corresponds to its activity. If we survey them species by species, too, this will be evident; horse, dog, and man have different pleasures, as Heraclitus says 'asses would prefer sweepings to gold'; for food is pleasanter than gold to asses. So the pleasures of creatures different in kind differ in kind, and it is plausible to suppose that those of a single species do not differ. But they vary to no small extent, in the case of men at least; the same things delight some people and pain others, and are painful and odious to some, and pleasant to and liked by others. This happens, too, in the case of sweet things; the same things do not seem sweet to a man in a fever and a healthy man-nor hot to a weak man and one in good condition. The same happens in other cases. But in all such matters that which appears to the good man is thought to be really so. If this is correct, as it seems to be, and virtue and the good man as such are the measure of each thing, those also will be pleasures which appear so to him, and those things pleasant which he enjoys. If the things he finds tiresome seem pleasant to some one, that is nothing surprising; for men may be ruined and spoilt in many ways; but the things are not pleasant, but only pleasant to these people and to people in this condition. Those which are admittedly disgraceful plainly should not be said to be pleasures, except to a perverted taste; but of those that are thought to be good what kind of pleasure or what pleasure should be said to be that proper to man? Is it not plain from the corresponding activities? The pleasures follow these. Whether, then, the perfect and supremely happy man has one or more activities, the pleasures that perfect these will be said in the strict sense to be pleasures proper to man, and the rest will be so in a secondary and fractional way, as are the activities.

6

Now that we have spoken of the virtues, the forms of friendship, and the varieties of pleasure, what remains is to discuss in outline the nature of happiness, since this is what we state the end of human nature to be. Our discussion will be the more concise if we first sum up what we have said already. We said, then, that it is not a disposition; for if it were it might belong to some one who was asleep throughout his life, living the life of a plant, or, again, to some one who was suffering the greatest misfortunes. If these implications are unacceptable, and we must rather class happiness as an activity, as we have said before, and if some activities are necessary, and desirable for the sake of something else, while others are so in themselves, evidently happiness must be placed among those desirable in themselves, not among those desirable for the sake of something else; for happiness does not lack anything, but is self-sufficient. Now those activities are desirable in themselves from which nothing is sought beyond the activity. And of this nature virtuous actions are thought to be; for to do noble and good deeds is a thing desirable for its own sake.

Pleasant amusements also are thought to be of this nature; we choose them not for the sake of other things; for we are injured rather than benefited by them, since we are led to neglect our bodies and our property. But most of the people who are deemed happy take refuge in such pastimes, which is the reason why those who are ready-witted at them are highly esteemed at the courts of tyrants; they make themselves pleasant companions in the tyrants' favourite pursuits, and that is the sort of man they want. Now these things are thought to be of the nature of happiness because people in despotic positions spend their leisure in them, but perhaps such people prove nothing; for virtue and reason, from which good activities flow, do not depend on despotic position; nor, if these people, who have never tasted pure and generous pleasure, take refuge in the bodily pleasures, should these for that reason be thought more desirable; for boys, too, think the things that are valued among themselves are the best. It is to be expected, then, that, as different things seem valuable to boys and to men, so they should to bad men and to good. Now, as we have often maintained, those things are both valuable and pleasant which are such to the good man; and to each man the activity in accordance with his own disposition is most desirable, and, therefore, to the good man that which is in accordance with virtue. Happiness, therefore, does not lie in amusement; it would, indeed, be strange if the end were amusement, and one were to take trouble and suffer hardship all one's life in order to amuse oneself. For, in a word, everything that we choose we choose for the sake of something else-except happiness, which is an end. Now to exert oneself and work for the sake of amusement seems silly and utterly childish. But to amuse oneself in order that one may exert oneself, as Anacharsis puts it, seems right; for amusement is a sort of relaxation, and we need relaxation because we cannot work continuously. Relaxation, then, is not an end; for it is taken for the sake of activity.

The happy life is thought to be virtuous; now a virtuous life requires exertion, and does not consist in amusement. And we say that serious things are better than laughable things and those connected with amusement, and that the activity of the better of any two things-whether it be two elements of our being or two men-is the more serious; but the activity of the better is ipso facto superior and more of the nature of happiness. And any chance person-even a slave-can enjoy the bodily pleasures no less than the best man; but no one assigns to a slave a share in happiness-unless he assigns to him also a share in human life. For happiness does not lie in such occupations, but, as we have said before, in virtuous activities.

7

If happiness is activity in accordance with virtue, it is reasonable that it should be in accordance with the highest virtue; and this will be that of the best thing in us. Whether it be reason or something else that is this element which is thought to be our natural ruler and guide and to take thought of things noble and divine, whether it be itself also divine or only the most divine element in us, the activity of this in accordance with its proper virtue will be perfect happiness. That this activity is contemplative we have already said.

Now this would seem to be in agreement both with what we said before and with the truth. For, firstly, this activity is the best (since not only is reason the best thing in us, but the objects of reason are the best of knowable objects); and secondly, it is the most continuous, since we can contemplate truth more continuously than we can do anything. And we think happiness has pleasure mingled with it, but the activity of philosophic wisdom is admittedly the pleasantest of virtuous activities; at all events the pursuit of it is thought to offer pleasures marvellous for their purity and their enduringness, and it is to be expected that those who know will pass their time more pleasantly than those who inquire. And the self-sufficiency that is spoken of must belong most to the contemplative activity. For while a philosopher, as well as a just man or one possessing any other virtue, needs the necessaries of life, when they are sufficiently equipped with things of that sort the just man needs people towards whom and with whom he shall act justly, and the temperate man, the brave man, and each of the others is in the same case, but the philosopher, even when by himself, can contemplate truth, and the better the wiser he is; he can perhaps do so better if he has fellow-workers, but still he is the most self-sufficient. And this activity alone would seem to be loved for its own sake; for nothing arises from it apart from the contemplating, while from practical activities we gain more or less apart from the action. And happiness is thought to depend on leisure; for we are busy that we may have leisure, and make war that we may live in peace. Now the activity of the practical virtues is exhibited in political or military affairs, but the actions concerned with these seem to be unleisurely. Warlike actions are completely so (for no one chooses to be at war, or provokes war, for the sake of being at war; any one would seem absolutely murderous if he were to make enemies of his friends in order to bring about battle and slaughter); but the action of the statesman is also unleisurely, and-apart from the political action itself-aims at despotic power and honours, or at all events happiness, for him and his fellow citizens-a happiness different from political action, and evidently sought as being different. So if among virtuous actions political and military actions are distinguished by nobility and greatness, and these are unleisurely and aim at an end and are not desirable for their own sake, but the activity of reason, which is contemplative, seems both to be superior in serious worth and to aim at no end beyond itself, and to have its pleasure proper to itself (and this augments the activity), and the self-sufficiency, leisureliness, unweariedness (so far as this is possible for man), and all the other attributes ascribed to the supremely happy man are evidently those connected with this activity, it follows that this will be the complete happiness of man, if it be allowed a complete term of life (for none of the attributes of happiness is incomplete).

But such a life would be too high for man; for it is not in so far as he is man that he will live so, but in so far as something divine is present in him; and by so much as this is superior to our composite nature is its activity superior to that which is the exercise of the other kind of virtue. If reason is divine, then, in comparison with man, the life according to it is divine in comparison with human life. But we must not follow those who advise us, being men, to think of human things, and, being mortal, of mortal things, but must, so far as we can, make ourselves immortal, and strain every nerve to live in accordance with the best thing in us; for even if it be small in bulk, much more does it in power and worth surpass everything. This would seem, too, to be each man himself, since it is the authoritative and better part of him. It would be strange, then, if he were to choose not the life of his self but that of something else. And what we said before' will apply now; that which is proper to each thing is by nature best and most pleasant for each thing; for man, therefore, the life according to reason is best and pleasantest, since reason more than anything else is man. This life therefore is also the happiest.

8

But in a secondary degree the life in accordance with the other kind of virtue is happy; for the activities in accordance with this befit our human estate. Just and brave acts, and other virtuous acts, we do in relation to each other, observing our respective duties with regard to contracts and services and all manner of actions and with regard to passions; and all of these seem to be typically human. Some of them seem even to arise from the body, and virtue of character to be in many ways bound up with the passions. Practical wisdom, too, is linked to virtue of character, and this to practical wisdom, since the principles of practical wisdom are in accordance with the moral virtues and rightness in morals is in accordance with practical wisdom. Being connected with the passions also, the moral virtues must belong to our composite nature; and the virtues of our composite nature are human; so, therefore, are the life and the happiness which correspond to these. The excellence of the reason is a thing apart; we must be content to say this much about it, for to describe it precisely is a task greater than our purpose requires. It would seem, however, also to need external equipment but little, or less than moral virtue does. Grant that both need the necessaries, and do so equally, even if the statesman's work is the more concerned with the body and things of that sort; for there will be little difference there; but in what they need for the exercise of their activities there will be much difference. The liberal man will need money for the doing of his liberal deeds, and the just man too will need it for the returning of services (for wishes are hard to discern, and even people who are not just pretend to wish to act justly); and the brave man will need power if he is to accomplish any of the acts that correspond to his virtue, and the temperate man will need opportunity; for how else is either he or any of the others to be recognized? It is debated, too, whether the will or the deed is more essential to virtue, which is assumed to involve both; it is surely clear that its perfection involves both; but for deeds many things are needed, and more, the greater and nobler the deeds are. But the man who is contemplating the truth needs no such thing, at least with a view to the exercise of his activity; indeed they are, one may say, even hindrances, at all events to his contemplation; but in so far as he is a man and lives with a number of people, he chooses to do virtuous acts; he will therefore need such aids to living a human life.

But that perfect happiness is a contemplative activity will appear from the following consideration as well. We assume the gods to be above all other beings blessed and happy; but what sort of actions must we assign to them? Acts of justice? Will not the gods seem absurd if they make contracts and return deposits, and so on? Acts of a brave man, then, confronting dangers and running risks because it is noble to do so? Or liberal acts? To whom will they give? It will be strange if they are really to have money or anything of the kind. And what would their temperate acts be? Is not such praise tasteless, since they have no bad appetites? If we were to run through them all, the circumstances of action would be found trivial and unworthy of gods. Still, every one supposes that they live and therefore that they are active; we cannot suppose them to sleep like Endymion. Now if you take away from a living being action, and still more production, what is left but contemplation? Therefore the activity of God, which surpasses all others in blessedness, must be contemplative; and of human activities, therefore, that which is most akin to this must be most of the nature of happiness.

This is indicated, too, by the fact that the other animals have no share in happiness, being completely deprived of such activity. For while the whole life of the gods is blessed, and that of men too in so far as some likeness of such activity belongs to them, none of the other animals is happy, since they in no way share in contemplation. Happiness extends, then, just so far as contemplation does, and those to whom contemplation more fully belongs are more truly happy, not as a mere concomitant but in virtue of the contemplation; for this is in itself precious. Happiness, therefore, must be some form of contemplation.

But, being a man, one will also need external prosperity; for our nature is not self-sufficient for the purpose of contemplation, but our body also must be healthy and must have food and other attention. Still, we must not think that the man who is to be happy will need many things or great things, merely because he cannot be supremely happy without external goods; for self-sufficiency and action do not involve excess, and we can do noble acts without ruling earth and sea; for even with moderate advantages one can act virtuously (this is manifest enough; for private persons are thought to do worthy acts no less than despots-indeed even more); and it is enough that we should have so much as that; for the life of the man who is active in accordance with virtue will be happy. Solon, too, was perhaps sketching well the happy man when he described him as moderately furnished with externals but as having done (as Solon thought) the noblest acts, and lived temperately; for one can with but moderate possessions do what one ought. Anaxagoras also seems to have supposed the happy man not to be rich nor a despot, when he said that he would not be surprised if the happy man were to seem to most people a strange person; for they judge by externals, since these are all they perceive. The opinions of the wise seem, then, to harmonize with our arguments. But while even such things carry some conviction, the truth in practical matters is discerned from the facts of life; for these are the decisive factor. We must therefore survey what we have already said, bringing it to the test of the facts of life, and if it harmonizes with the facts we must accept it, but if it clashes with them we must suppose it to be mere theory. Now he who exercises his reason and cultivates it seems to be both in the best state of mind and most dear to the gods. For if the gods have any care for human affairs, as they are thought to have, it would be reasonable both that they should delight in that which was best and most akin to them (i.e. reason) and that they should reward those who love and honour this most, as caring for the things that are dear to them and acting both rightly and nobly. And that all these attributes belong most of all to the philosopher is manifest. He, therefore, is the dearest to the gods. And he who is that will presumably be also the happiest; so that in this way too the philosopher will more than any other be happy.

9

If these matters and the virtues, and also friendship and pleasure, have been dealt with sufficiently in outline, are we to suppose that our programme has reached its end? Surely, as the saying goes, where there are things to be done the end is not to survey and recognize the various things, but rather to do them; with regard to virtue, then, it is not enough to know, but we must try to have and use it, or try any other way there may be of becoming good. Now if arguments were in themselves enough to make men good, they would justly, as Theognis says, have won very great rewards, and such rewards should have been provided; but as things are, while they seem to have power to encourage and stimulate the generous-minded among our youth, and to make a character which is gently born, and a true lover of what is noble, ready to be possessed by virtue, they are not able to encourage the many to nobility and goodness. For these do not by nature obey the sense of shame, but only fear, and do not abstain from bad acts because of their baseness but through fear of punishment; living by passion they pursue their own pleasures and the means to them, and and the opposite pains, and have not even a conception of what is noble and truly pleasant, since they have never tasted it. What argument would remould such people? It is hard, if not impossible, to remove by argument the traits that have long since been incorporated in the character; and perhaps we must be content if, when all the influences by which we are thought to become good are present, we get some tincture of virtue.

Now some think that we are made good by nature, others by habituation, others by teaching. Nature's part evidently does not depend on us, but as a result of some divine causes is present in those who are truly fortunate; while argument and teaching, we may suspect, are not powerful with all men, but the soul of the student must first have been cultivated by means of habits for noble joy and noble hatred, like earth which is to nourish the seed. For he who lives as passion directs will not hear argument that dissuades him, nor understand it if he does; and how can we persuade one in such a state to change his ways? And in general passion seems to yield not to argument but to force. The character, then, must somehow be there already with a kinship to virtue, loving what is noble and hating what is base.

But it is difficult to get from youth up a right training for virtue if one has not been brought up under right laws; for to live temperately and hardily is not pleasant to most people, especially when they are young. For this reason their nurture and occupations should be fixed by law; for they will not be painful when they have become customary. But it is surely not enough that when they are young they should get the right nurture and attention; since they must, even when they are grown up, practise and be habituated to them, we shall need laws for this as well, and generally speaking to cover the whole of life; for most people obey necessity rather than argument, and punishments rather than the sense of what is noble.

This is why some think that legislators ought to stimulate men to virtue and urge them forward by the motive of the noble, on the assumption that those who have been well advanced by the formation of habits will attend to such influences; and that punishments and penalties should be imposed on those who disobey and are of inferior nature, while the incurably bad should be completely banished. A good man (they think), since he lives with his mind fixed on what is noble, will submit to argument, while a bad man, whose desire is for pleasure, is corrected by pain like a beast of burden. This is, too, why they say the pains inflicted should be those that are most opposed to the pleasures such men love.

However that may be, if (as we have said) the man who is to be good must be well trained and habituated, and go on to spend his time in worthy occupations and neither willingly nor unwillingly do bad actions, and if this can be brought about if men live in accordance with a sort of reason and right order, provided this has force,-if this be so, the paternal command indeed has not the required force or compulsive power (nor in general has the command of one man, unless he be a king or something similar), but the law has compulsive power, while it is at the same time a rule proceeding from a sort of practical wisdom and reason. And while people hate men who oppose their impulses, even if they oppose them rightly, the law in its ordaining of what is good is not burdensome.

In the Spartan state alone, or almost alone, the legislator seems to have paid attention to questions of nurture and occupations; in most states such matters have been neglected, and each man lives as he pleases, Cyclops-fashion, 'to his own wife and children dealing law'. Now it is best that there should be a public and proper care for such matters; but if they are neglected by the community it would seem right for each man to help his children and friends towards virtue, and that they should have the power, or at least the will, to do this.

It would seem from what has been said that he can do this better if he makes himself capable of legislating. For public control is plainly effected by laws, and good control by good laws; whether written or unwritten would seem to make no difference, nor whether they are laws providing for the education of individuals or of groups-any more than it does in the case of music or gymnastics and other such pursuits. For as in cities laws and prevailing types of character have force, so in households do the injunctions and the habits of the father, and these have even more because of the tie of blood and the benefits he confers; for the children start with a natural affection and disposition to obey. Further, private education has an advantage over public, as private medical treatment has; for while in general rest and abstinence from food are good for a man in a fever, for a particular man they may not be; and a boxer presumably does not prescribe the same style of fighting to all his pupils. It would seem, then, that the detail is worked out with more precision if the control is private; for each person is more likely to get what suits his case.

But the details can be best looked after, one by one, by a doctor or gymnastic instructor or any one else who has the general knowledge of what is good for every one or for people of a certain kind (for the sciences both are said to be, and are, concerned with what is universal); not but what some particular detail may perhaps be well looked after by an unscientific person, if he has studied accurately in the light of experience what happens in each case, just as some people seem to be their own best doctors, though they could give no help to any one else. None the less, it will perhaps be agreed that if a man does wish to become master of an art or science he must go to the universal, and come to know it as well as possible; for, as we have said, it is with this that the sciences are concerned.

And surely he who wants to make men, whether many or few, better by his care must try to become capable of legislating, if it is through laws that we can become good. For to get any one whatever-any one who is put before us-into the right condition is not for the first chance comer; if any one can do it, it is the man who knows, just as in medicine and all other matters which give scope for care and prudence.

Must we not, then, next examine whence or how one can learn how to legislate? Is it, as in all other cases, from statesmen? Certainly it was thought to be a part of statesmanship. Or is a difference apparent between statesmanship and the other sciences and arts? In the others the same people are found offering to teach the arts and practising them, e.g. doctors or painters; but while the sophists profess to teach politics, it is practised not by any of them but by the politicians, who would seem to do so by dint of a certain skill and experience rather than of thought; for they are not found either writing or speaking about such matters (though it were a nobler occupation perhaps than composing speeches for the law-courts and the assembly), nor again are they found to have made statesmen of their own sons or any other of their friends. But it was to be expected that they should if they could; for there is nothing better than such a skill that they could have left to their cities, or could prefer to have for themselves, or, therefore, for those dearest to them. Still, experience seems to contribute not a little; else they could not have become politicians by familiarity with politics; and so it seems that those who aim at knowing about the art of politics need experience as well.

But those of the sophists who profess the art seem to be very far from teaching it. For, to put the matter generally, they do not even know what kind of thing it is nor what kinds of things it is about; otherwise they would not have classed it as identical with rhetoric or even inferior to it, nor have thought it easy to legislate by collecting the laws that are thought well of; they say it is possible to select the best laws, as though even the selection did not demand intelligence and as though right judgement were not the greatest thing, as in matters of music. For while people experienced in any department judge rightly the works produced in it, and understand by what means or how they are achieved, and what harmonizes with what, the inexperienced must be content if they do not fail to see whether the work has been well or ill made-as in the case of painting. Now laws are as it were the' works' of the political art; how then can one learn from them to be a legislator, or judge which are best? Even medical men do not seem to be made by a study of text-books. Yet people try, at any rate, to state not only the treatments, but also how particular classes of people can be cured and should be treated-distinguishing the various habits of body; but while this seems useful to experienced people, to the inexperienced it is valueless. Surely, then, while collections of laws, and of constitutions also, may be serviceable to those who can study them and judge what is good or bad and what enactments suit what circumstances, those who go through such collections without a practised faculty will not have right judgement (unless it be as a spontaneous gift of nature), though they may perhaps become more intelligent in such matters.

Now our predecessors have left the subject of legislation to us unexamined; it is perhaps best, therefore, that we should ourselves study it, and in general study the question of the constitution, in order to complete to the best of our ability our philosophy of human nature. First, then, if anything has been said well in detail by earlier thinkers, let us try to review it; then in the light of the constitutions we have collected let us study what sorts of influence preserve and destroy states, and what sorts preserve or destroy the particular kinds of constitution, and to what causes it is due that some are well and others ill administered. When these have been studied we shall perhaps be more likely to see with a comprehensive view, which constitution is best, and how each must be ordered, and what laws and customs it must use, if it is to be at its best. Let us make a beginning of our discussion.

Politics

Introduction

The Politics of Aristotle is the second part of a treatise of which the Ethics is the first part. It looks back to the Ethics as the Ethics looks forward to the Politics. For Aristotle did not separate, as we are inclined to do, the spheres of the statesman and the moralist. In the Ethics he has described the character necessary for the good life, but that life is for him essentially to be lived in society, and when in the last chapters of the Ethics he comes to the practical application of his inquiries, that finds expression not in moral exhortations addressed to the individual but in a description of the legislative opportunities of the statesman. It is the legislator's task to frame a society which shall make the good life possible. Politics for Aristotle is not a struggle between individuals or classes for power, nor a device for getting done such elementary tasks as the maintenance of order and security without too great encroachments on individual liberty. The state is "a community of well-being in families and aggregations of families for the sake of a perfect and self-sufficing life." The legislator is a craftsman whose material is society and whose aim is the good life.

In an early dialogue of Plato's, the Protagoras, Socrates asks Protagoras why it is not as easy to find teachers of virtue as it is to find teachers of swordsmanship, riding, or any other art. Protagoras' answer is that there are no special teachers of virtue, because virtue is taught by the whole community. Plato and Aristotle both accept the view of moral education implied in this answer. In a passage of the Republic (492 b) Plato repudiates the notion that the sophists have a corrupting moral influence upon young men. The public themselves, he says, are the real sophists and the most complete and thorough educators. No private education can hold out against the irresistible force of public opinion and the ordinary moral standards of society. But that makes it all the more essential that public opinion and social environment should not be left to grow up at haphazard as they ordinarily do, but should be made by the wise legislator the expression of the good and be informed in all their details by his knowledge. The legislator is the only possible teacher of virtue.

Such a programme for a treatise on government might lead us to expect in the Politics mainly a description of a Utopia or ideal state which might inspire poets or philosophers but have little direct effect upon political institutions. Plato's Republic is obviously impracticable, for its author had turned away in despair from existing politics. He has no proposals, in that dialogue at least, for making the best of things as they are. The first lesson his philosopher has to learn is to turn away from this world of becoming and decay, and to look upon the unchanging eternal world of ideas. Thus his ideal city is, as he says, a pattern laid up in heaven by which the just man may rule his life, a pattern therefore in the meantime for the individual and not for the statesman. It is a city, he admits in the Laws, for gods or the children of gods, not for men as they are.

Aristotle has none of the high enthusiasm or poetic imagination of Plato. He is even unduly impatient of Plato's idealism, as is shown by the criticisms in the second book. But he has a power to see the possibilities of good in things that are imperfect, and the patience of the true politician who has learned that if he would make men what they ought to be, he must take them as he finds them. His ideal is constructed not of pure reason or poetry, but from careful and sympathetic study of a wide range of facts. His criticism of Plato in the light of history, in Book II. chap, v., though as a criticism it is curiously inept, reveals his own attitude admirably: "Let us remember that we should not disregard the experience of ages; in the multitude of years, these things, if they were good, would certainly not have been unknown; for almost everything has been found out, although sometimes they are not put together; in other cases men do not use the knowledge which they have." Aristotle in his Constitutions had made a study of one hundred and fifty-eight constitutions of the states of his day, and the fruits of that study are seen in the continual reference to concrete political experience, which makes the Politics in some respects a critical history of the workings of the institutions of the Greek city state. In Books IV., V., and VI. the ideal state seems far away, and we find a dispassionate survey of imperfect states, the best ways of preserving them, and an analysis of the causes of their instability. It is as though Aristotle were saying: "I have shown you the proper and normal type of constitution, but if you will not have it and insist on living under a perverted form, you may as well know how to make the best of it." In this way the Politics, though it defines the state in the light of its ideal, discusses states and institutions as they are. Ostensibly it is merely a continuation of the Ethics, but it comes to treat political questions from a purely political standpoint.

This combination of idealism and respect for the teachings of experience constitutes in some ways the strength and value of the Politics, but it also makes it harder to follow. The large nation states to which we are accustomed make it difficult for us to think that the state could be constructed and modelled to express the good life. We can appreciate Aristotle's critical analysis of constitutions, but find it hard to take seriously his advice to the legislator. Moreover, the idealism and the empiricism of the Politics are never really reconciled by Aristotle himself.

It may help to an understanding of the Politics if something is said on those two points.

We are accustomed since the growth of the historical method to the belief that states are "not made but grow," and are apt to be impatient with the belief which Aristotle and Plato show in the powers of the lawgiver. But however true the maxim may be of the modern nation state, it was not true of the much smaller and more self-conscious Greek city. When Aristotle talks of the legislator, he is not talking in the air. Students of the Academy had been actually called on to give new constitutions to Greek states. For the Greeks the constitution was not merely as it is so often with us, a matter of political machinery. It was regarded as a way of life. Further, the constitution within the framework of which the ordinary process of administration and passing of decrees went on, was always regarded as the work of a special man or body of men, the lawgivers. If we study Greek history, we find that the position of the legislator corresponds to that assigned to him by Plato and Aristotle. All Greek states, except those perversions which Aristotle criticises as being "above law," worked under rigid constitutions, and the constitution was only changed when the whole people gave a commission to a lawgiver to draw up a new one. Such was the position of the AEsumnetes, whom Aristotle describes in Book III. chap, xiv., in earlier times, and of the pupils of the Academy in the fourth century. The lawgiver was not an ordinary politician. He was a state doctor, called in to prescribe for an ailing constitution. So Herodotus recounts that when the people of Cyrene asked the oracle of Delphi to help them in their dissensions, the oracle told them to go to Mantinea, and the Mantineans lent them Demonax, who acted as a "setter straight" and drew up a new constitution for Cyrene. So again the Milesians, Herodotus tells us, were long troubled by civil discord, till they asked help from Paros, and the Parians sent ten commissioners who gave Miletus a new constitution. So the Athenians, when they were founding their model new colony at Thurii, employed Hippodamus of Miletus, whom Aristotle mentions in Book II, as the best expert in town-planning, to plan the streets of the city, and Protagoras as the best expert in law-making, to give the city its laws. In the Laws Plato represents one of the persons of the dialogue as having been asked by the people of Gortyna to draw up laws for a colony which they were founding. The situation described must have occurred frequently in actual life. The Greeks thought administration should be democratic and law-making the work of experts. We think more naturally of law-making as the special right of the people and administration as necessarily confined to experts.

Aristotle's Politics, then, is a handbook for the legislator, the expert who is to be called in when a state wants help. We have called him a state doctor. It is one of the most marked characteristics of Greek political theory that Plato and Aristotle think of the statesman as one who has knowledge of what ought to be done, and can help those who call him in to prescribe for them, rather than one who has power to control the forces of society. The desire of society for the statesman's advice is taken for granted, Plato in the Republic says that a good constitution is only possible when the ruler does not want to rule; where men contend for power, where they have not learnt to distinguish between the art of getting hold of the helm of state and the art of steering, which alone is statesmanship, true politics is impossible.

With this position much that Aristotle has to say about government is in agreement. He assumes the characteristic Platonic view that all men seek the good, and go wrong through ignorance, not through evil will, and so he naturally regards the state as a community which exists for the sake of the good life. It is in the state that that common seeking after the good which is the profoundest truth about men and nature becomes explicit and knows itself. The state is for Aristotle prior to the family and the village, although it succeeds them in time, for only when the state with its conscious organisation is reached can man understand the secret of his past struggles after something he knew not what. If primitive society is understood in the light of the state, the state is understood in the light of its most perfect form, when the good after which all societies are seeking is realised in its perfection. Hence for Aristotle as for Plato, the natural state or the state as such is the ideal state, and the ideal state is the starting-point of political inquiry.

In accordance with the same line of thought, imperfect states, although called perversions, are regarded by Aristotle as the result rather of misconception and ignorance than of perverse will. They all represent, he says, some kind of justice. Oligarchs and democrats go wrong in their conception of the good. They have come short of the perfect state through misunderstanding of the end or through ignorance of the proper means to the end. But if they are states at all, they embody some common conception of the good, some common aspirations of all their members.

The Greek doctrine that the essence of the state consists in community of purpose is the counterpart of the notion often held in modern times that the essence of the state is force. The existence of force is for Plato and Aristotle a sign not of the state but of the state's failure. It comes from the struggle between conflicting misconceptions of the good. In so far as men conceive the good rightly they are united. The state represents their common agreement, force their failure to make that agreement complete. The cure, therefore, of political ills is knowledge of the good life, and the statesman is he who has such knowledge, for that alone can give men what they are always seeking.

If the state is the organisation of men seeking a common good, power and political position must be given to those who can forward this end. This is the principle expressed in Aristotle's account of political justice, the principle of "tools to those who can use them." As the aim of the state is differently conceived, the qualifications for government will vary. In the ideal state power will be given to the man with most knowledge of the good; in other states to the men who are most truly capable of achieving that end which the citizens have set themselves to pursue. The justest distribution of political power is that in which there is least waste of political ability.

Further, the belief that the constitution of a state is only the outward expression of the common aspirations and beliefs of its members, explains the paramount political importance which Aristotle assigns to education. It is the great instrument by which the legislator can ensure that the future citizens of his state will share those common beliefs which make the state possible. The Greeks with their small states had a far clearer apprehension than we can have of the dependence of a constitution upon the people who have to work it.

Such is in brief the attitude in which Aristotle approaches political problems, but in working out its application to men and institutions as they are, Aristotle admits certain compromises which are not really consistent with it.

1. Aristotle thinks of membership of a state as community in pursuit of the good. He wishes to confine membership in it to those who are capable of that pursuit in the highest and most explicit manner. His citizens, therefore, must be men of leisure, capable of rational thought upon the end of life. He does not recognise the significance of that less conscious but deep-seated membership of the state which finds its expression in loyalty and patriotism. His definition of citizen includes only a small part of the population of any Greek city. He is forced to admit that the state is not possible without the co-operation of men whom he will not admit to membership in it, either because they are not capable of sufficient rational appreciation of political ends, like the barbarians whom he thought were natural slaves, or because the leisure necessary for citizenship can only be gained by the work of the artisans who by that very work

make themselves incapable of the life which they make possible for others. "The artisan only attains excellence in proportion as he becomes a slave," and the slave is only a living instrument of the good life. He exists for the state, but the state does not exist for him.

2. Aristotle in his account of the ideal state seems to waver between two ideals. There is the ideal of an aristocracy and the ideal of what he calls constitutional government, a mixed constitution. The principle of "tools to those who can use them" ought to lead him, as it does Plato, to an aristocracy. Those who have complete knowledge of the good must be few, and therefore Plato gave entire power in his state into the hands of the small minority of philosopher guardians. It is in accordance with this principle that Aristotle holds that kingship is the proper form of government when there is in the state one man of transcendent virtue. At the same time, Aristotle always holds that absolute government is not properly political, that government is not like the rule of a shepherd over his sheep, but the rule of equals over equals. He admits that the democrats are right in insisting that equality is a necessary element in the state, though he thinks they do not admit the importance of other equally necessary elements. Hence he comes to say that ruling and being ruled over by turns is an essential feature of constitutional government, which he admits as an alternative to aristocracy. The end of the state, which is to be the standard of the distribution of political power, is conceived sometimes as a good for the apprehension and attainment of which "virtue" is necessary and sufficient (this is the principle of aristocracy), and sometimes as a more complex good, which needs for its attainment not only "virtue" but wealth and equality. This latter conception is the principle on which the mixed constitution is based. This in its distribution of political power gives some weight to "virtue," some to wealth, and some to mere number. But the principle of "ruling and being ruled by turns" is not really compatible with an unmodified principle of "tools to those who can use them." Aristotle is right in seeing that political government demands equality, not in the sense that all members of the state should be equal in ability or should have equal power, but in the sense that none of them can properly be regarded simply as tools with which the legislator works, that each has a right to say what will be made of his own life. The analogy between the legislator and the craftsman on which Plato insists, breaks down because the legislator is dealing with men like himself, men who can to some extent conceive their own end in life and cannot be treated merely as means to the end of the legislator. The sense of the value of "ruling and being ruled in turn" is derived from the experience that the ruler may use his power to subordinate the lives of the citizens of the state not to the common good but to his own private purposes. In modern terms, it is a simple, rough-and-ready attempt to solve that constant problem of politics, how efficient government is to be combined with popular control. This problem arises from the imperfection of human nature, apparent in rulers as well as in ruled, and if the principle which attempts to solve it be admitted as a principle of importance in the formation of the best constitution, then the starting-point of politics will be man's actual imperfection, not his ideal nature. Instead, then, of beginning with a state which would express man's ideal nature, and adapting it as well as may be to man's actual shortcomings from that ideal, we must recognise that the state and all political machinery are as much the expression of man's weakness as of his ideal possibilities. The state is possible only because men have common aspirations, but government, and political power, the existence of officials who are given authority to act in the name of the whole state, are necessary because men's community is imperfect, because man's social nature expresses itself in conflicting ways, in the clash of interests, the rivalry of parties, and the struggle of classes, instead of in the united seeking after a common good. Plato and Aristotle were familiar with the legislator who was called in by the whole people, and they tended therefore to take the general will or common consent of the people for granted. Most political questions are concerned with the construction and expression of the general will, and with attempts to ensure that the political machinery made to express the general will shall not be exploited for private or sectional ends.

Aristotle's mixed constitution springs from a recognition of sectional interests in the state. For the proper relation between the claims of "virtue," wealth, and numbers is to be based not upon their relative importance in the good life, but upon the strength of the parties which they represent. The mixed constitution is practicable in a state where the middle class is strong, as only the middle class can mediate between the rich and the poor. The mixed constitution will be stable if it represents the actual balance of power between different classes in the state. When we come to Aristotle's analysis of existing constitutions, we find that while he regards them as imperfect approximations to the ideal, he also thinks of them as the result of the struggle between classes. Democracy, he explains, is the government not of the many but of the poor; oligarchy a government not of the few but of the rich. And each class is thought of, not as trying to express an ideal, but as struggling to acquire power or maintain its position. If ever the class existed in unredeemed nakedness, it was in the Greek cities of the fourth century, and its existence is abundantly recognised by Aristotle. His account of the causes of revolutions in Book V. shows how far were the existing states of Greece from the ideal with which he starts. His analysis of the facts forces him to look upon them as the scene of struggling factions. The causes of revolutions are not described as primarily changes in the conception of the common good, but changes in the military or economic power of the several classes in the state. The aim which he sets before oligarchs or democracies is not the good life, but simple stability or permanence of the existing constitution.

With this spirit of realism which pervades Books IV., V., and VI. the idealism of Books I., II., VII., and VIII. is never reconciled. Aristotle is content to call existing constitutions perversions of the true form. But we cannot read the Politics without recognising and profiting from the insight into the nature of the state which is revealed throughout. Aristotle's failure does not lie in this, that he is both idealist and realist, but that he keeps these two tendencies too far apart. He thinks too much of his ideal state, as something to be reached once for all by knowledge, as a fixed type to which actual states approximate or from which they are perversions. But if we are to think of actual politics as intelligible in the light of the ideal, we must think of that ideal as progressively revealed in history, not as something to be discovered by turning our back on experience and having recourse to abstract reasoning. If we stretch forward from what exists to an ideal, it is to a better which may be in its turn transcended, not to a single immutable best. Aristotle found in the society of his time men who were not capable of political reflection, and who, as he thought, did their best work under superintendence. He therefore called them natural slaves. For, according to Aristotle, that is a man's natural condition in which he does his best work. But Aristotle also thinks of nature as something fixed and immutable; and therefore sanctions the institution of slavery, which assumes that what men are that they will always be, and sets up an artificial barrier to their ever becoming anything else. We see in Aristotle's defence of slavery how the conception of nature as the ideal can have a debasing influence upon views of practical politics. His high ideal of citizenship offers to those who can satisfy its claims the prospect of a fair life; those who fall short are deemed to be different in nature and shut out entirely from approach to the ideal.

A. D. LINDSAY.

Book I

Chapter I

As we see that every city is a society, and every society Ed. is established for some good purpose; for an apparent good is the spring of all human actions; it is evident that this is the principle upon which they are every one founded, and this is more especially true of that which has for its object the best possible, and is itself the most excellent, and comprehends all the rest. Now this is called a city, and the society thereof a political society; for those who think that the principles of a political, a regal, a family, and a herile government are the same are mistaken, while they suppose that each of these differ in the numbers to whom their power extends, but not in their constitution: so that with them a herile government is one composed of a very few, a domestic of more, a civil and a regal of still more, as if there was no difference between a large family and a small city, or that a regal government and a political one are the same, only that in the one a single person is continually at the head of public affairs; in the other, that each member of the state has in his turn a share in the government, and is at one time a magistrate, at another a private person, according to the rules of political science. But now this is not true, as will be evident to any one who will consider this question in the most approved method. As, in an inquiry into every other subject, it is necessary to separate the different parts of which it is compounded, till we arrive at their first elements, which are the most minute parts thereof; so by the same proceeding we shall acquire a knowledge of the primary parts of a city and see wherein they differ from each other, and whether the rules of art will give us any assistance in examining into each of these things which are mentioned.

Chapter II

Now if in this particular science any one would attend to its original seeds, and their first shoot, he would then as in others have the subject perfectly before him; and perceive, in the first place, that it is requisite that those should be joined together whose species cannot exist without each other, as the male and the female, for the business of propagation; and this not through choice, but by that natural impulse which acts both upon plants and animals also, for the purpose of their leaving behind them others like themselves. It is also from natural causes that some beings command and others obey, that each may obtain their mutual safety; for a being who is endowed with a mind capable of reflection and forethought is by nature the superior and governor, whereas he whose excellence is merely corporeal is formect to be a slave; whence it follows that the different state of master and slave is equally advantageous to both. But there is a natural difference between a female and a slave: for nature is not like the artists who make the Delphic swords for the use of the poor, but for every particular purpose she has her separate instruments, and thus her ends are most complete, for whatsoever is employed on one subject only, brings that one to much greater perfection than when employed on many; and yet among the barbarians, a female and a slave are upon a level in the community, the reason for which is, that amongst them there are none qualified by nature to govern, therefore their society can be nothing but between slaves of different sexes. For which reason the poets say, it is proper for the Greeks to govern the barbarians, as if a barbarian and a slave were by nature one. Now of these two societies the domestic is the first, and Hesiod is right when he says, "First a house, then a wife, then an ox for the plough," for the poor man has always an ox before a household slave. That society then which nature has established for daily support is the domestic, and those who compose it are called by Charondas *homosipuoi*, and by Epimenides the Cretan *homokapnoi*; but the society of many families, which was first instituted for their lasting, mutual advantage, is called a village, and a village is most naturally composed of the descendants of one family, whom some persons call homogalaktes, the children and the children's children thereof: for which reason cities were originally governed by kings, as the barbarian states now are, which are composed of those who had before submitted to kingly government; for every family is governed by the elder, as are the branches thereof, on account of their relationship thereunto, which is what Homer says, "Each one ruled his wife and child;" and in this scattered manner they formerly lived. And the opinion which universally prevails, that the gods themselves are subject to kingly government, arises from hence, that all men formerly were, and many are so now; and as they imagined themselves to be made in the likeness of the gods, so they supposed their manner of life must needs be the same. And when many villages so entirely join themselves together as in every respect to form but one society, that society is a city, and contains in itself, if I may so speak, the end and perfection of government: first founded that we might live, but continued that we may live happily. For which reason every city must be allowed to be the work of nature, if we admit that the original society between male and female is; for to this as their end all subordinate societies tend, and the end of everything is the nature of it. For what every being is in its most perfect state, that certainly is the nature of that being, whether it be a man, a horse, or a house: besides, whatsoever produces the final cause and the end which we desire, must be best; but a government complete in itself is that final cause and what is best. Hence it is evident that a city is a natural production, and that man is naturally a political animal, and that whosoever is naturally and not accidentally unfit for society, must be either inferior or superior to man: thus the man in Homer, who is reviled for being "without society, without law, without family." Such a one must naturally be of a quarrelsome disposition, and as solitary as the birds. The gift of speech also evidently proves that man is a more social animal than the bees, or any of the herding cattle: for nature, as we say, does nothing in vain, and man is the only animal who enjoys it. Voice indeed, as being the token of pleasure and pain, is imparted to others also, and thus much their nature is capable of, to perceive pleasure and pain, and to impart these sensations to others; but it is by speech that we are enabled to express what is useful for us, and what is hurtful, and of course what is just and what is unjust: for in this particular man differs from other animals, that he alone has a perception of good and evil, of just and unjust, and it is a participation of these common sentiments which forms a family and a city. Besides, the notion of a city naturally precedes that of a family or an individual, for the whole must necessarily be prior to the parts, for if you take away the whole man, you cannot say a foot or a hand remains, unless by equivocation, as supposing a hand of stone to be made, but that would only be a dead one; but everything is understood to be this or that by its energic qualities and powers, so that when these no longer remain, neither can that be said to be the same, but something of the same name. That a city then precedes an individual is plain, for if an individual is not in himself sufficient to compose a perfect government, he is to a city as other parts are to a whole; but he that is incapable of society, or so complete in himself as not to want it, makes no part of a city, as a beast or a god. There is then in all persons a natural impetus to associate with each other in this manner, and he who first founded civil society was the cause of the greatest good; for as by the completion of it man is the most excellent of all living beings, so without law and justice he would be the worst of all, for nothing is so difficult to subdue as injustice in arms: but these arms man is born with, namely, prudence and valour, which he may apply to the most opposite purposes, for he who abuses them will be the most wicked, the most cruel, the most lustful, and most gluttonous being imaginable; for justice is a political virtue, by the rules of it the state is regulated, and these rules are the criterion of what is right.

Chapter III

Since it is now evident of what parts a city is composed, it will be necessary to treat first of family government, for every city is made up of families, and every family has again its separate parts of which it is composed. When a family is complete, it consists of freemen and slaves; but as in every subject we should begin with examining into the smallest parts of which it consists, and as the first and smallest parts of a family are the master and slave, the husband and wife, the father and child, let us first inquire into these three, what each of them may be, and what they ought to be; that is to say, the herile, the nuptial, and the paternal. Let these then be considered as the three distinct parts of a family: some think that the providing what is necessary for the family is something different from the government of it, others that this is the greatest part of it; it shall be considered separately; but we will first speak of a master and a slave, that we may both understand the nature of those things which are absolutely necessary, and also try if we can learn anything better on this subject than what is already known. Some persons have thought that the power of the master over his slave originates from his superior knowledge, and that this knowledge is the same in the master, the magistrate, and the king, as we have already said; but others think that herile government is contrary to nature, and that it is the law which makes one man a slave and another free, but that in nature there is no difference; for which reason that power cannot be founded in justice, but in force.

Chapter IV

Since then a subsistence is necessary in every family, the means of procuring it certainly makes up part of the management of a family, for without necessaries it is impossible to live, and to live well. As in all arts which are brought to perfection it is necessary that they should have their proper instruments if they would complete their works, so is it in the art of managing a family: now of instruments some of them are alive, others inanimate; thus with respect to the pilot of the ship, the tiller is without life, the sailor is alive; for a servant is as an instrument in many arts. Thus property is as an instrument to living; an estate is a multitude of instruments; so a slave is an animated instrument, but every one that can minister of himself is more valuable than any other instrument; for if every instrument, at command, or from a preconception of its master's will, could accomplish its work (as the story goes of the statues of Daedalus; or what the poet tells us of the tripods of Vulcan, "that they moved of their own accord into the assembly of the gods "), the shuttle would then weave, and the lyre play of itself; nor would the architect want servants, or the master slaves. Now what are generally called instruments are the efficients of something else, but possessions are what we simply use: thus with a shuttle we make something else for our use; but we only use a coat, or a bed: since then making and using differ from each other in species, and they both require their instruments, it is necessary that these should be different from each other. Now life is itself what we use, and not what we employ as the efficient of something else; for which reason the services of a slave are for use. A possession may be considered in the same nature as a part of anything; now a part is not only a part of something, but also is nothing else; so is a possession; therefore a master is only the master of the slave, but no part of him; but the slave is not only the slave of the master, but nothing else but that. This fully explains what is the nature of a slave, and what are his capacities; for that being who by nature is nothing of himself, but totally another's, and is a man, is a slave by nature; and that man who is the property of another, is his mere chattel, though he continues a man; but a chattel is an instrument for use, separate from the body.

Chapter V

But whether any person is such by nature, and whether it is advantageous and just for any one to be a slave or no, or whether all slavery is contrary to nature, shall be considered hereafter; not that it is difficult to determine it upon general principles, or to understand it from matters of fact; for that some should govern, and others be governed, is not only necessary but useful, and from the hour of their birth some are marked out for those purposes, and others for the other, and there are many species of both sorts. And the better those are who are governed the better also is the government, as for instance of man, rather than the brute creation: for the more excellent the materials are with which the work is finished, the more excellent certainly is the work; and wherever there is a governor and a governed, there certainly is some work produced; for whatsoever is composed of many parts, which jointly become one, whether conjunct or separate, evidently show the marks of governing and governed; and this is true of every living thing in all nature; nay, even in some things which partake not of life, as in music; but this probably would be a disquisition too foreign to our present purpose. Every living thing in the first place is composed of soul and body, of these the one is by nature the governor, the other the governed; now if we would know what is natural, we ought to search for it in those subjects in which nature appears most perfect, and not in those which are corrupted; we should therefore examine into a man who is most perfectly formed both in soul and body, in whom this is evident, for in the depraved and vicious the body seems to rule rather than the soul, on account of their being corrupt and contrary to nature. We may then, as we affirm, perceive in an animal the first principles of herile and political government; for the soul governs the body as the master governs his slave; the mind governs the appetite with a political or a kingly power, which shows that it is both natural and advantageous that the body should be governed by the soul, and the pathetic part by the mind, and that part which is possessed of reason; but to have no ruling power, or an improper one, is hurtful to all; and this holds true not only of man, but of other animals also, for tame animals are naturally better than wild ones, and it is advantageous that both should be under subjection to man; for this is productive of their common safety: so is it naturally with the male and the female; the one is superior, the other inferior; the one governs, the other is governed; and the same rule must necessarily hold good with respect to all mankind. Those men therefore who are as much inferior to others as the body is to the soul, are to be thus disposed of, as the proper use of them is their bodies, in which their excellence consists; and if what I have said be true, they are slaves by nature, and it is advantageous to them to be always under government. He then is by nature formed a slave who is qualified to become the chattel of another person, and on that account is so, and who has just reason enough to know that there is such a faculty, without being indued with the use of it; for other animals have no perception of reason, but are entirely guided by appetite, and indeed they vary very little in their use from each other; for the advantage which we receive, both from slaves and tame animals, arises from their bodily strength administering to our necessities; for it is the intention of nature to make the bodies of slaves and freemen different from each other, that the one should be robust for their necessary purposes, the others erect, useless indeed for what slaves are employed in, but fit for civil life, which is divided into the duties of war and peace; though these rules do not always take place, for slaves have sometimes the bodies of freemen, sometimes the souls; if then it is evident that if some bodies are as much more excellent than others as the statues of the gods excel the human form, every one will allow that the inferior ought to be slaves to the superior; and if this is true with respect to the body, it is still juster to determine in the same manner, when we consider the soul; though it is not so easy to perceive the beauty of the soul as it is of the body. Since then some men are slaves by nature, and others are freemen, it is clear that where slavery is advantageous to any one, then it is just to make him a slave.

Chapter VI

But it is not difficult to perceive that those who maintain the contrary opinion have some reason on their side; for a man may become a slave two different ways; for he may be so by law also, and this law is a certain compact, by which whatsoever is taken in battle is adjudged to be the property of the conquerors: but many persons who are conversant in law call in question this pretended right, and say that it would be hard that a man should be compelled by violence to be the slave and subject of another who had the power to compel him, and was his superior in strength; and upon this subject, even of those who are wise, some think one way and some another; but the cause of this doubt and variety of opinions arises from hence, that great abilities, when accompanied with proper means, are generally able to succeed by force: for victory is always owing to a superiority in some advantageous circumstances; so that it seems that force never prevails but in consequence of great abilities. But still the dispute concerning the justice of it remains; for some persons think, that justice consists in benevolence, others think it just that the powerful should govern: in the midst of these contrary opinions, there are no reasons sufficient to convince us, that the right of being master and governor ought not to be placed with those who have the greatest abilities. Some persons, entirely resting upon the right which the law gives (for that which is legal is in some respects just), insist upon it that slavery occasioned by war is just, not that they say it is wholly so, for it may happen that the principle upon which the wars were commenced is unjust; moreover no one will say that a man who is unworthily in slavery is therefore a slave; for if so, men of the noblest families might happen to be slaves, and the descendants of slaves, if they should chance to be taken prisoners in war and sold: to avoid this difficulty they say that such persons should not be called slaves, but barbarians only should; but when they say this, they do nothing more than inquire who is a slave by nature, which was what we at first said; for we must acknowledge that there are some persons who, wherever they are, must necessarily be slaves, but others in no situation; thus also it is with those of noble descent: it is not only in their own country that they are Esteemed as such, but everywhere, but the barbarians are respected on this account at home only; as if nobility and freedom were of two sorts, the one universal, the other not so. Thus says the Helen of Theodectes:

> "Who dares reproach me with the name of slave? When from the immortal gods, on either side, I draw my lineage."

Those who express sentiments like these, shew only that they distinguish the slave and the freeman, the noble and the ignoble from each other by their virtues and their vices; for they think it reasonable, that as a man begets a man, and a beast a beast, so from a good man, a good man should be descended; and this is what nature desires to do, but frequently cannot accomplish it. It is evident then that this doubt has some reason in it, and that these persons are not slaves, and those freemen, by the appointment of nature; and also that in some instances it is sufficiently clear, that it is advantageous to both parties for this man to be a slave, and that to be a master, and that it is right and just, that some should be governed, and others govern, in the manner that nature intended; of which sort of government is that which a master exercises over a slave. But to govern ill is disadvantageous to both; for the same thing is useful to the part and to the whole, to the body and to the soul; but the slave is as it were a part of the master, as if he were an animated part of his body, though separate. For which reason a mutual utility and friendship may subsist between the master and the slave, I mean when they are placed by nature in that relation to each other, for the contrary takes place amongst those who are reduced to slavery by the law, or by conquest.

Chapter VII

It is evident from what has been said, that a herile and a political government are not the same, or that all governments are alike to each other, as some affirm; for one is adapted to the nature of freemen, the other to that of slaves. Domestic government is a monarchy, for that is what prevails in every house; but a political state is the government of free men and equals. The master is not so called from his knowing how to manage his slave, but because he is so; for the same reason a slave and a freeman have their respective appellations. There is also one sort of knowledge proper for a master, another for a slave; the slave's is of the nature of that which was taught by a slave at Syracuse; for he for a stipulated sum instructed the boys in all the business of a household slave, of which there are various sorts to be learnt, as the art of cookery, and other such-like services, of which some are allotted to some, and others to others; some employments being more honourable, others more necessary; according to the proverb, "One slave excels another, one master excels another:" in such-like things the knowledge of a slave consists. The knowledge of the master is to be able properly to employ his slaves, for the mastership of slaves is the employment, not the mere possession of them; not that this knowledge contains anything great or respectable; for what a slave ought to know how to do, that a master ought to know how to order; for which reason, those who have it in their power to be free from these low attentions, employ a steward for this business, and apply themselves either to public affairs or philosophy: the knowledge of procuring what is necessary for a family is different from that which belongs either to the master or the slave: and to do this justly must be either by war or hunting. And thus much of the difference between a master and a slave.

Chapter VIII

As a slave is a particular species of property, let us by all means inquire into the nature of property in general, and the acquisition of money, according to the manner we have proposed. In the first place then, some one may doubt whether the getting of money is the same thing as economy, or whether it is a part of it, or something subservient to it; and if so, whether it is as the art of making shuttles is to the art of weaving, or the art of making brass to that of statue founding, for they are not of the same service; for the one supplies the tools, the other the matter: by the matter I mean the subject out of which the work is finished, as wool for the cloth and brass for the statue. It is evident then that the getting of money is not the same thing as economy, for the business of the one is to furnish the means of the other to use them; and what art is there employed in the management of a family but economy, but whether this is a part of it, or something of a different species, is a doubt; for if it is the business of him who is to get money to find out how riches and possessions may be procured, and both these arise from various causes, we must first inquire whether the art of husbandry is part of money-getting or something different, and in general, whether the same is not true of every acquisition and every attention which relates to provision. But as there are many sorts of provision, so are the methods of living both of man and the brute creation very various; and as it is impossible to live without food, the difference in that particular makes the lives of animals so different from each other. Of beasts, some live in herds, others separate, as is most convenient for procuring themselves food; as some of them live upon flesh, others on fruit, and others on whatsoever they light on, nature having so distinguished their course of life, that they can very easily procure themselves subsistence; and as the same things are not agreeable to all, but one animal likes one thing and another another, it follows that the lives of those beasts who live upon flesh must be different from the lives of those who live on fruits; so is it with men, their lives differ greatly from each other; and of all these the shepherd's is the idlest, for they live upon the flesh of tame animals, without any trouble, while they are obliged to change their habitations on account of their flocks, which they are compelled to follow, cultivating, as it were, a living farm. Others live exercising violence over living creatures, one pursuing this thing, another that, these preying upon men; those who live near lakes and marshes and rivers, or the sea itself, on fishing, while others are fowlers, or hunters of wild beasts; but the greater part of mankind live upon the produce of the earth and its cultivated fruits; and the manner in which all those live who follow the direction of nature, and labour for their own subsistence, is nearly the same, without ever thinking to procure any provision by way of exchange or merchandise, such are shepherds, husband-men, robbers, fishermen, and hunters: some join different employments together, and thus live very agreeably; supplying those deficiencies which were wanting to make their subsistence depend upon themselves only: thus, for instance, the same person shall be a shepherd and a robber, or a husbandman and a hunter; and so with respect to the rest, they pursue that mode of life which necessity points out. This provision then nature herself seems to have furnished all animals with, as well immediately upon their first origin as also when they are arrived at a state of maturity; for at the first of these periods some of them are provided in the womb with proper nourishment, which continues till that which is born can get food for itself, as is the case with worms and birds; and as to those which bring forth their young alive, they have the means for their subsistence for a certain time within themselves, namely milk. It is evident then that we may conclude of those things that are, that plants are created for the sake of animals, and animals for the sake of men; the tame for our use and provision; the wild, at least the greater part, for our provision also, or for some other advantageous purpose, as furnishing us with clothes, and the like. As nature therefore makes nothing either imperfect or in vain, it necessarily follows that she has made all these things for men: for which reason what we gain in war is in a certain degree a natural acquisition; for hunting is a part of it, which it is necessary for us to employ against wild beasts; and those men who being intended by nature for slavery are unwilling to submit to it, on which occasion such a. war is by nature just: that species of acquisition then only which is according to nature is part of economy; and this ought to be at hand, or if not, immediately procured, namely, what is necessary to be kept in store to live upon, and which are useful as well for the state as the family. And true riches seem to consist in these; and the acquisition of those possessions which are necessary for a happy life is not infinite; though Solon says otherwise in this verse:

> "No bounds to riches can be fixed for man;"

for they may be fixed as in other arts; for the instruments of no art whatsoever are infinite, either in their number or their magnitude; but riches are a number of instruments in domestic and civil economy; it is therefore evident that the acquisition of certain things according to nature is a part both of domestic and civil economy, and for what reason.

Chapter IX

There is also another species of acquisition which they particularly call pecuniary, and with great propriety; and by this indeed it seems that there are no bounds to riches and wealth. Now many persons suppose, from their near relation to each other, that this is one and the same with that we have just mentioned, but it is not the same as that, though not very different; one of these is natural, the other is not, but rather owing to some art and skill; we will enter into a particular examination of this subject. The uses of every possession are two, both dependent upon the thing itself, but not in the same manner, the one supposing an inseparable connection with it, the other not; as a shoe, for instance, which may be either worn, or exchanged for something else, both these are the uses of the shoe; for he who exchanges a shoe with some man who wants one, for money or provisions, uses the shoe as a shoe, but not according to the original intention, for shoes were not at first made to be exchanged. The same thing holds true of all other possessions; for barter, in general, had its original beginning in nature, some men having a surplus, others too little of what was necessary for them: hence it is evident, that the selling provisions for money is not according to the natural use of things; for they were obliged to use barter for those things which they wanted; but it is plain that barter could have no place in the first, that is to say, in family society; but must have begun when the number of those who composed the community was enlarged: for the first of these had all things in common; but when they came to be separated they were obliged to exchange with each other many different things which both parties wanted. Which custom of barter is still preserved amongst many barbarous nations, who procure one necessary with another, but never sell anything; as giving and receiving wine for corn and the like. This sort of barter is not contradictory to nature, nor is it any species of money-getting; but is necessary in procuring that subsistence which is so consonant thereunto. But this barter introduced the use of money, as might be expected; for a convenient place from whence to import what you wanted, or to export what you had a surplus of, being often at a great distance, money necessarily made its way into commerce; for it is not everything which is naturally most useful that is easiest of carriage; for which reason they invented something to exchange with each other which they should mutually give and take, that being really valuable itself, should have the additional advantage of being of easy conveyance, for the purposes of life, as iron and silver, or anything else of the same nature: and this at first passed in value simply according to its weight or size; but in process of time it had a certain stamp, to save the trouble of weighing, which stamp expressed its value.

Money then being established as the necessary medium of exchange, another species of money-getting soon took place, namely, by buying and selling, at probably first in a simple manner, afterwards with more skill and experience, where and how the greatest profits might be made. For which reason the art of money-getting seems to be chiefly conversant about trade, and the business of it to be able to tell where the greatest profits can be made, being the means of procuring abundance of wealth and possessions: and thus wealth is very often supposed to consist in the quantity of money which any one possesses, as this is the medium by which all trade is conducted and a fortune made, others again regard it as of no value, as being of none by nature, but arbitrarily made so by compact; so that if those who use it should alter their sentiments, it would be worth nothing, as being of no service for any necessary purpose. Besides, he who abounds in money often wants necessary food; and it is impossible to say that any person is in good circumstances when with all his possessions he may perish with hunger.

Like Midas in the fable, who from his insatiable wish had everything he touched turned into gold. For which reason others endeavour to procure other riches and other property, and rightly, for there are other riches and property in nature; and these are the proper objects of economy: while trade only procures money, not by all means, but by the exchange of it, and for that purpose it is this which it is chiefly employed about, for money is the first principle and the end of trade; nor are there any bounds to be set to what is thereby acquired. Thus also there are no limits to the art of medicine, with respect to the health which it attempts to procure; the same also is true of all other arts; no line can be drawn to terminate their bounds, the several professors of them being desirous to extend them as far as possible. (But still the means to be employed for that purpose are limited; and these are the limits beyond which the art cannot proceed.) Thus in the art of acquiring riches there are no limits, for the object of that is money and possessions; but economy has a boundary, though this has not: for acquiring riches is not the business of that, for which reason it should seem that some boundary should be set to riches, though we see the contrary to this is what is practised; for all those who get riches add to their money without end; the cause of which is the near connection of these two arts with each other, which sometimes occasions the one to change employments with the other, as getting of money is their common object: for economy requires the possession of wealth, but not on its own account but with another view, to purchase things necessary therewith; but the other procures it merely to increase it: so that some persons are confirmed in their belief, that this is the proper object of economy, and think that for this purpose money should be saved and hoarded up without end; the reason for which disposition is, that they are intent upon living, but not upon living well; and this desire being boundless in its extent, the means which they aim at for that purpose are boundless also; and those who propose to live well, often confine that to the enjoyment of the pleasures of sense; so that as this also seems to depend upon what a man has, all their care is to get money, and hence arises the other cause for this art; for as this enjoyment is excessive in its degree, they endeavour to procure means proportionate to supply it; and if they cannot do this merely by the art of dealing in money, they will endeavour to do it by other ways, and apply all their powers to a purpose they were not by nature intended for. Thus, for instance, courage was intended to inspire fortitude, not to get money by; neither is this the end of the soldier's or the physician's art, but victory and health.

But such persons make everything subservient to money-getting, as if this was the only end; and to the end everything ought to refer.

We have now considered that art of money-getting which is not necessary, and have seen in what manner we became in want of it; and also that which is necessary, which is different from it; for that economy which is natural, and whose object is to provide food, is not like this unlimited in its extent, but has its bounds.

Chapter X

We have now determined what was before doubtful, whether or no the art of getting money is his business who is at the head of a family or a state, and though not strictly so, it is however very necessary; for as a politician does not make men, but receiving them from the hand of nature employs them to proper purposes; thus the earth, or the sea, or something else ought to supply them with provisions, and this it is the business of the master of the family to manage properly; for it is not the weaver's business to make yarn, but to use it, and to distinguish what is good and useful from what is bad and of no service; and indeed some one may inquire why getting money should be a part of economy when the art of healing is not, as it is as requisite that the family should be in health as that they should eat, or have anything else which is necessary; and as it is indeed in some particulars the business both of the master of the family, and he to whom the government of the state is entrusted, to see after the health of those under their care, but in others not, but the physician's; so also as to money; in some respects it is the business of the master of the family, in others not, but of the servant; but as we have already said, it is chiefly nature's, for it is her part to supply her offspring with food; for everything finds nourishment left for it in what produced it; for which reason the natural riches of all men arise from fruits and animals. Now money-making, as we say, being twofold, it may be applied to two purposes, the service of the house or retail trade; of which the first is necessary and commendable, the other justly censurable; for it has not its origin in nature, but by it men gain from each other; for usury is most reasonably detested, as it is increasing our fortune by money itself, and not employing it for the purpose it was originally intended, namely exchange.

And this is the explanation of the name (TOKOS), which means the breeding of money. For as offspring resemble their parents, so usury is money bred of money. Whence of all forms of money-making it is most against nature.

Chapter XI

Having already sufficiently considered the general principles of this subject, let us now go into the practical part thereof; the one is a liberal employment for the mind, the other necessary. These things are useful in the management of one's affairs; to be skilful in the nature of cattle, which are most profitable, and where, and how; as for instance, what advantage will arise from keeping horses, or oxen, or sheep, or any other live stock; it is also necessary to be acquainted with the comparative value of these things, and which of them in particular places are worth most; for some do better in one place, some in another. Agriculture also should be understood, and the management of arable grounds and orchards; and also the care of bees, and fish, and birds, from whence any profit may arise; these are the first and most proper parts of domestic management.

With respect to gaining money by exchange, the principal method of doing this is by merchandise, which is carried on in three different ways, either by sending the commodity for sale by sea or by land, or else selling it on the place where it grows; and these differ from each other in this, that the one is more profitable, the other safer. The second method is by usury. The third by receiving wages for work done, and this either by being employed in some mean art, or else in mere bodily labour. There is also a third species of improving a fortune, that is something between this and the first; for it partly depends upon nature, partly upon exchange; the subject of which is, things that are immediately from the earth, or their produce, which, though they bear no fruit, are yet useful, such as selling of timber and the whole art of metallurgy, which includes many different species, for there are various sorts of things dug out of the earth.

These we have now mentioned in general, but to enter into particulars concerning each of them, though it might be useful to the artist, would be tiresome to dwell on. Now of all the works of art, those are the most excellent wherein chance has the least to do, and those are the meanest which deprave the body, those the most servile in which bodily strength alone is chiefly wanted, those most illiberal which require least skill; but as there are books written on these subjects by some persons, as by Chares the Panian, and Apollodorus the Lemnian, upon husbandry and planting; and by others on other matters, let those who have occasion consult them thereon; besides, every person should collect together whatsoever he hears occasionally mentioned, by means of which many of those who aimed at making a fortune have succeeded in their intentions; for all these are useful to those who make a point of getting money, as in the contrivance of Thales the Milesian (which was certainly a gainful one, but as it was his it was attributed to his wisdom, though the method he used was a general one, and would universally succeed), when they reviled him for his poverty, as if the study of philosophy was useless: for they say that he, perceiving by his skill in astrology that there would be great plenty of olives that year, while it was yet winter, having got a little money, he gave earnest for all the oil works that were in Miletus and Chios, which he hired at a low price, there being no one to bid against him; but when the season came for making oil, many persons wanting them, he all at once let them upon what terms he pleased; and raising a large sum of money by that means, convinced them that it was easy for philosophers to be rich if they chose it, but that that was not what they aimed at; in this manner is Thales said to have shown his wisdom. It indeed is, as we have said, generally gainful for a person to contrive to make a monopoly of anything; for which reason some cities also take this method when they want money, and monopolise their commodities. There was a certain person in Sicily who laid out a sum of money which was deposited in his hand in buying up all the iron from the iron merchants; so that when the dealers came from the markets to purchase, there was no one had any to sell but himself; and though he put no great advance upon it, yet by laying out fifty talents he made an hundred. When Dionysius heard this he permitted him to take his money with him, but forbid him to continue any longer in Sicily, as being one who contrived means for getting money inconsistent with his affairs. This man's view and Thales's was exactly the same; both of them contrived to procure a monopoly for themselves: it is useful also for politicians to understand these things, for many states want to raise money and by such means, as well as private families, nay more so; for which reason some persons who are employed in the management of public affairs confine themselves to this province only.

Chapter XII

There are then three parts of domestic government, the masters, of which we have already treated, the fathers, and the husbands; now the government of the wife and children should both be that of free persons, but not the same; for the wife should be treated as a citizen of a free state, the children should be under kingly power; for the male is by nature superior to the female, except when something happens contrary to the usual course of nature, as is the elder and perfect to the younger and imperfect. Now in the generality of free states, the governors and the governed alternately change place; for an equality without any preference is what nature chooses; however, when one governs and another is governed, she endeavours that there should be a distinction between them in forms, expressions, and honours; according to what Amasis said of his laver. This then should be the established rule between the man and the woman. The government of children should be kingly; for the power of the father over the child is founded in affection and seniority, which is a species of kingly government; for which reason Homer very properly calls Jupiter "the father of gods and men," who was king of both these; for nature requires that a king should be of the same species with those whom he governs, though superior in some particulars, as is the case between the elder and the younger, the father and the son.

Chapter XIII

It is evident then that in the due government of a family, greater attention should be paid to the several members of it and their virtues than to the possessions or riches of it; and greater to the freemen than the slaves: but here some one may doubt whether there is any other virtue in a slave than his organic services, and of higher estimation than these, as temperance, fortitude, justice, and such-like habits, or whether they possess only bodily qualities: each side of the question has its difficulties; for if they possess these virtues, wherein do they differ from freemen? and that they do not, since they are men, and partakers of reason, is absurd. Nearly the same inquiry may be made concerning a woman and a child, whether these also have their proper virtues; whether a woman ought to be temperate, brave, and just, and whether a child is temperate or no; and indeed this inquiry ought to be general, whether the virtues of those who, by nature, either govern or are governed, are the same or different; for if it is necessary that both of them should partake of the fair and good, why is it also necessary that, without exception, the one should govern, the other always be governed? for this cannot arise from their possessing these qualities in different degrees; for to govern, and to be governed, are things different in species, but more or less are not. And yet it is wonderful that one party ought to have them, and the other not; for if he who is to govern should not be temperate and just, how can he govern well? or if he is to be governed, how can he be governed well? for he who is intemperate and a coward will never do what he ought: it is evident then that both parties ought to be virtuous; but there is a difference between them, as there is between those who by nature command and who by nature obey, and this originates in the soul; for in this nature has planted the governing and submitting principle, the virtues of which we say are different, as are those of a rational and an irrational being. It is plain then that the same principle may be extended farther, and that there are in nature a variety of things which govern and are governed; for a freeman is governed in a different manner from a slave, a male from a female, and a man from a child: and all these have parts of mind within them, but in a different manner. Thus a slave can have no power of determination, a woman but a weak one, a child an imperfect one. Thus also must it necessarily be with respect to moral virtues; all must be supposed to possess them, but not in the same manner, but as is best suited to every one's employment; on which account he who is to govern ought to be perfect in moral virtue, for his business is entirely that of an architect, and reason is the architect; while others want only that portion of it which may be sufficient for their station; from whence it is evident, that although moral virtue is common to all those we have spoken of, yet the temperance of a man and a woman are not the same, nor their courage, nor their justice, though Socrates thought otherwise; for the courage of the man consists in commanding, the woman's in obeying; and the same is true in other particulars: and this will be evident to those who will examine different virtues separately; for those who use general terms deceive themselves when they say, that virtue consists in a good disposition of mind, or doing what is right, or something of this sort. They do much better who enumerate the different virtues as Georgias did, than those who thus define them; and as Sophocles speaks of a woman, we think of all persons, that their 'virtues should be applicable to their characters, for says he,

"Silence is a woman's ornament,"

but it is not a man's; and as a child is incomplete, it is evident that his virtue is not to be referred to himself in his present situation, but to that in which he will be complete, and his preceptor. In like manner the virtue of a slave is to be referred to his master; for we laid it down as a maxim, that the use of a slave was to employ him in what you wanted; so that it is clear enough that few virtues are wanted in his station, only that he may not neglect his work through idleness or fear: some person may question if what I have said is true, whether virtue is not necessary for artificers in their calling, for they often through idleness neglect their work, but the difference between them is very great; for a slave is connected with you for life, but the artificer not so nearly: as near therefore as the artificer approaches to the situation of a slave, just so much ought he to have of the virtues of one; for a mean artificer is to a certain point a slave; but then a slave is one of those things which are by nature what they are, but this is not true of a shoemaker, or any other artist. It is evident then that a slave ought to be trained to those virtues which are proper for his situation by his master; and not by him who has the power of a master, to teach him any particular art. Those therefore are in the wrong who would deprive slaves of reason, and say that they have only to follow their orders; for slaves want more instruction than children, and thus we determine this matter. It is necessary, I am sensible, for every one who treats upon government, to enter particularly into the relations of husband and wife, and of parent and child, and to show what are the virtues of each and their respective connections with each other; what is right and what is wrong; and how the one ought to be followed, and the other avoided. Since then every family is part of a city, and each of those individuals is part of a family, and the virtue of the parts ought to correspond to the virtue of the whole; it is necessary, that both the wives and children of the community should be instructed correspondent to the nature thereof, if it is of consequence to the virtue of the state, that the wives and children therein should be virtuous, and of consequence it certainly is, for the wives are one half of the free persons; and of the children the succeeding citizens are to be formed. As then we have determined these points, we will leave the rest to be spoken to in another place, as if the subject was now finished; and beginning again anew, first consider the sentiments of those who have treated of the most perfect forms of government.

Book II

Chapter I

Since then we propose to inquire what civil society is of all others best for those who have it in their power to live entirely as they wish, it is necessary to examine into the polity of those states which are allowed to be well governed; and if there should be any others which some persons have described, and which appear properly regulated, to note what is right and useful in them; and when we point out wherein they have failed, let not this be imputed to an affectation of wisdom, for it is because there are great defects in all those which are already established, that I have been induced to undertake this work. We will begin with that part of the subject which naturally presents itself first to our consideration. The members of every state must of necessity have all things in common, or some things common, and not others, or nothing at all common. To have nothing in common is evidently impossible, for society itself is one species of community; and the first thing necessary thereunto is a common place of habitation, namely the city, which must be one, and this every citizen must have a share in. But in a government which is to be well founded, will it be best to admit of a community in everything which is capable thereof, or only in some particulars, but in others not? for it is possible that the citizens may have their wives, and children, and goods in common, as in Plato's Commonwealth; for in that Socrates affirms that all these particulars ought to be so. Which then shall we prefer? the custom which is already established, or the laws which are proposed in that treatise?

Chapter II

Now as a community of wives is attended with many other difficulties, so neither does the cause for which he would frame his government in this manner seem agreeable to reason, nor is it capable of producing that end which he has proposed, and for which he says it ought to take place; nor has he given any particular directions for putting it in practice. Now I also am willing to agree with Socrates in the principle which he proceeds upon, and admit that the city ought to be one as much as possible; and yet it is evident that if it is contracted too much, it will be no longer a city, for that necessarily supposes a multitude; so that if we proceed in this manner, we shall reduce a city to a family, and a family to a single person: for we admit that a family is one in a greater degree than a city, and a single person than a family; so that if this end could be obtained, it should never be put in practice, as it would annihilate the city; for a city does not only consist of a large number of inhabitants, but there must also be different sorts; for were they all alike, there could be no city; for a confederacy and a city are two different things; for a confederacy is valuable from its numbers, although all those who compose it are men of the same calling; for this is entered into for the sake of mutual defence, as we add an additional weight to make the scale go down. The same distinction prevails between a city and a nation when the people are not collected into separate villages, but live as the Arcadians. Now those things in which a city should be one are of different sorts, and in preserving an alternate reciprocation of power between these, the safety thereof consists (as I have already mentioned in my treatise on Morals), for amongst freemen and equals this is absolutely necessary; for all cannot govern at the same time, but either by the year, or according to some other regulation or time, by which means every one in his turn will be in office; as if the shoemakers and carpenters should exchange occupations, and not always be employed in the same calling. But as it is evidently better, that these should continue to exercise their respective trades; so also in civil society, where it is possible, it would be better that the government should continue in the same hands; but where it is not (as nature has made all men equal, and therefore it is just, be the administration good or bad, that all should partake of it), there it is best to observe a rotation, and let those who are their equals by turns submit to those who are at that time magistrates, as they will, in their turns, alternately be governors and governed, as if they were different men: by the same method different persons will execute different offices. From hence it is evident, that a city cannot be one in the manner that some persons propose; and that what has been said to be the greatest good which it could enjoy, is absolutely its destruction, which cannot be: for the good of anything is that which preserves it. For another reason also it is clear, that it is not for the best to endeavour to make a city too much one, because a family is more sufficient in itself than a single person, a city than a family; and indeed Plato supposes that a city owes its existence to that sufficiency in themselves which the members of it enjoy. If then this sufficiency is so desirable, the less the city is one the better.

Chapter III

But admitting that it is most advantageous for a city to be one as much as possible, it does not seem to follow that this will take place by permitting all at once to say this is mine, and this is not mine (though this is what Socrates regards as a proof that a city is entirely one), for the word All is used in two senses; if it means each individual, what Socrates proposes will nearly take place; for each person will say, this is his own son, and his own wife, and his own property, and of everything else that may happen to belong to him, that it is his own. But those who have their wives and children in common will not say so, but all will say so, though not as individuals; therefore, to use the word all is evidently a fallacious mode of speech; for this word is sometimes used distributively, and sometimes collectively, on account of its double meaning, and is the cause of inconclusive syllogisms in reasoning. Therefore for all persons to say the same thing was their own, using the word all in its distributive sense, would be well, but is impossible: in its collective sense it would by no means contribute to the concord of the state. Besides, there would be another inconvenience attending this proposal, for what is common to many is taken least care of; for all men regard more what is their own than what others share with them in, to which they pay less attention than is incumbent on every one: let me add also, that every one is more negligent of what another is to see to, as well as himself, than of his own private business; as in a family one is often worse served by many servants than by a few. Let each citizen then in the state have a thousand children, but let none of them be considered as the children of that individual, but let the relation of father and child be common to them all, and they will all be neglected. Besides, in consequence of this, whenever any citizen behaved well or ill, every person, be the number what it would, might say, this is my son, or this man's or that; and in this manner would they speak, and thus would they doubt of the whole thousand, or of whatever number the city consisted; and it would be uncertain to whom each child belonged, and when it was born, who was to take care of it: and which do you think is better, for every one to say this is mine, while they may apply it equally to two thousand or ten thousand; or as we say, this is mine in our present forms of government, where one man calls another his son, another calls that same person his brother, another nephew, or some other relation, either by blood or marriage, and first extends his care to him and his, while another regards him as one of the same parish and the same tribe; and it is better for any one to be a nephew in his private capacity than a son after that manner. Besides, it will be impossible to prevent some persons from suspecting that they are brothers and sisters, fathers and mothers to each other; for, from the mutual likeness there is between the sire and the offspring, they will necessarily conclude in what relation they stand to each other, which circumstance, we are informed by those writers who describe different parts of the world, does sometimes happen; for in Upper Africa there are wives in common who yet deliver their children to their respective fathers, being guided by their likeness to them. There are also some mares and cows which naturally bring forth their young so like the male, that we can easily distinguish by which of them they were impregnated: such was the mare called Just, in Pharsalia.

Chapter IV

Besides, those who contrive this plan of community cannot easily avoid the following evils; namely, blows, murders involuntary or voluntary, quarrels, and reproaches, all which it would be impious indeed to be guilty of towards our fathers and mothers, or those who are nearly related to us; though not to those who are not connected to us by any tie of affinity: and certainly these mischiefs must necessarily happen oftener amongst those who do not know how they are connected to each other than those who do; and when they do happen, if it is among the first of these, they admit of a legal expiation, but amongst the latter that cannot be done. It is also absurd for those who promote a community of children to forbid those who love each other from indulging themselves in the last excesses of that passion, while they do not restrain them from the passion itself, or those intercourses which are of all things most improper, between a Father and a son, a brother and a brother, and indeed the thing itself is most absurd. It is also ridiculous to prevent this intercourse between the nearest relations, for no other reason than the violence of the pleasure, while they think that the relation of father and daughter, the brother and sister, is of no consequence at all. It seems also more advantageous for the state, that the husbandmen should have their wives and children in common than the military, for there will be less affection among them in that case than when otherwise; for such persons ought to be under subjection, that they may obey the laws, and not seek after innovations. Upon the whole, the consequences of such a law as this would be directly contrary to those things which good laws ought to establish, and which Socrates endeavoured to establish by his regulations concerning women and children: for we think that friendship is the greatest good which can happen to any city, as nothing so much prevents seditions: and amity in a city is what Socrates commends above all things, which appears to be, as indeed he says, the effect of friendship; as we learn from Aristophanes in the Erotics, who says, that those who love one another from the excess of that passion, desire to breathe the same soul, and from being two to be blended into one: from whence it would necessarily follow, that both or one of them must be destroyed. But now in a city which admits of this community, the tie of friendship must, from that very cause, be extremely weak, when no father can say, this is my son; or son, this is my father; for as a very little of what is sweet, being mixed with a great deal of water is imperceptible after the mixture, so must all family connections, and the names they go by, be necessarily disregarded in such a community, it being then by no means necessary that the father should have any regard for him he called a son, or the brothers for those they call brothers. There are two things which principally inspire mankind with care and love of their offspring, knowing it is their own, and what ought to be the object of their affection, neither of which can take place in this sort of community. As for exchanging the children of the artificers and husbandmen with those of the military, and theirs reciprocally with these, it will occasion great confusion in whatever manner it shall be done; for of necessity, those who carry the children must know from whom they took and to whom they gave them; and by this means those evils which I have already mentioned will necessarily be the more likely to happen, as blows, incestuous love, murders, and the like; for those who are given from their own parents to other citizens, the military, for instance, will not call them brothers, sons, fathers, or mothers. The same thing would happen to those of the military who were placed among the other citizens; so that by this means every one would be in fear how to act in consequence of consanguinity. And thus let us determine concerning a community of wives and children.

Chapter V

We proceed next to consider in what manner property should be regulated in a state which is formed after the most perfect mode of government, whether it should be common or not; for this may be considered as a separate question from what had been determined concerning wives and children; I mean, whether it is better that these should be held separate, as they now everywhere are, or that not only possessions but also the usufruct of them should be in common; or that the soil should have a particular owner, but that the produce should be brought together and used as one common stock, as some nations at present do; or on the contrary, should the soil be common, and should it also be cultivated in common, while the produce is divided amongst the individuals for their particular use, which is said to be practised by some barbarians; or shall both the soil and the fruit be common? When the business of the husbandman devolves not on the citizen, the matter is much easier settled; but when those labour together who have a common right of possession, this may occasion several difficulties; for there may not be an equal proportion between their labour and what they consume; and those who labour hard and have but a small proportion of the produce, will certainly complain of those who take a large share of it and do but little for that. Upon the whole, as a community between man and man so entire as to include everything possible, and thus to have all things that man can possess in common, is very difficult, so is it particularly so with respect to property; and this is evident from that community which takes place between those who go out to settle a colony; for they frequently have disputes with each other upon the most common occasions, and come to blows upon trifles: we find, too, that we oftenest correct those slaves who are generally employed in the common offices of the family: a community of property then has these and other inconveniences attending it.

But the manner of life which is now established, more particularly when embellished with good morals and a system of equal laws, is far superior to it, for it will have the advantage of both; by both I mean properties being common, and divided also; for in some respects it ought to be in a manner common, but upon the whole private: for every man's attention being employed on his own particular concerns, will prevent mutual complaints against each other; nay, by this means industry will be increased, as each person will labour to improve his own private property; and it will then be, that from a principle of virtue they will mutually perform good offices to each other, according to the proverb, "All things are common amongst friends;" and in some cities there are traces of this custom to be seen, so that it is not impracticable, and particularly in those which are best governed; some things are by this means in a manner common, and others might be so; for there, every person enjoying his own private property, some things he assists his friend with, others are considered as in common; as in Lacedaemon, where they use each other's slaves, as if they were, so to speak, their own, as they do their horses and dogs, or even any provision they may want in a journey.

It is evident then that it is best to have property private, but to make the use of it common; but how the citizens are to be brought to it is the particular business of the legislator. And also with respect to pleasure, it is unspeakable how advantageous it is, that a man should think he has something which he may call his own; for it is by no means to no purpose, that each person should have an affection for himself, for that is natural, and yet to be a self-lover is justly censured; for we mean by that, not one that simply loves himself, but one that loves himself more than he ought; in like manner we blame a money-lover, and yet both money and self is what all men love. Besides, it is very pleasing to us to oblige and assist our friends and companions, as well as those whom we are connected with by the rights of hospitality; and this cannot be done without the establishment of private property, which cannot take place with those who make a city too much one; besides, they prevent every opportunity of exercising two principal virtues, modesty and liberality. Modesty with respect to the female sex, for this virtue requires you to abstain from her who is another's; liberality, which depends upon private property, for without that no one can appear liberal, or do any generous action; for liberality consists in imparting to others what is our own.

This system of polity does indeed recommend itself by its good appearance and specious pretences to humanity; and when first proposed to any one, must give him great pleasure, as he will conclude it to be a wonderful bond of friendship, connecting all to all; particularly when any one censures the evils which are now to be found in society, as arising from properties not being common, I mean the disputes which happen between man and man, upon their different contracts with each other; those judgments which are passed in court in consequence of fraud, and perjury, and flattering the rich, none of which arise from properties being private, but from the vices of mankind. Besides, those who live in one general community, and have all things in common, oftener dispute with each other than those who have their property separate; from the very small number indeed of those who have their property in common, compared with those where it is appropriated, the instances of their quarrels are but few. It is also but right to mention, not only the inconveniences they are preserved from who live in a communion of goods, but also the advantages they are deprived of; for when the whole comes to be considered, this manner of life will be found impracticable.

We must suppose, then, that Socrates's mistake arose from the principle he set out with being false; we admit, indeed, that both a family and a city ought to be one in some particulars, but not entirely; for there is a point beyond which if a city proceeds in reducing itself to one, it will be no longer a city.

There is also another point at which it will still continue to be a city, but it will approach so near to not being one, that it will be worse than none; as if any one should reduce the voices of those who sing in concert to one, or a verse to a foot. But the people ought to be made one, and a community, as I have already said, by education; as property at Lacedaemon, and their public tables at Crete, were made common by their legislators. But yet, whosoever shall introduce any education, and think thereby to make his city excellent and respectable, will be absurd, while he expects to form it by such regulations, and not by manners, philosophy, and laws. And whoever would establish a government upon a community of goods, ought to know that he should consult the experience of many years, which would plainly enough inform him whether such a scheme is useful; for almost all things have already been found out, but some have been neglected, and others which have been known have not been put in practice. But this would be most evident, if any one could see such a government really established: for it would be impossible to frame such a city without dividing and separating it into its distinct parts, as public tables, wards, and tribes; so that here the laws will do nothing more than forbid the military to engage in agriculture, which is what the Lacedaemonians are at present endeavouring to do.

Nor has Socrates told us (nor is it easy to say) what plan of government should be pursued with respect to the individuals in the state where there is a community of goods established; for though the majority of his citizens will in general consist of a multitude of persons of different occupations, of those he has determined nothing; whether the property of the husbandman ought to be in common, or whether each person should have his share to himself; and also, whether their wives and children ought to be in common: for if all things are to be alike common to all, where will be the difference between them and the military, or what would they get by submitting to their government? and upon what principles would they do it, unless they should establish the wise practice of the Cretans? for they, allowing everything else to their slaves, forbid them only gymnastic exercises and the use of arms. And if they are not, but these should be in the same situation with respect to their property which they are in other cities, what sort of a community will there be? in one city there must of necessity be two, and those contrary to each other; for he makes the military the guardians of the state, and the husbandman, artisans, and others, citizens; and all those quarrels, accusations, and things of the like sort, which he says are the bane of other cities, will be found in his also: notwithstanding Socrates says they will not want many laws in consequence of their education, but such only as may be necessary for regulating the streets, the markets, and the like, while at the same time it is the education of the military only that he has taken any care of. Besides, he makes the husbandmen masters of property upon paying a tribute; but this would be likely to make them far more troublesome and high-spirited than the Helots, the Penestise, or the slaves which others employ; nor has he ever determined whether it is necessary to give any attention to them in these particulars, nor thought of what is connected therewith, their polity, their education, their laws; besides, it is of no little consequence, nor is it easy to determine, how these should be framed so as to preserve the community of the military.

Besides, if he makes the wives common, while the property continues separate, who shall manage the domestic concerns with the same care which the man bestows upon his fields? nor will the inconvenience be remedied by making property as well as wives common; and it is absurd to draw a comparison from the brute creation, and say, that the same principle should regulate the connection of a man and a woman which regulates theirs amongst whom there is no family association.

It is also very hazardous to settle the magistracy as Socrates has done; for he would have persons of the same rank always in office, which becomes the cause of sedition even amongst those who are of no account, but more particularly amongst those who are of a courageous and warlike disposition; it is indeed evidently necessary that he should frame his community in this manner; for that golden particle which God has mixed up in the soul of man flies not from one to the other, but always continues with the same; for he says, that some of our species have gold, and others silver, blended in their composition from the moment of their birth: but those who are to be husbandmen and artists, brass and iron; besides, though he deprives the military of happiness, he says, that the legislator ought to make all the citizens happy; but it is impossible that the whole city can be happy, without all, or the greater, or some part of it be happy. For happiness is not like that numerical equality which arises from certain numbers when added together, although neither of them may separately contain it; for happiness cannot be thus added together, but must exist in every individual, as some properties belong to every integral; and if the military are not happy, who else are so? for the artisans are not, nor the multitude of those who are employed in inferior offices. The state which Socrates has described has all these defects, and others which are not of less consequence.

Chapter VI

It is also nearly the same in the treatise upon Laws which was writ afterwards, for which reason it will be proper in this place to consider briefly what he has there said upon government, for Socrates has thoroughly settled but very few parts of it; as for instance, in what manner the community of wives and children ought to be regulated, how property should be established, and government conducted.

Now he divides the inhabitants into two parts, husbandmen and soldiers, and from these he select a third part who are to be senators and govern the city; but he has not said whether or no the husbandman and artificer shall have any or what share in the government, or whether they shall have arms, and join with the others in war, or not. He thinks also that the women ought to go to war, and have the same education as the soldiers; as to other particulars, he has filled his treatise with matter foreign to the purpose; and with respect to education, he has only said what that of the guards ought to be.

As to his book of Laws, laws are the principal thing which that contains, for he has there said but little concerning government; and this government, which he was so desirous of framing in such a manner as to impart to its members a more entire community of goods than is to be found in other cities, he almost brings round again to be the same as that other government which he had first proposed; for except the community of wives and goods, he has framed both his governments alike, for the education of the citizens is to be the same in both; they are in both to live without any servile employ, and their common tables are to be the same, excepting that in that he says the women should have common tables, and that there should be a thousand men-at-arms, in this, that there should be five thousand.

All the discourses of Socrates are masterly, noble, new, and inquisitive; but that they are all true it may probably be too much to say. For now with respect to the number just spoken of, it must be acknowledged that he would want the country of Babylonia for them, or some one like it, of an immeasurable extent, to support five thousand idle persons, besides a much greater number of women and servants. Every one, it is true, may frame an hypothesis as he pleases, but yet it ought to be possible. It has been said, that a legislator should have two things in view when he frames his laws, the country and the people. He will also do well, if he has some regard to the neighbouring states, if he intends that his community should maintain any political intercourse with them, for it is not only necessary that they should understand that practice of war which is adapted to their own country, but to others also; for admitting that any one chooses not this life either in public or private, yet there is not the less occasion for their being formidable to their enemies, not only when they invade their country, but also when they retire out of it.

It may also be considered whether the quantity of each person's property may not be settled in a different manner from what he has done it in, by making it more determinate; for he says, that every one ought to have enough whereon to live moderately, as if any one had said to live well, which is the most comprehensive expression. Besides, a man may live moderately and miserably at the same time; he had therefore better have proposed, that they should live both moderately and liberally; for unless these two conspire, luxury will come in on the one hand, or wretchedness on the other, since these two modes of living are the only ones applicable to the employment of our substance; for we cannot say with respect to a man's fortune, that he is mild or courageous, but we may say that he is prudent and liberal, which are the only qualities connected therewith.

It is also absurd to render property equal, and not to provide for the increasing number of the citizens; but to leave that circumstance uncertain, as if it would regulate itself according to the number of women who should happen to be childless, let that be what it would because this seems to take place in other cities; but the case would not be the same in such a state which he proposes and those which now actually unite; for in these no one actually wants, as the property is divided amongst the whole community, be their numbers what they will; but as it could not then be divided, the supernumeraries, whether they were many or few, would have nothing at all. But it is more necessary than even to regulate property, to take care that the increase of the people should not exceed a certain number; and in determining that, to take into consideration those children who will die, and also those women who will be barren; and to neglect this, as is done in several cities, is to bring certain poverty on the citizens; and poverty is the cause of sedition and evil. Now Phidon the Corinthian, one of the oldest legislators, thought the families and the number of the citizens should continue the same; although it should happen that all should have allotments at the first, disproportionate to their numbers.

In Plato's Laws it is however different; we shall mention hereafter what we think would be best in these particulars. He has also neglected in that treatise to point out how the governors are to be distinguished from the governed; for he says, that as of one sort of wool the warp ought to be made, and of another the woof, so ought some to govern, and others to be governed. But since he admits, that all their property may be increased fivefold, why should he not allow the same increase to the country? he ought also to consider whether his allotment of the houses will be useful to the community, for he appoints two houses to each person, separate from each other; but it is inconvenient for a person to inhabit two houses. Now he is desirous to have his whole plan of government neither a democracy nor an oligarchy, but something between both, which he calls a polity, for it is to be composed of men-at-arms. If Plato intended to frame a state in which more than in any other everything should be common, he has certainly given it a right name; but if he intended it to be the next in perfection to that which he had already framed, it is not so; for perhaps some persons will give the preference to the Lacedaemonian form of government, or some other which may more completely have attained to the aristocratic form.

Some persons say, that the most perfect government should be composed of all others blended together, for which reason they commend that of Lacedaemon; for they say, that this is composed of an oligarchy, a monarchy, and a democracy, their kings representing the monarchical part, the senate the oligarchical; and, that in the ephori may be found the democratical, as these are taken from the people. But some say, that in the ephori is absolute power, and that it is their common meal and daily course of life, in which the democratical form is represented. It is also said in this treatise of Laws, that the best form of government must, be one composed of a democracy and a tyranny; though such a mixture no one else would ever allow to be any government at all, or if it is, the worst possible; those propose what is much better who blend many governments together; for the most perfect is that which is formed of many parts. But now in this government of Plato's there are no traces of a monarchy, only of an oligarchy and democracy; though he seems to choose that it should rather incline to an oligarchy, as is evident from the appointment of the magistrates; for to choose them by lot is common to both; but that a man of fortune must necessarily be a member of the assembly, or to elect the magistrates, or take part in the management of public affairs, while others are passed over, makes the state incline to an oligarchy; as does the endeavouring that the greater part of the rich may be in office, and that the rank of their appointments may correspond with their fortunes.

The same principle prevails also in the choice of their senate; the manner of electing which is favourable also to an oligarchy; for all are obliged to vote for those who are senators of the first class, afterwards they vote for the same number out of the second, and then out of the third; but this compulsion to vote at the election of senators does not extend to the third and fourth classes and the first and second class only are obliged to vote for the fourth. By this means he says he shall necessarily have an equal number of each rank, but he is mistaken-for the majority will always consist of those of the first rank, and the most considerable people; and for this reason, that many of the commonalty not being obliged to it, will not attend the elections. From hence it is evident, that such a state will not consist of a democracy and a monarchy, and this will be further proved by what we shall say when we come particularly to consider this form of government.

There will also great danger arise from the manner of electing the senate, when those who are elected themselves are afterwards to elect others; for by this means, if a certain number choose to combine together, though not very considerable, the election will always fall according to their pleasure. Such are the things which Plato proposes concerning government in his book of Laws.

Chapter VII

There are also some other forms of government, which have been proposed either by private persons, or philosophers, or politicians, all of which come much nearer to those which have been really established, or now exist, than these two of Plato's; for neither have they introduced the innovation of a community of wives and children, and public tables for the women, but have been contented to set out with establishing such rules as are absolutely necessary.

There are some persons who think, that the first object of government should be to regulate well everything relating to private property; for they say, that a neglect herein is the source of all seditions whatsoever. For this reason, Phaleas the Chalcedonian first proposed, that the fortunes of the citizens should be equal, which he thought was not difficult to accomplish when a community was first settled, but that it was a work of greater difficulty in one that had been long established; but yet that it might be effected, and an equality of circumstances introduced by these means, that the rich should give marriage portions, but never receive any, while the poor should always receive, but never give.

But Plato, in his treatise of Laws, thinks that a difference in circumstances should be permitted to a certain degree; but that no citizen should be allowed to possess more than five times as much as the lowest census, as we have already mentioned. But legislators who would establish this principle are apt to overlook what they ought to consider; that while they regulate the quantity of provisions which each individual shall possess, they ought also to regulate the number of his children; for if these exceed the allotted quantity of provision, the law must necessarily be repealed; and yet, in spite of the repeal, it will have the bad effect of reducing many from wealth to poverty, so difficult is it for innovators not to fall into such mistakes. That an equality of goods was in some degree serviceable to strengthen the bands of society, seems to have been known to some of the ancients; for Solon made a law, as did some others also, to restrain persons from possessing as much land as they pleased. And upon the same principle there are laws which forbid men to sell their property, as among the Locrians, unless they can prove that some notorious misfortune has befallen them. They were also to preserve their ancient patrimony, which custom being broken through by the Leucadians, made their government too democratic; for by that means it was no longer necessary to be possessed of a certain fortune to be qualified to be a magistrate. But if an equality of goods is established, this may be either too much, when it enables the people to live luxuriously, or too little, when it obliges them to live hard. Hence it is evident, that it is not proper for the legislator to establish an equality of circumstances, but to fix a proper medium. Besides, if any one should regulate the division of property in such a manner that there should be a moderate sufficiency for all, it would be of no use; for it is of more consequence that the citizen should entertain a similarity of sentiments than an equality of circumstances; but this can never be attained unless they are properly educated under the direction of the law. But probably Phaleas may say, that this in what he himself mentions; for he both proposes a equality of property and one plan of education in his city. But he should have said particularly what education he intended, nor is it of any service to have this to much one; for this education may be one, and yet such as will make the citizens over-greedy, to grasp after honours, or riches, or both. Besides, not only an inequality of possessions, but also of honours, will occasion seditions, but this upon contrary grounds; for the vulgar will be seditious if there be an inequality of goods, by those of more elevated sentiments, if there is an equality of honours.

"When good and bad do equal honours share."

For men are not guilty of crimes for necessaries only (for which he thinks an equality of goods would be a sufficient remedy, as they would then have no occasion to steal cold or hunger), but that they may enjoy what they desire, and not wish for it in vain; for if their desire extend beyond the common necessaries of life, they were be wicked to gratify them; and not only so, but if their wishes point that way, they will do the same to enjoy those pleasures which are free from the alloy of pain. What remedy then shall we find for these three disorders. And first, to prevent stealing from necessity, let every one be supplied with a moderate subsistence, which may make the addition of his own industry necessary; second to prevent stealing to procure the luxuries of life, temperance be enjoined; and thirdly, let those who wish for pleasure in itself seek for it only in philosophy, all others want the assistance of men.

Since then men are guilty of the greatest crimes from ambition, and not from necessity, no one, for instance aims at being a tyrant to keep him from the cold, hence great honour is due to him who kills not a thief, but tyrant; so that polity which Phaleas establishes would only be salutary to prevent little crimes. He has also been very desirous to establish such rules as will conduce to perfect the internal policy of his state, and he ought also to have done the same with respect to its neighbours and all foreign nations; for the considerations of the military establishment should take place in planning every government, that it may not be unprovided in case of a war, of which he has said nothing; so also with respect to property, it ought not only to be adapted to the exigencies of the state, but also to such dangers as may arise from without.

Thus it should not be so much as to tempt those who are near, and more powerful to invade it, while those who possess it are not able to drive out the invaders, nor so little as that the state should not be able to go to war with those who are quite equal to itself, and of this he has determined nothing; it must indeed be allowed that it is advantageous to a community to be rather rich than poor; probably the proper boundary is this, not to possess enough to make it worth while for a more powerful neighbour to attack you, any more than he would those who had not so much as yourself; thus when Autophradatus proposed to besiege Atarneus, Eubulus advised him to consider what time it would require to take the city, and then would have him determine whether it would answer, for that he should choose, if it would even take less than he proposed, to quit the place; his saying this made Autophradatus reflect upon the business and give over the siege. There is, indeed, some advantage in an equality of goods amongst the citizens to prevent seditions; and yet, to say truth, no very great one; for men of great abilities will stomach their being put upon a level with the rest of the community. For which reason they will very often appear ready for every commotion and sedition; for the wickedness of mankind is insatiable. For though at first two oboli might be sufficient, yet when once it is become customary, they continually want something more, until they set no limits to their expectations; for it is the nature of our desires to be boundless, and many live only to gratify them. But for this purpose the first object is, not so much to establish an equality of fortune, as to prevent those who are of a good disposition from desiring more than their own, and those who are of a bad one from being able to acquire it; and this may be done if they are kept in an inferior station, and not exposed to injustice. Nor has he treated well the equality of goods, for he has extended his regulation only to land; whereas a man's substance consists not only in this, but also in slaves, cattle, money, and all that variety of things which fall under the name of chattels; now there must be either an equality established in all these, or some certain rule, or they must be left entirely at large. It appears too by his laws, that he intends to establish only a small state, as all the artificers are to belong to the public, and add nothing to the complement of citizens; but if all those who are to be employed in public works are to be the slaves of the public, it should be done in the same manner as it is at Epidamnum, and as Diophantus formerly regulated it at Athens. From these particulars any one may nearly judge whether Phaleas's community is well or ill established.

Chapter VIII

Hippodamus, the son of Euruphon a Milesian, contrived the art of laying out towns, and separated the Pireus. This man was in other respects too eager after notice, and seemed to many to live in a very affected manner, with his flowing locks and his expensive ornaments, and a coarse warm vest which he wore, not only in the winter, but also in the hot weather. As he was very desirous of the character of a universal scholar, he was the first who, not being actually engaged in the management of public affairs, sat himself to inquire what sort of government was best; and he planned a state, consisting of ten thousand persons, divided into three parts, one consisting of artisans, another of husbandmen, and the third of soldiers; he also divided the lands into three parts, and allotted one to sacred purposes, another to the public, and the third to individuals. The first of these was to supply what was necessary for the established worship of the gods; the second was to be allotted to the support of the soldiery; and the third was to be the property of the husbandman. He thought also that there need only be three sorts of laws, corresponding to the three sorts of actions which can be brought, namely, for assault, trespasses, or death. He ordered also that there should be a particular court of appeal, into which all causes might be removed which were supposed to have been unjustly determined elsewhere; which court should be composed of old men chosen for that purpose. He thought also [1268 that they should not pass sentence by votes; but that every one should bring with him a tablet, on which he should write, that he found the party guilty, if it was so, but if not, he should bring a plain tablet; but if he acquitted him of one part of the indictment but not of the other, he should express that also on the tablet; for he disapproved of that general custom already established, as it obliges the judges to be guilty of perjury if they determined positively either on the one side or the other. He also made a law, that those should be rewarded who found out anything for the good of the city, and that the children of those who fell in battle should be educated at the public expense; which law had never been proposed by any other legislator, though it is at present in use at Athens as well as in other cities, he would have the magistrates chosen out of the people in general, by whom he meant the three parts before spoken of; and that those who were so elected should be the particular guardians of what belonged to the public, to strangers, and to orphans.

These are the principal parts and most worthy of notice in Hippodamus's plan. But some persons might doubt the propriety of his division of the citizens into three parts; for the artisans, the husbandmen, and the soldiers are to compose one community, where the husbandmen are to have no arms, and the artisans neither arms nor land, which would in a manner render them slaves to the soldiery. It is also impossible that the whole community should partake of all the honourable employments in it-for the generals and the guardians of the state must necessarily be appointed out of the soldiery, and indeed the most honourable magistrates; but as the two other parts will not have their share in the government, how can they be expected to have any affection for it? But it is necessary that the soldiery should be superior to the other two parts, and this superiority will not be easily gained without they are very numerous; and if they are so, why should the community consist of any other members? why should any others have a right to elect the magistrates? Besides, of what use are the husbandmen to this community? Artisans, 'tis true, are necessary, for these every city wants, and they can live upon their business. If the husbandmen indeed furnished the soldiers with provisions, they would be properly part of the community; but these are supposed to have their private property, and to cultivate it for their own use. Moreover, if the soldiers themselves are to cultivate that common land which is appropriated for their support, there will be no distinction between the soldier and the husbandman, which the legislator intended there should be; and if there should be any others who are to cultivate the private property of the husbandman and the common lands of the military, there will be a fourth order in the state which will have no share in it, and always entertain hostile sentiments towards it. If any one should propose that the same persons should cultivate their own lands and the public ones also, then there would be a deficiency of provisions to supply two families, as the lands would not immediately yield enough for themselves and the soldiers also; and all these things would occasion great confusion.

Nor do I approve of his method of determining causes, when he would have the judge split the case which comes simply before him; and thus, instead of being a judge, become an arbitrator. Now when any matter is brought to arbitration, it is customary for many persons to confer together upon the business that is before them; but when a cause is brought before judges it is not so; and many legislators take care that the judges shall not have it in their power to communicate their sentiments to each other. Besides, what can prevent confusion on the bench when one judge thinks a fine should be different from what another has set it at; one proposing twenty minae, another ten, or be it more or less, another four, and another five; and it is evident, that in this manner they will differ from each other, while some will give the whole damages sued for, and others nothing; in this situation, how shall their determinations be settled? Besides, a judge cannot be obliged to perjure himself who simply acquits or condemns, if the action is fairly and justly brought; for he who acquits the party does not say that he ought not to pay any fine at all, but that he ought not to pay a fine of twenty minae. But he that condemns him is guilty of perjury if he sentences him to pay twenty minae while he believes the damages ought not to be so much.

Now with respect to these honours which he proposes to bestow on those who can give any information useful to the community, this, though very pleasing in speculation, is what the legislator should not settle, for it would encourage informers, and probably occasion commotions in the state. And this proposal of his gives rise also to further conjectures and inquiries; for some persons have doubted whether it is useful or hurtful to alter the established law of any country, if even for the better; for which reason one cannot immediately determine upon what he here says, whether it is advantageous to alter the law or not. We know, indeed, that it is possible to propose to new model both the laws and government as a common good; and since we have mentioned this subject, it may be very proper to enter into a few particulars concerning it, for it contains some difficulties, as I have already said, and it may appear better to alter them, since it has been found useful in other sciences.

Thus the science of physic is extended beyond its ancient bounds; so is the gymnastic, and indeed all other arts and powers; so that one may lay it down for certain that the same thing will necessarily hold good in the art of government. And it may also be affirmed, that experience itself gives a proof of this; for the ancient laws are too simple and barbarous; which allowed the Greeks to wear swords in the city, and to buy their wives of each. other. And indeed all the remains of old laws which we have are very simple; for instance, a law in Cuma relative to murder. If any person who prosecutes another for murder can produce a certain number of witnesses to it of his own relations, the accused person shall be held guilty. Upon the whole, all persons ought to endeavour to follow what is right, and not what is established; and it is probable that the first men, whether they sprung out of the earth, or were saved from some general calamity, had very little understanding or knowledge, as is affirmed of these aborigines; so that it would be absurd to continue in the practice of their rules. Nor is it, moreover, right to permit written laws always to remain without alteration; for as in all other sciences, so in politics, it is impossible to express everything in writing with perfect exactness; for when we commit anything to writing we must use general terms, but in every action there is something particular to itself, which these may not comprehend; from whence it is evident, that certain laws will at certain times admit of alterations. But if we consider this matter in another point of view, it will appear to require great caution; for when the advantage proposed is trifling, as the accustoming the people easily to abolish their laws is of bad consequence, it is evidently better to pass over some faults which either the legislator or the magistrates may have committed; for the alterations will not be of so much service as a habit of disobeying the magistrates will be of disservice. Besides, the instance brought from the arts is fallacious; for it is not the same thing to alter the one as the other. For a law derives all its strength from custom, and this requires long time to establish; so that, to make it an easy matter to pass from the established laws to other new ones, is to weaken the power of laws. Besides, here is another question; if the laws are to be altered, are they all to be altered, and in every government or not, and whether at the pleasure of one person or many? all which particulars will make a great difference; for which reason we will at present drop the inquiry, to pursue it at some other time.

Chapter IX

There are two considerations which offer themselves with respect to the government established at Lacedaemon and Crete, and indeed in almost all other states whatsoever; one is whether their laws do or do not promote the best establishment possible? the other is whether there is anything, if we consider either the principles upon which it is founded or the executive part of it, which prevents the form of government that they had proposed to follow from being observed; now it is allowed that in every well-regulated state the members of it should be free from servile labour; but in what manner this shall be effected is not so easy to determine; for the Penestse have very often attacked the Thessalians, and the Helots the Lacedaemonians, for they in a manner continually watch an opportunity for some misfortune befalling them. But no such thing has ever happened to the Cretans; the reason for which probably is, that although they are engaged in frequent wars with the neighbouring cities, yet none of these would enter into an alliance with the revolters, as it would be disadvantageous for them, who themselves also have their villains. But now there is perpetual enmity between the Lacedaemonians and all their neighbours, the Argives, the Messenians, and the Arcadians. Their slaves also first revolted from the Thessalians while they were engaged in wars with their neighbours the Acheans, the Perrabeans, and the Magnesians. It seems to me indeed, if nothing else, yet something very troublesome to keep upon proper terms with them; for if you are remiss in your discipline they grow insolent, and think themselves upon an equality with their masters; and if they are hardly used they are continually plotting against you and hate you. It is evident, then, that those who employ slaves have not as yet hit upon the right way of managing them.

As to the indulging of women in any particular liberties, it is hurtful to the end of government and the prosperity of the city; for as a man and his wife are the two parts of a family, if we suppose a city to be divided into two parts, we must allow that the number of men and women will be equal.

In whatever city then the women are not under good regulations, we must look upon one half of it as not under the restraint of law, as it there happened; for the legislator, desiring to make his whole city a collection of warriors with respect to the men, he most evidently accomplished his design; but in the meantime the women were quite neglected, for they live without restraint in every improper indulgence and luxury. So that in such a state riches will necessarily be in general esteem, particularly if the men are governed by their wives, which has been the case with many a brave and warlike people except the Celts, and those other nations, if there are any such, who openly practise pederasty. And the first mythologists seem not improperly to have joined Mars and Venus together; for all nations of this character are greatly addicted either to the love of women or of boys, for which reason it was thus at Lacedaemon; and many things in their state were done by the authority of the women. For what is the difference, if the power is in the hands of the women, or in the hands of those whom they themselves govern? it must turn to the same account. As this boldness of the women can be of no use in any common occurrences, if it was ever so, it must be in war; but even here we find that the Lacedaemonian women were of the greatest disservice, as was proved at the time of the Theban invasion, when they were of no use at all, as they are in other cities, but made more disturbance than even the enemy.

The origin of this indulgence which the Lacedaemonian women enjoy is easily accounted for, from the long time the men were absent from home upon foreign expeditions against the Argives, and afterwards the Arcadians and Messenians, so that, when these wars were at an end, their military life, in which there is no little virtue, prepared them to obey the precepts of their law-giver; but we are told, that when Lycurgus endeavoured also to reduce the women to an obedience to his laws, upon their refusal he declined it. It may indeed be said that the women were the causes of these things, and of course all the fault was theirs. But we are not now considering where the fault lies, or where it does not lie, but what is right and what is wrong; and when the manners of the women are not well regulated, as I have already said, it must not only occasion faults which are disgraceful to the state, but also increase the love of money. In the next place, fault may be found with his unequal division of property, for some will have far too much, others too little; by which means the land will come into few hands, which business is badly regulated by his laws. For he made it infamous for any one either to buy or sell their possessions, in which he did right; but he permitted any one that chose it to give them away, or bequeath them, although nearly the same consequences will arise from one practice as from the other. It is supposed that near two parts in five of the whole country is the property of women, owing to their being so often sole heirs, and having such large fortunes in marriage; though it would be better to allow them none, or a little, or a certain regulated proportion. Now every one is permitted to make a woman his heir if he pleases; and if he dies intestate, he who succeeds as heir at law gives it to whom he pleases. From whence it happens that although the country is able to support fifteen hundred horse and thirty thousand foot, the number does not amount to one thousand.

And from these facts it is evident, that this particular is badly regulated; for the city could not support one shock, but was ruined for want of men. They say, that during the reigns of their ancient kings they used to present foreigners with the freedom of their city, to prevent there being a want of men while they carried on long wars; it is also affirmed that the number of Spartans was formerly ten thousand; but be that as it will, an equality of property conduces much to increase the number of the people. The law, too, which he made to encourage population was by no means calculated to correct this inequality; for being willing that the Spartans should be as numerous as possible, to make them desirous of having large families he ordered that he who had three children should be excused the night-watch, and that he who had four should pay no taxes: though it is very evident, that while the land was divided in this manner, that if the people increased there must many of them be very poor.

Nor was he less blamable for the manner in which he constituted the ephori; for these magistrates take cognisance of things of the last importance, and yet they are chosen out of the people in general; so that it often happens that a very poor person is elected to that office, who, from that circumstance, is easily bought. There have been many instances of this formerly, as well as in the late affair at Andros. And these men, being corrupted with money, went as far as they could to ruin the city: and, because their power was too great and nearly tyrannical, their kings were obliged to natter them, which contributed greatly to hurt the state; so that it altered from an aristocracy to a democracy. This magistracy is indeed the great support of the state; for the people are easy, knowing that they are eligible to the first office in it; so that, whether it took place by the intention of the legislator, or whether it happened by chance, this is of great service to their affairs; for it is necessary that every member of the state should endeavour that each part of the government should be preserved, and continue the same. And upon this principle their kings have always acted, out of regard to their honour; the wise and good from their attachment to the senate, a seat wherein they consider as the reward of virtue; and the common people, that they may support the ephori, of whom they consist. And it is proper that these magistrates should be chosen out of the whole community, not as the custom is at present, which is very ridiculous. The ephori are the supreme judges in causes of the last consequence; but as it is quite accidental what sort of persons they may be, it is not right that they should determine according to their own opinion, but by a written law or established custom. Their way of life also is not consistent with the manners of the city, for it is too indulgent; whereas that of others is too severe; so that they cannot support it, but are obliged privately to act contrary to law, that they may enjoy some of the pleasures of sense. There are also great defects in the institution of their senators. If indeed they were fitly trained to the practice of every human virtue, every one would readily admit that they would be useful to the government; but still it might be debated whether they should be continued judges for life, to determine points of the greatest moment, since the mind has its old age as well as the body; but as they are so brought up, that even the legislator could not depend upon them as good men, their power must be inconsistent with the safety of the state: for it is known that the members of that body have been guilty both of bribery and partiality in many public affairs; for which reason it had been much better if they had been made answerable for their conduct, which they are not. But it may be said the ephori seem to have a check upon all the magistrates. They have indeed in this particular very great power; but I affirm that they should not be entrusted with this control in the manner they are. Moreover, the mode of choice which they make use of at the election of their senators is very childish. Nor is it right for any one to solicit for a place he is desirous of; for every person, whether he chooses it or not, ought to execute any office he is fit for. But his intention was evidently the same in this as in the other parts of his government. For making his citizens ambitious after honours, with men of that disposition he has filled his senate, since no others will solicit for that office; and yet the principal part of those crimes which men are deliberately guilty of arise from ambition and avarice.

We will inquire at another time whether the office of a king is useful to the state: thus much is certain, that they should be chosen from a consideration of their conduct and not as they are now. But that the legislator himself did not expect to make all his citizens honourable and completely virtuous is evident from this, that he distrusts them as not being good men; for he sent those upon the same embassy that were at variance with each other; and thought, that in the dispute of the kings the safety of the state consisted. Neither were their common meals at first well established: for these should rather have been provided at the public expense, as at Crete, where, as at Lacedaemon, every one was obliged to buy his portion, although he might be very poor, and could by no means bear the expense, by which means the contrary happened to what the legislator desired: for he intended that those public meals should strengthen the democratic part of his government: but this regulation had quite the contrary effect, for those who were very poor could not take part in them; and it was an observation of their forefathers, that the not allowing those who could not contribute their proportion to the common tables to partake of them, would be the ruin of the state. Other persons have censured his laws concerning naval affairs, and not without reason, as it gave rise to disputes. For the commander of the fleet is in a manner set up in opposition to the kings, who are generals of the army for life.

There is also another defect in his laws worthy of censure, which Plato has given in his book of Laws; that the whole constitution was calculated only for the business of war: it is indeed excellent to make them conquerors; for which reason the preservation of the state depended thereon. The destruction of it commenced with their victories: for they knew not how to be idle, or engage in any other employment than war. In this particular also they were mistaken, that though they rightly thought, that those things which are the objects of contention amongst mankind are better procured by virtue than vice, yet they wrongfully preferred the things themselves to virtue. Nor was the public revenue well managed at Sparta, for the state was worth nothing while they were obliged to carry on the most extensive wars, and the subsidies were very badly raised; for as the Spartans possessed a large extent of country, they were not exact upon each other as to what they paid in. And thus an event contrary to the legislator's intention took place; for the state was poor, the individuals avaricious. Enough of the Lacedaemonian government; for these seem the chief defects in it.

Chapter X

The government of Crete bears a near resemblance to this, in some few particulars it is not worse, but in general it is far inferior in its contrivance. For it appears and is allowed in many particulars the constitution of Lacedaemon was formed in imitation of that of Crete; and in general most new things are an improvement upon the old. For they say, that when Lycurgus ceased to be guardian to King Charilles he went abroad and spent a long time with his relations in Crete, for the Lycians are a colony of the Lacedaemonians; and those who first settled there adopted that body of laws which they found already established by the inhabitants; in like manner also those who now live near them have the very laws which Minos first drew up.

This island seems formed by nature to be the mistress of Greece, for it is entirely surrounded by a navigable ocean which washes almost all the maritime parts of that country, and is not far distant on the one side from Peloponnesus, on the other, which looks towards Asia, from Triopium and Rhodes. By means of this situation Minos acquired the empire of the sea and the islands; some of which he subdued, in others planted colonies: at last he died at Camicus while he was attacking Sicily. There is this analogy between the customs of the Lacedaemonians and the Cretans, the Helots cultivate the grounds for the one, the domestic slaves for the other. Both states have their common meals, and the Lacedaemonians called these formerly not *psiditia* but *andpia*, as the Cretans do; which proves from whence the custom arose. In this particular their governments are also alike: the ephori have the same power with those of Crete, who are called *kosmoi*; with this difference only, that the number of the one is five, of the other ten. The senators are the same as those whom the Cretans call the council. There was formerly also a kingly power in Crete; but it was afterwards dissolved, and the command of their armies was given to the *kosmoi*. Every one also has a vote in their public assembly; but this has only the power of confirming what has already passed the council and the *kosmoi*.

The Cretans conducted their public meals better than the Lacedaemonians, for at Lacedaemon each individual was obliged to furnish what was assessed upon him; which if he could not do, there was a law which deprived him of the rights of a citizen, as has been already mentioned: but in Crete they were furnished by the community; for all the corn and cattle, taxes and contributions, which the domestic slaves were obliged to furnish, were divided into parts and allotted to the gods, the exigencies of the state, and these public meals; so that all the men, women, and children were maintained from a common stock. The legislator gave great attention to encourage a habit of eating sparingly, as very useful to the citizens. He also endeavoured, that his community might not be too populous, to lessen the connection with women, by introducing the love of boys: whether in this he did well or ill we shall have some other opportunity of considering. But that the public meals were better ordered at Crete than at Lacedaemon is very evident.

The institution of the *kosmoi*, was still worse than that of the ephori: for it contained all the faults incident to that magistracy and some peculiar to itself; for in both cases it is uncertain who will be elected: but the Lacedaemonians have this advantage which the others have not, that as all are eligible, the whole community have a share in the highest honours, and therefore all desire to preserve the state: whereas among the Cretans the *kosmoi* are not chosen out of the people in general, but out of some certain families, and the senate out of the *kosmoi*. And the same observations which may be made on the senate at Lacedaemon may be applied to these; for their being under no control, and their continuing for life, is an honour greater than they merit; and to have their proceedings not regulated by a written law, but left to their own discretion, is dangerous. (As to there being no insurrections, although the people share not in the management of public affairs, this is no proof of a well-constituted government, as the *kosmoi* have no opportunity of being bribed like the ephori, as they live in an island far from those who would corrupt them.) But the method they take to correct that fault is absurd, impolitic, and tyrannical: for very often either their fellow-magistrates or some private persons conspire together and turn out the *kosmoi*. They are also permitted to resign their office before their time is elapsed, and if all this was done by law it would be well, and not at the pleasure of the individuals, which is a bad rule to follow. But what is worst of all is, that general confusion which those who are in power introduce to impede the ordinary course of justice; which sufficiently shows what is the nature of the government, or rather lawless force: for it is usual with the principal persons amongst them to collect together some of the common people and their friends, and then revolt and set up for themselves, and come to blows with each other. And what is the difference, if a state is dissolved at once by such violent means, or if it gradually so alters in process of time as to be no longer the same constitution? A state like this would ever be exposed to the invasions of those who were powerful and inclined to attack it; but, as has been already mentioned, its situation preserves it, as it is free from the inroads of foreigners; and for this reason the family slaves still remain quiet at Crete, while the Helots are perpetually revolting: for the Cretans take no part in foreign affairs, and it is but lately that any foreign troops have made an attack upon the island; and their ravages soon proved the ineffectualness of their laws. And thus much for the government of Crete.

Chapter XI

The government of Carthage seems well established, and in many respects superior to others; in some particulars it bears a near resemblance to the Lacedaemonians; and indeed these three states, the Cretans, the Lacedaemonians and the Carthaginians are in some things very like each other, in others they differ greatly. Amongst many excellent constitutions this may show how well their government is framed, that although the people are admitted to a share in the administration, the form of it remains unaltered, without any popular insurrections, worth notice, on the one hand, or degenerating into a tyranny on the other. Now the Carthaginians have these things in common with the Lacedaemonians: public tables for those who are connected together by the tie of mutual friendship, after the manner of their Phiditia; they have also a magistracy, consisting of an hundred and four persons, similar to the ephori, or rather selected with more judgment; for amongst the Lacedaemonians, all the citizens are eligible, but amongst the Carthaginians, they are chosen out of those of the better sort: there is also some analogy between the king and the senate in both these governments, though the Carthaginian method of appointing their kings is best, for they do not confine themselves to one family; nor do they permit the election to be at large, nor have they any regard to seniority; for if amongst the candidates there are any of greater merit than the rest, these they prefer to those who may be older; for as their power is very extensive, if they are persons of no account, they may be very hurtful to the state, as they have always been to the Lacedaemonians; also the greater part of those things which become reprehensible by their excess are common to all those governments which we have described.

Now of those principles on which the Carthaginians have established their mixed form of government, composed of an aristocracy and democracy, some incline to produce a democracy, others an oligarchy: for instance, if the kings and the senate are unanimous upon any point in debate, they can choose whether they will bring it before the people or no; but if they disagree, it is to these they must appeal, who are not only to hear what has been approved of by the senate, but are finally to determine upon it; and whosoever chooses it, has a right to speak against any matter whatsoever that may be proposed, which is not permitted in other cases. The five, who elect each other, have very great and extensive powers; and these choose the hundred, who are magistrates of the highest rank: their power also continues longer than any other magistrates, for it commences before they come into office, and is prolonged after they are out of it; and in this particular the state inclines to an oligarchy: but as they are not elected by lot, but by suffrage, and are not permitted to take money, they are the greatest supporters imaginable of an aristocracy.

The determining all causes by the same magistrates, and not orae in one court and another in another, as at Lacedaemon, has the same influence. The constitution of Carthage is now shifting from an aristocracy to an oligarchy, in consequence of an opinion which is favourably entertained by many, who think that the magistrates in the community ought not to be persons of family only, but of fortune also; as it is impossible for those who are in bad circumstances to support the dignity of their office, or to be at leisure to apply to public business. As choosing men of fortune to be magistrates make a state incline to an oligarchy, and men of abilities to an aristocracy, so is there a third method of proceeding which took place in the polity of Carthage; for they have an eye to these two particulars when they elect their officers, particularly those of the highest rank, their kings and their generals. It must be admitted, that it was a great fault in their legislator not to guard against the constitution's degenerating from an aristocracy; for this is a most necessary thing to provide for at first, that those citizens who have the best abilities should never be obliged to do anything unworthy their character, but be always at leisure to serve the public, not only when in office, but also when private persons; for if once you are obliged to look among the wealthy, that you may have men at leisure to serve you, your greatest offices, of king and general, will soon become venal; in consequence of which, riches will be more honourable than virtue and a love of money be the ruling principle in the city-for what those who have the chief power regard as honourable will necessarily be the object which the citizens in general will aim at; and where the first honours are not paid to virtue, there the aristocratic form of government cannot flourish: for it is reasonable to conclude, that those who bought their places should generally make an advantage of what they laid out their money for; as it is absurd to suppose, that if a man of probity who is poor should be desirous of gaining something, a bad man should not endeavour to do the same, especially to reimburse himself; for which reason the magistracy should be formed of those who are most able to support an aristocracy. It would have been better for the legislature to have passed over the poverty of men of merit, and only to have taken care to have ensured them sufficient leisure, when in office, to attend to public affairs.

It seems also improper, that one person should execute several offices, which was approved of at Carthage; for one business is best done by one person; and it is the duty of the legislator to look to this, and not make the same person a musician and a shoemaker: so that where the state is not small it is more politic and more popular to admit many persons to have a share in the government; for, as I just now said, it is not only more usual, but everything is better and sooner done, when one thing only is allotted to one person: and this is evident both in the army and navy, where almost every one, in his turn, both commands and is under command. But as their government inclines to an oligarchy, they avoid the ill effects of it by always appointing some of the popular party to the government of cities to make their fortunes. Thus they consult this fault in their constitution and render it stable; but this is depending on chance; whereas the legislator ought to frame his government, that there the no room for insurrections. But now, if there should be any general calamity, and the people should revolt from their rulers, there is no remedy for reducing them to obedience by the laws. And these are the particulars of the Lacedaemonian, the Cretan, and the Carthaginian governments which seem worthy of commendation.

Chapter XII

Some of those persons who have written upon government had never any share in public affairs, but always led a private life. Everything worthy of notice in their works we have already spoke to. Others were legislators, some in their own cities, others were employed in regulating the governments of foreign states. Some of them only composed a body of laws; others formed the constitution also, as Lycurgus; and Solon, who did both. The Lacedaemonians have been already mentioned. Some persons think that Solon was an excellent legislator, who could dissolve a pure oligarchy, and save the people from that slavery which hung over them, and establish the ancient democratic form of government in his country; wherein every part of it was so framed as to be well adapted to the whole. In the senate of Areopagus an oligarchy was preserved; by the manner of electing their magistrates, an aristocracy; and in their courts of justice, a democracy.

Solon seems not to have altered the established form of government, either with respect to the senate or the mode of electing their magistrates; but to have raised the people to great consideration in the state by allotting the supreme judicial department to them; and for this some persons blame him, as having done what would soon overturn that balance of power he intended to establish; for by trying all causes whatsoever before the people, who were chosen by lot to determine them, it was necessary to flatter a tyrannical populace who had got this power; which contributed to bring the government to that pure democracy it now is.

Both Ephialtes and Pericles abridged the power of the Areopagites, the latter of whom introduced the method of paying those who attended the courts of justice: and thus every one who aimed at being popular proceeded increasing the power of the people to what we now see it. But it is evident that this was not Solon's intention, but that it arose from accident; for the people being the cause of the naval victory over the Medes, assumed greatly upon it, and enlisted themselves under factious demagogues, although opposed by the better part of the citizens. He thought it indeed most necessary to entrust the people with the choice of their magistrates and the power of calling them to account; for without that they must have been slaves and enemies to the other citizens: but he ordered them to elect those only who were persons of good account and property, either out of those who were worth five hundred medimns, or those who were called xeugitai, or those of the third census, who were called horsemen.

As for those of the fourth, which consisted of mechanics, they were incapable of any office. Zaleucus was the legislator of the Western Locrians, as was Charondas, the Catanean, of his own cities, and those also in Italy and Sicily which belonged to the Calcidians. Some persons endeavour to prove that Onomacritus, the Locrian, was the first person of note who drew up laws; and that he employed himself in that business while he was at Crete, where he continued some time to learn the prophetic art: and they say, that Thales was his companion; and that Lycurgus and Zaleucus were the scholars of Thales, and Charondas of Zaleucus; but those who advance this, advance what is repugnant to chronology. Philolaus also, of the family of the Bacchiades, was a Theban legislator. This man was very fond of Diocles, a victor in the Olympic games, and when he left his country from a disgust at an improper passion which his mother Alithoe had entertained for him, and settled at Thebes, Philolaus followed him, where they both died, and where they still show their tombs placed in view of each other, but so disposed, that one of them looks towards Corinth, the other does not; the reason they give for this is, that Diodes, from his detestation of his mother's passion, would have his tomb so placed that no one could see Corinth from it; but Philolaus chose that it might be seen from his: and this was the cause of their living at Thebes.

As Philolaus gave them laws concerning many other things, so did he upon adoption, which they call adoptive laws; and this he in particular did to preserve the number of families. Charondas did nothing new, except in actions for perjury, which he was the first person who took into particular consideration. He also drew up his laws with greater elegance and accuracy than even any of our present legislators. Philolaus introduced the law for the equal distribution of goods; Plato that for the community of women, children, and goods, and also for public tables for the women; and one concerning drunkenness, that they might observe sobriety in their symposiums. He also made a law concerning their warlike exercises; that they should acquire a habit of using both hands alike, as it was necessary that one hand should be as useful as the other.

As for Draco's laws, they were published when the government was already established, and they have nothing particular in them worth mentioning, except their severity on account of the enormity of their punishments. Pittacus was the author of some laws, but never drew up any form of government; one of which was this, that if a drunken man beat any person he should be punished more than if he did it when sober; for as people are more apt to be abusive when drunk than sober, he paid no consideration to the excuse which drunkenness might claim, but regarded only the common benefit. Andromadas Regmus was also a lawgiver to the Thracian talcidians. There are some laws of his concerning murders and heiresses extant, but these contain nothing that any one can say is new and his own. And thus much for different sorts of governments, as well those which really exist as those which different persons have proposed.

Book III

Chapter I

Every one who inquires into the nature of government, and what are its different forms, should make this almost his first question, What is a city? For upon this there is a dispute: for some persons say the city did this or that, while others say, not the city, but the oligarchy, or the tyranny. We see that the city is the only object which both the politician and legislator have in view in all they do: but government is a certain ordering of those who inhabit a city. As a city is a collective body, and, like other wholes, composed of many parts, it is evident our first inquiry must be, what a citizen is: for a city is a certain number of citizens. So that we must consider whom we ought to call citizen, and who is one; for this is often doubtful: for every one will not allow that this character is applicable to the same person; for that man who would be a citizen in a republic would very often not be one in an oligarchy. We do not include in this inquiry many of those who acquire this appellation out of the ordinary way, as honorary persons, for instance, but those only who have a natural right to it.

Now it is not residence which constitutes a man a citizen; for in this sojourners and slaves are upon an equality with him; nor will it be sufficient for this purpose, that you have the privilege of the laws, and may plead or be impleaded, for this all those of different nations, between whom there is a mutual agreement for that purpose, are allowed; although it very often happens, that sojourners have not a perfect right therein without the protection of a patron, to whom they are obliged to apply, which shows that their share in the community is incomplete. In like manner, with respect to boys who are not yet enrolled, or old men who are past war, we admit that they are in some respects citizens, but not completely so, but with some exceptions, for these are not yet arrived to years of maturity, and those are past service; nor is there any difference between them. But what we mean is sufficiently intelligible and clear, we want a complete citizen, one in whom there is no deficiency to be corrected to make him so. As to those who are banished, or infamous, there may be the same objections made and the same answer given. There is nothing that more characterises a complete citizen than having a share in the judicial and executive part of the government.

With respect to offices, some are fixed to a particular time, so that no person is, on any account, permitted to fill them twice; or else not till some certain period has intervened; others are not fixed, as a juryman's, and a member of the general assembly: but probably some one may say these are not offices, nor have the citizens in these capacities any share in the government; though surely it is ridiculous to say that those who have the principal power in the state bear no office in it. But this objection is of no weight, for it is only a dispute about words; as there is no general term which can be applied both to the office of a juryman and a member of the assembly. For the sake of distinction, suppose we call it an indeterminate office: but I lay it down as a maxim, that those are citizens who could exercise it. Such then is the description of a citizen who comes nearest to what all those who are called citizens are. Every one also should know, that of the component parts of those things which differ from each other in species, after the first or second remove, those which follow have either nothing at all or very little common to each.

Now we see that governments differ from each other in their form, and that some of them are defective, others as excellent as possible: for it is evident, that those which have many deficiencies and degeneracies in them must be far inferior to those which are without such faults. What I mean by degeneracies will be hereafter explained. Hence it is clear that the office of a citizen must differ as governments do from each other: for which reason he who is called a citizen has, in a democracy, every privilege which that station supposes. In other forms of government he may enjoy them; but not necessarily: for in some states the people have no power; nor have they any general assembly, but a few select men.

The trial also of different causes is allotted to different persons; as at Lacedaemon all disputes concerning contracts are brought before some of the ephori: the senate are the judges in cases of murder, and so on; some being to be heard by one magistrate, others by another: and thus at Carthage certain magistrates determine all causes. But our former description of a citizen will admit of correction; for in some governments the office of a juryman and a member of the general assembly is not an indeterminate one; but there are particular persons appointed for these purposes, some or all of the citizens being appointed jurymen or members of the general assembly, and this either for all causes and all public business whatsoever, or else for some particular one: and this may be sufficient to show what a citizen is; for he who has a right to a share in the judicial and executive part of government in any city, him we call a citizen of that place; and a city, in one word, is a collective body of such persons sufficient in themselves to all the purposes of life.

Chapter II

In common use they define a citizen to be one who is sprung from citizens on both sides, not on the father's or the mother's only. Others carry the matter still further, and inquire how many of his ancestors have been citizens, as his grandfather, great-grandfather, etc., but some persons have questioned how the first of the family could prove themselves citizens, according to this popular and careless definition. Gorgias of Leontium, partly entertaining the same doubt, and partly in jest, says, that as a mortar is made by a mortar-maker, so a citizen is made by a citizen-maker, and a Larisssean by a Larisssean-maker. This is indeed a very simple account of the matter; for if citizens are so, according to this definition, it will be impossible to apply it to the first founders or first inhabitants of states, who cannot possibly claim in right either of their father or mother. It is probably a matter of still more difficulty to determine their rights as citizens who are admitted to their freedom after any revolution in the state. As, for instance, at Athens, after the expulsion of the tyrants, when Clisthenes enrolled many foreigners and city-slaves amongst the tribes; and the doubt with respect to them was, not whether they were citizens or no, but whether they were legally so or not. Though indeed some persons may have this further doubt, whether a citizen can be a citizen when he is illegally made; as if an illegal citizen, and one who is no citizen at all, were in the same predicament: but since we see some persons govern unjustly, whom yet we admit to govern, though not justly, and the definition of a citizen is one who exercises certain offices, for such a one we have defined a citizen to be, it is evident, that a citizen illegally created yet continues to be a citizen, but whether justly or unjustly so belongs to the former inquiry.

Chapter III

It has also been doubted what was and what was not the act of the city; as, for instance, when a democracy arises out of an aristocracy or a tyranny; for some persons then refuse to fulfil their contracts; as if the right to receive the money was in the tyrant and not in the state, and many other things of the same nature; as if any covenant was founded for violence and not for the common good. So in like manner, if anything is done by those who have the management of public affairs where a democracy is established, their actions are to be considered as the actions of the state, as well as in the oligarchy or tyranny.

And here it seems very proper to consider this question, When shall we say that a city is the same, and when shall we say that it is different?

It is but a superficial mode of examining into this question to begin with the place and the people; for it may happen that these may be divided from that, or that some one of them may live in one place, and some in another (but this question may be regarded as no very knotty one; for, as a city may acquire that appellation on many accounts, it may be solved many ways); and in like manner, when men inhabit one common place, when shall we say that they inhabit the same city, or that the city is the same? for it does not depend upon the walls; for I can suppose Peloponnesus itself surrounded with a wall, as Babylon was, and every other place, which rather encircles many nations than one city, and that they say was taken three days when some of the inhabitants knew nothing of it: but we shall find a proper time to determine this question; for the extent of a city, how large it should be, and whether it should consist of more than one people, these are particulars that the politician should by no means be unacquainted with. This, too, is a matter of inquiry, whether we shall say that a city is the same while it is inhabited by the same race of men, though some of them are perpetually dying, others coming into the world, as we say that a river or a fountain is the same, though the waters are continually changing; or when a revolution takes place shall we say the men are the same, but the city is different: for if a city is a community, it is a community of citizens; but if the mode of government should alter, and become of another sort, it would seem a necessary consequence that the city is not the same; as we regard the tragic chorus as different from the comic, though it may probably consist of the same performers: thus every other community or composition is said to be different if the species of composition is different; as in music the same hands produce different harmony, as the Doric and Phrygian. If this is true, it is evident, that when we speak of a city as being the same we refer to the government there established; and this, whether it is called by the same name or any other, or inhabited by the same men or different. But whether or no it is right to dissolve the community when the constitution is altered is another question.

Chapter IV

What has been said, it follows that we should consider whether the same virtues which constitute a good man make a valuable citizen, or different; and if a particular inquiry is necessary for this matter we must first give a general description of the virtues of a good citizen; for as a sailor is one of those who make up a community, so is a citizen, although the province of one sailor may be different from another's (for one is a rower, another a steersman, a third a boatswain, and so on, each having their several appointments), it is evident that the most accurate description of any one good sailor must refer to his peculiar abilities, yet there are some things in which the same description may be applied to the whole crew, as the safety of the ship is the common business of all of them, for this is the general centre of all their cares: so also with respect to citizens, although they may in a few particulars be very different, yet there is one care common to them all, the safety of the community, for the community of the citizens composes the state; for which reason the virtue of a citizen has necessarily a reference to the state. But if there are different sorts of governments, it is evident that those actions which constitute the virtue of an excellent citizen in one community will not constitute it in another; wherefore the virtue of such a one cannot be perfect: but we say, a man is good when his virtues are perfect; from whence it follows, that an excellent citizen does not possess that virtue which constitutes a good man. Those who are any ways doubtful concerning this question may be convinced of the truth of it by examining into the best formed states: for, if it is impossible that a city should consist entirely of excellent citizens (while it is necessary that every one should do well in his calling, in which consists his excellence, as it is impossible that all the citizens should have the same qualifications) it is impossible that the virtue of a citizen and a good man should be the same; for all should possess the virtue of an excellent citizen: for from hence necessarily arise the perfection of the city: but that every one should possess the virtue of a good man is impossible without all the citizens in a well-regulated state were necessarily virtuous. Besides, as a city is composed of dissimilar parts, as an animal is of life and body; the soul of reason and appetite; a family of a man and his wife-property of a master and a slave; in the same manner, as a city is composed of all these and many other very different parts, it necessarily follows that the virtue of all the citizens cannot be the same; as the business of him who leads the band is different from the other dancers. From all which proofs it is evident that the virtues of a citizen cannot be one and the same. But do we never find those virtues united which constitute a good man and excellent citizen? for we say, such a one is an excellent magistrate and a prudent and good man; but prudence is a necessary qualification for all those who engage in public affairs. Nay, some persons affirm that the education of those who are intended to command should, from the beginning, be different from other citizens, as the children of kings are generally instructed in riding and warlike exercises; and thus Euripides says:

"...No showy arts Be mine, but teach me what the state requires."

As if those who are to rule were to have an education peculiar to themselves. But if we allow, that the virtues of a good man and a good magistrate may be the same, and a citizen is one who obeys the magistrate, it follows that the virtue of the one cannot in general be the same as the virtue of the other, although it may be true of some particular citizen; for the virtue of the magistrate must be different from the virtue of the citizen. For which reason Jason declared that was he deprived of his kingdom he should pine away with regret, as not knowing how to live a private man. But it is a great recommendation to know how to command as well as to obey; and to do both these things well is the virtue of an accomplished citizen. If then the virtue of a good man consists only in being able to command, but the virtue of a good citizen renders him equally fit for the one as well as the other, the commendation of both of them is not the same. It appears, then, that both he who commands and he who obeys should each of them learn their separate business: but that the citizen should be master of and take part in both these, as any one may easily perceive; in a family government there is no occasion for the master to know how to perform the necessary offices, but rather to enjoy the labour of others; for to do the other is a servile part. I mean by the other, the common family business of the slave.

There are many sorts of slaves; for their employments are various: of these the handicraftsmen are one, who, as their name imports, get their living by the labour of their hands, and amongst these all mechanics are included; for which reasons such workmen, in some states, were not formerly admitted into any share in the government; till at length democracies were established: it is not therefore proper for any man of honour, or any citizen, or any one who engages in public affairs, to learn these servile employments without they have occasion for them for their own use; for without this was observed the distinction between a master and a slave would be lost. But there is a government of another sort, in which men govern those who are their equals in rank, and freemen, which we call a political government, in which men learn to command by first submitting to obey, as a good general of horse, or a commander-in-chief, must acquire a knowledge of their duty by having been long under the command of another, and the like in every appointment in the army: for well is it said, no one knows how to command who has not himself been under command of another. The virtues of those are indeed different, but a good citizen must necessarily be endowed with them; he ought also to know in what manner freemen ought to govern, as well as be governed: and this, too, is the duty of a good man. And if the temperance and justice of him who commands is different from his who, though a freeman, is under command, it is evident that the virtues of a good citizen cannot be the same as justice, for instance but must be of a different species in these two different situations, as the temperance and courage of a man and a woman are different from each other; for a man would appear a coward who had only that courage which would be graceful in a woman, and a woman would be thought a talker who should take as large a part in the conversation as would become a man of consequence.

The domestic employments of each of them are also different; it is the man's business to acquire subsistence, the woman's to take care of it. But direction and knowledge of public affairs is a virtue peculiar to those who govern, while all others seem to be equally requisite for both parties; but with this the governed have no concern, it is theirs to entertain just notions: they indeed are like flute-makers, while those who govern are the musicians who play on them.

And thus much to show whether the virtue of a good man and an excellent citizen is the same, or if it is different, and also how far it is the same, and how far different.

Chapter V

But with respect to citizens there is a doubt remaining, whether those only are truly so who are allowed to share in the government, or whether the mechanics also are to be considered as such? for if those who are not permitted to rule are to be reckoned among them, it is impossible that the virtue of all the citizens should be the same, for these also are citizens; and if none of them are admitted to be citizens, where shall they be ranked? for they are neither sojourners nor foreigners? or shall we say that there will no inconvenience arise from their not being citizens, as they are neither slaves nor freedmen: for this is certainly true, that all those are not citizens who are necessary to the existence of a city, as boys are not citizens in the same manner that men are, for those are perfectly so, the others under some conditions; for they are citizens, though imperfect ones: for in former times among some people the mechanics were either slaves or foreigners, for which reason many of them are so now: and indeed the best regulated states will not permit a mechanic to be a citizen; but if it be allowed them, we cannot then attribute the virtue we have described to every citizen or freeman, but to those only who are disengaged from servile offices. Now those who are employed by one person in them are slaves; those who do them for money are mechanics and hired servants: hence it is evident on the least reflection what is their situation, for what I have said is fully explained by appearances. Since the number of communities is very great, it follows necessarily that there will be many different sorts of citizens, particularly of those who are governed by others, so that in one state it may be necessary to admit mechanics and hired servants to be citizens, but in others it may be impossible; as particularly in an aristocracy, where honours are bestowed on virtue and dignity: for it is impossible for one who lives the life of a mechanic or hired servant to acquire the practice of virtue. In an oligarchy also hired servants are not admitted to be citizens; because there a man's right to bear any office is regulated by his fortune; but mechanics are, for many citizens are very rich.

There was a law at Thebes that no one could have a share in the government till he had been ten years out of trade. In many states the law invites strangers to accept the freedom of the city; and in some democracies the son of a free-woman is himself free. The same is also observed in many others with respect to natural children; but it is through want of citizens regularly born that they admit such: for these laws are always made in consequence of a scarcity of inhabitants; so, as their numbers increase, they first deprive the children of a male or female slave of this privilege, next the child of a free-woman, and last of all they will admit none but those whose fathers and mothers were both free.

That there are many sorts of citizens, and that he may be said to be as completely who shares the honours of the state, is evident from what has been already said. Thus Achilles, in Homer, complains of Agamemnon's treating him like an unhonoured stranger; for a stranger or sojourner is one who does not partake of the honours of the state: and whenever the right to the freedom of the city is kept obscure, it is for the sake of the inhabitants. From what has been said it is plain whether the virtue of a good man and an excellent citizen is the same or different: and we find that in some states it is the same, in others not; and also that this is not true of each citizen, but of those only who take the lead, or are capable of taking the lead, in public affairs, either alone or in conjunction with others.

Chapter VI

Having established these points, we proceed next to consider whether one form of government only should be established, or more than one; and if more, how many, and of what sort, and what are the differences between them. The form of government is the ordering and regulating of the city, and all the offices in it, particularly those wherein the supreme power is lodged; and this power is always possessed by the administration; but the administration itself is that particular form of government which is established in any state: thus in a democracy the supreme power is lodged in the whole people; on the contrary, in an oligarchy it is in the hands of a few. We say then, that the form of government in these states is different, and we shall find the same thing hold good in others. Let us first determine for whose sake a city is established; and point out the different species of rule which man may submit to in social life.

I have already mentioned in my treatise on the management of a family, and the power of the master, that man is an animal naturally formed for society, and that therefore, when he does not want any foreign assistance, he will of his own accord desire to live with others; not but that mutual advantage induces them to it, as far as it enables each person to live more agreeably; and this is indeed the great object not only to all in general, but also to each individual: but it is not merely matter of choice, but they join in society also, even that they may be able to live, which probably is not without some share of merit, and they also support civil society, even for the sake of preserving life, without they are grievously overwhelmed with the miseries of it: for it is very evident that men will endure many calamities for the sake of living, as being something naturally sweet and desirable. It is easy to point out the different modes of government, and we have already settled them in our exoteric discourses. The power of the master, though by nature equally serviceable, both to the master and to the slave, yet nevertheless has for its object the benefit of the master, while the benefit of the slave arises accidentally; for if the slave is destroyed, the power of the master is at an end: but the authority which a man has over his wife, and children, and his family, which we call domestic government, is either for the benefit of those who are under subjection, or else for the common benefit of the whole: but its particular object is the benefit of the governed, as we see in other arts; in physic, for instance, and the gymnastic exercises, wherein, if any benefit arise to the master, it is accidental; for nothing forbids the master of the exercises from sometimes being himself one of those who exercises, as the steersman is always one of the sailors; but both the master of the exercises and the steersman consider the good of those who are under their government. Whatever good may happen to the steersman when he is a sailor, or to the master of the exercises when he himself makes one at the games, is not intentional, or the object of their power; thus in all political governments which are established to preserve and defend the equality of the citizens it is held right to rule by turns. Formerly, as was natural, every one expected that each of his fellow-citizens should in his turn serve the public, and thus administer to his private good, as he himself when in office had done for others; but now every one is desirous of being continually in power, that he may enjoy the advantage which he makes of public business and being in office; as if places were a never-failing remedy for every complaint, and were on that account so eagerly sought after.

It is evident, then, that all those governments which have a common good in view are rightly established and strictly just, but those who have in view only the good of the rulers are all founded on wrong principles, and are widely different from what a government ought to be, for they are tyranny over slaves, whereas a city is a community of freemen.

Chapter VII

Having established these particulars, we come to consider next the different number of governments which there are, and what they are; and first, what are their excellencies: for when we have determined this, their defects will be evident enough.

It is evident that every form of government or administration, for the words are of the same import, must contain a supreme power over the whole state, and this supreme power must necessarily be in the hands of one person, or a few, or many; and when either of these apply their power for the common good, such states are well governed; but when the interest of the one, the few, or the many who enjoy this power is alone consulted, then ill; for you must either affirm that those who make up the community are not citizens, or else let these share in the advantages of government. We usually call a state which is governed by one person for the common good, a kingdom; one that is governed by more than one, but by a few only, an aristocracy; either because the government is in the hands of the most worthy citizens, or because it is the best form for the city and its inhabitants. When the citizens at large govern for the public good, it is called a state; which is also a common name for all other governments, and these distinctions are consonant to reason; for it will not be difficult to find one person, or a very few, of very distinguished abilities, but almost impossible to meet with the majority of a people eminent for every virtue; but if there is one common to a whole nation it is valour; for this is created and supported by numbers: for which reason in such a state the profession of arms will always have the greatest share in the government.

Now the corruptions attending each of these governments are these; a kingdom may degenerate into a tyranny, an aristocracy into an oligarchy, and a state into a democracy. Now a tyranny is a monarchy where the good of one man only is the object of government, an oligarchy considers only the rich, and a democracy only the poor; but neither of them have a common good in view.

Chapter VIII

It will be necessary to enlarge a little more upon the nature of each of these states, which is not without some difficulty, for he who would enter into a philosophical inquiry into the principles of them, and not content himself with a superficial view of their outward conduct, must pass over and omit nothing, but explain the true spirit of each of them. A tyranny then is, as has been said, a monarchy, where one person has an absolute and despotic power over the whole community and every member therein: an oligarchy, where the supreme power of the state is lodged with the rich: a democracy, on the contrary, is where those have it who are worth little or nothing. But the first difficulty that arises from the distinctions which we have laid down is this, should it happen that the majority of the inhabitants who possess the power of the state (for this is a democracy) should be rich, the question is, how does this agree with what we have said? The same difficulty occurs, should it ever happen that the poor compose a smaller part of the people than the rich, but from their superior abilities acquire the supreme power; for this is what they call an oligarchy; it should seem then that our definition of the different states was not correct: nay, moreover, could any one suppose that the majority of the people were poor, and the minority rich, and then describe the state in this manner, that an oligarchy was a government in which the rich, being few in number, possessed the supreme power, and that a democracy was a state in which the poor, being many in number, possessed it, still there will be another difficulty; for what name shall we give to those states we have been describing? I mean, that in which the greater number are rich, and that in which the lesser number are poor (where each of these possess the supreme power), if there are no other states than those we have described. It seems therefore evident to reason, that whether the supreme power is vested in the hands of many or few may be a matter of accident; but that it is clear enough, that when it is in the hands of the few, it will be a government of the rich; when in the hands of the many, it will be a government of the poor; since in all countries there are many poor and few rich: it is not therefore the cause that has been already assigned (namely, the number of people in power) that makes the difference between the two governments; but an oligarchy and democracy differ in this from each other, in the poverty of those who govern in the one, and the riches I28oa of those who govern in the other; for when the government is in the hands of the rich, be they few or be they more, it is an oligarchy; when it is in the hands of the poor, it is a democracy: but, as we have already said, the one will be always few, the other numerous, but both will enjoy liberty; and from the claims of wealth and liberty will arise continual disputes with each other for the lead in public affairs.

Chapter IX

Let us first determine what are the proper limits of an oligarchy and a democracy, and what is just in each of these states; for all men have some natural inclination to justice; but they proceed therein only to a certain degree; nor can they universally point out what is absolutely just; as, for instance, what is equal appears just, and is so; but not to all; only among those who are equals: and what is unequal appears just, and is so; but not to all, only amongst those who are unequals; which circumstance some people neglect, and therefore judge ill; the reason for which is, they judge for themselves, and every one almost is the worst judge in his own cause. Since then justice has reference to persons, the same distinctions must be made with respect to persons which are made with respect to things, in the manner that I have already described in my Ethics.

As to the equality of the things, these they agree in; but their dispute is concerning the equality of the persons, and chiefly for the reason above assigned; because they judge ill in their own cause; and also because each party thinks, that if they admit what is right in some particulars, they have done justice on the whole: thus, for instance, if some persons are unequal in riches, they suppose them unequal in the whole; or, on the contrary, if they are equal in liberty, they suppose them equal in the whole: but what is absolutely just they omit; for if civil society was founded for the sake of preserving and increasing property, every one's right in the city would be equal to his fortune; and then the reasoning of those who insist upon an oligarchy would be valid; for it would not be right that he who contributed one mina should have an equal share in the hundred along with him who brought in all the rest, either of the original money or what was afterwards acquired.

Nor was civil society founded merely to preserve the lives of its members; but that they might live well: for otherwise a state might be composed of slaves, or the animal creation: but this is not so; for these have no share in the happiness of it; nor do they live after their own choice; nor is it an alliance mutually to defend each other from injuries, or for a commercial intercourse: for then the Tyrrhenians and Carthaginians, and all other nations between whom treaties of commerce subsist, would be citizens of one city; for they have articles to regulate their exports and imports, and engagements for mutual protection, and alliances for mutual defence; but yet they have not all the same magistrates established among them, but they are different among the different people; nor does the one take any care, that the morals of the other should be as they ought, or that none of those who have entered into the common agreements should be unjust, or in any degree vicious, only that they do not injure any member of the confederacy. But whosoever endeavours to establish wholesome laws in a state, attends to the virtues and the vices of each individual who composes it; from whence it is evident, that the first care of him who would found a city, truly deserving that name, and not nominally so, must be to have his citizens virtuous; for otherwise it is merely an alliance for self-defence; differing from those of the same cast which are made between different people only in place: for law is an agreement and a pledge, as the sophist Lycophron says, between the citizens of their intending to do justice to each other, though not sufficient to make all the citizens just and good: and that this is faact is evident, for could any one bring different places together, as, for instance, enclose Megara and Corinth in a wall, yet they would not be one city, not even if the inhabitants intermarried with each other, though this inter-community contributes much to make a place one city. Besides, could we suppose a set of people to live separate from each other, but within such a distance as would admit of an intercourse, and that there were laws subsisting between each party, to prevent their injuring one another in their mutual dealings, supposing one a carpenter, another a husbandman, shoemaker, and the like, and that their numbers were ten thousand, still all that they would have together in common would be a tariff for trade, or an alliance for mutual defence, but not the same city. And why? not because their mutual intercourse is not near enough, for even if persons so situated should come to one place, and every one should live in his own house as in his native city, and there should be alliances subsisting between each party to mutually assist and prevent any injury being done to the other, still they would not be admitted to be a city by those who think correctly, if they preserved the same customs when they were together as when they were separate.

It is evident, then, that a city is not a community of place; nor established for the sake of mutual safety or traffic with each other; but that these things are the necessary consequences of a city, although they may all exist where there is no city: but a city is a society of people joining together with their families and their children to live agreeably for the sake of having their lives as happy and as independent as possible: and for this purpose it is necessary that they should live in one place and intermarry with each other: hence in all cities there are family-meetings, clubs, sacrifices, and public entertainments to promote friendship; for a love of sociability is friendship itself; so that the end then for which a city is established is, that the inhabitants of it may live happy, and these things are conducive to that end: for it is a community of families and villages for the sake of a perfect independent life; that is, as we have already said, for the sake of living well and happily. It is not therefore founded for the purpose of men's merely living together, but for their living as men ought; for which reason those who contribute most to this end deserve to have greater power in the city than those who are their equals in family and freedom, but their inferiors in civil virtue, or those who excel them in wealth but are below them in worth. It is evident from what has been said, that in all disputes upon government each party says something that is just.

Chapter X

It may also be a doubt where the supreme power ought to be lodged. Shall it be with the majority, or the wealthy, with a number of proper persons, or one better than the rest, or with a tyrant? But whichever of these we prefer some difficulty will arise. For what? shall the poor have it because they are the majority? they may then divide among themselves, what belongs to the rich: nor is this unjust; because truly it has been so judged by the supreme power. But what avails it to point out what is the height of injustice if this is not? Again, if the many seize into their own hands everything which belongs to the few, it is evident that the city will be at an end. But virtue will never destroy what is virtuous; nor can what is right be the ruin of the state: therefore such a law can never be right, nor can the acts of a tyrant ever be wrong, for of necessity they must all be just; for he, from his unlimited power, compels every one to obey his command, as the multitude oppress the rich. Is it right then that the rich, the few, should have the supreme power? and what if they be guilty of the same rapine and plunder the possessions of the majority, that will be as right as the other: but that all things of this sort are wrong and unjust is evident. Well then, these of the better sort shall have it: but must not then all the other citizens live unhonoured, without sharing the offices of the city; for the offices of a city are its honours, and if one set of men are always in power, it is evident that the rest must be without honour. Well then, let it be with one person of all others the fittest for it: but by this means the power will be still more contracted, and a greater number than before continue unhonoured. But some one may say, that it is wrong to let man have the supreme power and not the law, as his soul is subject to so many passions. But if this law appoints an aristocracy, or a democracy, how will it help us in our present doubts? for those things will happen which we have already mentioned.

Chapter XI

Other particulars we will consider separately; but it seems proper to prove, that the supreme power ought to be lodged with the many, rather than with those of the better sort, who are few; and also to explain what doubts (and probably just ones) may arise: now, though not one individual of the many may himself be fit for the supreme power, yet when these many are joined together, it does not follow but they may be better qualified for it than those; and this not separately, but as a collective body; as the public suppers exceed those which are given at one person's private expense: for, as they are many, each person brings in his share of virtue and wisdom; and thus, coming together, they are like one man made up of a multitude, with many feet, many hands, and many intelligences: thus is it with respect to the manners and understandings of the multitude taken together; for which reason the public are the best judges of music and poetry; for some understand one part, some another, and all collectively the whole; and in this particular men of consequence differ from each of the many; as they say those who are beautiful do from those who are not so, and as fine pictures excel any natural objects, by collecting the several beautiful parts which were dispersed among different originals into one, although the separate parts, as the eye or any other, might be handsomer than in the picture.

But if this distinction is to be made between every people and every general assembly, and some few men of consequence, it may be doubtful whether it is true; nay, it is clear enough that, with respect to a few, it is not; since the same conclusion might be applied even to brutes: and indeed wherein do some men differ from brutes? Not but that nothing prevents what I have said being true of the people in some states. The doubt then which we have lately proposed, with all its consequences, may be settled in this manner; it is necessary that the freemen who compose the bulk of the people should have absolute power in some things; but as they are neither men of property, nor act uniformly upon principles of virtue, it is not safe to trust them with the first offices in the state, both on account of their iniquity and their ignorance; from the one of which they will do what is wrong, from the other they will mistake: and yet it is dangerous to allow them no power or share in the government; for when there are many poor people who are incapable of acquiring the honours of their country, the state must necessarily have many enemies in it; let them then be permitted to vote in the public assemblies and to determine causes; for which reason Socrates, and some other legislators, gave them the power of electing the officers of the state, and also of inquiring into their conduct when they came out of office, and only prevented their being magistrates by themselves; for the multitude when they are collected together have all of them sufficient understanding for these purposes, and, mixing among those of higher rank, are serviceable to the city, as some things, which alone are improper for food, when mixed with others make the whole more wholesome than a few of them would be.

But there is a difficulty attending this form of government, for it seems, that the person who himself was capable of curing any one who was then sick, must be the best judge whom to employ as a physician; but such a one must be himself a physician; and the same holds true in every other practice and art: and as a physician ought to give an account of his practice to a physician, so ought it to be in other arts: those whose business is physic may be divided into three sorts, the first of these is he who makes up the medicines; the second prescribes, and is to the other as the architect is to the mason; the third is he who understands the science, but never practises it: now these three distinctions may be found in those who understand all other arts; nor have we less opinion of their judgment who are only instructed in the principles of the art than of those who practise it: and with respect to elections the same method of proceeding seems right; for to elect a proper person in any science is the business of those who are skilful therein; as in geometry, of geometricians; in steering, of steersmen: but if some individuals should know something of particular arts and works, they do not know more than the professors of them: so that even upon this principle neither the election of magistrates, nor the censure of their conduct, should be entrusted to the many.

But probably all that has been here said may not be right; for, to resume the argument I lately used, if the people are not very brutal indeed, although we allow that each individual knows less of these affairs than those who have given particular attention to them, yet when they come together they will know them better, or at least not worse; besides, in some particular arts it is not the workman only who is the best judge; namely, in those the works of which are understood by those who do not profess them: thus he who builds a house is not the only judge of it, for the master of the family who inhabits it is a better; thus also a steersman is a better judge of a tiller than he who made it; and he who gives an entertainment than the cook. What has been said seems a sufficient solution of this difficulty; but there is another that follows: for it seems absurd that the power of the state should be lodged with those who are but of indifferent morals, instead of those who are of excellent characters. Now the power of election and censure are of the utmost consequence, and this, as has been said, in some states they entrust to the people; for the general assembly is the supreme court of all, and they have a voice in this, and deliberate in all public affairs, and try all causes, without any objection to the meanness of their circumstances, and at any age: but their treasurers, generals, and other great officers of state are taken from men of great fortune and worth. This difficulty also may be solved upon the same principle; and here too they may be right, for the power is not in the man who is member of the assembly, or council, but the assembly itself, and the council, and the people, of which each individual of the whole community are the parts, I mean as senator, adviser, or judge; for which reason it is very right, that the many should have the greatest powers in their own hands; for the people, the council, and the judges are composed of them, and the property of all these collectively is more than the property of any person or a few who fill the great offices of the state: and thus I determine these points.

The first question that we stated shows plainly, that the supreme power should be lodged in laws duly made and that the magistrate or magistrates, either one or more, should be authorised to determine those cases which the laws cannot particularly speak to, as it is impossible for them, in general language, to explain themselves upon everything that may arise: but what these laws are which are established upon the best foundations has not been yet explained, but still remains a matter of some question: but the laws of every state will necessarily be like every state, either trifling or excellent, just or unjust; for it is evident, that the laws must be framed correspondent to the constitution of the government; and, if so, it is plain, that a well-formed government will have good laws, a bad one, bad ones.

Chapter XII

Since in every art and science the end aimed at is always good, so particularly in this, which is the most excellent of all, the founding of civil society, the good wherein aimed at is justice; for it is this which is for the benefit of all. Now, it is the common opinion, that justice is a certain equality; and in this point all the philosophers are agreed when they treat of morals: for they say what is just, and to whom; and that equals ought to receive equal: but we should know how we are to determine what things are equal and what unequal; and in this there is some difficulty, which calls for the philosophy of the politician. Some persons will probably say, that the employments of the state ought to be given according to every particular excellence of each citizen, if there is no other difference between them and the rest of the community, but they are in every respect else alike: for justice attributes different things to persons differing from each other in their character, according to their respective merits. But if this is admitted to be true, complexion, or height, or any such advantage will be a claim for a greater share of the public rights. But that this is evidently absurd is clear from other arts and sciences; for with respect to musicians who play on the flute together, the best flute is not given to him who is of the best family, for he will play never the better for that, but the best instrument ought to be given to him who is the best artist.

If what is now said does not make this clear, we will explain it still further: if there should be any one, a very excellent player on the flute, but very deficient in family and beauty, though each of them are more valuable endowments than a skill in music, and excel this art in a higher degree than that player excels others, yet the best flutes ought to be given to him; for the superiority in beauty and fortune should have a reference to the business in hand; but these have none. Moreover, according to this reasoning, every possible excellence might come in comparison with every other; for if bodily strength might dispute the point with riches or liberty, even any bodily strength might do it; so that if one person excelled in size more than another did in virtue, and his size was to qualify him to take place of the other's virtue, everything must then admit of a comparison with each other; for if such a size is greater than virtue by so much, it is evident another must be equal to it: but, since this is impossible, it is plain that it would be contrary to common sense to dispute a right to any office in the state from every superiority whatsoever: for if one person is slow and the other swift, neither is the one better qualified nor the other worse on that account, though in the gymnastic races a difference in these particulars would gain the prize; but a pretension to the offices of the state should be founded on a superiority in those qualifications which are useful to it: for which reason those of family, independency, and fortune, with great propriety, contend with each other for them; for these are the fit persons to fill them: for a city can no more consist of all poor men than it can of all slaves But if such persons are requisite, it is evident that those also who are just and valiant are equally so; for without justice and valour no state can be supported, the former being necessary for its existence, the latter for its happiness.

Chapter XIII

It seems, then, requisite for the establishment of a state, that all, or at least many of these particulars should be well canvassed and inquired into; and that virtue and education may most justly claim the right of being considered as the necessary means of making the citizens happy, as we have already said. As those who are equal in one particular are not therefore equal in all, and those who are unequal in one particular are not therefore unequal in all, it follows that all those governments which are established upon a principle which supposes they are, are erroneous.

We have already said, that all the members of the community will dispute with each other for the offices of the state; and in some particulars justly, but not so in general; the rich, for instance, because they have the greatest landed property, and the ultimate right to the soil is vested in the community; and also because their fidelity is in general most to be depended on. The freemen and men of family will dispute the point with each other, as nearly on an equality; for these latter have a right to a higher regard as citizens than obscure persons, for honourable descent is everywhere of great esteem: nor is it an improper conclusion, that the descendants of men of worth will be men of worth themselves; for noble birth is the fountain of virtue to men of family: for the same reason also we justly say, that virtue has a right to put in her pretensions. Justice, for instance, is a virtue, and so necessary to society, that all others must yield her the precedence.

Let us now see what the many have to urge on their side against the few; and they may say, that if, when collectively taken, they are compared with them, they are stronger, richer, and better than they are. But should it ever happen that all these should inhabit the same city, I mean the good, the rich, the noble, as well as the many, such as usually make up the community, I ask, will there then be any reason to dispute concerning who shall govern, or will there not? for in every community which we have mentioned there is no dispute where the supreme power should be placed; for as these differ from each other, so do those in whom that is placed; for in one state the rich enjoy it, in others the meritorious, and thus each according to their separate manners. Let us however consider what is to be done when all these happen at the same time to inhabit the same city. If the virtuous should be very few in number, how then shall we act? shall we prefer the virtuous on account of their abilities, if they are capable of governing the city? or should they be so many as almost entirely to compose the state?

There is also a doubt concerning the pretensions of all those who claim the honours of government: for those who found them either on fortune or family have nothing which they can justly say in their defence; since it is evident upon their principle, that if any one person can be found richer than all the rest, the right of governing all these will be justly vested in this one person. In the same manner, one man who is of the best family will claim it from those who dispute the point upon family merit: and probably in an aristocracy the same dispute might arise on the score of virtue, if there is one man better than all the other men of worth who are in the same community; it seems just, by the same reasoning, that he should enjoy the supreme power. And upon this principle also, while the many suppose they ought to have the supreme command, as being more powerful than the few, if one or more than one, though a small number should be found stronger than themselves, these ought rather to have it than they.

All these things seem to make it plain, that none of these principles are justly founded on which these persons would establish their right to the supreme power; and that all men whatsoever ought to obey them: for with respect to those who claim it as due to their virtue or their fortune, they might have justly some objection to make; for nothing hinders but that it may sometimes happen, that the many may be better or richer than the few, not as individuals, but in their collective capacity.

As to the doubt which some persons have proposed and objected, we may answer it in this manner; it is this, whether a legislator, who would establish the most perfect system of laws, should calculate them for the use of the better part of the citizens, or the many, in the circumstances we have already mentioned? The rectitude of anything consists in its equality; that therefore which is equally right will be advantageous to the whole state, and to every member of it in common.

Now, in general, a citizen is one who both shares in the government and also in his turn submits to be governed; their condition, it is true, is different in different states: the best is that in which a man is enabled to choose and to persevere in a course of virtue during his whole life, both in his public and private state. But should there be one person, or a very few, eminent for an uncommon degree of virtue, though not enough to make up a civil state, so that the virtue of the many, or their political abilities, should be too inferior to come in comparison with theirs, if more than one; or if but one, with his only; such are not to be considered as part of the city; for it would be doing them injustice to rate them on a level with those who are so far their inferiors in virtue and political abilities, that they appear to them like a god amongst men. From whence it is evident, that a system of laws must be calculated for those who are equal to each other in nature and power. Such men, therefore, are not the object of law; for they are themselves a law: and it would be ridiculous in any one to endeavour to include them in the penalties of a law: for probably they might say what Antisthenes tells us the lions did to the hares when they demanded to be admitted to an equal share with them in the government. And it is on this account that democratic states have established the ostracism; for an equality seems the principal object of their government. For which reason they compel all those who are very eminent for their power, their fortune, their friendships, or any other cause which may give them too great weight in the government, to submit to the ostracism, and leave the city for a stated time; as the fabulous histories relate the Argonauts served Hercules, for they refused to take him with them in the ship Argo on account of his superior valour. For which reason those who hate a tyranny and find fault with the advice which Periander gave to Thrasybulus, must not think there was nothing to be said in its defence; for the story goes, that Periander said nothing to the messenger in answer to the business he was consulted about, but striking off those ears of corn which were higher than the rest, reduced the whole crop to a level; so that the messenger, without knowing the cause of what was done, related the fact to Thrasybulus, who understood by it that he must take off all the principal men in the city. Nor is this serviceable to tyrants only; nor is it tyrants only who do it; for the same thing is practised both in oligarchies and democracies: for the ostracism has in a manner nearly the same power, by restraining and banishing those who are too great; and what is done in one city is done also by those who have the supreme power in separate states; as the Athenians with respect to the Samians, the Chians, and the Lesbians; for when they suddenly acquired the superiority over all Greece, they brought the other states into subjection, contrary to the treaties which subsisted between them. The King of Persia also very often reduces the Medes and Babylonians when they assume upon their former power: and this is a principle which all governments whatsoever keep in their eye; even those which are best administered, as well as those which are not, do it; these for the sake of private utility, the others for the public good.

The same thing is to be perceived in the other arts and sciences; for a painter would not represent an animal with a foot disproportionally large, though he had drawn it remarkably beautiful; nor would the shipwright make the prow or any other part of the vessel larger than it ought to be; nor will the master of the band permit any who sings louder and better than the rest to sing in concert with them. There is therefore no reason that a monarch should not act in agreement with free states, to support his own power, if they do the same thing for the benefit of their respective communities; upon which account when there is any acknowledged difference in the power of the citizens, the reason upon which the ostracism is founded will be politically just; but it is better for the legislator so to establish his state at the beginning as not to want this remedy: but if in course of time such an inconvenience should arise, to endeavour to amend it by some such correction. Not that this was the use it was put to: for many did not regard the benefit of their respective communities, but made the ostracism a weapon in the hand of sedition.

It is evident, then, that in corrupt governments it is partly just and useful to the individual, though probably it is as clear that it is not entirely just: for in a well-governed state there may be great doubts about the use of it, not on account of the pre-eminence which one may have in strength, riches, or connection: but when the pre-eminence is virtue, what then is to be done? for it seems not right to turn out and banish such a one; neither does it seem right to govern him, for that would be like desiring to share the power with Jupiter and to govern him: nothing then remains but what indeed seems natural, and that is for all persons quietly to submit to the government of those who are thus eminently virtuous, and let them be perpetually kings in the separate states.

Chapter XIV

What has been now said, it seems proper to change our subject and to inquire into the nature of monarchies; for we have already admitted them to be one of those species of government which are properly founded. And here let us consider whether a kingly government is proper for a city or a country whose principal object is the happiness of the inhabitants, or rather some other. But let us first determine whether this is of one kind only, or more; and it is easy to know that it consists of many different species, and that the forms of government are not the same in all: for at Sparta the kingly power seems chiefly regulated by the laws; for it is not supreme in all circumstances; but when the king quits the territories of the state he is their general in war; and all religious affairs are entrusted to him: indeed the kingly power with them is chiefly that of a general who cannot be called to an account for his conduct, and whose command is for life: for he has not the power of life and death, except as a general; as they frequently had in their expeditions by martial law, which we learn from Homer; for when Agamemnon is affronted in council, he restrains his resentment, but when he is in the field and armed with this power, he tells the Greeks:

> "Whoe'er I know shall shun th' impending fight,
> To dogs and vultures soon shall be a prey; For death is mine...."

This, then, is one species of monarchical government in which the kingly power is in a general for life; and is sometimes hereditary, sometimes elective: besides, there is also another, which is to be met with among some of the barbarians, in which the kings are invested with powers nearly equal to a tyranny, yet are, in some respects, bound by the laws and the customs of their country; for as the barbarians are by nature more prone to slavery than the Greeks, and those in Asia more than those in Europe, they endure without murmuring a despotic government; for this reason their governments are tyrannies; but yet not liable to be overthrown, as being customary and according to law. Their guards also are such as are used in a kingly government, not a despotic one; for the guards of their kings are his citizens, but a tyrant's are foreigners. The one commands, in the manner the law directs, those who willingly obey; the other, arbitrarily, those who consent not. The one, therefore, is guarded by the citizens, the other against them.

These, then, are the two different sorts of these monarchies, and another is that which in ancient Greece they called *aesumnetes*; which is nothing more than an elective tyranny; and its difference from that which is to be found amongst the barbarians consists not in its not being according to law, but only in its not being according to the ancient customs of the country. Some persons possessed this power for life, others only for a particular time or particular purpose, as the people of Mitylene elected Pittacus to oppose the exiles, who were headed by Antimenides and Alcaeus the poet, as we learn from a poem of his; for he upbraids the Mitylenians for having chosen Pittacus for their tyrant, and with one voice extolling him to the skies who was the ruin of a rash and devoted people. These sorts of government then are, and ever were, despotic, on account of their being tyrannies; but inasmuch as they are elective, and over a free people, they are also kingly.

A fourth species of kingly government is that which was in use in the heroic times, when a free people submitted to a kingly government, according to the laws and customs of their country. For those who were at first of benefit to mankind, either in arts or arms, or by collecting them into civil society, or procuring them an establishment, became the kings of a willing people, and established an hereditary monarchy. They were particularly their generals in war, and presided over their sacrifices, excepting such only as belonged to the priests: they were also the supreme judges over the people; and in this case some of them took an oath, others did not; they did, the form of swearing was by their sceptre held out.

In ancient times the power of the kings extended to everything whatsoever, both civil, domestic, and foreign; but in after-times they relinquished some of their privileges, and others the people assumed, so that, in some states, they left their kings only the right of presiding over the sacrifices; and even those whom it were worth while to call by that name had only the right of being commander-in-chief in their foreign wars.

These, then, are the four sorts of kingdoms: the first is that of the heroic times; which was a government over a free people, with its rights in some particulars marked out; for the king was their general, their judge, and their high priest. The second, that of the barbarians; which is an hereditary despotic government regulated by laws: the third is that which they call aesumnetic, which is an elective tyranny. The fourth is the Lacedaemonian; and this, in few words, is nothing more than an hereditary generalship: and in these particulars they differ from each other. There is a fifth species of kingly government, which is when one person has a supreme power over all things whatsoever, in the manner that every state and every city has over those things which belong to the public: for as the master of a family is king in his own house, so such a king is master of a family in his own city or state.

Chapter XV

But the different sorts of kingly governments may, if I may so say, be reduced to two; which we will consider more particularly. The last spoken of, and the Lacedaemonian, for the chief of the others are placed between these, which are as it were at the extremities, they having less power than an absolute government, and yet more than the Lacedaemonians; so that the whole matter in question may be reduced to these two points; the one is, whether it is advantageous to the citizens to have the office of general continue in one person for life, and whether it should be confined to any particular families or whether every one should be eligible: the other, whether it is advantageous for one person to have the supreme power over everything or not. But to enter into the particulars concerning the office of a Lacedaemonian general would be rather to frame laws for a state than to consider the nature and utility of its constitution, since we know that the appointing of a general is what is done in every state. Passing over this question then, we will proceed to consider the other part of their government, which is the polity of the state; and this it will be necessary to examine particularly into, and to go through such questions as may arise.

Now the first thing which presents itself to our consideration is this, whether it is best to be governed by a good man, or by good laws? Those who prefer a kingly government think that laws can only speak a general language, but cannot adapt themselves to particular circumstances; for which reason it is absurd in any science to follow written rule; and even in Egypt the physician was allowed to alter the mode of cure which the law prescribed to him, after the fourth day; but if he did it sooner it was at his own peril: from whence it is evident, on the very same account, that a government of written laws is not the best; and yet general reasoning is necessary to all those who are to govern, and it will be much more perfect in those who are entirely free from passions than in those to whom they are natural. But now this is a quality which laws possess; while the other is natural to the human soul. But some one will say in answer to this, that man will be a better judge of particulars. It will be necessary, then, for a king to be a lawgiver, and that his laws should be published, but that those should have no authority which are absurd, as those which are not, should. But whether is it better for the community that those things which cannot possibly come under the cognisance of the law either at all or properly should be under the government of every worthy citizen, as the present method is, when the public community, in their general assemblies, act as judges and counsellors, where all their determinations are upon particular cases, for one individual, be he who he will, will be found, upon comparison, inferior to a whole people taken collectively: but this is what a city is, as a public entertainment is better than one man's portion: for this reason the multitude judge of many things better than any one single person. They are also less liable to corruption from their numbers, as water is from its quantity: besides, the judgment of an individual must necessarily be perverted if he is overcome by anger or any other passion; but it would be hard indeed if the whole community should be misled by anger. Moreover, let the people be free, and they will do nothing but in conformity to the law, except only in those cases which the law cannot speak to. But though what I am going to propose may not easily be met with, yet if the majority of the state should happen to be good men, should they prefer one uncorrupt governor or many equally good, is it not evident that they should choose the many? But there may be divisions among these which cannot happen when there is but one. In answer to this it may be replied that all their souls will be as much animated with virtue as this one man's.

If then a government of many, and all of them good men, compose an aristocracy, and the government of one a kingly power, it is evident that the people should rather choose the first than the last; and this whether the state is powerful or not, if many such persons so alike can be met with: and for this reason probable it was, that the first governments were generally monarchies; because it was difficult to find a number of persons eminently virtuous, more particularly as the world was then divided into small communities; besides, kings were appointed in return for the benefits they had conferred on mankind; but such actions are peculiar to good men: but when many persons equal in virtue appeared at the time, they brooked not a superiority, but sought after an equality and established a free state; but after this, when they degenerated, they made a property of the public; which probably gave rise to oligarchies; for they made wealth meritorious, and the honours of government were reserved for the rich: and these afterwards turned to tyrannies and these in their turn gave rise to democracies; for the power of the tyrants continually decreasing, on account of their rapacious avarice, the people grew powerful enough to frame and establish democracies: and as cities after that happened to increase, probably it was not easy for them to be under any other government than a democracy. But if any person prefers a kingly government in a state, what is to be done with the king's children? Is the family also to reign? But should they have such children as some persons usually have, it will be very detrimental. It may be said, that then the king who has it in his power will never permit such children to succeed to his kingdom. But it is not easy to trust to that; for it is very hard and requires greater virtue than is to be met with in human nature. There is also a doubt concerning the power with which a king should be entrusted: whether he should be allowed force sufficient to compel those who do not choose to be obedient to the laws, and how he is to support his government? for if he is to govern according to law and do nothing of his own will which is contrary thereunto, at the same time it will be necessary to protect that power with which he guards the law, This matter however may not be very difficult to determine; for he ought to have a proper power, and such a one is that which will be sufficient to make the king superior to any one person or even a large part of the community, but inferior to the whole, as the ancients always appointed guards for that person whom they created aesumnetes or tyrant; and some one advised the Syracusians, when Dionysius asked for guards, to allow him such.

Chapter XVI

We will next consider the absolute monarch that we have just mentioned, who does everything according to his own will: for a king governing under the direction of laws which he is obliged to follow does not of himself create any particular species of government, as we have already said: for in every state whatsoever, either aristocracy or democracy, it is easy to appoint a general for life; and there are many who entrust the administration of affairs to one person only; such is the government at Dyrrachium, and nearly the same at Opus. As for an absolute monarchy as it is called, that is to say, when the whole state is wholly subject to the will of one person, namely the king, it seems to many that it is unnatural that one man should have the entire rule over his fellow-citizens when the state consists of equals: for nature requires that the same right and the same rank should necessarily take place amongst all those who are equal by nature: for as it would be hurtful to the body for those who are of different constitutions to observe the same regimen, either of diet or clothing, so is it with respect to the honours of the state as hurtful, that those who are equal in merit should be unequal in rank; for which reason it is as much a man's duty to submit to command as to assume it, and this also by rotation; for this is law, for order is law; and it is more proper that law should govern than any one of the citizens: upon the same principle, if it is advantageous to place the supreme power in some particular persons, they should be appointed to be only guardians, and the servants of the laws, for the supreme power must be placed somewhere; but they say, that it is unjust that where all are equal one person should continually enjoy it. But it seems unlikely that man should be able to adjust that which the law cannot determine; it may be replied, that the law having laid down the best rules possible, leaves the adjustment and application of particulars to the discretion of the magistrate; besides, it allows anything to be altered which experience proves may be better established. Moreover, he who would place the supreme power in mind, would place it in God and the laws; but he who entrusts man with it, gives it to a wild beast, for such his appetites sometimes make him; for passion influences those who are in power, even the very best of men: for which reason law is reason without desire.

The instance taken from the arts seems fallacious: wherein it is said to be wrong for a sick person to apply for a remedy to books, but that it would be far more eligible to employ those who are skilful in physic; for these do nothing contrary to reason from motives of friendship but earn their money by curing the sick, whereas those who have the management of public affairs do many things through hatred or favour. And, as a proof of what we have advanced, it may be observed, that whenever a sick person suspects that his physician has been persuaded by his enemies to be guilty of any foul practice to him in his profession, he then rather chooses to apply to books for his cure: and not only this but even physicians themselves when they are ill call in other physicians: and those who teach others the gymnastic exercises, exercise with those of the same profession, as being incapable from self-partiality to form a proper judgment of what concerns themselves. From whence it is evident, that those who seek for what is just, seek for a mean; now law is a mean. Moreover; the moral law is far superior and conversant with far superior objects than the written law; for the supreme magistrate is safer to be trusted to than the one, though he is inferior to the other. But as it is impossible that one person should have an eye to everything himself, it will be necessary that the supreme magistrate should employ several subordinate ones under him; why then should not this be done at first, instead of appointing one person in this manner? Besides, if, according to what has been already said, the man of worth is on that account fit to govern, two men of worth are certainly better than one: as, for instance, in Homer, "Let two together go:" and also Agamemnon's wish; "Were ten such faithful counsel mine!" Not but that there are even now some particular magistrates invested with supreme power to decide, as judges, those things which the law cannot, as being one of those cases which comes not properly under its jurisdiction; for of those which can there is no doubt: since then laws comprehend some things, but not all, it is necessary to enquire and consider which of the two is preferable, that the best man or the best law should govern; for to reduce every subject which can come under the deliberation of man into a law is impossible.

No one then denies, that it is necessary that there should be some person to decide those cases which cannot come under the cognisance of a written law: but we say, that it is better to have many than one; for though every one who decides according to the principles of the law decides justly; yet surely it seems absurd to suppose, that one person can see better with two eyes, and hear better with two ears, or do better with two hands and two feet, than many can do with many: for we see that absolute monarchs now furnish themselves with many eyes and ears and hands and feet; for they entrust those who are friends to them and their government with part of their power; for if they are not friends to the monarch, they will not do what he chooses; but if they are friends to him, they are friends also to his government: but a friend is an equal and like his friend: if then he thinks that such should govern, he thinks that his equal also should govern. These are nearly the objections which are usually made to a kingly power.

Chapter XVII

Probably what we have said may be true of some persons, but not of others; for some men are by nature formed to be under the government of a master; others, of a king; others, to be the citizens of a free state, just and useful; but a tyranny is not according to nature, nor the other perverted forms of government; for they are contrary to it. But it is evident from what has been said, that among equals it is neither advantageous nor right that one person should be lord over all where there are no established laws, but his will is the law; or where there are; nor is it right that one who is good should have it over those who are good; or one who is not good over those who are not good; nor one who is superior to the rest in worth, except in a particular manner, which shall be described, though indeed it has been already mentioned. But let us next determine what people are best qualified for a kingly government, what for an aristocratic, and what for a democratic. And, first, for a kingly; and it should be those who are accustomed by nature to submit the civil government of themselves to a family eminent for virtue: for an aristocracy, those who are naturally framed to bear the rule of free men, whose superior virtue makes them worthy of the management of others: for a free state, a war-like people, formed by nature both to govern and be governed by laws which admit the poorest citizen to share the honours of the commonwealth according to his worth. But whenever a whole family or any one of another shall happen so far to excel in virtue as to exceed all other persons in the community, then it is right that the kingly power should be in them, or if it is an individual who does so, that he should be king and lord of all; for this, as we have just mentioned, is not only correspondent to that principle of right which all founders of all states, whether aristocracies, oligarchies, or democracies, have a regard to (for in placing the supreme power they all think it right to fix it to excellence, though not the same); but it is also agreeable to what has been already said; as it would not be right to kill, or banish, or ostracise such a one for his superior merit. Nor would it be proper to let him have the supreme power only in turn; for it is contrary to nature that what is highest should ever be lowest: but this would be the case should such a one ever be governed by others. So that there can nothing else be done but to submit, and permit him continually to enjoy the supreme power. And thus much with respect to kingly power in different states, and whether it is or is not advantageous to them, and to what, and in what manner.

Chapter XVIII

Since then we have said that there are three sorts of regular governments, and of these the best must necessarily be that which is administered by the best men (and this must be that which happens to have one man, or one family, or a number of persons excelling all the rest in virtue, who are able to govern and be governed in such a manner as will make life most agreeable, and we have already shown that the virtue of a good man and of a citizen in the most perfect government will be the same), it is evident, that in the same manner, and for those very qualities which would procure a man the character of good, any one would say, that the government of a state was a well-established aristocracy or kingdom; so that it will be found to be education and morals that are almost the whole which go to make a good man, and the same qualities will make a good citizen or good king.

These particulars being treated of, we will now proceed to consider what sort of government is best, how it naturally arises, and how it is established; for it is necessary to make a proper inquiry concerning this.

Book IV

Chapter I

In every art and science which is not conversant in parts but in some one genus in which it is complete, it is the business of that art alone to determine what is fitted to its particular genus; as what particular exercise is fitted to a certain particular body, and suits it best: for that body which is formed by nature the most perfect and superior to others necessarily requires the best exercise-and also of what one kind that must be which will suit the generality; and this is the business of the gymnastic arts: and although any one should not desire to acquire an exact knowledge and skill in these exercises, yet it is not, on that account, the less necessary that he who professes to be a master and instruct the youth in them should be perfect therein: and we see that this is what equally befalls the healing, shipbuilding, cloth-making, and indeed all other arts; so that it evidently belongs to the same art to find out what kind of government is best, and would of all others be most correspondent to our wish, while it received no molestation from without: and what particular species of it is adapted to particular persons; for there are many who probably are incapable of enjoying the best form: so that the legislator, and he who is truly a politician, ought to be acquainted not only with that which is most perfect imaginable, but also that which is the best suited to any given circumstances. There is, moreover, a third sort, an imaginary one, and he ought, if such a one should be presented to his consideration, to be able to discern what sort of one it would be at the beginning; and, when once established, what would be the proper means to preserve it a long time. I mean, for instance, if a state should happen not to have the best form of government, or be deficient in what was necessary, or not receive every advantage possible, but something less. And, besides all this, it is necessary to know what sort of government is best fitting for all cities: for most of those writers who have treated this subject, however speciously they may handle other parts of it, have failed in describing the practical parts: for it is not enough to be able to perceive what is best without it is what can be put in practice. It should also be simple, and easy for all to attain to. But some seek only the most subtile forms of government. Others again, choosing rather to treat of what is common, censure those under which they live, and extol the excellence of a particular state, as the Lacedaemonian, or some other: but every legislator ought to establish such a form of government as from the present state and disposition of the people who are to receive it they will most readily submit to and persuade the community to partake of: for it is not a business of less trouble to correct the mistakes of an established government than to form a new one; as it is as difficult to recover what we have forgot as to learn anything afresh. He, therefore, who aspires to the character of a legislator, ought, besides all we have already said, to be able to correct the mistakes of a government already established, as we have before mentioned. But this is impossible to be done by him who does not know how many different forms of government there are: some persons think that there is only one species both of democracy and oligarchy; but this is not true: so that every one should be acquainted with the difference of these governments, how great they are, and whence they arise; and should have equal knowledge to perceive what laws are best, and what are most suitable to each particular government: for all laws are, and ought to be, framed agreeable to the state that is to be governed by them, and not the state to the laws: for government is a certain ordering in a state which particularly respects the magistrates in what manner they shall be regulated, and where the supreme power shall be placed; and what shall be the final object which each community shall have in view; but the laws are something different from what regulates and expresses the form of the constitution-it is their office to direct the conduct of the magistrate in the execution of his office and the punishment of offenders. From whence it is evident, that the founders of laws should attend both to the number and the different sorts of government; for it is impossible that the same laws should be calculated for all sorts of oligarchies and all sorts of democracies, for of both these governments there are many species, not one only.

Chapter II

Since, then, according to our first method in treating of the different forms of government, we have divided those which are regular into three sorts, the kingly, the aristocratical, the free states, and shown the three excesses which these are liable to: the kingly, of becoming tyrannical; the aristocratical, oligarchical; and the free state, democratical: and as we have already treated of the aristocratical and kingly; for to enter into an inquiry what sort of government is best is the same thing as to treat of these two expressly; for each of them desires to be established upon the principles of virtue: and as, moreover, we have already determined wherein a kingly power and an aristocracy differ from each other, and when a state may be said to be governed by a king, it now remains that we examine into a free state, and also these other governments, an oligarchy, a democracy, and a tyranny; and it is evident of these three excesses which must be the worst of all, and which next to it; for, of course, the excesses of the best and most holy must be the worst; for it must necessarily happen either that the name of king only will remain, or else that the king will assume more power than belongs to him, from whence tyranny will arise, the worst excess imaginable, a government the most contrary possible to a free state. The excess next hurtful is an oligarchy; for an aristocracy differs much from this sort of government: that which is least so is a democracy. This subject has been already treated of by one of those writers who have gone before me, though his sentiments are not the same as mine: for he thought, that of all excellent constitutions, as a good oligarchy or the like, a democracy was the worst, but of all bad ones, the best.

Now I affirm, that all these states have, without exception, fallen into excess; and also that he should not have said that one oligarchy was better than another, but that it was not quite so bad. But this question we shall not enter into at present. We shall first inquire how many different sorts of free states there are; since there are many species of democracies and oligarchies; and which of them is the most comprehensive, and most desirable after the best form of government; or if there is any other like an aristocracy, well established; and also which of these is best adapted to most cities, and which of them is preferable for particular persons: for, probably, some may suit better with an oligarchy than a democracy, and others better with a democracy than an oligarchy; and afterwards in what manner any one ought to proceed who desires to establish either of these states, I mean every species of democracy, and also of oligarchy. And to conclude, when we shall have briefly gone through everything that is necessary, we will endeavour to point out the sources of corruption, and stability, in government, as well those which are common to all as those which are peculiar to each state, and from what causes they chiefly arise.

Chapter III

The reason for there being many different sorts of governments is this, that each state consists of a great number of parts; for, in the first place, we see that all cities are made up of families: and again, of the multitude of these some must be rich, some poor, and others in the middle station; and that, both of the rich and poor, some will be used to arms, others not. We see also, that some of the common people are husbandmen, others attend the market, and others are artificers. There is also a difference between the nobles in their wealth, and the dignity in which they live: for instance, in the number of horses they breed; for this cannot be supported without a large fortune: for which reason, in former times, those cities whose strength consisted in horse became by that means oligarchies; and they used horse in their expeditions against the neighbouring cities; as the Eretrians the Chalcidians, the Magnetians, who lived near the river Meander, and many others in Asia. Moreover, besides the difference of fortune, there is that which arises from family and merit; or, if there are any other distinctions which make part of the city, they have been already mentioned in treating of an aristocracy, for there we considered how many parts each city must necessarily be composed of; and sometimes each of these have a share in the government, sometimes a few, sometimes more.

It is evident then, that there must be many forms of government, differing from each other in their particular constitution: for the parts of which they are composed each differ from the other. For government is the ordering of the magistracies of the state; and these the community share between themselves, either as they can attain them by force, or according to some common equality which there is amongst them, as poverty, wealth, or something which they both partake of. There must therefore necessarily be as many different forms of governments as there are different ranks in the society, arising from the superiority of some over others, and their different situations. And these seem chiefly to be two, as they say, of the winds: namely, the north and the south; and all the others are declinations from these. And thus in politics, there is the government of the many and the government of the few; or a democracy and an oligarchy: for an aristocracy may be considered as a species of oligarchy, as being also a government of the few; and what we call a free state may be considered as a democracy: as in the winds they consider the west as part of the north, and the east as part of the south: and thus it is in music, according to some, who say there are only two species of it, the Doric and the Phrygian, and all other species of composition they call after one of these names; and many people are accustomed to consider the nature of government in the same light; but it is both more convenient and more correspondent to truth to distinguish governments as I have done, into two species: one, of those which are established upon proper principles; of which there may be one or two sorts: the other, which includes all the different excesses of these; so that we may compare the best form of government to the most harmonious piece of music; the oligarchic and despotic to the more violent tunes; and the democratic to the soft and gentle airs.

Chapter IV

We ought not to define a democracy as some do, who say simply, that it is a government where the supreme power is lodged in the people; for even in oligarchies the supreme power is in the majority. Nor should they define an oligarchy a government where the supreme power is in the hands of a few: for let us suppose the number of a people to be thirteen hundred, and that of these one thousand were rich, who would not permit the three hundred poor to have any share in the government, although they were free, and their equal in everything else; no one would say, that this government was a democracy. In like manner, if the poor, when few in number, should acquire the power over the rich, though more than themselves, no one would say, that this was an oligarchy; nor this, when the rest who are rich have no share in the administration. We should rather say, that a democracy is when the supreme power is in the hands of the freemen; an oligarchy, when it is in the hands of the rich: it happens indeed that in the one case the many will possess it, in the other the few; because there are many poor and few rich. And if the power of the state was to be distributed according to the size of the citizens, as they say it is in Ethiopia, or according to their beauty, it would be an oligarchy: for the number of those who are large and beautiful is small.

Nor are those things which we have already mentioned alone sufficient to describe these states; for since there are many species both of a democracy and an oligarchy, the matter requires further consideration; as we cannot admit, that if a few persons who are free possess the supreme power over the many who are not free, that this government is a democracy: as in Apollonia, in Ionia, and in Thera: for in each of these cities the honours of the state belong to some few particular families, who first founded the colonies. Nor would the rich, because they are superior in numbers, form a democracy, as formerly at Colophon; for there the majority had large possessions before the Lydian war: but a democracy is a state where the freemen and the poor, being the majority, are invested with the power of the state. An oligarchy is a state where the rich and those of noble families, being few, possess it.

We have now proved that there are various forms of government and have assigned a reason for it; and shall proceed to show that there are even more than these, and what they are, and why; setting out with the principle we have already laid down. We admit that every city consists not of one, but many parts: thus, if we should endeavour to comprehend the different species of animals we should first of all note those parts which every animal must have, as a certain sensorium, and also what is necessary to acquire and retain food, as a mouth and a belly; besides certain parts to enable it to move from place to place. If, then, these are the only parts of an animal and there are differences between them; namely, in their various sorts of stomachs, bellies, and sensoriums: to which we must add their motive powers; the number of the combinations of all these must necessarily make up the different species of animals. For it is not possible that the same kind of animal should have any very great difference in its mouth or ears; so that when all these are collected, who happen to have these things similar in all, they make up a species of animals of which there are as many as there are of these general combinations of necessary parts.

The same thing is true of what are called states; for a city is not made of one but many parts, as has already been often said; one of which is those who supply it with provisions, called husbandmen, another called mechanics, whose employment is in the manual arts, without which the city could not be inhabited; of these some are busied about what is absolutely necessary, others in what contribute to the elegancies and pleasures of life; the third sort are your exchange-men, I mean by these your buyers, sellers, merchants, and victuallers; the fourth are your hired labourers or workmen; the fifth are the men-at-arms, a rank not less useful than the other, without you would have the community slaves to every invader; but what cannot defend itself is unworthy of the name of a city; for a city is self-sufficient, a slave not. So that when Socrates, in Plato's Republic, says that a city is necessarily composed of four sorts of people, he speaks elegantly but not correctly, and these are, according to him, weavers, husbandmen, shoe-makers, and builders; he then adds, as if these were not sufficient, smiths, herdsmen for what cattle are necessary, and also merchants and victuallers, and these are by way of appendix to his first list; as if a city was established for necessity, and not happiness, or as if a shoe-maker and a husbandman were equally useful. He reckons not the military a part before the increase of territory and joining to the borders of the neighbouring powers will make war necessary: and even amongst them who compose his four divisions, or whoever have any connection with each other, it will be necessary to have some one to distribute justice, and determine between man and man. If, then, the mind is a more valuable part of man than the body, every one would wish to have those things more regarded in his city which tend to the advantage of these than common matters, such are war and justice; to which may be added council, which is the business of civil wisdom (nor is it of any consequence whether these different employments are filled by different persons or one, as the same man is oftentimes both a soldier and a husbandman): so that if both the judge and the senator are parts of the city, it necessarily follows that the soldier must be so also. The seventh sort are those who serve the public in expensive employments at their own charge: these are called the rich. The eighth are those who execute the different offices of the state, and without these it could not possibly subsist: it is therefore necessary that there should be some persons capable of governing and filling the places in the city; and this either for life or in rotation: the office of senator, and judge, of which we have already sufficiently treated, are the only ones remaining. If, then, these things are necessary for a state, that it may be happy and just, it follows that the citizens who engage in public affairs should be men of abilities therein. Several persons think, that different employments may be allotted to the same person; as a soldier's, a husbandman's, and an artificer's; as also that others may be both senators and judges.

Besides, every one supposes himself a man of political abilities, and that he is qualified for almost every department in the state. But the same person cannot at once be poor and rich: for which reason the most obvious division of the city is into two parts, the poor and rich; moreover, since for the generality the one are few, the other many, they seem of all the parts of a city most contrary to each other; so that as the one or the other prevail they form different states; and these are the democracy and the oligarchy.

But that there are many different states, and from what causes they arise, has been already mentioned: and that there are also different species both of democracies and oligarchies we will now show. Though this indeed is evident from what we have already said: there are also many different sorts of common people, and also of those who are called gentlemen. Of the different sorts of the first are husbandmen, artificers, exchange-men, who are employed in buying and selling, seamen, of which some are engaged in war, some in traffic, some in carrying goods and passengers from place to place, others in fishing, and of each of these there are often many, as fishermen at Tarentum and Byzantium, masters of galleys at Athens, merchants at AEgina and Chios, those who let ships on freight at Tenedos; we may add to these those who live by their manual labour and have but little property; so that they cannot live without some employ: and also those who are not free-born on both sides, and whatever other sort of common people there may be. As for gentlemen, they are such as are distinguished either by their fortune, their birth, their abilities, or their education, or any such-like excellence which is attributed to them.

The most pure democracy is that which is so called principally from that equality which prevails in it: for this is what the law in that state directs; that the poor shall be in no greater subjection than the rich; nor that the supreme power shall be lodged with either of these, but that both shall share it. For if liberty and equality, as some persons suppose, are chiefly to be found in a democracy, it must be most so by every department of government being alike open to all; but as the people are the majority, and what they vote is law, it follows that such a state must be a democracy. This, then, is one species thereof. Another is, when the magistrates are elected by a certain census; but this should be but small, and every one who was included in it should be eligible, but as soon as he was below it should lose that right. Another sort is, in which every citizen who is not infamous has a share in the government, but where the government is in the laws. Another, where every citizen without exception has this right. Another is like these in other particulars, but there the people govern, and not the law: and this takes place when everything is determined by a majority of votes, and not by a law; which happens when the people are influenced by the demagogues: for where a democracy is governed by stated laws there is no room for them, but men of worth fill the first offices in the state: but where the power is not vested in the laws, there demagogues abound: for there the people rule with kingly power: the whole composing one body; for they are supreme, not as individuals but in their collective capacity.

Homer also discommends the government of many; but whether he means this we are speaking of, or where each person exercises his power separately, is uncertain. When the people possess this power they desire to be altogether absolute, that they may not be under the control of the law, and this is the time when flatterers are held in repute. Nor is there any difference between such a people and monarchs in a tyranny: for their manners are the same, and they both hold a despotic power over better persons than themselves. For their decrees are like the others' edicts; their demagogues like the others' flatterers: but their greatest resemblance consists in the mutual support they give to each other, the flatterer to the tyrant, the demagogue to the people: and to them it is owing that the supreme power is lodged in the votes of the people, and not in the laws; for they bring everything before them, as their influence is owing to their being supreme whose opinions they entirely direct; for these are they whom the multitude obey. Besides, those who accuse the magistrates insist upon it, that the right of determining on their conduct lies in the people, who gladly receive their complaints as the means of destroying all their offices.

Any one, therefore, may with great justice blame such a government as being a democracy, and not a free state; for where the government is not in the laws, then there is no free state, for the law ought to be supreme over all things; and particular incidents which arise should be determined by the magistrates or the state. If, therefore, a democracy is to be reckoned a free state, it is evident that any such establishment which centres all power in the votes of the people cannot, properly speaking, be a democracy: for their decrees cannot be general in their extent. Thus, then, we may describe the several species of democracies.

Chapter V

Of the different species of oligarchies one is, when the right to the offices is regulated by a certain census; so that the poor, although the majority, have no share in it; while all those who are included therein take part in the management of public affairs. Another sort is, when the magistrates are men of very small fortune, who upon any vacancy do themselves fill it up: and if they do this out of the community at large, the state approaches to an aristocracy; if out of any particular class of people, it will be an oligarchy. Another sort of oligarchy is, when the power is an hereditary nobility. The fourth is, when the power is in the same hands as the other, but not under the control of law; and this sort of oligarchy exactly corresponds to a tyranny in monarchies, and to that particular species of democracies which I last mentioned in treating of that state: this has the particular name of a dynasty. These are the different sorts of oligarchies and democracies.

It should also be known, that it often happens that a free state, where the supreme power is in the laws, may not be democratic, and yet in consequence of the established manners and customs of the people, may be governed as if it was; so, on the other hand, where the laws may countenance a more democratic form of government, these may make the state inclining to an oligarchy; and this chiefly happens when there has been any alteration in the government; for the people do not easily change, but love their own ancient customs; and it is by small degrees only that one thing takes place of another; so that the ancient laws will remain, while the power will be in the hands of those who have brought about a revolution in the state.

Chapter VI

It is evident from what has been said, that there are as many different sorts of democracies and oligarchies as I have reckoned up: for, of necessity, either all ranks of the people which I have enumerated must have a share in the government, or some only, and others not; for when the husbandmen, and those only who possess moderate fortunes, have the supreme power, they will govern according to law; for as they must get their livings by their employs, they have but little leisure for public business: they will therefore establish proper laws, and never call public assemblies but when there is a necessity for them; and they will readily let every one partake with them in the administration of public affairs as soon as they possess that fortune which the law requires for their qualification: every one, therefore, who is qualified will have his share in the government: for to exclude any would be to make the government an oligarchy, and for all to have leisure to attend without they had a subsistence would be impossible: for these reasons, therefore, this government is a species of democracy. Another species is distinguished by the mode of electing their magistrates, in which every one is eligible, to whose birth there are no objections, provided he is supposed to have leisure to attend: for which reason in such a democracy the supreme power will be vested in the laws, as there will be nothing paid to those who go to the public assemblies. A third species is where every freeman has a right to a share in the government, which he will not accept for the cause already assigned; for which reason here also the supreme power will be in the law. The fourth species of democracy, the last which was established in order of time, arose when cities were greatly enlarged to what they were at first, and when the public revenue became something considerable; for then the populace, on account of their numbers, were admitted to share in the management of public affairs, for then even the poorest people were at leisure to attend to them, as they received wages for so doing; nay, they were more so than others, as they were not hindered by having anything of their own to mind, as the rich had; for which reason these last very often did not frequent the public assemblies and the courts of justice: thus the supreme power was lodged in the poor, and not in the laws. These are the different sorts of democracies, and such are the causes which necessarily gave birth to them.

The first species of oligarchy is, when the generality of the state are men of moderate and not too large property; for this gives them leisure for the management of public affairs: and, as they are a numerous body, it necessarily follows that the supreme power must be in the laws, and not in men; for as they are far removed from a monarchical government, and have not sufficient fortune to neglect their private affairs, while they are too many to be supported by the public, they will of course determine to be governed by the laws, and not by each other. But if the men of property in the state are but few, and their property is large, then an oligarchy of the second sort will take place; for those who have most power will think that they have a right to lord it over the others; and, to accomplish this, they will associate to themselves some who have an inclination for public affairs, and as they are not powerful enough to govern without law, they will make a law for that purpose. And if those few who have large fortunes should acquire still greater power, the oligarchy will then alter into one of the third sort; for they will get all the offices of the state into their own hands by a law which directs the son to succeed upon the death of his father; and, after that, when, by means of their increasing wealth and powerful connections, they extend still further their oppression, a monarchical dynasty will directly succeed wherein men will be supreme, and not the law; and this is the fourth species of an oligarchy correspondent to the last-mentioned class of democracies.

Chapter VII

There are besides two other states, a democracy and an oligarchy, one of which all speak of, and it is always esteemed a species of the four sorts; and thus they reckon them up; a monarchy, an oligarchy, a democracy, and this fourth which they call an aristocracy. There is also a fifth, which bears a name that is also common to the other four, namely, a state: but as this is seldom to be met with, it has escaped those who have endeavoured to enumerate the different sorts of governments, which they fix at four only, as does Plato in his Republic.

An aristocracy, of which I have already treated in the first book, is rightly called so; for a state governed by the best men, upon the most virtuous principles, and not upon any hypothesis, which even good men may propose, has alone a right to be called an aristocracy, for it is there only that a man is at once a good man and a good citizen; while in other states men are good only relative to those states. Moreover, there are some other states which are called by the same name, that differ both from oligarchies and free states, wherein not only the rich but also the virtuous have a share in the administration; and have therefore acquired the name of aristocracies; for in those governments wherein virtue is not their common care, there are still men of worth and approved goodness. Whatever state, then, like the Carthaginians, favours the rich, the virtuous, and the citizens at large, is a sort of aristocracy: when only the two latter are held in esteem, as at Lacedaemon, and the state is jointly composed of these, it is a virtuous democracy. These are the two species of aristocracies after the first, which is the best of all governments. There is also a third, which is, whenever a free state inclines to the dominion of a few.

Chapter VIII

It now remains for us to treat of that government which is particularly called a free state, and also of a tyranny; and the reason for my choosing to place that free state here is, because this, as well as those aristocracies already mentioned, although they do not seem excesses, yet, to speak true, they have all departed from what a perfect government is. Nay, they are deviations both of them equally from other forms, as I said at the beginning. It is proper to mention a tyranny the last of all governments, for it is of all others the least like one: but as my intention is to treat of all governments in general, for this reason that also, as I have said, will be taken into consideration in its proper place.

I shall now inquire into a free state and show what it is; and we shall the better understand its positive nature as we have already described an oligarchy and a democracy; for a free state is indeed nothing more than a mixture of them, and it has been usual to call those which incline most to a democracy, a free state; those which incline most to an oligarchy, an aristocracy, because those who are rich are generally men of family and education; besides, they enjoy those things which others are often guilty of crimes to procure: for which reason they are regarded as men of worth and honour and note.

Since, then, it is the genius of an aristocracy to allot the larger part of the government to the best citizens, they therefore say, that an oligarchy is chiefly composed of those men who are worthy and honourable: now it seems impossible that where the government is in the hands of the good, there the laws should not be good, but bad; or, on the contrary, that where the government is in the hands of the bad, there the laws should be good; nor is a government well constituted because the laws are, without at the same time care is taken that they are observed; for to enforce obedience to the laws which it makes is one proof of a good constitution in the state-another is, to have laws well calculated for those who are to abide by them; for if they are improper they must be obeyed: and this may be done two ways, either by their being the best relative to the particular state, or the best absolutely. An aristocracy seems most likely to confer the honours of the state on the virtuous; for virtue is the object of an aristocracy, riches of an oligarchy, and liberty of a democracy; for what is approved of by the majority will prevail in all or in each of these three different states; and that which seems good to most of those who compose the community will prevail: for what is called a state prevails in many communities, which aim at a mixture of rich and poor, riches and liberty: as for the rich, they are usually supposed to take the place of the worthy and honourable. As there are three things which claim an equal rank in the state, freedom, riches, and virtue (for as for the fourth, rank, it is an attendant on two of the others, for virtue and riches are the origin of family), it is evident, that the conjuncture of the rich and the poor make up a free state; but that all three tend to an aristocracy more than any other, except that which is truly so, which holds the first rank.

We have already seen that there are governments different from a monarchy, a democracy, and an oligarchy; and what they are, and wherein they differ from each other; and also aristocracies and states properly so called, which are derived from them; and it is evident that these are not much unlike each other.

Chapter IX

We shall next proceed to show how that government which is peculiarly called a state arises alongside of democracy and oligarchy, and how it ought to be established; and this will at the same time show what are the proper boundaries of both these governments, for we must mark out wherein they differ from one another, and then from both these compose a state of such parts of each of them as will show from whence they were taken.

There are three different ways in which two states may be blended and joined together; for, in the first place, all those rules may be adopted which the laws of each of them have ordered; as for instance in the judicial department, for in an oligarchy the rich are fined if they do not come to the court as jurymen, but the poor are not paid for their attendance; but in democracies they are, while the rich are not fined for their neglect. Now these things, as being common to both, are fit to be observed in a free state which is composed of both. This, then, is one way in which they may be joined together. In the second place, a medium may be taken between the different methods which each state observes; for instance, in a democracy the right to vote in the public assembly is either confined by no census at all, or limited by a very small one; in an oligarchy none enjoy it but those whose census is high: therefore, as these two practices are contrary to each other, a census between each may be established in such a state. In the third place, different laws of each community may be adopted; as, for instance, as it seems correspondent to the nature of a democracy, that the magistrates should be chosen by lot, but an aristocracy by vote, and in the one state according to a census, but not in the other: let, then, an aristocracy and a free state copy something from each of them; let them follow an oligarchy in choosing their magistrates by vote, but a democracy in not admitting of any census, and thus blend together the different customs of the two governments. But the best proof of a happy mixture of a democracy and an oligarchy is this, when a person may properly call the same state a democracy and an oligarchy. It is evident that those who speak of it in this manner are induced to it because both these governments are there well blended together: and indeed this is common to all mediums, that the extremes of each side should be discerned therein, as at Lacedaemon; for many affirm that it is a democracy from the many particulars in which it follows that form of government; as for instance, in the first place, in the bringing up of their children, for the rich and poor are brought up in the same manner; and their education is such that the children of the poor may partake of it; and the same rules are observed when they are youths and men, there is no distinction between a rich person and a poor one; and in their public tables the same provision is served to all. The rich also wear only such clothes as the poorest man is able to purchase. Moreover, with respect to two magistracies of the highest rank, one they have a right to elect to, the other to fill; namely, the senate and the ephori. Others consider it as an oligarchy, the principles of which it follows in many things, as in choosing all their officers by vote, and not by lot; in there being but a few who have a right to sit in judgment on capital causes and the like. Indeed, a state which is well composed of two others ought to resemble them both, and neither, Such a state ought to have its means of preservation in itself, and not without; and when I say in itself, I do not mean that it should owe this to the forbearance of their neighbours, for this may happen to a bad government, but to every member of the community's not being willing that there should be the least alteration in their constitution. Such is the method in which a free state or aristocracy ought to be established.

Chapter X

It now remains to treat of a tyranny; not that there is much to be said on that subject, but as it makes part of our plan, since we enumerated it amongst our different sorts of governments. In the beginning of this work we inquired into the nature of kingly government, and entered into a particular examination of what was most properly called so, and whether it was advantageous to a state or not, and what it should be, and how established; and we divided a tyranny into two pieces when we were upon this subject, because there is something analogous between this and a kingly government, for they are both of them established by law; for among some of the barbarians they elect a monarch with absolute power, and formerly among the Greeks there were some such, whom they called sesumnetes. Now these differ from each other; for some possess only kingly power regulated by law, and rule those who voluntarily submit to their government; others rule despotically according to their own will. There is a third species of tyranny, most properly so called, which is the very opposite to kingly power; for this is the government of one who rules over his equals and superiors without being accountable for his conduct, and whose object is his own advantage, and not the advantage of those he governs;

for which reason he rules by compulsion, for no freemen will ever willingly submit to such a government. These are the different species of tyrannies, their principles, and their causes.

Chapter XI

We proceed now to inquire what form of government and what manner of life is best for communities in general, not adapting it to that superior virtue which is above the reach of the vulgar, or that education which every advantage of nature and fortune only can furnish, nor to those imaginary plans which may be formed at pleasure; but to that mode of life which the greater part of mankind can attain to, and that government which most cities may establish: for as to those aristocracies which we have now mentioned, they are either too perfect for a state to support, or one so nearly alike to that state we now going to inquire into, that we shall treat of them both as one.

The opinions which we form upon these subjects must depend upon one common principle: for if what I have said in my treatise on Morals is true, a happy life must arise from an uninterrupted course of virtue; and if virtue consists in a certain medium, the middle life must certainly be the happiest; which medium is attainable by every one. The boundaries of virtue and vice in the state must also necessarily be the same as in a private person; for the form of government is the life of the city. In every city the people are divided into three sorts; the very rich, the very poor, and those who are between them. If this is universally admitted, that the mean is best, it is evident that even in point of fortune mediocrity is to be preferred; for that state is most submissive to reason; for those who are very handsome, or very strong, or very noble, or very rich; or, on the contrary; those who are very poor, or very weak, or very mean, with difficulty obey it; for the one are capricious and greatly flagitious, the other rascally and mean, the crimes of each arising from their different excesses: nor will they go through the different offices of the state; which is detrimental to it: besides, those who excel in strength, in riches, or friends, or the like, neither know how nor are willing to submit to command: and this begins at home when they are boys; for there they are brought up too delicately to be accustomed to obey their preceptors: as for the very poor, their general and excessive want of what the rich enjoy reduces them to a state too mean: so that the one know not how to command, but to be commanded as slaves, the others know not how to submit to any command, nor to command themselves but with despotic power.

A city composed of such men must therefore consist of slaves and masters, not freemen; where one party must hate, and the other despise, where there could be no possibility of friendship or political community: for community supposes affection; for we do not even on the road associate with our enemies. It is also the genius of a city to be composed as much as possible of equals; which will be most so when the inhabitants are in the middle state: from whence it follows, that that city must be best framed which is composed of those whom we say are naturally its proper members. It is men of this station also who will be best assured of safety and protection; for they will neither covet what belongs to others, as the poor do; nor will others covet what is theirs, as the poor do what belongs to the rich; and thus, without plotting against any one, or having any one plot against them, they will live free from danger: for which reason Phocylides wisely wishes for the middle state, as being most productive of happiness. It is plain, then, that the most perfect political community must be amongst those who are in the middle rank, and those states are best instituted wherein these are a larger and more respectable part, if possible, than both the other; or, if that cannot be, at least than either of them separate; so that being thrown into the balance it may prevent either scale from preponderating.

It is therefore the greatest happiness which the citizens can enjoy to possess a moderate and convenient fortune; for when some possess too much, and others nothing at all, the government must either be in the hands of the meanest rabble or else a pure oligarchy; or, from the excesses of both, a tyranny; for this arises from a headstrong democracy or an oligarchy, but very seldom when the members of the community are nearly on an equality with each other. We will assign a reason for this when we come to treat of the alterations which different states are likely to undergo. The middle state is therefore best, as being least liable to those seditions and insurrections which disturb the community; and for the same reason extensive governments are least liable to these inconveniences; for there those in a middle state are very numerous, whereas in small ones it is easy to pass to the two extremes, so as hardly to have any in a medium remaining, but the one half rich, the other poor: and from the same principle it is that democracies are more firmly established and of longer continuance than oligarchies; but even in those when there is a want of a proper number of men of middling fortune, the poor extend their power too far, abuses arise, and the government is soon at an end.

We ought to consider as a proof of what I now advance, that the best lawgivers themselves were those in the middle rank of life, amongst whom was Solon, as is evident from his poems, and Lycurgus, for he was not a king, and Charondas, and indeed most others. What has been said will show us why of so many free states some have changed to democracies, others to oligarchies: for whenever the number of those in the middle state has been too small, those who were the more numerous, whether the rich or the poor, always overpowered them and assumed to themselves the administration of public affairs; from hence arose either a democracy or an oligarchy. Moreover, when in consequence of their disputes and quarrels with each other, either the rich get the better of the poor, or the poor of the rich, neither of them will establish a free state; but, as the record of their victory, one which inclines to their own principles, and form either a democracy or an oligarchy.

Those who made conquests in Greece, having all of them an eye to the respective forms of government in their own cities, established either democracies or oligarchies, not considering what was serviceable to the state, but what was similar to their own; for which reason a government has never been established where the supreme power has been placed amongst those of the middling rank, or very seldom; and, amongst a few, one man only of those who have yet been conquerors has been persuaded to give the preference to this order of men: it is indeed an established custom with the inhabitants of most cities not to desire an equality, but either to aspire to govern, or when they are conquered, to submit.

Thus we have shown what the best state is, and why. It will not be difficult to perceive of the many states which there are, for we have seen that there are various forms both of democracies and oligarchies, to which we should give the first place, to which the second, and in the same manner the next also; and to observe what are the particular excellences and defects of each, after we have first described the best possible; for that must be the best which is nearest to this, that worst which is most distant from the medium, without any one has a particular plan of his own which he judges by. I mean by this, that it may happen, that although one form of government may be better than another, yet there is no reason to prevent another from being preferable thereunto in particular circumstances and for particular purposes.

Chapter XII

After what has been said, it follows that we should now show what particular form of government is most suitable for particular persons; first laying this down as a general maxim, that that party which desires to support the actual administration of the state ought always to be superior to that which would alter it. Every city is made up of quality and quantity: by quality I mean liberty, riches, education, and family, and by quantity its relative populousness: now it may happen that quality may exist in one of those parts of which the city is composed, and quantity in another; thus the number of the ignoble may be greater than the number of those of family, the number of the poor than that of the rich; but not so that the quantity of the one shall overbalance the quality of the other; those must be properly adjusted to each other; for where the number of the poor exceeds the proportion we have mentioned, there a democracy will rise up, and if the husbandry should have more power than others, it will be a democracy of husbandmen; and the democracy will be a particular species according to that class of men which may happen to be most numerous: thus, should these be the husbandmen, it will be of these, and the best; if of mechanics and those who hire themselves out, the worst possible: in the same manner it may be of any other set between these two. But when the rich and the noble prevail more by their quality than they are deficient in quantity, there an oligarchy ensues; and this oligarchy may be of different species, according to the nature of the prevailing party. Every legislator in framing his constitution ought to have a particular regard to those in the middle rank of life; and if he intends an oligarchy, these should be the object of his laws; if a democracy, to these they should be entrusted; and whenever their number exceeds that of the two others, or at least one of them, they give stability to the constitution; for there is no fear that the rich and the poor should agree to conspire together against them, for neither of these will choose to serve the other. If any one would choose to fix the administration on the widest basis, he will find none preferable to this; for to rule by turns is what the rich and the poor will not submit to, on account of their hatred to each other. It is, moreover, allowed that an arbitrator is the most proper person for both parties to trust to; now this arbitrator is the middle rank.

Those who would establish aristocratical governments are mistaken not only in giving too much power to the rich, but also in deceiving the common people; for at last, instead of an imaginary good, they must feel a real evil, for the encroachments of the rich are more destructive to the state than those of the poor.

Chapter XIII

There are five particulars in which, under fair pretences, the rich craftily endeavour to undermine the rights of the people, these are their public assemblies, their offices of state, their courts of justice, their military power, and their gymnastic exercises. With respect to their public assemblies, in having them open to all, but in fining the rich only, or others very little, for not attending; with respect to offices, in permitting the poor to swear off, but not granting this indulgence to those who are within the census; with respect to their courts of justice, in fining the rich for non-attendance, but the poor not at all, or those a great deal, and these very little, as was done by the laws of Charondas. In some places every citizen who was enrolled had a right to attend the public assemblies and to try causes; which if they did not do, a very heavy fine was laid upon them; that through fear of the fine they might avoid being enrolled, as they were then obliged to do neither the one nor the other. The same spirit of legislation prevailed with respect to their bearing arms and their gymnastic exercises; for the poor are excused if they have no arms, but the rich are fined; the same method takes place if they do not attend their gymnastic exercises, there is no penalty on one, but there is on the other: the consequence of which is, that the fear of this penalty induces the rich to keep the one and attend the other, while the poor do neither. These are the deceitful contrivances of oligarchical legislators.

The contrary prevails in a democracy; for there they make the poor a proper allowance for attending the assemblies and the courts, but give the rich nothing for doing it: whence it is evident, that if any one would properly blend these customs together, they must extend both the pay and the fine to every member of the community, and then every one would share in it, whereas part only now do. The citizens of a free state ought to consist of those only who bear arms: with respect to their census it is not easy to determine exactly what it ought to be, but the rule that should direct upon this subject should be to make it as extensive as possible, so that those who are enrolled in it make up a greater part of the people than those who are not; for those who are poor, although they partake not of the offices of the state, are willing to live quiet, provided that no one disturbs them in their property: but this is not an easy matter; for it may not always happen, that those who are at the head of public affairs are of a humane behaviour. In time of war the poor are accustomed to show no alacrity without they have provisions found them; when they have, then indeed they are willing to fight.

In some governments the power is vested not only in those who bear arms, but also in those who have borne them. Among the Malienses the state was composed of these latter only, for all the officers were soldiers who had served their time. And the first states in Greece which succeeded those where kingly power was established, were governed by the military. First of all the horse, for at that time the strength and excellence of the army depended on the horse, for as to the heavy-armed foot they were useless without proper discipline; but the art of tactics was not known to the ancients, for which reason their strength lay in their horse: but when cities grew larger, and they depended more on their foot, greater numbers partook of the freedom of the city; for which reason what we call republics were formerly called democracies. The ancient governments were properly oligarchies or kingdoms; for on account of the few persons in each state, it would have been impossible to have found a sufficient number of the middle rank; so these being but few, and those used to subordination, they more easily submitted to be governed.

We have now shown why there are many sorts of governments, and others different from those we have treated of: for there are more species of democracies than one, and the like is true of other forms, and what are their differences, and whence they arise; and also of all others which is the best, at least in general; and which is best suited for particular people.

Chapter XIV

We will now proceed to make some general reflections upon the governments next in order, and also to consider each of them in particular; beginning with those principles which appertain to each: now there are three things in all states which a careful legislator ought well to consider, which are of great consequence to all, and which properly attended to the state must necessarily be happy; and according to the variation of which the one will differ from the other. The first of these is the public assembly; the second the officers of the state, that is, who they ought to be, and with what power they should be entrusted, and in what manner they should be appointed; the third, the judicial department.

Now it is the proper business of the public assembly to determine concerning war and peace, making or breaking off alliances, to enact laws, to sentence to death, banishment, or confiscation of goods, and to call the magistrates to account for their behaviour when in office. Now these powers must necessarily be entrusted to the citizens in general, or all of them to some; either to one magistrate or more; or some to one, and some to another, or some to all, but others to some: to entrust all to all is in the spirit of a democracy, for the people aim at equality. There are many methods of delegating these powers to the citizens at large, one of which is to let them execute them by turn, and not altogether, as was done by Tellecles, the Milesian, in his state. In others the supreme council is composed of the different magistrates, and they succeed to the offices of the community by proper divisions of tribes, wards, and other very small proportions, till every one in his turn goes through them: nor does the whole community ever meet together, without it is when new laws are enacted, or some national affair is debated, or to hear what the magistrates have to propose to them. Another method is for the people to meet in a collective body, but only for the purpose of holding the comitia, making laws, determining concerning war or peace, and inquiring into the conduct of their magistrates, while the remaining part of the public business is conducted by the magistrates, who have their separate departments, and are chosen out of the whole community either by vote or ballot. Another method is for the people in general to meet for the choice of the magistrates, and to examine into their conduct; and also to deliberate concerning war and alliances, and to leave other things to the magistrates, whoever happen to be chosen, whose particular employments are such as necessarily require persons well skilled therein. A fourth method is for every person to deliberate upon every subject in public assembly, where the magistrates can determine nothing of themselves, and have only the privilege of giving their opinions first; and this is the method of the most pure democracy, which is analogous to the proceedings in a dynastic oligarchy and a tyrannic monarchy.

These, then, are the methods in which public business is conducted in a democracy. When the power is in the hands of part of the community only, it is an oligarchy and this also admits of different customs; for whenever the officers of the state are chosen out of those who have a moderate fortune, and these from that circumstance are many, and when they depart not from that line which the law has laid down, but carefully follow it, and when all within the census are eligible, certainly it is then an oligarchy, but founded on true principles of government from its moderation. When the people in general do not partake of the deliberative power, but certain persons chosen for that purpose, who govern according to law; this also, like the first, is an oligarchy. When those who have the deliberative power elect each other, and the son succeeds to the father, and when they can supersede the laws, such a government is of necessity a strict oligarchy. When some persons determine on one thing, and others on another, as war and peace, and when all inquire into the conduct of their magistrates, and other things are left to different officers, elected either by vote or lot, then the government is an aristocracy or a free state. When some are chosen by vote and others by lot, and these either from the people in general, or from a certain number elected for that purpose, or if both the votes and the lots are open to all, such a state is partly an aristocracy, partly a free government itself. These are the different methods in which the deliberative power is vested in different states, all of whom follow some regulation here laid down. It is advantageous to a democracy, in the present sense of the word, by which I mean a state wherein the people at large have a supreme power, even over the laws, to hold frequent public assemblies; and it will be best in this particular to imitate the example of oligarchies in their courts of justice; for they fine those who are appointed to try causes if they do not attend, so should they reward the poor for coming to the public assemblies: and their counsels will be best when all advise with each other, the citizens with the nobles, the nobles with the citizens. It is also advisable when the council is to be composed of part of the citizens, to elect, either by vote or lot, an equal number of both ranks. It is also proper, if the common people in the state are very numerous, either not to pay every one for his attendance, but such a number only as will make them equal to the nobles, or to reject many of them by lot.

In an oligarchy they should either call up some of the common people to the council, or else establish a court, as is done in some other states, whom they call pre-advisers or guardians of the laws, whose business should be to propose first what they should afterwards enact. By this means the people would have a place in the administration of public affairs, without having it in their power to occasion any disorder in the government. Moreover, the people may be allowed to have a vote in whatever bill is proposed, but may not themselves propose anything contrary thereto; or they may give their advice, while the power of determining may be with the magistrates only. It is also necessary to follow a contrary practice to what is established in democracies, for the people should be allowed the power of pardoning, but not of condemning, for the cause should be referred back again to the magistrates: whereas the contrary takes place in republics; for the power of pardoning is with the few, but not of condemning, which is always referred to the people at large. And thus we determine concerning the deliberative power in any state, and in whose hands it shall be.

Chapter XV

We now proceed to consider the choice of magistrates; for this branch of public business contains many different Parts, as how many there shall be, what shall be their particular office, and with respect to time how long each of them shall continue in place; for some make it six months, others shorter, others for a year, others for a much longer time; or whether they should be perpetual or for a long time, or neither; for the same person may fill the same office several times, or he may not be allowed to enjoy it even twice, but only once: and also with respect to the appointment of magistrates, who are to be eligible, who is to choose them, and in what manner; for in all these particulars we ought properly to distinguish the different ways which may be followed; and then to show which of these is best suited to such and such governments.

Now it is not easy to determine to whom we ought properly to give the name of magistrate, for a government requires many persons in office; but every one of those who is either chosen by vote or lot is not to be reckoned a magistrate. The priests, for instance, in the first place; for these are to be considered as very different from civil magistrates: to these we may add the choregi and heralds; nay, even ambassadors are elected: there are some civil employments which belong to the citizens; and these are either when they are all engaged in one thing, as when as soldiers they obey their general, or when part of them only are, as in governing the women or educating the youth; and also some economic, for they often elect corn-meters: others are servile, and in which, if they are rich, they employ slaves. But indeed they are most properly called magistrates, who are members of the deliberative council, or decide causes, or are in some command, the last more especially, for to command is peculiar to magistrates. But to speak truth, this question is of no great consequence, nor is it the province of the judges to decide between those who dispute about words; it may indeed be an object of speculative inquiry; but to inquire what officers are necessary in a state, and how many, and what, though not most necessary, may yet be advantageous in a well-established government, is a much more useful employment, and this with respect to all states in general, as well as to small cities.

In extensive governments it is proper to allot one employment to one person, as there are many to serve the public in so numerous a society, where some may be passed over for a long time, and others never be in office but once; and indeed everything is better done which has the whole attention of one person, than when that attention is divided amongst many; but in small states it is necessary that a few of the citizens should execute many employments; for their numbers are so small it will not be convenient to have many of them in office at the same time; for where shall we find others to succeed them in turn? Small states will sometimes want the same magistrates and the same laws as large ones; but the one will not want to employ them so often as the other; so that different charges may be intrusted to the same person without any inconvenience, for they will not interfere with each other, and for want of sufficient members in the community it will be necessary. If we could tell how many magistrates are necessary in every city, and how many, though not necessary, it is yet proper to have, we could then the better know how many different offices one might assign to one magistrate. It is also necessary to know what tribunals in different places should have different things under their jurisdiction, and also what things should always come under the cognisance of the same magistrate; as, for instance, decency of manners, shall the clerk of the market take cognisance of that if the cause arises in the market, and another magistrate in another place, or the same magistrate everywhere: or shall there be a distinction made of the fact, or the parties? as, for instance, in decency of manners, shall it be one cause when it relates to a man, another when it relates to a woman?

In different states shall the magistrates be different or the same? I mean, whether in a democracy, an oligarchy, an aristocracy, and a monarchy, the same persons shall have the same power? or shall it vary according to the different formation of the government? as in an aristocracy the offices of the state are allotted to those who are well educated; in an oligarchy to those who are rich; in a democracy to the freemen? Or shall the magistrates differ as the communities differ? For it may happen that the very same may be sometimes proper, sometimes otherwise: in this state it may be necessary that the magistrate have great powers, in that but small. There are also certain magistrates peculiar to certain states-as the pre-advisers are not proper in a democracy, but a senate is; for one such order is necessary, whose business shall be to consider beforehand and prepare those bills which shall be brought before the people that they may have leisure to attend to their own affairs; and when these are few in number the state inclines to an oligarchy. The pre-advisers indeed must always be few for they are peculiar to an oligarchy: and where there are both these offices in the same state, the pre-adviser's is superior to the senator's, the one having only a democratical power, the other an oligarchical: and indeed the power of the senate is lost in those democracies, in which the people, meeting in one public assembly, take all the business into their own hands; and this is likely to happen either when the community in general are in easy circumstances, or when they are paid for their attendance; for they are then at leisure often to meet together and determine everything for themselves. A magistrate whose business is to control the manners of the boys, or women, or who takes any department similar to this, is to be found in an aristocracy, not in a democracy; for who can forbid the wives of the poor from appearing in public? neither is such a one to be met with in an oligarchy; for the women there are too delicate to bear control. And thus much for this subject. Let us endeavour to treat at large of the establishment of magistrates, beginning from first principles. Now, they differ from each other in three ways, from which, blended together, all the varieties which can be imagined arise. The first of these differences is in those who appoint the magistrates, the second consists in those who are appointed, the third in the mode of appointment; and each of these three differ in three manners; for either all the citizens may appoint collectively, or some out of their whole body, or some out of a particular order in it, according to fortune, family, or virtue, or some other rule (as at Megara, where the right of election was amongst those who had returned together to their country, and had reinstated themselves by force of arms) and this either by vote or lot. Again, these several modes may be differently formed together, as some magistrates may be chosen by part of the community, others by the whole; some out of part, others out of the whole; some by vote, others by lot: and each of these different modes admit of a four-fold subdivision; for either all may elect all by vote or by lot; and when all elect, they may either proceed without any distinction, or they may elect by a certain division of tribes, wards, or companies, till they have gone through the whole community: and some magistrates may be elected one way, and others another. Again, if some magistrates are elected either by vote or lot of all the citizens, or by the vote of some and the lot of some, or some one way and some another; that is to say, some by the vote of all, others by the lot of all, there will then be twelve different methods of electing the magistrates, without blending the two together. Of these there are two adapted to a democracy; namely, to have all the magistrates chosen out of all the people, either by vote or lot, or both; that is to say, some of them by lot, some by vote. In a free state the whole community should not elect at the same time, but some out of the whole, or out of some particular rank; and this either by lot, or vote, or both: and they should elect either out of the whole community, or out of some particular persons in it, and this both by lot and vote. In an oligarchy it is proper to choose some magistrates out of the whole body of the citizens, some by vote, some by lot, others by both: by lot is most correspondent to that form of government. In a free aristocracy, some magistrates should be chosen out of the community in general, others out of a particular rank, or these by choice, those by lot. In a pure oligarchy, the magistrates should be chosen out of certain ranks, and by certain persons, and some of those by lot, others by both methods; but to choose them out of the whole community is not correspondent to the nature of this government. It is proper in an aristocracy for the whole community to elect their magistrates out of particular persons, and this by vote. These then are all the different ways of electing of magistrates; and they have been allotted according to the nature of the different communities; but what mode of proceeding is proper for different communities, or how the offices ought to be established, or with what powers shall be particularly explained. I mean by the powers of a magistrate, what should be his particular province, as the management of the finances or the laws of the state; for different magistrates have different powers, as that of the general of the army differs from the clerk of the market.

Chapter XVI

Of the three parts of which a government is formed, we now come to consider the judicial; and this also we shall divide in the same manner as we did the magisterial, into three parts. Of whom the judges shall consist, and for what causes, and how. When I say of whom, I mean whether they shall be the whole people, or some particulars; by for what causes I mean, how many different courts shall be appointed; by how, whether they shall be elected by vote or lot. Let us first determine how many different courts there ought to be. Now these are eight. The first of these is the court of inspection over the behaviour of the magistrates when they have quitted their office; the second is to punish those who have injured the public; the third is to take cognisance of those causes in which the state is a party; the fourth is to decide between magistrates and private persons, who appeal from a fine laid upon them; the fifth is to determine disputes which may arise concerning contracts of great value; the sixth is to judge between foreigners, and of murders, of which there are different species; and these may all be tried by the same judges or by different ones; for there are murders of malice prepense and of chance-medley; there is also justifiable homicide, where the fact is admitted, and the legality of it disputed.

There is also another court called at Athens the Court of Phreattae, which determines points relating to a murder committed by one who has run away, to decide whether he shall return; though such an affair happens but seldom, and in very large cities; the seventh, to determine causes wherein strangers are concerned, and this whether they are between stranger and stranger or between a stranger and a citizen. The eighth and last is for small actions, from one to five drachma's, or a little more; for these ought also to be legally determined, but not to be brought before the whole body of the judges. But without entering into any particulars concerning actions for murder, and those wherein strangers are the parties, let us particularly treat of those courts which have the jurisdiction of those matters which more particularly relate to the affairs of the community and which if not well conducted occasion seditions and commotions in the state. Now, of necessity, either all persons must have a right to judge of all these different causes, appointed for that purpose, either by vote or lot, or all of all, some of them by vote, and others by lot, or in some causes by vote, in others by lot. Thus there will be four sorts of judges. There will be just the same number also if they are chosen out of part of the people only; for either all the judges must be chosen out of that part either by vote or lot, or some by lot and some by vote, or the judges in particular causes must be chosen some by vote, others by lot; by which means there will be the same number of them also as was mentioned. Besides, different judges may be joined together; I mean those who are chosen out of the whole people or part of them or both; so that all three may sit together in the same court, and this either by vote, lot, or both. And thus much for the different sorts of judges. Of these appointments that which admits all the community to be judges in all causes is most suitable to a democracy; the second, which appoints that certain persons shall judge all causes, to an oligarchy; the third, which appoints the whole community to be judges in some causes, but particular persons in others, to an aristocracy or free state.

Book V

Chapter I

We have now gone through those particulars we proposed to speak of; it remains that we next consider from what causes and how alterations in government arise, and of what nature they are, and to what the destruction of each state is owing; and also to what form any form of polity is most likely to shift into, and what are the means to be used for the general preservation of governments, as well as what are applicable to any particular state; and also of the remedies which are to be applied either to all in general, or to any one considered separately, when they are in a state of corruption: and here we ought first to lay down this principle, that there are many governments, all of which approve of what is just and what is analogically equal; and yet have failed from attaining thereunto, as we have already mentioned; thus democracies have arisen from supposing that those who are equal in one thing are so in every other circumstance; as, because they are equal in liberty, they are equal in everything else; and oligarchies, from supposing that those who are unequal in one thing are unequal in all; that when men are so in point of fortune, that inequality extends to everything else. Hence it follows, that those who in some respects are equal with others think it right to endeavour to partake of an equality with them in everything; and those who are superior to others endeavour to get still more; and it is this more which is the inequality: thus most states, though they have some notion of what is just, yet are almost totally wrong; and, upon this account, when either party has not that share in the administration which answers to his expectations, he becomes seditious: but those who of all others have the greatest right to be so are the last that are; namely, those who excel in virtue; for they alone can be called generally superior. There are, too, some persons of distinguished families who, because they are so, disdain to be on an equality with others, for those esteem themselves noble who boast of their ancestors' merit and fortune: these, to speak truth, are the origin and fountain from whence seditions arise. The alterations which men may propose to make in governments are two; for either they may change the state already established into some other, as when they propose to erect an oligarchy where there is a democracy; or a democracy, or free state, where there is an oligarchy, or an aristocracy from these, or those from that; or else, when they have no objection to the established government, which they like very well, but choose to have the sole management in it themselves; either in the hands of a few or one only. They will also raise commotions concerning the degree in which they would have the established power; as if, for instance, the government is an oligarchy, to have it more purely so, and in the same manner if it is a democracy, or else to have it less so; and, in like manner, whatever may be the nature of the government, either to extend or contract its powers; or else to make some alterations in some parts of it; as to establish or abolish a particular magistracy, as some persons say Lysander endeavoured to abolish the kingly power in Sparta; and Pausanias that of the ephori. Thus in Epidamnus there was an alteration in one part of the constitution, for instead of the philarchi they established a senate. It is also necessary for all the magistrates at Athens; to attend in the court of the Helisea when any new magistrate is created: the power of the archon also in that state partakes of the nature of an oligarchy: inequality is always the occasion of sedition, but not when those who are unequal are treated in a different manner correspondent to that inequality. Thus kingly power is unequal when exercised over equals. Upon the whole, those who aim after an equality are the cause of seditions. Equality is twofold, either in number or value. Equality in number is when two things contain the same parts or the same quantity; equality in value is by proportion as two exceeds one, and three two by the same number-thus by proportion four exceeds two, and two one in the same degree, for two is the same part of four that one is of two; that is to say, half. Now, all agree in what is absolutely and simply just; but, as we have already said they dispute concerning proportionate value; for some persons, if they are equal in one respect, think themselves equal in all; others, if they are superior in one thing, think they may claim the superiority in all; from whence chiefly arise two sorts of governments, a democracy and an oligarchy; for nobility and virtue are to be found only amongst a few; the contrary amongst the many; there being in no place a hundred of the first to be met with, but enough of the last everywhere. But to establish a government entirely upon either of these equalities is wrong, and this the example of those so established makes evident, for none of them have been stable; and for this reason, that it is impossible that whatever is wrong at the first and in its principles should not at last meet with a bad end: for which reason in some things an equality of numbers ought to take place, in others an equality in value. However, a democracy is safer and less liable to sedition than an oligarchy; for in this latter it may arise from two causes, for either the few in power may conspire against each other or against the people; but in a democracy only one; namely, against the few who aim at exclusive power; but there is no instance worth speaking of, of a sedition of the people against themselves. Moreover, a government composed of men of moderate fortunes comes much nearer to a democracy than an oligarchy, and is the safest of all such states.

Chapter II

Since we are inquiring into the causes of seditions and revolutions in governments, we must begin entirely with the first principles from whence they arise. Now these, so to speak, are nearly three in number; which we must first distinguish in general from each other, and endeavour to show in what situation people are who begin a sedition; and for what causes; and thirdly, what are the beginnings of political troubles and mutual quarrels with each other. Now that cause which of all others most universally inclines men to desire to bring about a change in government is that which I have already mentioned; for those who aim at equality will be ever ready for sedition, if they see those whom they esteem their equals possess more than they do, as well as those also who are not content with equality but aim at superiority, if they think that while they deserve more than, they have only equal with, or less than, their inferiors. Now, what they aim at may be either just or unjust; just, when those who are inferior are seditious, that they may be equal; unjust, when those who are equal are so, that they may be superior. These, then, are the situations in which men will be seditious: the causes for which they will be so are profit and honour; and their contrary: for, to avoid dishonour or loss of fortune by mulcts, either on their own account or their friends, they will raise a commotion in the state. The original causes which dispose men to the things which I have mentioned are, taken in one manner, seven in number, in another they are more; two of which are the same with those that have been already mentioned: but influencing in a different manner; for profit and honour sharpen men against each other; not to get the possession of them for themselves (which was what I just now supposed), but when they see others, some justly, others unjustly, engrossing them. The other causes are haughtiness, fear, eminence, contempt, disproportionate increase in some part of the state. There are also other things which in a different manner will occasion revolutions in governments; as election intrigues, neglect, want of numbers, a too great dissimilarity of circumstances.

Chapter III

What influence ill-treatment and profit have for this purpose, and how they may be the causes of sedition, is almost self-evident; for when the magistrates are haughty and endeavour to make greater profits than their office gives them, they not only occasion seditions amongst each other, but against the state also who gave them their power; and this their avarice has two objects, either private property or the property of the state. What influence honours have, and how they may occasion sedition, is evident enough; for those who are themselves unhonoured while they see others honoured, will be ready for any disturbance: and these things are done unjustly when any one is either honoured or discarded contrary to their deserts, justly when they are according to them. Excessive honours are also a cause of sedition when one person or more are greater than the state and the power of the government can permit; for then a monarchy or a dynasty is usually established: on which account the ostracism was introduced in some places, as at Argos and Athens: though it is better to guard against such excesses in the founding of a state, than when they have been permitted to take place, to correct them afterward. Those who have been guilty of crimes will be the cause of sedition, through fear of punishment; as will those also who expect an injury, that they may prevent it; as was the case at Rhodes, when the nobles conspired against the people on account of the decrees they expected would pass against them. Contempt also is a cause of sedition and conspiracies; as in oligarchies, where there are many who have no share in the administration. The rich also even in democracies, despising the disorder and anarchy which will arise, hope to better themselves by the same means which happened at Thebes after the battle of Oenophyta, where, in consequence of bad administration, the democracy was destroyed; as it was at Megara, where the power of the people was lost through anarchy and disorder; the same thing happened at Syracuse before the tyranny of Gelon; and at Rhodes there was the same sedition before the popular government was overthrown. Revolutions in state will also arise from a disproportionate increase; for as the body consists of many parts, it ought to increase proportion-ably to preserve its symmetry, which would otherwise be destroyed; as if the foot was to be four cubits long, and the rest of the body but two palms; it might otherwise be changed into an animal of a different form, if it increase beyond proportion not only in quantity, but also in disposition of parts; so also a city consists of parts, some of which may often increase without notice, as the number of poor in democracies and free states. They will also sometimes happen by accident, as at Tarentum, a little after the Median war, where so many of the nobles were killed in a battle by the Iapygi, that from a free state the government was turned into a democracy; and at Argos, where so many of the citizens were killed by Cleomenes the Spartan, that they were obliged to admit several husbandmen to the freedom of the state: and at Athens, through the unfortunate event of the infantry battles, the number of the nobles was reduced by the soldiers being chosen from the list of citizens in the Lacedaemonian wars. Revolutions also sometimes take place in a democracy, though seldomer; for where the rich grow numerous or properties increase, they become oligarchies or dynasties. Governments also sometimes alter without seditions by a combination of the meaner people; as at Hersea: for which purpose they changed the mode of election from votes to lots, and thus got themselves chosen: and by negligence, as when the citizens admit those who are not friends to the constitution into the chief offices of the state, which happened at Orus, when the oligarchy of the archons was put an end to at the election of Heracleodorus, who changed that form of government into a democratic free state. By little and little, I mean by this, that very often great alterations silently take place in the form of government from people's overlooking small matters; as at Ambracia, where the census was originally small, but at last became nothing at all, as if a little and nothing at all were nearly or entirely alike. That state also is liable to seditions which is composed of different nations, till their differences are blended together and undistinguishable; for as a city cannot be composed of every multitude, so neither can it in every given time; for which reason all those republics which have hitherto been originally composed of different people or afterwards admitted their neighbours to the freedom of their city, have been most liable to revolutions; as when the Achaeans joined with the Traezenians in founding Sybaris; for soon after, growing more powerful than the Traezenians, they expelled them from the city; from whence came the proverb of Sybarite wickedness: and again, disputes from a like cause happened at Thurium between the Sybarites and those who had joined with them in building the city; for they assuming upon these, on account of the country being their own, were driven out. And at Byzantium the new citizens, being detected in plots against the state, were driven out of the city by force of arms. The Antisseans also, having taken in those who were banished from Chios, afterwards did the same thing; and also the Zancleans, after having taken in the people of Samos. The Appolloniats, in the Euxine Sea, having admitted their sojourners to the freedom of their city, were troubled with seditions: and the Syracusians, after the expulsion of their tyrants, having enrolled strangers and mercenaries amongst their citizens, quarrelled with each other and came to an open rupture: and the people of Amphipolis, having taken in a colony of Chalcidians, were the greater part of them driven out of the city by them. Many persons occasion seditions in oligarchies because they think themselves ill-used in not sharing the honours of the state with their equals, as I have already mentioned; but in democracies the principal people do the same because they have not more than an equal share with others who are not equal to them. The situation of the place will also sometimes occasion disturbances in the state when the ground is not well adapted for one city; as at Clazomene, where the people who lived in that part of the town called Chytrum quarrelled with them who lived in the island, and the Colophonians with the Notians. At Athens too the disposition of the citizens is not the same, for those who live in the Piraeus are more attached to a popular government than those who live in the city properly so called; for as the interposition of a rivulet, however small, will occasion the line of the phalanx to fluctuate, so any trifling disagreement will be the cause of seditions; but they will not so soon flow from anything else as from the disagreement between virtue and vice, and next to that between poverty and riches, and so on in order, one cause having more influence than another; one of which that I last mentioned.

Chapter IV

But seditions in government do not arise for little things, but from them; for their immediate cause is something of moment. Now, trifling quarrels are attended with the greatest consequences when they arise between persons of the first distinction in the state, as was the case with the Syracusians in a remote period; for a revolution in the government was brought about by a quarrel between two young men who were in office, upon a love affair; for one of them being absent, the other seduced his mistress; he in his turn, offended with this, persuaded his friend's wife to come and live with him; and upon this the whole city took part either with the one or the other, and the government was overturned: therefore every one at the beginning of such disputes ought to take care to avoid the consequences; and to smother up all quarrels which may happen to arise amongst those in power, for the mischief lies in the beginning; for the beginning is said to be half of the business, so that what was then but a little fault will be found afterwards to bear its full proportion to what follows. Moreover, disputes between men of note involve the whole city in their consequences; in Hestiaea, after the Median war: two brothers having a dispute about their paternal estate; he who was the poorer, from the other's having concealed part of the effects, and some money which his father had found, engaged the popular party on his side, while the other, who was rich, the men of fashion. And at Delphos, a quarrel about a wedding was the beginning of all the seditions that afterwards arose amongst them; for the bridegroom, being terrified by some unlucky omen upon waiting upon the bride, went away without marrying her; which her relations resenting, contrived secretly to convey some sacred money into his pocket while he was sacrificing, and then killed him as an impious person. At Mitylene also, a dispute, which arose concerning a right of heritage, was the beginning of great evils, and a war with the Athenians, in which Paches took their city, for Timophanes, a man of fortune, leaving two daughters, Doxander, who was circumvented in procuring them in marriage for his two sons, began a sedition, and excited the Athenians to attack them, being the host of that state. There was also a dispute at Phocea, concerning a right of inheritance, between Mnasis, the father of Mnasis, and Euthucrates, the father of Onomarchus, which brought on the Phoceans the sacred war. The government too of Epidamnus was changed from a quarrel that arose from an intended marriage; for a certain man having contracted his daughter in marriage, the father of the young person to whom she was contracted, being archon, punishes him, upon which account he, resenting the affront, associated himself with those who were excluded from any share in the government, and brought about a revolution. A government may be changed either into an oligarchy, democracy, or a free state;

when the magistrates, or any part of the city acquire great credit, or are increased in power, as the court of Areopagus at Athens, having procured great credit during the Median war, added firmness to their administration; and, on the other hand, the maritime force, composed of the commonalty, having gained the victory at Salamis, by their power at sea, got the lead in the state, and strengthened the popular party: and at Argos, the nobles, having gained great credit by the battle of Mantinea against the Lacedaemonians, endeavoured to dissolve the democracy. And at Syracuse, the victory in their war with the Athenians being owing to the common people, they changed their free state into a democracy: and at Chalcis, the people having taken off the tyrant Phocis, together with the nobles, immediately seized the government: and at Ambracia also the people, having expelled the tyrant Periander, with his party, placed the supreme power in themselves. And this in general ought to be known, that whosoever has been the occasion of a state being powerful, whether private persons, or magistrates, a certain tribe, or any particular part of the citizens, or the multitude, be they who they will, will be the cause of disputes in the state. For either some persons, who envy them the honours they have acquired, will begin to be seditious, or they, on account of the dignity they have acquired, will not be content with their former equality. A state is also liable to commotions when those parts of it which seem to be opposite to each other approach to an equality, as the rich and the common people; so that the part which is between them both is either nothing at all, or too little to be noticed; for if one party is so much more powerful than the other, as to be evidently stronger, that other will not be willing to hazard the danger: for which reason those who are superior in excellence and virtue will never be the cause of seditions; for they will be too few for that purpose when compared to the many. In general, the beginning and the causes of seditions in all states are such as I have now described, and revolutions therein are brought about in two ways, either by violence or fraud: if by violence, either at first by compelling them to submit to the change when it is made. It may also be brought about by fraud in two different ways, either when the people, being at first deceived, willingly consent to an alteration in their government, and are afterwards obliged by force to abide by it: as, for instance, when the four hundred imposed upon the people by telling them that the king of Persia would supply them with money for the war against the Lacedaemonians; and after they had been guilty of this falsity, they endeavoured to keep possession of the supreme power; or when they are at first persuaded and afterwards consent to be governed: and by one of these methods which I have mentioned are all revolutions in governments brought about.

Chapter V

We ought now to inquire into those events which will arise from these causes in every species of government. Democracies will be most subject to revolutions from the dishonesty of their demagogues; for partly, by informing against men of property, they induce them to join together through self-defence, for a common fear will make the greatest enemies unite; and partly by setting the common people against them: and this is what any one may continually see practised in many states. In the island of Cos, for instance, the democracy was subverted by the wickedness of the demagogues, for the nobles entered into a combination with each other. And at Rhodes the demagogues, by distributing of bribes, prevented the people from paying the trierarchs what was owing to them, who were obliged by the number of actions they were harassed with to conspire together and destroy the popular state. The same thing was brought about at Heraclea, soon after the settlement of the city, by the same persons; for the citizens of note, being ill treated by them, quitted the city, but afterwards joining together they returned and overthrew the popular state. Just in the same manner the democracy was destroyed in Megara; for there the demagogues, to procure money by confiscations, drove out the nobles, till the number of those who were banished was considerable, who, returning, got the better of the people in a battle, and established an oligarchy. The like happened at Cume, during the time of the democracy, which Thrasymachus destroyed; and whoever considers what has happened in other states may perceive the same revolutions to have arisen from the same causes. The demagogues, to curry favour with the people, drive the nobles to conspire together, either by dividing their estates, or obliging them to spend them on public services, or by banishing them, that they may confiscate the fortunes of the wealthy. In former times, when the same person was both demagogue and general, the democracies were changed into tyrannies; and indeed most of the ancient tyrannies arose from those states: a reason for which then subsisted, but not now; for at that time the demagogues were of the soldiery; for they were not then powerful by their eloquence; but, now the art of oratory is cultivated, the able speakers are at present the demagogues; but, as they are unqualified to act in a military capacity, they cannot impose themselves on the people as tyrants, if we except in one or two trifling instances. Formerly, too, tyrannies were more common than now, on account of the very extensive powers with which some magistrates were entrusted: as the prytanes at Miletus; for they were supreme in many things of the last consequence; and also because at that time the cities were not of that very great extent, the people in general living in the country, and being employed in husbandry, which gave them, who took the lead in public affairs, an opportunity, if they had a turn for war, to make themselves tyrants; which they all did when they had gained the confidence of the people; and this confidence was their hatred to the rich. This was the case of Pisistratus at Athens, when he opposed the Pediaci: and of Theagenes in Megara, who slaughtered the cattle belonging to the rich, after he had seized those who kept them by the riverside. Dionysius also, for accusing Daphnseus and the rich, was thought worthy of being raised to a tyranny, from the confidence which the people had of his being a popular man in consequence of these enmities. A government shall also alter from its ancient and approved democratic form into one entirely new, if there is no census to regulate the election of magistrates; for, as the election is with the people, the demagogues who are desirous of being in office, to flatter them, will endeavour with all their power to make the people superior even to the laws. To prevent this entirely, or at least in a great measure, the magistrates should be elected by the tribes, and not by the people at large. These are nearly the revolutions to which democracies are liable, and also the causes from whence they arise.

Chapter VI

There are two things which of all others most evidently occasion a revolution in an oligarchy; one is, when the people are ill used, for then every individual is ripe for sedition; more particularly if one of the oligarchy should happen to be their leader; as Lygdamis, at Naxus, who was afterwards tyrant of that island. Seditions also which arise from different causes will differ from each other; for sometimes a revolution is brought about by the rich who have no share in the administration, which is in the hands of a very few indeed: and this happened at Massilia, Ister, Heraclea, and other cities; for those who had no share in the government ceased not to raise disputes till they were admitted to it: first the elder brothers, and then the younger also: for in some places the father and son are never in office at the same time; in others the elder and younger brother: and where this is observed the oligarchy partakes something of a free state. At Ister it was changed into a democracy; in Heraclea, instead of being in the hands of a few, it consisted of six hundred. At Cnidus the oligarchy was destroyed by the nobles quarrelling with each other, because the government was in the hands of so few: for there, as we have just mentioned, if the father was in office, the son could not; or, if there were many brothers, the eldest only; for the people, taking advantage of their disputes, elected one of the nobles for their general, and got the victory: for where there are seditions government is weak. And formerly at Erithria, during the oligarchy of the Basilides, although the state flourished greatly under their excellent management, yet because the people were displeased that the power should be in the hands of so few, they changed the government. Oligarchies also are subject to revolutions, from those who are in office therein, from the quarrels of the demagogues with each other. The demagogues are of two sorts; one who flatter the few when they are in power: for even these have their demagogues; such was Charicles at Athens, who had great influence over the thirty; and, in the same manner, Phrynichus over the four hundred. The others are those demagogues who have a share in the oligarchy, and flatter the people: such were the state-guardians at Larissa, who flattered the people because they were elected by them. And this will always happen in every oligarchy where the magistrates do not elect themselves, but are chosen out of men either of great fortune or certain ranks, by the soldiers or by the people; as was the custom at Abydos. And when the judicial department is not in the hands of the supreme power, the demagogues, favouring the people in their causes, overturn the government; which happened at Heraclea in Pontus: and also when some desire to contract the power of the oligarchy into fewer hands; for those who endeavour to support an equality are obliged to apply to the people for assistance. An oligarchy is also subject to revolutions when the nobility spend their fortunes by luxury; for such persons are desirous of innovations, and either endeavour to be tyrants themselves or to support others in being so, as Hypparinus supported Dionysius of Syracuse. And at Amphipolis one Cleotimus collected a colony of Chalcidians, and when they came set them to quarrel with the rich: and at AEgina a certain person who brought an action against Chares attempted on that account to alter the government. Sometimes they will try to raise commotions, sometimes they will rob the public, and then quarrel with each other, or else fight with those who endeavour to detect them; which was the case at Apollonia in Pontus. But if the members of an oligarchy agree among themselves the state is not very easily destroyed without some external force. Pharsalus is a proof of this, where, though the place is small, yet the citizens have great power, from the prudent use they make of it. An oligarchy also will be destroyed when they create another oligarchy under it; that is, when the management of public affairs is in the hands of a few, and not equally, but when all of them do not partake of the supreme power, as happened once at Elis, where the supreme power in general was in the hands of a very few out of whom a senate was chosen, consisting but of ninety, who held their places for life; and their mode of election was calculated to preserve the power amongst each other's families, like the senators at Lacedaemon. An oligarchy is liable to a revolution both in time of war and peace; in war, because through a distrust in the citizens the government is obliged to employ mercenary troops, and he to whom they give the command of the army will very often assume the tyranny, as Timophanes did at Corinth; and if they appoint more than one general, they will very probably establish a dynasty: and sometimes, through fear of this, they are forced to let the people in general have some share in the government, because they are obliged to employ them. In peace, from their want of confidence in each other, they will entrust the guardianship of the state to mercenaries and their general, who will be an arbiter between them, and sometimes become master of both, which happened at Larissa, when Simos and the Aleuadae had the chief power. The same thing happened at Abydos, during the time of the political clubs, of which Iphiades' was one. Commotions also will happen in an oligarchy from one party's overbearing and insulting another, or from their quarrelling about their law-suits or marriages. How their marriages, for instance, will have that effect has been already shown: and in Eretria, Diagoras destroyed the oligarchy of the knights upon the same account. A sedition also arose at Heraclea, from a certain person being condemned by the court; and at Thebes, in consequence of a man's being guilty of adultery; the punishment indeed which Eurytion suffered at Heraclea was just, yet it was illegally executed: as was that at Thebes upon Archias; for their enemies endeavoured to have them publicly bound in the pillory. Many revolutions also have been brought about in oligarchies by those who could not brook the despotism which those persons assumed who were in power, as at Cnidus and Chios. Changes also may happen by accident in what we call a free state and in an oligarchy; wheresoever the senators, judges, and magistrates are chosen according to a certain census; for it often happens that the highest census is fixed at first; so that a few only could have a share in the government, in an oligarchy, or in a free state those of moderate fortunes only; when the city grows rich, through peace or some other happy cause, it becomes so little that every one's fortune is equal to the census, so that the whole community may partake of all the honours of government; and this change sometimes happens by little and little, and insensible approaches, sometimes quicker. These are the revolutions and seditions that arise in oligarchies, and the causes to which they are owing: and indeed both democracies and oligarchies sometimes alter, not into governments of a contrary form, but into those of the same government; as, for instance, from having the supreme power in the law to vest it in the ruling party, or the contrariwise.

Chapter VII

Commotions also arise in aristocracies, from there being so few persons in power (as we have already observed they do in oligarchies, for in this particular an aristocracy is most near an oligarchy, for in both these states the administration of public affairs is in the hands of a few; not that this arises from the same cause in both, though herein they chiefly seem alike): and these will necessarily be most likely to happen when the generality of the people are high-spirited and think themselves equal to each other in merit; such were those at Lacedasmon, called the Partheniae (for these were, as well as others, descendants of citizens), who being detected in a conspiracy against the state, were sent to found Tarentum. They will happen also when some great men are disgraced by those who have received higher honours than themselves, to whom they are no ways inferior in abilities, as Lysander by the kings: or when an ambitious man cannot get into power, as Cinadon, who, in the reign of Agesilaus, was chief in a conspiracy against the Spartans: and also when some are too poor and others too rich, which will most frequently happen in time of war; as at Lacedaemon during the Messenian war, which is proved by a poem of Tyrtaeus, called "Eunomia;" for some persons being reduced thereby, desired that the lands might be divided: and also when some person of very high rank might still be higher if he could rule alone, which seemed to be Pausanias's intention at Lacedaemon, when he was their general in the Median war, and Anno's at Carthage. But free states and aristocracies are mostly destroyed from want of a fixed administration of public affairs; the cause of which evil arises at first from want of a due mixture of the democratic and the oligarchic parts in a free state; and in an aristocracy from the same causes, and also from virtue not being properly joined to power; but chiefly from the two first, I mean the undue mixture of the democratic and oligarchic parts; for these two are what all free states endeavour to blend together, and many of those which we call aristocracies, in this particular these states differ from each other, and on this account the one of them is less stable than the other, for that state which inclines most to an oligarchy is called an aristocracy, and that which inclines most to a democracy is called a free state; on which account this latter is more secure than the former, for the wider the foundation the securer the building, and it is ever best to live where equality prevails. But the rich, if the community gives them rank, very often endeavour to insult and tyrannise over others. On the whole, whichever way a government inclines, in that it will settle, each party supporting their own. Thus a free state will become a democracy; an aristocracy an oligarchy; or the contrary, an aristocracy may change into a democracy (for the poor, if they think themselves injured, directly take part with the contrary side) and a free state into an oligarchy. The only firm state is that where every one enjoys that equality he has a right to and fully possesses what is his own. And what I have been speaking of happened to the Thurians; for the magistrates being elected according to a very high census, it was altered to a lower, and they were subdivided into more courts, but in consequence of the nobles possessing all the land, contrary to law; the state was too much of an oligarchy, which gave them an opportunity of encroaching greatly on the rest of the people; but these, after they had been well inured to war, so far got the better of their guards as to expel every one out of the country who possessed more than he ought. Moreover, as all aristocracies are free oligarchies, the nobles therein endeavour to have rather too much power, as at Lacedaemon, where property is now in the hands of a few, and the nobles have too much liberty to do as they please and make such alliances as they please. Thus the city of the Locrians was ruined from an alliance with Dionysius; which state was neither a democracy nor well-tempered aristocracy. But an aristocracy chiefly approaches to a secret change by its being destroyed by degrees, as we have already said of all governments in general; and this happens from the cause of the alteration being trifling; for whenever anything which in the least regards the state is treated with contempt, after that something else, and this of a little more consequence, will be more easily altered, until the whole fabric of government is entirely subverted, which happened in the government of Thurium; for the law being that they should continue soldiers for five years, some young men of a martial disposition, who were in great esteem amongst their officers, despising those who had the management of public affairs, and imagining they could easily accomplish their intention, first endeavoured to abolish this law, with a view of having it lawful to continue the same person perpetually in the military, perceiving that the people would readily appoint them. Upon this, the magistrates who are called counselors first joined together with an intention to oppose it but were afterwards induced to agree to it, from a belief that if that law was not repealed they would permit the management of all other public affairs to remain in their hands; but afterwards, when they endeavoured to restrain some fresh alterations that were making, they found that they could do nothing, for the whole form of government was altered into a dynasty of those who first introduced the innovations. In short, all governments are liable to be destroyed either from within or from without; from without when they have for their neighbour a state whose policy is contrary to theirs, and indeed if it has great power the same thing will happen if it is not their neighbour; of which both the Athenians and the Lacedaemonians are a proof; for the one, when conquerors everywhere destroyed the oligarchies; the other the democracies. These are the chief causes of revolutions and dissensions in governments.

Chapter VIII

We are now to consider upon what the preservation of governments in general and of each state in particular depends; and, in the first place, it is evident that if we are right in the causes we have assigned for their destruction, we know also the means of their preservation; for things contrary produce contraries: but destruction and preservation are contrary to each other. In well-tempered governments it requires as much care as anything whatsoever, that nothing be done contrary to law: and this ought chiefly to be attended to in matters of small consequence; for an illegality that approaches insensibly, approaches secretly, as in a family small expenses continually repeated consume a man's income; for the understanding is deceived thereby, as by this false argument; if every part is little, then the whole is little: now, this in one sense is true, in another is false, for the whole and all the parts together are large, though made up of small parts. The first therefore of anything is what the state ought to guard against. In the next place, no credit ought to be given to those who endeavour to deceive the people with false pretences; for they will be confuted by facts. The different ways in which they will attempt to do this have been already mentioned. You may often perceive both aristocracies and oligarchies continuing firm, not from the stability of their forms of government, but from the wise conduct of the magistrates, both towards those who have a part in the management of public affairs, and those also who have not: towards those who have not, by never injuring them; and also introducing those who are of most consequence amongst them into office; nor disgracing those who are desirous of honour; or encroaching on the property of individuals; towards those who have, by behaving to each other upon an equality; for that equality which the favourers of a democracy desire to have established in the state is not only just, but convenient also, amongst those who are of the same rank: for which reason, if the administration is in the hands of many, those rules which are established in democracies will be very useful; as to let no one continue in office longer than six months: that all those who are of the same rank may have their turn; for between these there is a sort of democracy: for which reason demagogues are most likely to arise up amongst them, as we have already mentioned: besides, by this means both aristocracies and democracies will be the less liable to be corrupted into dynasties, because it will not be so easy for those who are magistrates for a little to do as much mischief as they could in a long time: for it is from hence that tyrannies arise in democracies and oligarchies; for either those who are most powerful in each state establish a tyranny, as the demagogues in the one, the dynasties in the other, or the chief magistrates who have been long in power. Governments are sometimes preserved not only by having the means of their corruption at a great distance, but also by its being very near them; for those who are alarmed at some impending evil keep a stricter hand over the state; for which reason it is necessary for those who have the guardianship of the constitution to be able to awaken the fears of the people, that they may preserve it, and not like a night-guard to be remiss in protecting the state, but to make the distant danger appear at hand. Great care ought also to be used to endeavour to restrain the quarrels and disputes of the nobles by laws, as well as to prevent those who are not already engaged in them from taking a part therein; for to perceive an evil at its very first approach is not the lot of every one, but of the politician. To prevent any alteration taking place in an oligarchy or free state on account of the census, if that happens to continue the same while the quantity of money is increased, it will be useful to take a general account of the whole amount of it in former times, to compare it with the present, and to do this every year in those cities where the census is yearly, in larger communities once in three or five years; and if the whole should be found much larger or much less than it was at the time when the census was first established in the state, let there be a law either to extend or contract it, doing both these according to its increase or decrease; if it increases making the census larger, if it decreases smaller: and if this latter is not done in oligarchies and free states, you will have a dynasty arise in the one, an oligarchy in the other: if the former is not, free states will be changed into democracies, and oligarchies into free states or democracies. It is a general maxim in democracies, oligarchies, monarchies, and indeed in all governments, not to let any one acquire a rank far superior to the rest of the community, but rather to endeavour to confer moderate honours for a continuance than great ones for a short time; for these latter spoil men, for it is not every one who can bear prosperity: but if this rule is not observed, let not those honours which were conferred all at once be all at once taken away, but rather by degrees. But, above all things, let this regulation be made by the law, that no one shall have too much power, either by means of his fortune or friends; but if he has, for his excess therein, let it be contrived that he shall quit the country. Now, as many persons promote innovations, that they may enjoy their own particular manner of living, there ought to be a particular officer to inspect the manners of every one, and see that these are not contrary to the genius of the state in which he lives, whether it may be an oligarchy, a democracy, or any other form of government; and, for the same reason, those should be guarded against who are most prosperous in the city: the means of doing which is by appointing those who are otherwise to the business and the offices of the state. I mean, to oppose men of account to the common people, the poor to the rich, and to blend both these into one body, and to increase the numbers of those who are in the middle rank; and this will prevent those seditions which arise from an inequality of condition. But above all, in every state it is necessary, both by the laws and every other method possible, to prevent those who are employed by the public from being venal, and this particularly in an oligarchy; for then the people will not be so much displeased from seeing themselves excluded from a share in the government (nay, they will rather be glad to have leisure to attend their private affairs) as at suspecting that the officers of the state steal the public money, then indeed they are afflicted with double concern, both because they are deprived of the honours of the state, and pillaged by those who enjoy them. There is one method of blending together a democracy and an aristocracy, if office brought no profit; by which means both the rich and the poor will enjoy what they desire; for to admit all to a share in the government is democratical; that the rich should be in office is aristocratical. This must be done by letting no public employment whatsoever be attended with any emolument; for the poor will not desire to be in office when they can get nothing by it, but had rather attend to their own affairs: but the rich will choose it, as they want nothing of the community. Thus the poor will increase their fortunes by being wholly employed in their own concerns; and the principal part of the people will not be governed by the lower sort. To prevent the exchequer from being defrauded, let all public money be delivered out openly in the face of the whole city, and let copies of the accounts be deposited in the different wards tribes, and divisions. But, as the magistrates are to execute their offices without any advantages, the law ought to provide proper honours for those who execute them well. In democracies also it is necessary that the rich should be protected, by not permitting their lands to be divided, nor even the produce of them, which in some states is done unperceivably. It would be also better if the people would prevent them when they offer to exhibit a number of unnecessary and yet expensive public entertainments of plays, music, processions, and the like. In an oligarchy it is necessary to take great care of the poor, and allot them public employments which are gainful; and, if any of the rich insult them, to let their punishment be severer than if they insulted one of their own rank; and to let estates pass by affinity, and not gift: nor to permit any person to have more than one; for by this means property will be more equally divided, and the greater part of the poor get into better circumstances. It is also serviceable in a democracy and an oligarchy to allot those who take no part in public affairs an equality or a preference in other things; the rich in a democracy, to the poor in an oligarchy: but still all the principal offices in the state to be filled only by those who are best qualified to discharge them.

Chapter IX

There are three qualifications necessary for those who fill the first departments in government; first of all, an affection for the established constitution; second place, abilities every way completely equal to the business of their office; in the third, virtue and justice correspondent to the nature of that particular state they are placed in; for if justice is not the same in all states, it is evident that there must be different species thereof. There may be some doubt, when all these qualifications do not in the same persons, in what manner the choice shall be made; as for instance, suppose that one person is an accomplished general, but a bad man and no friend to the constitution; another is just and a friend to it, which shall one prefer? we should then consider of two qualities, which of them the generality possess in a greater degree, which in a less; for which reason in the choice of a general we should regard his courage more than his virtue as the more uncommon quality; as there are fewer capable of conducting an army than there are good men: but, to protect the state or manage the finances, the contrary rule should be followed; for these require greater virtue than the generality are possessed of, but only that knowledge which is common to all. It may be asked, if a man has abilities equal to his appointment in the state, and is affectionate to the constitution, what occasion is there for being virtuous, since these two things alone are sufficient to enable him to be useful to the public? it is, because those who possess those qualities are often deficient in prudence; for, as they often neglect their own affairs, though they know them and love themselves, so nothing will prevent their serving the public in the same manner. In short, whatsoever the laws contain which we allow to be useful to the state contributes to its preservation: but its first and principal support is (as has been often insisted upon) to have the number of those who desire to preserve it greater than those who wish to destroy it. Above all things that ought not to be forgotten which many governments now corrupted neglect; namely, to preserve a mean. For many things seemingly favourable to a democracy destroy a democracy, and many things seemingly favourable to an oligarchy destroy an oligarchy. Those who think this the only virtue extend it to excess, not considering that as a nose which varies a little from perfect straightness, either towards a hook nose or a flat one, may yet be beautiful and agreeable to look at; but if this particularity is extended beyond measure, first of all the properties of the part is lost, but at last it can hardly be admitted to be a nose at all, on account of the excess of the rise or sinking: thus it is with other parts of the human body; so also the same thing is true with respect to states; for both an oligarchy and a democracy may something vary from their most perfect form and yet be well constituted; but if any one endeavours to extend either of them too far, at first he will make the government the worse for it, but at last there will be no government at all remaining. The lawgiver and the politician therefore should know well what preserves and what destroys a democracy or an oligarchy, for neither the one nor the other can possibly continue without rich and poor: but that whenever an entire equality of circumstances prevails, the state must necessarily become of another form; so that those who destroy these laws, which authorise an inequality in property, destroy the government. It is also an error in democracies for the demagogues to endeavour to make the common people superior to the laws; and thus by setting them at variance with the rich, dividing one city into two; whereas they ought rather to speak in favour of the rich. In oligarchies, on the contrary, it is wrong to support those who are in administration against the people. The oaths also which they take in an oligarchy ought to be contrary to what they now are; for, at present, in some places they swear, "I will be adverse to the common people, and contrive all I can against them;" whereas they ought rather to suppose and pretend the contrary; expressing in their oaths, that they will not injure the people. But of all things which I have mentioned, that which contributes most to preserve the state is, what is now most despised, to educate your children for the state; for the most useful laws, and most approved by every statesman, will be of no service if the citizens are not accustomed to and brought up in the principles of the constitution; of a democracy, if that is by law established; of an oligarchy, if that is; for if there are bad morals in one man, there are in the city. But to educate a child fit for the state, it must not be done in the manner which would please either those who have the power in an oligarchy or those who desire a democracy, but so as they may be able to conduct either of these forms of governments. But now the children of the magistrates in an oligarchy are brought up too delicately, and the children of the poor hardy with exercise and labour; so that they are both desirous of and able to promote innovations. In democracies of the purest form they pursue a method which is contrary to their welfare; the reason of which is, that they define liberty wrong: now, there are two things which seem to be the objects of a democracy, that the people in general should possess the supreme power, and all enjoy freedom; for that which is just seems to be equal, and what the people think equal, that is a law: now, their freedom and equality consists in every one's doing what they please: that is in such a democracy every one may live as he likes; "as his inclination guides," in the words of Euripides: but this is wrong, for no one ought to think it slavery to live in subjection to government, but protection. Thus I have mentioned the causes of corruption in different states, and the means of their preservation.

Chapter X

It now remains that we speak of monarchies, their causes of corruption, and means of preservation; and indeed almost the same things which have been said of other governments happen to kingdoms and tyrannies; for a kingdom partakes of an aristocracy, a tyranny of the worst species of an oligarchy and democracy; for which reason it is the worst that man can submit to, as being composed of two, both of which are bad, and collectively retains all the corruptions and all the defects of both these states. These two species of monarchies arise from principles contrary to each other: a kingdom is formed to protect the better sort of people against the multitude, and kings are appointed out of those, who are chosen either for their superior virtue and actions flowing from virtuous principles, or else from their noble descent; but a tyrant is chosen out of the meanest populace; an enemy to the better sort, that the common people may not be oppressed by them. That this is true experience convinces us; for the generality of tyrants were indeed mere demagogues, who gained credit with the people by oppressing the nobles. Some tyrannies were established in this manner after the cities were considerably enlarged-others before that time, by kings who exceeded the power which their country allowed them, from a desire of governing despotically: others were founded by those who were elected to the superior offices in the state; for formerly the people appointed officers for life, who came to be at the head of civil and religious affairs, and these chose one out of their body in whom the supreme power over all the magistrates was placed. By all these means it was easy to establish a tyranny, if they chose it; for their power was ready at hand, either by their being kings, or else by enjoying the honours of the state; thus Phidon at Argos and other tyrants enjoyed originally the kingly power; Phalaris and others in Ionia, the honours of the state. Pansetius at Leontium, Cypselus at Corinth, Pisistratus at Athens, Dionysius at Syracuse, and others, acquired theirs by having been demagogues. A kingdom, as we have said, partakes much of the nature of an aristocracy, and is bestowed according to worth, as either virtue, family, beneficent actions, or these joined with power; for those who have been benefactors to cities and states, or have it in their powers to be so, have acquired this honour, and those who have prevented a people from falling into slavery by war, as Codrus, or those who have freed them from it, as Cyrus, or the founders of cities, or settlers of colonies, as the kings of Sparta, Macedon, and Molossus. A king desires to be the guardian of his people, that those who have property may be secure in the possession of it, and that the people in general meet with no injury; but a tyrant, as has been often said, has no regard to the common good, except for his own advantage; his only object is pleasure, but a king's is virtue: what a tyrant therefore is ambitious of engrossing is wealth, but a king rather honour. The guards too of a king are citizens, a tyrant's foreigners.

That a tyranny contains all that is bad both in a democracy and an oligarchy is evident; with an oligarchy it has for its end gain, as the only means of providing the tyrant with guards and the luxuries of life; like that it places no confidence in the people; and therefore deprives them of the use of arms: it is also common to them both to persecute the populace, to drive them out of the city and their own habitations. With a democracy it quarrels with the nobles, and destroys them both publicly and privately, or drives them into banishment, as rivals and an impediment to the government; hence naturally arise conspiracies both amongst those who desire to govern and those who desire not to be slaves; hence arose Periander's advice to Thrasybulus to take off the tallest stalks, hinting thereby, that it was necessary to make away with the eminent citizens. We ought then in reason, as has been already said, to account for the changes which arise in a monarchy from the same causes which produce them in other states: for, through injustice received, fear, and contempt, many of those who are under a monarchical government conspire against it; but of all species of injustice, injurious contempt has most influence on them for that purpose: sometimes it is owing to their being deprived of their private fortunes. The dissolution too of a kingdom and a tyranny are generally the same; for monarchs abound in wealth and honour, which all are desirous to obtain. Of plots: some aim at the life of those who govern, others at their government; the first arises from hatred to their persons; which hatred may be owing to many causes, either of which will be sufficient to excite their anger, and the generality of those who are under the influence of that passion will join in a conspiracy, not for the sake of their own advancement, but for revenge. Thus the plot against the children of Pisistratus arose from their injurious treatment of Harmodius's sister, and insulting him also; for Harmodius resenting the injury done to his sister, and Aristogiton the injury done to Harmodius. Periander the tyrant of Ambracia also lost his life by a conspiracy, for some improper liberties he took with a boy in his cups: and Philip was slain by Pausanias for neglecting to revenge him of the affront he had received from Attains; as was Amintas the Little by Darda, for insulting him on account of his age; and the eunuch by Evagoras the Cyprian in revenge for having taken his son's wife away from him....

Many also who have had their bodies scourged with stripes have, through resentment, either killed those who caused them to be inflicted or conspired against them, even when they had kingly power, as at Mitylene Megacles, joining with his friends, killed the Penthelidee, who used to go about striking those they met with clubs. Thus, in later times, Smendes killed

Penthilus for whipping him and dragging him away from his wife. Decamnichus also was the chief cause of the conspiracy against Archelaus, for he urged others on: the occasion of his resentment was his having delivered him to Euripides the poet to be scourged; for Euripides was greatly offended with him for having said something of the foulness of his breath. And many others have been killed or conspired against on the same account. Fear too is a cause which produces the same effects, as well in monarchies as in other states: thus Artabanes conspired against Xerxes through fear of punishment for having hanged Darius according to his orders, whom he supposed he intended to pardon, as the order was given at supper-time. Some kings also have been dethroned and killed in consequence of the contempt they were held in by the people; as some one conspired against Sardanapalus, having seen him spinning with his wife, if what is related of him is true, or if not of him, it may very probably be true of some one else. Dion also conspired against Dionysius the Younger, seeing his subjects desirous of a conspiracy, and that he himself was always drunk: and even a man's friends will do this if they despise him; for from the confidence he places in them, they think that they shall not be found out. Those also who think they shall gain his throne will conspire against a king through contempt; for as they are powerful themselves, and despise the danger, on account of their own strength, they will readily attempt it. Thus a general at the head of his army will endeavour to dethrone the monarch, as Cyrus did Astyages, despising both his manner of life and his forces; his forces for want of action, his life for its effeminacy: thus Suthes, the Thracian, who was general to Amadocus, conspired against him. Sometimes more than one of these causes will excite men to enter into conspiracies, as contempt and desire of gain; as in the instance of Mithridates against Ariobarzanes. Those also who are of a bold disposition, and have gained military honours amongst kings, will of all others be most like to engage in sedition; for strength and courage united inspire great bravery: whenever, therefore, these join in one person, he will be very ready for conspiracies, as he will easily conquer. Those who conspire against a tyrant through love of glory and honour have a different motive in view from what I have already mentioned; for, like all others who embrace danger, they have only glory and honour in view, and think, not as some do, of the wealth and pomp they may acquire, but engage in this as they would in any other noble action, that they may be illustrious and distinguished, and destroy a tyrant, not to succeed in his tyranny, but to acquire renown. No doubt but the number of those who act upon this principle is small, for we must suppose they regard their own safety as nothing in case they should not succeed, and must embrace the opinion of Dion (which few can do) when he made war upon Dionysius with a very few troops; for he said, that let the advantage he made be ever so little it would satisfy him to have gained it; and that, should it be his lot to die the moment he had gained footing in his country, he should think his death sufficiently glorious. A tyranny also is exposed to the same destruction as all other states are, from too powerful neighbours: for it is evident, that an opposition of principles will make them desirous of subverting it; and what they desire, all who can, do: and there is a principle of opposition in one state to another, as a democracy against a tyranny, as says Hesiod, "a potter against a potter;" for the extreme of a democracy is a tyranny; a kingly power against an aristocracy, from their different forms of government-for which reason the Lacedaemonians destroyed many tyrannies; as did the Syracusians during the prosperity of their state. Nor are they only destroyed from without, but also from within, when those who have no share in the power bring about a revolution, as happened to Gelon, and lately to Dionysius; to the first, by means of Thrasybulus, the brother of Hiero, who nattered Gelon's son, and induced him to lead a life of pleasure, that he himself might govern; but the family joined together and endeavoured to support the tyranny and expel Thrasybulus; but those whom they made of their party seized the opportunity and expelled the whole family. Dion made war against his relation Dionysius, and being assisted by the people, first expelled and then killed him. As there are two causes which chiefly induce men to conspire against tyrants, hatred and contempt, one of these, namely hatred, seems inseparable from them. Contempt also is often the cause of their destruction: for though, for instance, those who raised themselves to the supreme power generally preserved it;

but those who received it from them have, to speak truth, almost immediately all of them lost it; for, falling into an effeminate way of life, they soon grew despicable, and generally fell victims to conspiracies. Part of their hatred may be very fitly ascribed to anger; for in some cases this is their motive to action: for it is often a cause which impels them to act more powerfully than hatred, and they proceed with greater obstinacy against those whom they attack, as this passion is not under the direction of reason. Many persons also indulge this passion through contempt; which occasioned the fall of the Pisistratidae and many others. But hatred is more powerful than anger; for anger is accompanied with grief, which prevents the entrance of reason; but hatred is free from it. In short, whatever causes may be assigned as the destruction of a pure oligarchy unmixed with any other government and an extreme democracy, the same may be applied to a tyranny; for these are divided tyrannies.

Kingdoms are seldom destroyed by any outward attack; for which reason they are generally very stable; but they have many causes of subversion within; of which two are the principal; one is when those who are in power excite a sedition, the other when they endeavour to establish a tyranny by assuming greater power than the law gives them. A kingdom, indeed, is not what we ever see erected in our times, but rather monarchies and tyrannies; for a kingly government is one that is voluntarily submitted to, and its supreme power admitted upon great occasions: but where many are equal, and there are none in any respect so much better than another as to be qualified for the greatness and dignity of government over them, then these equals will not willingly submit to be commanded; but if any one assumes the government, either by force or fraud, this is a tyranny. To what we have already said we shall add, the causes of revolutions in an hereditary kingdom. One of these is, that many of those who enjoy it are naturally proper objects of contempt only: another is, that they are insolent while their power is not despotic; but they possess kingly honours only. Such a state is soon destroyed; for a king exists but while the people are willing to obey, as their submission to him is voluntary, but to a tyrant involuntary. These and such-like are the causes of the destruction of monarchies.

Chapter XI

Monarchies, in a word, are preserved by means contrary to what I have already mentioned as the cause of their destruction; but to speak to each separately: the stability of a kingdom will depend upon the power of the king's being kept within moderate bounds; for by how much the less extensive his power is, by so much the longer will his government continue; for he will be less despotic and more upon an equality of condition with those he governs; who, on that account, will envy him the less.

It was on this account that the kingdom of the Molossi continued so long; and the Lacedaemonians from their government's being from the beginning divided into two parts, and also by the moderation introduced into the other parts of it by Theopompus, and his establishment of the ephori; for by taking something from the power he increased the duration of the kingdom, so that in some measure he made it not less, but bigger; as they say he replied to his wife, who asked him if he was not ashamed to deliver down his kingdom to his children reduced from what he received it from his ancestors? No, says he, I give it him more lasting. Tyrannies are preserved two ways most opposite to each other, one of which is when the power is delegated from one to the other, and in this manner many tyrants govern in their states. Report says that Periander founded many of these. There are also many of them to be met with amongst the Persians. What has been already mentioned is as conducive as anything can be to preserve a tyranny; namely, to keep down those who are of an aspiring disposition, to take off those who will not submit, to allow no public meals, no clubs, no education, nothing at all, but to guard against everything that gives rise to high spirits or mutual confidence; nor to suffer the learned meetings of those who are at leisure to hold conversation with each other; and to endeavour by every means possible to keep all the people strangers to each other; for knowledge increases mutual confidence; and to oblige all strangers to appear in public, and to live near the city-gate, that all their actions may be sufficiently seen; for those who are kept like slaves seldom entertain any noble thoughts: in short, to imitate everything which the Persians and barbarians do, for they all contribute to support slavery; and to endeavour to know what every one who is under their power does and says; and for this purpose to employ spies: such were those women whom the Syracusians called potagogides Hiero also used to send out listeners wherever there was any meeting or conversation; for the people dare not speak with freedom for fear of such persons; and if any one does, there is the less chance of its being concealed; and to endeavour that the whole community should mutually accuse and come to blows with each other, friend with friend, the commons with the nobles, and the rich with each other. It is also advantageous for a tyranny that all those who are under it should be oppressed with poverty, that they may not be able to compose a guard; and that, being employed in procuring their daily bread, they may have no leisure to conspire against their tyrants. The Pyramids of Egypt are a proof of this, and the votive edifices of the Cyposelidse, and the temple of Jupiter Olympus, built by the Pisistratidae, and the works of Polycrates at Samos; for all these produced one end, the keeping the people poor. It is necessary also to multiply taxes, as at Syracuse; where Dionysius in the space of five years collected all the private property of his subjects into his own coffers. A tyrant also should endeavour to engage his subjects in a war, that they may have employment and continually depend upon their general. A king is preserved by his friends, but a tyrant is of all persons the man who can place no confidence in friends, as every one has it in his desire and these chiefly in their power to destroy him. All these things also which are done in an extreme democracy should be done in a tyranny, as permitting great licentiousness to the women in the house, that they may reveal their husbands' secrets; and showing great indulgence to slaves also for the same reason; for slaves and women conspire not against tyrants: but when they are treated with kindness, both of them are abettors of tyrants, and extreme democracies also; and the people too in such a state desire to be despotic. For which reason flatterers are in repute in both these: the demagogue in the democracy, for he is the proper flatterer of the people; among tyrants, he who will servilely adapt himself to their humours; for this is the business of flatterers. And for this reason tyrants always love the worst of wretches, for they rejoice in being flattered, which no man of a liberal spirit will submit to; for they love the virtuous, but flatter none. Bad men too are fit for bad purposes; "like to like," as the proverb says. A tyrant also should show no favour to a man of worth or a freeman; for he should think, that no one deserved to be thought these but himself; for he who supports his dignity, and is a friend to freedom, encroaches upon the superiority and the despotism of the tyrant: such men, therefore, they naturally hate, as destructive to their government. A tyrant also should rather admit strangers to his table and familiarity than citizens, as these are his enemies, but the others have no design against him. These and such-like are the supports of a tyranny, for it comprehends whatsoever is wicked. But all these things may be comprehended in three divisions, for there are three objects which a tyranny has in view; one of which is, that the citizens should be of poor abject dispositions; for such men never propose to conspire against any one. The second is, that they should have no confidence in each other; for while they have not this, the tyrant is safe enough from destruction. For which reason they are always at enmity with those of merit, as hurtful to their government; not only as they scorn to be governed despotically, but also because they can rely upon each other's fidelity, and others can rely upon theirs, and because they will not inform against their associates, nor any one else. The third is, that they shall be totally without the means of doing anything; for no one undertakes what is impossible for him to perform: so that without power a tyranny can never be destroyed. These, then, are the three objects which the inclinations of tyrants desire to see accomplished; for all their tyrannical plans tend to promote one of these three ends, that their people may neither have mutual confidence, power, nor spirit. This, then, is one of the two methods of preserving tyrannies: the other proceeds in a way quite contrary to what has been already described, and which may be discerned from considering to what the destruction of a kingdom is owing; for as one cause of that is, making the government approach near to a tyranny, so the safety of a tyranny consists in making the government nearly kingly; preserving only one thing, namely power, that not only the willing, but the unwilling also, must be obliged to submit; for if this is once lost, the tyranny is at an end. This, then, as the foundation, must be preserved: in other particulars carefully do and affect to seem like a king; first, appear to pay a great attention to what belongs to the public; nor make such profuse presents as will offend the people; while they are to supply the money out of the hard labour of their own hands, and see it given in profusion to mistresses, foreigners, and fiddlers; keeping an exact account both of what you receive and pay; which is a practice some tyrants do actually follow, by which means they seem rather fathers of families than tyrants: nor need you ever fear the want of money while you have the supreme power of the state in your own hands. It is also much better for those tyrants who quit their kingdom to do this than to leave behind them money they have hoarded up; for their regents will be much less desirous of making innovations, and they are more to be dreaded by absent tyrants than the citizens; for such of them as he suspects he takes with him, but these regents must be left behind. He should also endeavour to appear to collect such taxes and require such services as the exigencies of the state demand, that whenever they are wanted they may be ready in time of war; and particularly to take care that he appear to collect and keep them not as his own property, but the public's. His appearance also should not be severe, but respectable, so that he should inspire those who approach him with veneration and not fear; but this will not be easily accomplished if he is despised. If, therefore, he will not take the pains to acquire any other, he ought to endeavour to be a man of political abilities, and to fix that opinion of himself in the judgment of his subjects. He should also take care not to appear to be guilty of the least offence against modesty, nor to suffer it in those under him: nor to permit the women of his family to treat others haughtily; for the haughtiness of women has been the ruin of many tyrants. With respect to the pleasures of sense, he ought to do directly contrary to the practice of some tyrants at present; for they do not only continually indulge themselves in them for many days together, but they seem also to desire to have other witnesses of it, that they may wonder at their happiness; whereas he ought really to be moderate in these, and, if not, to appear to others to avoid them-for it is not the sober man who is exposed either to plots or contempt, but the drunkard; not the early riser, but the sluggard. His conduct in general should also be contrary to what is reported of former tyrants; for he ought to improve and adorn his city, so as to seem a guardian and not a tyrant; and, moreover., always to seem particularly attentive to the worship of the gods; for from persons of such a character men entertain less fears of suffering anything illegal while they suppose that he who governs them is religious and reverences the gods; and they will be less inclined to raise insinuations against such a one, as being peculiarly under their protection: but this must be so done as to give no occasion for any suspicion of hypocrisy. He should also take care to show such respect to men of merit in every particular, that they should not think they could be treated with greater distinction by their fellow-citizens in a free state. He should also let all honours flow immediately from himself, but every censure from his subordinate officers and judges. It is also a common protection of all monarchies not to make one person too great, or, certainly, not many; for they will support each other: but, if it is necessary to entrust any large powers to one person, to take care that it is not one of an ardent spirit; for this disposition is upon every opportunity most ready for a revolution: and, if it should seem necessary to deprive any one of his power, to do it by degrees, and not reduce him all at once. It is also necessary to abstain from all kinds of insolence; more particularly from corporal punishment; which you must be most cautious never to exercise over those who have a delicate sense of honour; for, as those who love money are touched to the quick when anything affects their property, so are men of honour and principle when they receive any disgrace: therefore, either never employ personal punishment, or, if you do, let it be only in the manner in which a father would correct his son, and not with contempt; and, upon the whole, make amends for any seeming disgrace by bestowing greater honours. But of all persons who are most likely to entertain designs against the person of a tyrant, those are chiefly to be feared and guarded against who regard as nothing the loss of their own lives, so that they can but accomplish their purpose: be very careful therefore of those who either think themselves affronted, or those who are dear to them; for those who are excited by anger to revenge regard as nothing their own persons: for, as Heraclitus says, it is dangerous to fight with an angry man who will purchase with his life the thing he aims at. As all cities are composed of two sorts of persons, the rich and the poor, it is necessary that both these should find equal protection from him who governs them, and that the one party should not have it in their power to injure the other; but that the tyrant should attach to himself that party which is the most powerful; which, if he does, he will have no occasion either to make his slaves free, or to deprive citizens of their arms; for the strength of either of the parties added to his own forces will render him superior to any conspiracy. It would be superfluous to go through all particulars; for the rule of conduct which the tyrant ought to pursue is evident enough, and that is, to affect to appear not the tyrant, but the king; the guardian of those he governs, not their plunderer, but their protector, and to affect the middle rank in life, not one superior to all others: he should, therefore, associate his nobles with him and soothe his people; for his government will not only be necessarily more honourable and worthy of imitation, as it will be over men of worth, and not abject wretches who perpetually both hate and fear him; but it will be also more durable. Let him also frame his life so that his manners may be consentaneous to virtue, or at least let half of them be so, that he may not be altogether wicked, but only so in part.

Chapter XII

Indeed an oligarchy and a tyranny are of all governments of the shortest duration. The tyranny of Orthagoras and his family at Sicyon, it is true, continued longer than any other: the reason for which was, that they used their power with moderation, and were in many particulars obedient to the laws; and, as Clisthenes was an able general, he never fell into contempt, and by the care he took that in many particulars his government should be popular. He is reported also to have presented a person with a crown who adjudged the victory to another; and some say that it is the statue of that judge which is placed in the forum.

They say also, that Pisistratus submitted to be summoned into the court of the Areopagites. The second that we shall mention is the tyranny of the Cypselidse, at Corinth, which continued seventy-seven years and six months; for Cypselus was tyrant there thirty years, Periander forty-four, and Psammetichus, the son of Georgias, three years; the reason for which was, that Cypselus was a popular man, and governed without guards. Periander indeed ruled like a tyrant, but then he was an able general. The third was that of the Pisistradidae at Athens; but it was not continual: for Pisistratus himself was twice expelled; so that out of thirty-three years he was only fifteen in power, and his son eighteen; so that the whole time was thirty-three years. Of the rest we shall mention that of Hiero, and Gelo at Syracuse; and this did not continue long, for both their reigns were only eighteen years; for Gelo died in the eighth year of his tyranny, and Hiero in his tenth. Thrasybulus fell in his eleventh month, and many other tyrannies have continued a very short time. We have now gone through the general cases of corruption and means of preservation both in free states and monarchies. In Plato's Republic, Socrates is introduced treating upon the changes which different governments are liable to: but his discourse is faulty; for he does not particularly mention what changes the best and first governments are liable to; for he only assigns the general cause, of nothing being immutable, but that in time everything will alter *****

**** he conceives that nature will then produce bad men, who will not submit to education, and in this, probably, he is not wrong; for it is certain that there are some persons whom it is impossible by any education to make good men; but why should this change be more peculiar to what he calls the best-formed government, than to all other forms, and indeed to all other things that exist? and in respect to his assigned time, as the cause of the alteration of all things, we find that those which did not begin to exist at the same time cease to be at the same time; so that, if anything came into beginning the day before the solstice, it must alter at the same time. Besides, why should such a form of government be changed into the Lacedaemonian? for, in general, when governments alter, they alter into the contrary species to what they before were, and not into one like their former. And this reasoning holds true of other changes; for he says, that from the Lacedaemonian form it changes into an oligarchy, and from thence into a democracy, and from a democracy into a tyranny: and sometimes a contrary change takes place, as from a democracy into an oligarchy, rather than into a monarchy. With respect to a tyranny he neither says whether there will be any change in it; or if not, to what cause it will be owing; or if there is, into what other state it will alter: but the reason of this is, that a tyranny is an indeterminate government; and, according to him, every state ought to alter into the first, and most perfect, thus the continuity and circle would be preserved. But one tyranny often changed into another; as at Syria, from Myron's to Clisthenes'; or into an oligarchy, as was Antileo's at Chalcas; or into a democracy, as was Gelo's at Syracuse; or into an aristocracy, as was Charilaus's at Lacedaemon, and at Carthage. An oligarchy is also changed into a tyranny; such was the rise of most of the ancient tyrannies in Sicily; at Leontini, into the tyranny of Panaetius; at Gela, into that of Cleander; at Rhegium into that of Anaxilaus; and the like in many other cities. It is absurd also to suppose, that a state is changed into an oligarchy because those who are in power are avaricious and greedy of money, and not because those who are by far richer than their fellow citizens think it unfair that those who have nothing should have an equal share in the rule of the state with themselves, who possess so much-for in many oligarchies it is not allowable to be employed in money-getting, and there are many laws to prevent it. But in Carthage, which is a democracy, money-getting is creditable, and yet their form of government remains unaltered. It is also absurd to say, that in an oligarchy there are two cities, one of the poor and another of the rich; for why should this happen to them more than to the Lacedaemonians, or any other state where all possess not equal property, or where all are not equally good? for though no one member of the community should be poorer than he was before, yet a democracy might nevertheless change into an oligarchy; if the rich should be more powerful than the poor, and the one too negligent, and the other attentive: and though these changes are owing to many causes, yet he mentions but one only, that the citizens become poor by luxury, and paying interest-money; as if at first they were all rich, or the greater part of them: but this is not so, but when some of those who have the principal management of public affairs lose their fortunes, they will endeavour to bring about a revolution; but when others do, nothing of consequence will follow, nor when such states do alter is there any more reason for their altering into a democracy than any other. Besides, though some of the members of the community may not have spent their fortunes, yet if they share not in the honours of the state, or if they are ill-used and insulted, they will endeavour to raise seditions, and bring about a revolution, that they may be allowed to do as they like; which, Plato says, arises from too much liberty. Although there are many oligarchies and democracies, yet Socrates, when he is treating of the changes they may undergo, speaks of them as if there was but one of each sort.

Book VI

Chapter I

We have already shown what is the nature of the supreme council in the state, and wherein one may differ from another, and how the different magistrates should be regulated; and also the judicial department, and what is best suited to what state; and also to what causes both the destruction and preservation of governments are owing.

As there are very many species of democracies, as well as of other states, it will not be amiss to consider at the same time anything which we may have omitted to mention concerning either of them, and to allot to each that mode of conduct which is peculiar to and advantageous for them; and also to inquire into the combinations of all these different modes of government which we have mentioned; for as these are blended together the government is altered, as from an aristocracy to be an oligarchy, and from a free state to be a democracy. Now, I mean by those combinations of government (which I ought to examine into, but have not yet done), namely, whether the deliberative department and the election of magistrates is regulated in a manner correspondent to an oligarchy, or the judicial to an aristocracy, or the deliberative part only to an oligarchy, and the election of magistrates to an aristocracy, or whether, in any other manner, everything is not regulated according to the nature of the government. But we will first consider what particular sort of democracy is fitted to a particular city, and also what particular oligarchy to a particular people; and of other states, what is advantageous to what. It is also necessary to show clearly, not only which of these governments is best for a state, but also how it ought to be established there, and other things we will treat of briefly.

And first, we will speak of a democracy; and this will at the same time show clearly the nature of its opposite which some persons call an oligarchy; and in doing this we must examine into all the parts of a democracy, and everything that is connected therewith; for from the manner in which these are compounded together different species of democracies arise: and hence it is that they are more than one, and of various natures. Now, there are two causes which occasion there being so many democracies; one of which is that which we have already mentioned; namely, there being different sorts of people; for in one country the majority are husbandmen, in another mechanics, and hired servants; if the first of these is added to the second, and the third to both of them, the democracy will not only differ in the particular of better or worse, but in this, that it will be no longer the same government; the other is that which we will now speak of. The different things which are connected with democracies and seem to make part of these states, do, from their being joined to them, render them different from others: this attending a few, that more, and another all. It is necessary that he who would found any state which he may happen to approve of, or correct one, should be acquainted with all these particulars. All founders of states endeavour to comprehend within their own plan everything of nearly the same kind with it; but in doing this they err, in the manner I have already described in treating of the preservation and destruction of governments. I will now speak of these first principles and manners, and whatever else a democratical state requires.

Chapter II

Now the foundation of a democratical state is liberty, and people have been accustomed to say this as if here only liberty was to be found; for they affirm that this is the end proposed by every democracy. But one part of liberty is to govern and be governed alternately; for, according to democratical justice, equality is measured by numbers, and not by worth: and this being just, it is necessary that the supreme power should be vested in the people at large; and that what the majority determine should be final: so that in a democracy the poor ought to have more power than the rich, as being the greater number; for this is one mark of liberty which all framers of a democracy lay down as a criterion of that state; another is, to live as every one likes; for this, they say, is a right which liberty gives, since he is a slave who must live as he likes not. This, then, is another criterion of a democracy. Hence arises the claim to be under no command whatsoever to any one, upon any account, any otherwise than by rotation, and that just as far only as that person is, in his turn, under his also. This also is conducive to that equality which liberty demands. These things being premised, and such being the government, it follows that such rules as the following should be observed in it, that all the magistrates should be chosen out of all the people, and all to command each, and each in his turn all: that all the magistrates should be chosen by lot, except to those offices only which required some particular knowledge and skill: that no census, or a very small one, should be required to qualify a man for any office: that none should be in the same employment twice, or very few, and very seldom, except in the army: that all their appointments should be limited to a very short time, or at least as many as possible: that the whole community should be qualified to judge in all causes whatsoever, let the object be ever so extensive, ever so interesting, or of ever so high a nature; as at Athens, where the people at large judge the magistrates when they come out of office, and decide concerning public affairs as well as private contracts: that the supreme power should be in the public assembly; and that no magistrate should be allowed any discretionary power but in a few instances, and of no consequence to public business. Of all magistrates a senate is best suited to a democracy, where the whole community is not paid for giving their attendance; for in that case it loses its power; for then the people will bring all causes before them, by appeal, as we have already mentioned in a former book. In the next place, there should, if possible, be a fund to pay all the citizens-who have any share in the management of public affairs, either as members of the assembly, judges, and magistrates; but if this cannot be done, at least the magistrates, the judges the senators, and members of the supreme assembly, and also those officers who are obliged to eat at a common table ought to be paid. Moreover, as an oligarchy is said to be a government of men of family, fortune, and education; so, on the contrary, a democracy is a government in the hands of men of no birth, indigent circumstances, and mechanical employments. In this state also no office should be for life; and, if any such should remain after the government has been long changed into a democracy, they should endeavour by degrees to diminish the power; and also elect by lot instead of vote. These things, then, appertain to all democracies; namely, to be established on that principle of justice which is homogeneous to those governments; that is, that all the members of the state, by number, should enjoy an equality, which seems chiefly to constitute a democracy, or government of the people: for it seems perfectly equal that the rich should have no more share in the government than the poor, nor be alone in power; but that all should be equal, according to number; for thus, they think, the equality and liberty of the state best preserved.

Chapter III

In the next place we must inquire how this equality is to be procured. Shall the qualifications be divided so that five hundred rich should be equal to a thousand poor, or shall the thousand have equal power with the five hundred? or shall we not establish our equality in this manner? but divide indeed thus, and afterwards taking an equal number both out of the five hundred and the thousand, invest them with the power of creating the magistrates and judges. Is this state then established according to perfect democratical justice, or rather that which is guided by numbers only? For the defenders of a democracy say, that that is just which the majority approve of: but the favourers of an oligarchy say, that that is just which those who have most approve of; and that we ought to be directed by the value of property. Both the propositions are unjust; for if we agree with what the few propose we erect a tyranny: for if it should happen that an individual should have more than the rest who are rich, according to oligarchical justice, this man alone has a right to the supreme power; but if superiority of numbers is to prevail, injustice will then be done by confiscating the property of the rich, who are few, as we have already said. What then that equality is, which both parties will admit, must be collected from the definition of right which is common to them both; for they both say that what the majority of the state approves of ought to be established. Be it so; but not entirely: but since a city happens to be made up of two different ranks of people, the rich and the poor, let that be established which is approved of by both these, or the greater part: but should there be opposite sentiments, let that be established which shall be approved of by the greater part: but let this be according to the census; for instance, if there should be ten of the rich and twenty of the poor, and six of the first and fifteen of the last should agree upon any measure, and the remaining four of the rich should join with the remaining five of the poor in opposing it, that party whose census when added together should determine which opinion should be law, and should these happen to be equal, it should be regarded as a case similar to an assembly or court of justice dividing equally upon any question that comes before them, who either determine it by lot or some such method. But although, with respect to what is equal and just, it may be very difficult to establish the truth, yet it is much easier to do than to persuade those who have it in their power to encroach upon others to be guided thereby; for the weak always desire what is equal and just, but the powerful pay no regard thereunto.

Chapter IV

There are four kinds of democracies. The best is that which is composed of those first in order, as we have already said, and this also is the most ancient of any. I call that the first which every one would place so, was he to divide the people; for the best part of these are the husbandmen. We see, then, that a democracy may be framed where the majority live by tillage or pasturage; for, as their property is but small, they will not be at leisure perpetually to hold public assemblies, but will be continually employed in following their own business, not having otherwise the means of living; nor will they be desirous of what another enjoys, but will rather like to follow their own business than meddle with state affairs and accept the offices of government, which will be attended with no great profit; for the major part of mankind are rather desirous of riches than honour (a proof of this is, that they submitted to the tyrannies in ancient times, and do now submit to the oligarchies, if no one hinders them in their usual occupations, or deprives them of their property; for some of them soon get rich, others are removed from poverty); besides, their having the right of election and calling their magistrates to account for their conduct when they come out of office, will satisfy their desire of honours, if any of them entertain that passion: for in some states, though the commonalty have not the right of electing the magistrates, yet it is vested in part of that body chosen to represent them: and it is sufficient for the people at large to possess the deliberative power: and this ought to be considered as a species of democracy; such was that formerly at Mantinsea: for which reason it is proper for the democracy we have been now treating of to have a power (and it has been usual for them to have it) of censuring their magistrates when out of office, and sitting in judgment upon all causes: but that the chief magistrates should be elected, and according to a certain census, which should vary with the rank of their office, or else not by a census, but according to their abilities for their respective appointments. A state thus constituted must be well constituted; for the magistracies will be always filled with the best men with the approbation of the people; who will not envy their superiors: and these and the nobles should be content with this part in the administration; for they will not be governed by their inferiors. They will be also careful to use their power with moderation, as there are others to whom full power is delegated to censure their conduct; for it is very serviceable to the state to have them dependent upon others, and not to be permitted to do whatsoever they choose; for with such a liberty there would be no check to that evil particle there is in every one: therefore it is necessary and most for the benefit of the state that the offices thereof should be filled by the principal persons in it, whose characters are unblemished, and that the people are not oppressed. It is now evident that this is the best species of democracy, and on what account; because the people are such and have such powers as they ought to have. To establish a democracy of husbandmen some of those laws which were observed in many ancient states are universally useful; as, for instance, on no account to permit any one to possess more than a certain quantity of land, or within a certain distance from the city. Formerly also, in some states, no one was allowed to sell their original lot of land. They also mention a law of one Oxylus, which forbade any one to add to their patrimony by usury. We ought also to follow the law of the Aphutaeans, as useful to direct us in this particular we are now speaking of; for they having but very little ground, while they were a numerous people, and at the same time were all husbandmen, did not include all their lands within the census, but divided them in such a manner that, according to the census, the poor had more power than the rich. Next to the commonalty of husbandmen is one of shepherds and herdsmen; for they have many things in common with them, and, by their way of life, are excellently qualified to make good soldiers, stout in body, and able to continue in the open air all night. The generality of the people of whom other democracies are composed are much worse than these; for their lives are wretched nor have they any business with virtue in anything they do; these are your mechanics, your exchange-men, and hired servants; as all these sorts of men frequent the exchange and the citadel, they can readily attend the public assembly; whereas the husbandmen, being more dispersed in the country, cannot so easily meet together; nor are they equally desirous of doing it with these others! When a country happens to be so situated that a great part of the land lies at a distance from the city, there it is easy to establish a good democracy or a free state for the people in general will be obliged to live in the country; so that it will be necessary in such a democracy, though there may be an exchange-mob at hand, never to allow a legal assembly without the inhabitants of the country attend. We have shown in what manner the first and best democracy ought to be established, and it will be equally evident as to the rest, for from these we should proceed as a guide, and always separate the meanest of the people from the rest. But the last and worst, which gives to every citizen without distinction a share in every part of the administration, is what few citizens can bear, nor is it easy to preserve for any long time, unless well supported by laws and manners. We have already noticed almost every cause that can destroy either this or any other state. Those who have taken the lead in such a democracy have endeavoured to support it, and make the people powerful by collecting together as many persons as they could and giving them their freedom, not only legitimately but naturally born, and also if either of their parents were citizens, that is to say, if either their father or mother; and this method is better suited to this state than any other: and thus the demagogues have usually managed. They ought, however, to take care, and do this no longer than the common people are superior to the nobles and those of the middle rank, and then stop; for, if they proceed still further, they will make the state disorderly, and the nobles will ill brook the power of the common people, and be full of resentment against it; which was the cause of an insurrection at Cyrene: for a little evil is overlooked, but when it becomes a great one it strikes the eye. It is, moreover, very-useful in such a state to do as Clisthenes did at Athens, when he was desirous of increasing the power of the people, and as those did who established the democracy in Cyrene; that is, to institute many tribes and fraternities, and to make the religious rites of private persons few, and those common; and every means is to be contrived to associate and blend the people together as much as possible; and that all former customs be broken through. Moreover, whatsoever is practised in a tyranny seems adapted to a democracy of this species; as, for instance, the licentiousness of the slaves, the women, and the children; for this to a certain degree is useful in such a state; and also to overlook every one's living as they choose; for many will support such a government: for it is more agreeable to many to live without any control than as prudence would direct.

Chapter V

It is also the business of the legislator and all those who would support a government of this sort not to make it too great a work, or too perfect; but to aim only to render it stable: for, let a state be constituted ever so badly, there is no difficulty in its continuing a few days: they should therefore endeavour to procure its safety by all those ways which we have described in assigning the causes of the preservation and destruction of governments; avoiding what is hurtful, and by framing such laws, written and unwritten, as contain those things which chiefly tend to the preservation of the state; nor to suppose that that is useful either for a democratic or an oligarchic form of government which contributes to make them more purely so, but what will contribute to their duration: but our demagogues at present, to flatter the people, occasion frequent confiscations in the courts; for which reason those who have the welfare of the state really at heart should act directly opposite to what they do, and enact a law to prevent forfeitures from being divided amongst the people or paid into the treasury, but to have them set apart for sacred uses: for those who are of a bad disposition would not then be the less cautious, as their punishment would be the same; and the community would not be so ready to condemn those whom they sat in judgment on when they were to get nothing by it: they should also take care that the causes which are brought before the public should be as few as possible, and punish with the utmost severity those who rashly brought an action against any one; for it is not the commons but the nobles who are generally prosecuted: for in all things the citizens of the same state ought to be affectionate to each other, at least not to treat those who have the chief power in it as their enemies. Now, as the democracies which have been lately established are very numerous, and it is difficult to get the common people to attend the public assemblies without they are paid for it, this, when there is not a sufficient public revenue, is fatal to the nobles; for the deficiencies therein must be necessarily made up by taxes, confiscations, and fines imposed by corrupt courts of justice: which things have already destroyed many democracies. Whenever, then, the revenues of the state are small, there should be but few public assemblies and but few courts of justice: these, however, should have very extensive jurisdictions, but should continue sitting a few days only, for by this means the rich would not fear the expense, although they should receive nothing for their attendance, though the poor did; and judgment also would be given much better; for the rich will not choose to be long absent from their own affairs, but will willingly be so for a short time: and, when there are sufficient revenues, a different conduct ought to be pursued from what the demagogues at present follow; for now they divide the surplus of the public money amongst the poor; these receive it and again want the same supply, while the giving it is like pouring water into a sieve: but the true patriot in a democracy ought to take care that the majority of the community are not too poor, for this is the cause of rapacity in that government; he therefore should endeavour that they may enjoy perpetual plenty; and as this also is advantageous to the rich, what can be saved out of the public money should be put by, and then divided at once amongst the poor, if possible, in such a quantity as may enable every one of them to purchase a little field, and, if that cannot be done, at least to give each of them enough to procure the implements of trade and husbandry; and if there is not enough for all to receive so much at once, then to divide it according to tribes or any other allotment. In the meantime let the rich pay them for necessary services, but not be obliged to find them in useless amusements. And something like this was the manner in which they managed at Carthage, and preserved the affections of the people; for by continually sending some of their community into colonies they procured plenty. It is also worthy of a sensible and generous nobility to divide the poor amongst them, and supplying them with what is necessary, induce them to work; or to imitate the conduct of the people at Tarentum: for they, permitting the poor to partake in common of everything which is needful for them, gain the affections of the commonalty. They have also two different ways of electing their magistrates; for some are chosen by vote, others by lot; by the last, that the people at large may have some share in the administration; by the former, that the state may be well governed: the same may be accomplished if of the same magistrates you choose some by vote, others by lot. And thus much for the manner in which democracies ought to be established.

Chapter VI

What has been already said will almost of itself sufficiently show how an oligarchy ought to be founded; for he who would frame such a state should have in his view a democracy to oppose it; for every species of oligarchy should be founded on principles diametrically opposite to some species of democracy.

The first and best-framed oligarchy is that which approaches near to what we call a free state; in which there ought to be two different census, the one high, the other low: from those who are within the latter the ordinary officers of the state ought to be chosen; from the former the supreme magistrates: nor should any one be excluded from a part of the administration who was within the census; which should be so regulated that the commonalty who are included in it should by means thereof be superior to those who have no share in the government; for those who are to have the management of public affairs ought always to be chosen out of the better sort of the people. Much in the same manner ought that oligarchy to be established which is next in order: but as to that which is most opposite to a pure democracy, and approaches nearest to a dynasty and a tyranny, as it is of all others the worst, so it requires the greatest care and caution to preserve it: for as bodies of sound and healthy constitutions and ships which are well manned and well found for sailing can bear many injuries without perishing, while a diseased body or a leaky ship with an indifferent crew cannot support the least shock; so the worst-established governments want most looking after. A number of citizens is the preservation of a democracy; for these are opposed to those rights which are founded in rank: on the contrary, the preservation of an oligarchy depends upon the due regulation of the different orders in the society.

Chapter VII

As the greater part of the community are divided into four sorts of people; husbandmen, mechanics, traders, and hired servants; and as those who are employed in war may likewise be divided into four; the horsemen, the heavy-armed soldier, the light-armed, and the sailor, where the nature of the country can admit a great number of horse; there a powerful oligarchy may be easily established: for the safety of the inhabitants depends upon a force of that sort; but those who can support the expense of horsemen must be persons of some considerable fortune. Where the troops are chiefly heavy-armed, there an oligarchy, inferior in power to the other, may be established; for the heavy-armed are rather made up of men of substance than the poor: but the light-armed and the sailors always contribute to support a democracy: but where the number of these is very great and a sedition arises, the other parts of the community fight at a disadvantage; but a remedy for this evil is to be learned from skilful generals, who always mix a proper number of light-armed soldiers with their horse and heavy-armed: for it is with those that the populace get the better of the men of fortune in an insurrection; for these being lighter are easily a match for the horse and the heavy-armed: so that for an oligarchy to form a body of troops from these is to form it against itself: but as a city is composed of persons of different ages, some young and some old, the fathers should teach their sons, while they were very young, a light and easy exercise; but, when they are grown up, they should be perfect in every warlike exercise. Now, the admission of the people to any share in the government should either be (as I said before) regulated by a census, or else, as at Thebes, allowed to those who for a certain time have ceased from any mechanic employment, or as at Massalia, where they are chosen according to their worth, whether citizens or foreigners. With respect to the magistrates of the highest rank which it may be necessary to have in a state, the services they are bound to do the public should be expressly laid down, to prevent the common people from being desirous of accepting their employments, and also to induce them to regard their magistrates with favour when they know what a price they pay for their honours. It is also necessary that the magistrates, upon entering into their offices, should make magnificent sacrifices and erect some public structure, that the people partaking of the entertainment, and seeing the city ornamented with votive gifts in their temples and public structures, may see with pleasure the stability of the government: add to this also, that the nobles will have their generosity recorded: but now this is not the conduct which those who are at present at the head of an oligarchy pursue, but the contrary; for they are not more desirous of honour than of gain; for which reason such oligarchies may more properly be called little democracies. Thus we have explained on what principles a democracy and an oligarchy ought to be established.

Chapter VIII

After what has been said I proceed next to treat particularly of the magistrates; of what nature they should be, how many, and for what purpose, as I have already mentioned: for without necessary magistrates no state can exist, nor without those which contribute to its dignity and good order can exist happily: now it is necessary that in small states the magistrates should be few; in a large one, many: also to know well what offices may be joined together, and what ought to be separated. The first thing necessary is to establish proper regulators in the markets; for which purpose a certain magistrate should be appointed to inspect their contracts and preserve good order; for of necessity, in almost every city there must be both buyers and sellers to supply each other's mutual wants: and this is what is most productive of the comforts of life; for the sake of which men seem to have joined together in one community. A second care, and nearly related to the first, is to have an eye both to the public and private edifices in the city, that they may be an ornament; and also to take care of all buildings which are likely to fall: and to see that the highways are kept in proper repair; and also that the landmarks between different estates are preserved, that there may be no disputes on that account; and all other business of the same nature. Now, this business may be divided into several branches, over each of which in populous cities they appoint a separate person; one to inspect the buildings, another the fountains, another the harbours; and they are called the inspectors of the city. A third, which is very like the last, and conversant nearly about the same objects, only in the country, is to take care of what is done out of the city. The officers who have this employment we call inspectors of the lands, or inspectors of the woods; but the business of all three of them is the same. There must also be other officers appointed to receive the public revenue and to deliver it out to those who are in the different departments of the state: these are called receivers or quaestors. There must also be another, before whom all private contracts and sentences of courts should be enrolled, as well as proceedings and declarations. Sometimes this employment is divided amongst many, but there is one supreme over the rest; these are called proctors, notaries, and the like. Next to these is an officer whose business is of all others the most necessary, and yet most difficult; namely, to take care that sentence is executed upon those who are condemned; and that every one pays the fines laid on him; and also to have the charge of those who are in prison. This office is very disagreeable on account of the odium attending it, so that no one will engage therein without it is made very profitable, or, if they do, will they be willing to execute it according to law; but it is most necessary, as it is of no service to pass judgment in any cause without that judgment is carried into execution: for without this human society could not subsist: for which reason it is best that this office should not be executed by one person, but by some of the magistrates of the other courts. In like manner, the taking care that those fines which are ordered by the judges are levied should be divided amongst different persons. And as different magistrates judge different causes, let the causes of the young be heard by the young: and as to those which are already brought to a hearing, let one person pass sentence, and another see it executed: as, for instance, let the magistrates who have the care of the public buildings execute the sentence which the inspectors of the markets have passed, and the like in other cases: for by so much the less odium attends those who carry the laws into execution, by so much the easier will they be properly put in force: therefore for the same persons to pass the sentence and to execute it will subject them to general hatred; and if they pass it upon all, they will be considered as the enemies of all. Thus one person has often the custody of the prisoner's body, while another sees the sentence against him executed, as the eleven did at Athens: for which reason it is prudent to separate these offices, and to give great attention thereunto as equally necessary with anything we have already mentioned; for it will certainly happen that men of character will decline accepting this office, and worthless persons cannot properly be entrusted with it, as having themselves rather an occasion for a guard than being qualified to guard others. This, therefore, ought by no means to be a separate office from others; nor should it be continually allotted to any individuals, but the young men; where there is a city-guard, the youths ought in turns to take these offices upon them. These, then, as the most necessary magistrates, ought to be first mentioned: next to these are others no less necessary, but of much higher rank, for they ought to be men of great skill and fidelity. These are they who have the guard of the city, and provide everything that is necessary for war; whose business it is, both in war and peace, to defend the walls and the gates, and to take care to muster and marshal the citizens. Over all these there are sometimes more officers, sometimes fewer: thus in little cities there is only one whom they call either general or polemarch; but where there are horse and light-armed troops, and bowmen, and sailors, they sometimes put distinct commanders over each of these; who again have others under them, according to their different divisions; all of which join together to make one military body: and thus much for this department. Since some of the magistrates, if not all, have business with the public money, it is necessary that there should be other officers, whose employment should be nothing else than to take an account of what they have, and correct any mismanagement therein. But besides all these magistrates there is one who is supreme over them all, who very often has in his own power the disposal of the public revenue and taxes; who presides over the people when the supreme power is in them; for there must be some magistrate who has a power to summon them together, and to preside as head of the state. These are sometimes called preadvisers; but where there are many, more properly a council. These are nearly the civil magistrates which are requisite to a government: but there are other persons whose business is confined to religion; as the priests, and those who are to take care of the temples, that they are kept in proper repair, or, if they fall down, that they may be rebuilt; and whatever else belongs to public worship. This charge is sometimes entrusted to one person, as in very small cities: in others it is delegated to many, and these distinct from the priesthood, as the builders or keepers of holy places, and officers of the sacred revenue. Next to these are those who are appointed to have the general care of all those public sacrifices to the tutelar god of the state, which the laws do not entrust to the priests: and these in different states have different appellations. To enumerate in few words the different departments of all those magistrates who are necessary: these are either religion, war, taxes, expenditures, markets, public buildings, harbours, highways. Belonging to the courts of justice there are scribes to enroll private contracts; and there must also be guards set over the prisoners, others to see the law is executed, council on either side, and also others to watch over the conduct of those who are to decide the causes. Amongst the magistrates also may finally be reckoned those who are to give their advice in public affairs. But separate states, who are peculiarly happy and have leisure to attend to more minute particulars, and are very attentive to good order, require particular magistrates for themselves; such as those who have the government of the women; who are to see the laws are executed; who take care of the boys and preside over their education. To these may be added those who have the care of their gymnastic exercises, their theatres, and every other public spectacle which there may happen to be. Some of these, however, are not of general use; as the governors of the women: for the poor are obliged to employ their wives and children in servile offices for want of slaves. As there are three magistrates to whom some states entrust the supreme power; namely, guardians of the laws, preadvisers, and senators; guardians of the laws suit best to an aristocracy, preadvisers to an oligarchy, and a senate to a democracy. And thus much briefly concerning all magistrates.

Book VII

Chapter I

He who proposes to make that inquiry which is necessary concerning what government is best, ought first to determine what manner of living is most eligible; for while this remains uncertain it will also be equally uncertain what government is best: for, provided no unexpected accidents interfere, it is highly probable, that those who enjoy the best government will live the most happily according to their circumstances; he ought, therefore, first to know what manner of life is most desirable for all; and afterwards whether this life is the same to the man and the citizen, or different. As I imagine that I have already sufficiently shown what sort of life is best in my popular discourses on that subject, I think I may very properly repeat the same here; as most certainly no one ever called in question the propriety of one of the divisions; namely, that as what is good, relative to man, may be divided into three sorts, what is external, what appertains to the body, and what to the soul, it is evident that all these must conspire to make a man happy: for no one would say that a man was happy who had no fortitude, no temperance, no justice, no prudence; but was afraid of the flies that flew round him: nor would abstain from the meanest theft if he was either hungry or dry, or would murder his dearest friend for a farthing; and also was in every particular as wanting in his understanding as an infant or an idiot. These truths are so evident that all must agree to them; though some may dispute about the quantity and the degree: for they may think, that a very little virtue is sufficient for happiness; but for riches, property, power, honour, and all such things, they endeavour to increase them without bounds: but to such we reply, that it is easy to prove from what experience teaches us in these cases, that these external goods produce not virtue, but virtue them. As to a happy life, whether it is to be found in pleasure or virtue or both, certain it is, that those whose morals are most pure, and whose understandings are best cultivated, will enjoy more of it, although their fortune is but moderate than those do who own an exuberance of wealth, are deficient in those; and this utility any one who reflects may easily convince himself of; for whatsoever is external has its boundary, as a machine, and whatsoever is useful in its excess is either necessarily hurtful, or at best useless to the possessor; but every good quality of the soul the higher it is in degree, so much the more useful it is, if it is permitted on this subject to use the word useful as well as noble. It is also very evident, that the accidents of each subject take place of each other, as the subjects themselves, of which we allow they are accidents, differ from each other in value; so that if the soul is more noble than any outward possession, as the body, both in itself and with respect to us, it must be admitted of course that the best accidents of each must follow the same analogy. Besides, it is for the sake of the soul that these things are desirable; and it is on this account that wise men should desire them, not the soul for them. Let us therefore be well assured, that every one enjoys as much happiness as he possesses virtue and wisdom, and acts according to their dictates; since for this we have the example of GOD Himself, *who is completely happy, not from any external good, but in Himself, and because such is His nature.* For good fortune is something different from happiness, as every good which depends not on the mind is owing to chance or fortune; but it is not from fortune that any one is wise and just: hence it follows, that that city is happiest which is the best and acts best: for no one can do well who acts not well; nor can the deeds either of man or city be praiseworthy without virtue and wisdom; for whatsoever is just, or wise, or prudent in a man, the same things are just, wise, and prudent in a city.

Thus much by way of introduction; for I could not but just touch upon this subject, though I could not go through a complete investigation of it, as it properly belongs to another question: let us at present suppose so much, that a man's happiest life, both as an individual and as a citizen, is a life of virtue, accompanied with those enjoyments which virtue usually procures. If there are any who are not convinced by what I have said, their doubts shall be answered hereafter, at present we shall proceed according to our intended method.

Chapter II

It now remains for us to say whether the happiness of any individual man and the city is the same or different: but this also is evident; for whosoever supposes that riches will make a person happy, must place the happiness of the city in riches if it possesses them; those who prefer a life which enjoys a tyrannic power over others will also think, that the city which has many others under its command is most happy: thus also if any one approves a man for his virtue, he will think the most worthy city the happiest: but here there are two particulars which require consideration, one of which is, whether it is the most eligible life to be a member of the community and enjoy the rights of a citizen, or whether to live as a stranger, without interfering in public affairs; and also what form of government is to be preferred, and what disposition of the state is best; whether the whole community should be eligible to a share in the administration, or only the greater part, and some only: as this, therefore, is a subject of political examination and speculation, and not what concerns the individual, and the first of these is what we are at present engaged in, the one of these I am not obliged to speak to, the other is the proper business of my present design. It is evident that government must be the best which is so established, that every one therein may have it in his power to act virtuously and live happily: but some, who admit that a life of virtue is most eligible, still doubt which is preferable a public life of active virtue, or one entirely disengaged from what is without and spent in contemplation; which some say is the only one worthy of a philosopher; and one of these two different modes of life both now and formerly seem to have been chosen by all those who were the most virtuous men; I mean the public or philosophic. And yet it is of no little consequence on which side the truth lies; for a man of sense must naturally incline to the better choice; both as an individual and a citizen. Some think that a tyrannic government over those near us is the greatest injustice; but that a political one is not unjust: but that still is a restraint on the pleasures and tranquillity of life. Others hold the quite contrary opinion, and think that a public and active life is the only life for man: for that private persons have no opportunity of practising any one virtue, more than they have who are engaged in public life the management of the state. These are their sentiments; others say, that a tyrannical and despotical mode of government is the only happy one; for even amongst some free states the object of their laws seems to be to tyrannise over their neighbours: so that the generality of political institutions, wheresoever dispersed, if they have any one common object in view, have all of them this, to conquer and govern. It is evident, both from the laws of the Lacedaemonians and Cretans, as well as by the manner in which they educated their children, that all which they had in view was to make them soldiers: besides, among all nations, those who have power enough and reduce others to servitude are honoured on that account; as were the Scythians, Persians, Thracians, and Gauls: with some there are laws to heighten the virtue of courage; thus they tell us that at Carthage they allowed every person to wear as many rings for distinction as he had served campaigns. There was also a law in Macedonia, that a man who had not himself killed an enemy should be obliged to wear a halter; among the Scythians, at a festival, none were permitted to drink out of the cup was carried about who had not done the same thing. Among the Iberians, a warlike nation, they fixed as many columns upon a man's tomb as he had slain enemies: and among different nations different things of this sort prevail, some of them established by law, others by custom. Probably it may seem too absurd to those who are willing to take this subject into their consideration to inquire whether it is the business of a legislator to be able to point out by what means a state may govern and tyrannise over its neighbours, whether they will, or will not: for how can that belong either to the politician or legislator which is unlawful? for that cannot be lawful which is done not only justly, but unjustly also: for a conquest may be unjustly made. But we see nothing of this in the arts: for it is the business neither of the physician nor the pilot to use either persuasion or force, the one to his patients, the other to his passengers: and yet many seem to think a despotic government is a political one, and what they would not allow to be just or proper, if exercised over themselves, they will not blush to exercise over others; for they endeavour to be wisely governed themselves, but think it of no consequence whether others are so or not: but a despotic power is absurd, except only where nature has framed the one party for dominion, the other for subordination; and therefore no one ought to assume it over all in general, but those only which are the proper objects thereof: thus no one should hunt men either for food or sacrifice, but what is fit for those purposes, and these are wild animals which are eatable.

Now a city which is well governed might be very happy in itself while it enjoyed a good system of laws, although it should happen to be so situated as to have no connection with any other state, though its constitution should not be framed for war or conquest; for it would then have no occasion for these. It is evident therefore that the business of war is to be considered as commendable, not as a final end, but as the means of procuring it. It is the duty of a good legislator to examine carefully into his state; and the nature of the people, and how they may partake of every intercourse, of a good life, and of the happiness which results from it: and in this respect some laws and customs differ from others. It is also the duty of a legislator, if he has any neighbouring states to consider in what manner he shall oppose each of them, or what good offices he shall show them. But what should be the final end of the best governments will be considered hereafter.

Chapter III

We will now speak to those who, while they agree that a life of virtue is most eligible, yet differ in the use of it addressing ourselves to both these parties; for there are some who disapprove of all political governments, and think that the life of one who is really free is different from the life of a citizen, and of all others most eligible: others again think that the citizen is the best; and that it is impossible for him who does nothing to be well employed; but that virtuous activity and happiness are the same thing. Now both parties in some particulars say what is right, in others what is wrong, thus, that the life of a freeman is better than the life of a slave is true, for a slave, as a slave, is employed in nothing honourable; for the common servile employments which he is commanded to perform have nothing virtuous in them; but, on the other hand, it is not true that a submission to all sorts of governments is slavery; for the government of freemen differs not more from the government of slaves than slavery and freedom differ from each other in their nature; and how they do has been already mentioned. To prefer doing of nothing to virtuous activity is also wrong, for happiness consists in action, and many noble ends are produced by the actions of the just and wise. From what we have already determined on this subject, some one probably may think, that supreme power is of all things best, as that will enable a man to command very many useful services from others; so that he who can obtain this ought not to give it up to another, but rather to seize it: and, for this purpose, the father should have no attention or regard for the son, or the son for the father, or friend for friend; for what is best is most eligible: but to be a member of the community and be in felicity is best. What these persons advance might probably be true, if the supreme good was certainly theirs who plunder and use violence to others: but it is most unlikely that it should be so; for it is a mere supposition: for it does not follow that their actions are honourable who thus assume the supreme power over others, without they were by nature as superior to them as a man to a woman, a father to a child, a master to a slave: so that he who so far forsakes the paths of virtue can never return back from whence he departed from them: for amongst equals whatever is fair and just ought to be reciprocal; for this is equal and right; but that equals should not partake of what is equal, or like to like, is contrary to nature: but whatever is contrary to nature is not right; therefore, if there is any one superior to the rest of the community in virtue and abilities for active life, him it is proper to follow, him it is right to obey, but the one alone will not do, but must be joined to the other also: and, if we are right in what we have now said, it follows that happiness consists in virtuous activity, and that both with respect to the community as well as the individual an active life is the happiest: not that an active life must necessarily refer to other persons, as some think, or that those studies alone are practical which are pursued to teach others what to do; for those are much more so whose final object is in themselves, and to improve the judgment and understanding of the man; for virtuous activity has an end, therefore is something practical; nay, those who contrive the plan which others follow are more particularly said to act, and are superior to the workmen who execute their designs. But it is not necessary that states which choose to have no intercourse with others should remain inactive; for the several members thereof may have mutual intercourse with each other; for there are many opportunities for this among the different citizens; the same thing is true of every individual: for, was it otherwise, neither could the Deity nor the universe be perfect; to neither of whom can anything external separately exist. Hence it is evident that that very same life which is happy for each individual is happy also for the state and every member of it.

Chapter IV

As I have now finished what was introductory to this subject, and considered at large the nature of other states, it now remains that I should first say what ought to be the establishment of a city which one should form according to one's wish; for no good state can exist without a moderate proportion of what is necessary. Many things therefore ought to be forethought of as desirable, but none of them such as are impossible: I mean relative to the number of citizens and the extent of the territory: for as other artificers, such as the weaver and the shipwright, ought to have such materials as are fit for their work, since so much the better they are, by so much superior will the work itself necessarily be; so also ought the legislator and politician endeavour to procure proper materials for the business they have in hand. Now the first and principal instrument of the politician is the number of the people; he should therefore know how many, and what they naturally ought to be: in like manner the country, how large, and what it is. Most persons think that it is necessary for a city to be large to be happy: but, should this be true, they cannot tell what is a large one and what a small one; for according to the multitude of the inhabitants they estimate the greatness of it; but they ought rather to consider its strength than its numbers; for a state has a certain object in view, and from the power which it has in itself of accomplishing it, its greatness ought to be estimated; as a person might say, that Hippocrates was a greater physician, though not a greater man, than one that exceeded him in the size of his body: but if it was proper to determine the strength of the city from the number of the inhabitants, it should never be collected from the multitude in general who may happen to be in it; for in a city there must necessarily be many slaves, sojourners, and foreigners; but from those who are really part of the city and properly constitute its members; a multitude of these is indeed a proof of a large city, but in a state where a large number of mechanics inhabit, and but few soldiers, such a state cannot be great; for the greatness of the city, and the number of men in it, are not the same thing. This too is evident from fact, that it is very difficult, if not impossible, to govern properly a very numerous body of men; for of all the states which appear well governed we find not one where the rights of a citizen are open to an indiscriminate multitude. And this is also evident from the nature of the thing; for as law is a certain order, so good law is of course a certain good order: but too large a multitude are incapable of this, unless under the government of that DIVINE POWER which comprehends the universe. Not but that, as quantity and variety are usually essential to beauty, the perfection of a city consists in the largeness of it as far as that largeness is consistent with that order already mentioned: but still there is a determinate size to all cities, as well as everything else, whether animals, plants, or machines, for each of these, if they are neither too little nor too big, have their proper powers; but when they have not their due growth, or are badly constructed, as a ship a span long is not properly a ship, nor one of two furlongs length, but when it is of a fit size; for either from its smallness or from its largeness it may be quite useless: so is it with a city; one that is too small has not in itself the power of self-defence, but this is essential to a city: one that is too large is capable of self-defence in what is necessary; but then it is a nation and not a city: for it will be very difficult to accommodate a form of government to it: for who would choose to be the general of such an unwieldy multitude, or who could be their herald but a stentor? The first thing therefore necessary is, that a city should consist of such numbers as will be sufficient to enable the inhabitants to live happily in their political community: and it follows, that the more the inhabitants exceed that necessary number the greater will the city be: but this must not be, as we have already said, without bounds; but what is its proper limit experience will easily show, and this experience is to be collected from the actions both of the governors and the governed. Now, as it belongs to the first to direct the inferior magistrates and to act as judges, it follows that they can neither determine causes with justice nor issue their orders with propriety without they know the characters of their fellow-citizens: so that whenever this happens not to be done in these two particulars, the state must of necessity be badly managed; for in both of them it is not right to determine too hastily and without proper knowledge, which must evidently be the case where the number of the citizens is too many: besides, it is more easy for strangers and sojourners to assume the rights of citizens, as they will easily escape detection in so great a multitude. It is evident, then, that the best boundary for a city is that wherein the numbers are the greatest possible, that they may be the better able to be sufficient in themselves, while at the same time they are not too large to be under the eye and government of the magistrates. And thus let us determine the extent of a city.

Chapter V

What we have said concerning a city may nearly be applied to a country; for as to what soil it should be, every one evidently will commend it if it is such as is sufficient in itself to furnish what will make the inhabitants happy; for which purpose it must be able to supply them with all the necessaries of life; for it is the having these in plenty, without any want, which makes them content. As to its extent, it should be such as may enable the inhabitants to live at their ease with freedom and temperance. Whether we have done right or wrong in fixing this limit to the territory shall be considered more minutely hereafter, when we come particularly to inquire into property, and what fortune is requisite for a man to live on, and how and in what manner they ought to employ it; for there are many doubts upon this question, while each party insists upon their own plan of life being carried to an excess, the one of severity, the other of indulgence. What the situation of the country should be it is not difficult to determine, in some particulars respecting that we ought to be advised by those who are skilful in military affairs. It should be difficult of access to an enemy, but easy to the inhabitants: and as we said, that the number of inhabitants ought to be such as can come under the eye of the magistrate, so should it be with the country; for then it is easily defended. As to the position of the city, if one could place it to one's wish, it is convenient to fix it on the seaside: with respect to the country, one situation which it ought to have has been already mentioned, namely, that it should be so placed as easily to give assistance to all places, and also to receive the necessaries of life from all parts, and also wood, or any other materials which may happen to be in the country.

Chapter VI

But with respect to placing a city in the neighbourhood of the sea, there are some who have many doubts whether it is serviceable or hurtful to a well-regulated state; for they say, that the resort of persons brought up under a different system of government is disserviceable to the state, as well by impeding the laws as by their numbers; for a multitude of merchants must necessarily arise from their trafficking backward and forward upon the seas, which will hinder the well-governing of the city: but if this inconvenience should not arise, it is evident that it is better, both on account of safety and also for the easier acquisition of the necessaries of life, that both the city and the country should be near the sea; for it is necessary that those who are to sustain the attack of the enemy should be ready with their assistance both by land and by sea, and to oppose any inroad, both ways if possible but if not, at least where they are most powerful, which they may do while they possess both. A maritime situation is also useful for receiving from others what your own country will not produce, and exporting those necessaries of your own growth which are more than you have occasion for; but a city ought to traffic to supply its own wants, and not the wants of others; for those who themselves furnish an open market for every one, do it for the sake of gain; which it is not proper for a well-established state to do, neither should they encourage such a commerce. Now, as we see that many places and cities have docks and harbours lying very convenient for the city, while those who frequent them have no communication with the citadel, and yet they are not too far off, but are surrounded by walls and such-like fortifications, it is evident, that if any good arises from such an intercourse the city will receive it, but if anything hurtful, it will be easy to restrain it by a law declaring and deputing whom the state will allow to have an intercourse with each other, and whom not. As to a naval power, it is by no means doubtful that it is necessary to have one to a certain degree; and this not only for the sake of the city itself, but also because it may be necessary to appear formidable to some of the neighbouring states, or to be able to assist them as well by sea as by land; but to know how great that force should be, the health of the state should be inquired into, and if that appears vigorous and enables her to take the lead of other communities, it is necessary that her force should correspond with her actions. As for that multitude of people which a maritime power creates, they are by no means necessary to a state, nor ought they to make a part of the citizens; for the mariners and infantry, who have the command, are freemen, and upon these depends a naval engagement: but when there are many servants and husbandmen, there they will always have a number of sailors, as we now see happens to some states, as in Heraclea, where they man many triremes, though the extent of their city is much inferior to some others. And thus we determine concerning the country, the port, the city, the sea, and a maritime power: as to the number of the citizens, what that ought to be we have already said.

Chapter VII

We now proceed to point out what natural disposition the members of the community ought to be of: but this any one will easily perceive who will cast his eye over the states of Greece, of all others the most celebrated, and also the other different nations of this habitable world. Those who live in cold countries, as the north of Europe, are full of courage, but wanting in understanding and the arts: therefore they are very tenacious of their liberty; but, not being politicians, they cannot reduce their neighbours under their power: but the Asiatics, whose understandings are quick, and who are conversant in the arts, are deficient in courage; and therefore are always conquered and the slaves of others: but the Grecians, placed as it were between these two boundaries, so partake of them both as to be at the same time both courageous and sensible; for which reason Greece continues free, and governed in the best manner possible, and capable of commanding the whole world, could they agree upon one system of policy. Now this is the difference between the Grecians and other nations, that the latter have but one of these qualities, whereas in the former they are both happily blended together. Hence it is evident, that those persons ought to be both sensible and courageous who will readily obey a legislator, the object of whose laws is virtue. As to what some persons say, that the military must be mild and tender to those they know, but severe and cruel to those they know not, it is courage which makes any one lovely; for that is the faculty of the soul which we most admire: as a proof of this, our resentment rises higher against our friends and acquaintance than against those we know not: for which reason Archilaus accusing his friends says very properly to himself, Shall my friends insult me? The spirit of freedom and command also is what all inherit who are of this disposition for courage is commanding and invincible. It also is not right for any one to say, that you should be severe to those you know not; for this behaviour is proper for no one: nor are those who are of a noble disposition harsh in their manners, excepting only to the wicked; and when they are particularly so, it is, as has been already said, against their friends, when they think they have injured them; which is agreeable to reason: for when those who think they ought to receive a favour from any one do not receive it, beside the injury done them, they consider what they are deprived of: hence the saying, "Cruel are the wars of brothers;" and this, "Those who have greatly loved do greatly hate." And thus we have nearly determined how many the inhabitants of a city ought to be, and what their natural disposition, and also the country how large, and of what sort is necessary; I say nearly, because it is needless to endeavour at as great accuracy in those things which are the objects of the senses as in those which are inquired into by the understanding only.

Chapter VIII

As in natural bodies those things are not admitted to be parts of them without which the whole would not exist, so also it is evident that in a political state everything that is necessary thereunto is not to be considered as a part of it, nor any other community from whence one whole is made; for one thing ought to be common and the same to the community, whether they partake of it equally or unequally, as, for instance, food, land, or the like; but when one thing is for the benefit of one person, and another for the benefit of another, in this there is nothing like a community, excepting that one makes it and the other uses it; as, for instance, between any instrument employed in making any work, and the workmen, as there is nothing common between the house and the builder, but the art of the builder is employed on the house. Thus property is necessary for states, but property is no part of the state, though many species of it have life; but a city is a community of equals, for the purpose of enjoying the best life possible: but the happiest life is the best which consists in the perfect practice of virtuous energies: as therefore some persons have great, others little or no opportunity of being employed in these, it is evident that this is the cause of the difference there is between the different cities and communities there are to be found; for while each of these endeavour to acquire what is best by various and different means, they give rise to different modes of living and different forms of government. We are now to consider what those things are without which a city cannot possibly exist; for what we call parts of the city must of necessity inhere in it: and this we shall plainly understand, if we know the number of things necessary to a city: first, the inhabitants must have food: secondly, arts, for many instruments are necessary in life: thirdly, arms, for it is necessary that the community should have an armed force within themselves, both to support their government against those of their own body who might refuse obedience to it, and also to defend it from those who might attempt to attack it from without: fourthly, a certain revenue, as well for the internal necessities of the state as for the business of war: fifthly, which is indeed the chief concern, a religious establishment: sixthly in order, but first of all in necessity, a court to determine both criminal and civil causes. These things are absolutely necessary, so to speak, in every state; for a city is a number of people not accidentally met together, but with a purpose of ensuring to themselves sufficient independency and self-protection; and if anything necessary for these purposes is wanting, it is impossible that in such a situation these ends can be obtained. It is necessary therefore that a city should be capable of acquiring all these things: for this purpose a proper number of husbandmen are necessary to procure food, also artificers and soldiers, and rich men, and priests and judges, to determine what is right and proper.

Chapter IX

Having determined thus far, it remains that we consider whether all these different employments shall be open to all; for it is possible to continue the same persons always husbandmen, artificers, judges, or counsellors; or shall we appoint different persons to each of those employments which we have already mentioned; or shall some of them be appropriated to particulars, and others of course common to all? but this does not take place in every state, for, as we have already said, it is possible that all may be common to all, or not, but only common to some; and this is the difference between one government and another: for in democracies the whole community partakes of everything, but in oligarchies it is different.

Since we are inquiring what is the best government possible, and it is admitted to be that in which the citizens are happy; and that, as we have already said, it is impossible to obtain happiness without virtue; it follows, that in the best-governed states, where the citizens are really men of intrinsic and not relative goodness, none of them should be permitted to exercise any mechanic employment or follow merchandise, as being ignoble and destructive to virtue; neither should they be husband-men, that they may be at leisure to improve in virtue and perform the duty they owe to the state. With respect to the employments of a soldier, a senator, and a judge, which are evidently necessary to the community, shall they be allotted to different persons, or shall the same person execute both? This question, too, is easily answered: for in some cases the same persons may execute them, in others they should be different, where the different employments require different abilities, as when courage is wanting for one, judgment for the other, there they should be allotted to different persons; but when it is evident, that it is impossible to oblige those who have arms in their hands, and can insist on their own terms, to be always under command; there these different employments should be trusted to one person; for those who have arms in their hands have it in their option whether they will or will not assume the supreme power: to these two (namely, those who have courage and judgment) the government must be entrusted; but not in the same manner, but as nature directs; what requires courage to the young, what requires judgment to the old; for with the young is courage, with the old is wisdom: thus each will be allotted the part they are fit for according to their different merits. It is also necessary that the landed property should belong to these men; for it is necessary that the citizens should be rich, and these are the men proper for citizens; for no mechanic ought to be admitted to the rights of a citizen, nor any other sort of people whose employment is not entirely noble, honourable, and virtuous; this is evident from the principle we at first set out with; for to be happy it is necessary to be virtuous; and no one should say that a city is happy while he considers only one part of its citizens, but for that purpose he ought to examine into all of them. It is evident, therefore, that the landed property should belong to these, though it may be necessary for them to have husbandmen, either slaves, barbarians, or servants. There remains of the different classes of the people whom we have enumerated, the priests, for these evidently compose a rank by themselves; for neither are they to be reckoned amongst the husbandmen nor the mechanics; for reverence to the gods is highly becoming every state: and since the citizens have been divided into orders, the military and the council, and it is proper to offer due worship to the gods, and since it is necessary that those who are employed in their service should have nothing else to do, let the business of the priesthood be allotted to those who are in years. We have now shown what is necessary to the existence of a city, and of what parts it consists, and that husbandmen, mechanic, and mercenary servants are necessary to a city; but that the parts of it are soldiers and sailors, and that these are always different from those, but from each other only occasionally.

Chapter X

It seems neither now nor very lately to have been known to those philosophers who have made politics their study, that a city ought to be divided by families into different orders of men; and that the husbandmen and soldiers should be kept separate from each other; which custom is even to this day preserved in Egypt and in Crete; also Sesostris having founded it in Egypt, Minos in Crete. Common meals seem also to have been an ancient regulation, and to have been established in Crete during the reign of Minos, and in a still more remote period in Italy; for those who are the best judges in that country say that one Italus being king of AEnotria., from whom the people, changing their names, were called Italians instead of AEnotrians, and that part of Europe was called Italy which is bounded by the Scylletic Gulf on the one side and the Lametic on the other, the distance between which is about half a day's journey. This Italus, they relate, made the AEnotrians, who were formerly shepherds, husbandmen, and gave them different laws from what they had before, and to have been the first who established common meals, for which reason some of his descendants still use them, and observe some of his laws. The Opici inhabit that part which lies towards the Tyrrhenian Sea, who both now are and formerly were called Ausonians. The Chones inhabited the part toward Iapigia and the Ionian Sea which is called Syrtis. These Chones were descended from the AEnotrians. Hence arose the custom of common meals, but the separation of the citizens into different families from Egypt: for the reign of Sesostris is of much higher antiquity than that of Minos. As we ought to think that most other things were found out in a long, nay, even in a boundless time (reason teaching us that want would make us first invent that which was necessary, and, when that was obtained, then those things which were requisite for the conveniences and ornament of life), so should we conclude the same with respect to a political state; now everything in Egypt bears the marks of the most remote antiquity, for these people seem to be the most ancient of all others, and to have acquired laws and political order; we should therefore make a proper use of what is told us of them, and endeavour to find out what they have omitted. We have already said, that the landed property ought to belong to the military and those who partake of the government of the state; and that therefore the husbandmen should be a separate order of people; and how large and of what nature the country ought to be: we will first treat of the division of the land, and of the husbandmen, how many and of what sort they ought to be; since we by no means hold that property ought to be common, as some persons have said, only thus far, in friendship, it should be their custom to let no citizen want subsistence. As to common meals, it is in general agreed that they are proper in well-regulated cities; my reasons for approving of them shall be mentioned hereafter: they are what all the citizens ought to partake of; but it will not be easy for the poor, out of what is their own, to furnish as much as they are ordered to do, and supply their own house besides. The expense also of religious worship should be defrayed by the whole state. Of necessity therefore the land ought to be divided into two parts, one of which should belong to the community in general, the other to the individuals separately; and each of these parts should again be subdivided into two: half of that which belongs to the public should be appropriated to maintain the worship of the gods, the other half to support the common meals. Half of that which belongs to the individuals should be at the extremity of the country, the other half near the city, so that these two portions being allotted to each person, all would partake of land in both places, which would be both equal and right; and induce them to act in concert with greater harmony in any war with their neighbours: for when the land is not divided in this manner, one party neglects the inroads of the enemy on the borders, the other makes it a matter of too much consequence and more than is necessary; for which reason in some places there is a law which forbids the inhabitants of the borders to have any vote in the council when they are debating upon a war which is made against them as their private interest might prevent their voting impartially. Thus therefore the country ought to be divided and for the reasons before mentioned. Could one have one's choice, the husbandmen should by all means be slaves, not of the same nation, or men of any spirit; for thus they would be laborious in their business, and safe from attempting any novelties: next to these barbarian servants are to be preferred, similar in natural disposition to these we have already mentioned. Of these, let those who are to cultivate the private property of the individual belong to that individual, and those who are to cultivate the public territory belong to the public. In what manner these slaves ought to be used, and for what reason it is very proper that they should have the promise of their liberty made them, as a reward for their services, shall be mentioned hereafter.

Chapter XI

We have already mentioned, that both the city and all the country should communicate both with the sea and the continent as much as possible. There are these four things which we should be particularly desirous of in the position of the city with respect to itself: in the first place, health is to be consulted as the first thing necessary: now a city which fronts the east and receives the winds which blow from thence is esteemed most healthful; next to this that which has a northern position is to be preferred, as best in winter. It should next be contrived that it may have a proper situation for the business of government and for defence in war: that in war the citizens may have easy access to it; but that it may be difficult of access to, and hardly to be taken by, the enemy. In the next place particularly, that there may be plenty of water, and rivers near at hand: but if those cannot be found, very large cisterns must be prepared to save rain-water, so that there may be no want of it in case they should be driven into the town in time of war. And as great care should be taken of the health of the inhabitants, the first thing to be attended to is, that the city should have a good situation and a good position; the second is, that they may have good water to drink; and this not be negligently taken care of; for what we chiefly and most frequently use for the support of the body must principally influence the health of it; and this influence is what the air and water naturally have: for which reason in all wise governments the waters ought to be appropriated to different purposes, and if they are not equally good, and if there is not a plenty of necessary water, that which is to drink should be separated from that which is for other uses. As to fortified places, what is proper for some governments is not proper for all; as, for instance, a lofty citadel is proper for a monarchy and an oligarchy; a city built upon a plain suits a democracy; neither of these for an aristocracy, but rather many strong places. As to the form of private houses, those are thought to be best and most useful for their different purposes which are distinct and separate from each other, and built in the modern manner, after the plan of Hippodamus: but for safety in time of war, on the contrary, they should be built as they formerly were; for they were such that strangers could not easily find their way out of them, and the method of access to them such as an enemy could with difficulty find out if he proposed to besiege them. A city therefore should have both these sorts of buildings, which may easily be contrived if any one will so regulate them as the planters do their rows of vines; not that the buildings throughout the city should be detached from each other, only in some parts of it; thus elegance and safety will be equally consulted. With respect to walls, those who say that a courageous people ought not to have any, pay too much respect to obsolete notions; particularly as we may see those who pride themselves therein continually confuted by facts. It is indeed disreputable for those who are equal, or nearly so, to the enemy, to endeavour to take refuge within their walls-but since it very often happens, that those who make the attack are too powerful for the bravery and courage of those few who oppose them to resist, if you would not suffer the calamities of war and the insolence of the enemy, it must be thought the part of a good soldier to seek for safety under the shelter and protection of walls more especially since so many missile weapons and machines have been most ingeniously invented to besiege cities with. Indeed to neglect surrounding a city with a wall would be similar to choosing a country which is easy of access to an enemy, or levelling the eminences of it; or as if an individual should not have a wall to his house lest it should be thought that the owner of it was a coward: nor should this be left unconsidered, that those who have a city surrounded with walls may act both ways, either as if it had or as if it had not; but where it has not they cannot do this. If this is true, it is not only necessary to have walls, but care must be taken that they may be a proper ornament to the city, as well as a defence in time of war; not only according to the old methods, but the modern improvements also: for as those who make offensive war endeavour by every way possible to gain advantages over their adversaries, so should those who are upon the defensive employ all the means already known, and such new ones as philosophy can invent, to defend themselves: for those who are well prepared are seldom first attacked.

Chapter XII

As the citizens in general are to eat at public tables in certain companies, and it is necessary that the walls should have bulwarks and towers in proper places and at proper distances, it is evident that it will be very necessary to have some of these in the towers; let the buildings for this purpose be made the ornaments of the walls. As to temples for public worship, and the hall for the public tables of the chief magistrates, they ought to be built in proper places, and contiguous to each other, except those temples which the law or the oracle orders to be separate from all other buildings; and let these be in such a conspicuous eminence, that they may have every advantage of situation, and in the neighbourhood of that part of the city which is best fortified. Adjoining to this place there ought to be a large square, like that which they call in Thessaly The Square of Freedom, in which nothing is permitted to be bought or sold; into which no mechanic nor husbandman, nor any such person, should be permitted to enter, unless commanded by the magistrates. It will also be an ornament to this place if the gymnastic exercises of the elders are performed in it. It is also proper, that for performing these exercises the citizens should be divided into distinct classes, according to their ages, and that the young persons should have proper officers to be with them, and that the seniors should be with the magistrates; for having them before their eyes would greatly inspire true modesty and ingenuous fear. There ought to be another square separate from this for buying and selling, which should be so situated as to be commodious for the reception of goods both by sea and land. As the citizens may be divided into magistrates and priests, it is proper that the public tables of the priests should be in buildings near the temples. Those of the magistrates who preside over contracts, indictments, and such-like, and also over the markets, and the public streets near the square, or some public way, I mean the square where things are bought and sold; for I intended the other for those who are at leisure, and this for necessary business. The same order which I have directed here should be observed also in the country; for there also their magistrates such as the surveyors of the woods and overseers of the grounds, must necessarily have their common tables and their towers, for the purpose of protection against an enemy. There ought also to be temples erected at proper places, both to the gods and the heroes; but it is unnecessary to dwell longer and most minutely on these particulars-for it is by no means difficult to plan these things, it is rather so to carry them into execution; for the theory is the child of our wishes, but the practical part must depend upon fortune; for which reason we shall decline saying anything farther upon these subjects.

Chapter XIII

We will now show of what numbers and of what sort of people a government ought to consist, that the state may be happy and well administered. As there are two particulars on which the excellence and perfection of everything depend, one of these is, that the object and end proposed should be proper; the other, that the means to accomplish it should be adapted to that purpose; for it may happen that these may either agree or disagree with each other; for the end we propose may be good, but in taking the means to obtain it we may err; at other times we may have the right and proper means in our power, but the end may be bad, and sometimes we may mistake in both; as in the art of medicine the physician does not sometimes know in what situation the body ought to be, to be healthy; nor what to do to procure the end he aims at. In every art and science, therefore, we should be master of this knowledge, namely, the proper end, and the means to obtain it. Now it is evident that all persons are desirous to live well and be happy; but that some have the means thereof in their own power, others not; and this either through nature or fortune; for many ingredients are necessary to a happy life; but fewer to those who are of a good than to those who are of a bad disposition. There are others who continually have the means of happiness in their own power, but do not rightly apply them. Since we propose to inquire what government is best, namely, that by which a state may be best administered, and that state is best administered where the people are the happiest, it is evident that happiness is a thing we should not be unacquainted with. Now, I have already said in my treatise on Morals (if I may here make any use of what I have there shown), that happiness consists in the energy and perfect practice of virtue; and this not relatively, but simply; I mean by relatively, what is necessary in some certain circumstances; by simply, what is good and fair in itself: of the first sort are just punishments, and restraints in a just cause; for they arise from virtue and are necessary, and on that account are virtuous; though it is more desirable that neither any state nor any individual should stand in need of them; but those actions which are intended either to procure honour or wealth are simply good; the others eligible only to remove an evil; these, on the contrary, are the foundation and means of relative good. A worthy man indeed will bear poverty, disease, and other unfortunate accidents with a noble mind; but happiness consists in the contrary to these (now we have already determined in our treatise on Morals, that he is a man of worth who considers what is good because it is virtuous as what is simply good; it is evident, therefore, that all the actions of such a one must be worthy and simply good): this has led some persons to conclude, that the cause of happiness was external goods; which would be as if any one should suppose that the playing well upon the lyre was owing to the instrument, and not to the art. It necessarily follows from what has been said, that some things should be ready at hand and others procured by the legislator; for which reason in founding a city we earnestly wish that there may be plenty of those things which are supposed to be under the dominion of fortune (for some things we admit her to be mistress over); but for a state to be worthy and great is not only the work of fortune but of knowledge and judgment also. But for a state to be worthy it is necessary that those citizens which are in the administration should be worthy also; but as in our city every citizen is to be so, we must consider how this may be accomplished; for if this is what every one could be, and not some individuals only, it would be more desirable; for then it would follow, that what might be done by one might be done by all. Men are worthy and good three ways; by nature, by custom, by reason. In the first place, a man ought to be born a man, and not any other animal; that is to say, he ought to have both a body and soul; but it avails not to be only born with some things, for custom makes great alterations; for there are some things in nature capable of alteration either way which are fixed by custom, either for the better or the worse. Now, other animals live chiefly a life of nature; and in very few things according to custom; but man lives according to reason also, which he alone is endowed with; wherefore he ought to make all these accord with each other; for if men followed reason, and were persuaded that it was best to obey her, they would act in many respects contrary to nature and custom. What men ought naturally to be, to make good members of a community, I have already determined; the rest of this discourse therefore shall be upon education; for some things are acquired by habit, others by hearing them.

Chapter XIV

As every political community consists of those who govern and of those who are governed, let us consider whether during the continuance of their lives they ought to be the same persons or different; for it is evident that the mode of education should be adapted to this distinction. Now, if one man differed from another as much, as we believe, the gods and heroes differ from men: in the first place, being far their superiors in body; and, secondly, in the soul: so that the superiority of the governors over the governed might be evident beyond a doubt, it is certain that it would be better for the one always to govern, the other always to be governed: but, as this is not easy to obtain, and kings are not so superior to those they govern as Scylax informs us they are in India, it is evident that for many reasons it is necessary that all in their turns should both govern and be governed: for it is just that those who are equal should have everything alike; and it is difficult for a state to continue which is founded in injustice; for all those in the country who are desirous of innovation will apply themselves to those who are under the government of the rest, and such will be their numbers in the state, that it will be impossible for the magistrates to get the better of them. But that the governors ought to excel the governed is beyond a doubt; the legislator therefore ought to consider how this shall be, and how it may be contrived that all shall have their equal share in the administration. Now, with respect to this it will be first said, that nature herself has directed us in our choice, laying down the selfsame thing when she has made some young, others old: the first of whom it becomes to obey, the latter to command; for no one when he is young is offended at his being under government, or thinks himself too good for it; more especially when he considers that he himself shall receive the same honours which he pays when he shall arrive at a proper age. In some respects it must be acknowledged that the governors and the governed are the same, in others they are different; it is therefore necessary that their education should be in some respect the same, in others different: as they say, that he will be a good governor who has first learnt to obey. Now of governments, as we have already said, some are instituted for the sake of him who commands; others for him who obeys: of the first sort is that of the master over the servant; of the latter, that of freemen over each other. Now some things which are commanded differ from others; not in the business, but in the end proposed thereby: for which reason many works, even of a servile nature, are not disgraceful for young freemen to perform; for many things which are ordered to be done are not honourable or dishonourable so much in their own nature as in the end which is proposed, and the reason for which they are undertaken. Since then we have determined, that the virtue of a good citizen and good governor is the same as of a good man; and that every one before he commands should have first obeyed, it is the business of the legislator to consider how his citizens may be good men, what education is necessary to that purpose, and what is the final object of a good life. The soul of man may be divided into two parts; that which has reason in itself, and that which hath not, but is capable of obeying its dictates: and according to the virtues of these two parts a man is said to be good: but of those virtues which are the ends, it will not be difficult for those to determine who adopt the division I have already given; for the inferior is always for the sake of the superior; and this is equally evident both in the works of art as well as in those of nature; but that is superior which has reason. Reason itself also is divided into two parts, in the manner we usually divide it; the theoretic and the practical; which division therefore seems necessary for this part also: the same analogy holds good with respect to actions; of which those which are of a superior nature ought always to be chosen by those who have it in their power; for that is always most eligible to every one which will procure the best ends. Now life is divided into labour and rest, war and peace; and of what we do the objects are partly necessary and useful, partly noble: and we should give the same preference to these that we do to the different parts of the soul and its actions, as war to procure peace; labour, rest; and the useful, the noble. The politician, therefore, who composes a body of laws ought to extend his views to everything; the different parts of the soul and their actions; more particularly to those things which are of a superior nature and ends; and, in the same manner, to the lives of men and their different actions.

They ought to be fitted both for labour and war, but rather for rest and peace; and also to do what is necessary and useful, but rather what is fair and noble. It is to those objects that the education of the children ought to tend, and of all the youths who want instruction. All the Grecian states which now seem best governed, and the legislators who founded those states, appear not to have framed their polity with a view to the best end, or to every virtue, in their laws and education; but eagerly to have attended to what is useful and productive of gain: and nearly of the same opinion with these are some persons who have written lately, who, by praising the Lacedaemonian state, show they approve of the intention of the legislator in making war and victory the end of his government. But how contrary to reason this is, is easily proved by argument, and has already been proved by facts (but as the generality of men desire to have an extensive command, that they may have everything desirable in the greater abundance; so Thibron and others who have written on that state seem to approve of their legislator for having procured them an extensive command by continually enuring them to all sorts of dangers and hardships): for it is evident, since the Lacedemonians have now no hope that the supreme power will be in their own hand, that neither are they happy nor was their legislator wise. This also is ridiculous, that while they preserved an obedience to their laws, and no one opposed their being governed by them, they lost the means of being honourable: but these people understand not rightly what sort of government it is which ought to reflect honour on the legislator; for a government of freemen is nobler than despotic power, and more consonant to virtue. Moreover, neither should a city be thought happy, nor should a legislator be commended, because he has so trained the people as to conquer their neighbours; for in this there is a great inconvenience: since it is evident that upon this principle every citizen who can will endeavour to procure the supreme power in his own city; which crime the Lacedaemonians accuse Pausanias of, though he enjoyed such great honours.

Such reasoning and such laws are neither political, useful nor true: but a legislator ought to instil those laws on the minds of men which are most useful for them, both in their public and private capacities. The rendering a people fit for war, that they may enslave their inferiors ought not to be the care of the legislator; but that they may not themselves be reduced to slavery by others. In the next place, he should take care that the object of his government is the safety of those who are under it, and not a despotism over all: in the third place, that those only are slaves who are fit to be only so. Reason indeed concurs with experience in showing that all the attention which the legislator pays to the business of war, and all other rules which he lays down, should have for their object rest and peace; since most of those states (which we usually see) are preserved by war; but, after they have acquired a supreme power over those around them, are ruined; for during peace, like a sword, they lose their brightness: the fault of which lies in the legislator, who never taught them how to be at rest.

Chapter XV

As there is one end common to a man both as an individual and a citizen, it is evident that a good man and a good citizen must have the same object in view; it is evident that all the virtues which lead to rest are necessary; for, as we have often said, the end of war is peace, of labour, rest; but those virtues whose object is rest, and those also whose object is labour, are necessary for a liberal life and rest; for we want a supply of many necessary things that we may be at rest. A city therefore ought to be temperate, brave, and patient; for, according to the proverb, "Rest is not for slaves;" but those who cannot bravely face danger are the slaves of those who attack them. Bravery, therefore, and patience are necessary for labour, philosophy for rest, and temperance and justice in both; but these chiefly in time of peace and rest; for war obliges men to be just and temperate; but the enjoyment of pleasure, with the rest of peace, is more apt to produce insolence; those indeed who are easy in their circumstances, and enjoy everything that can make them happy, have great occasion for the virtues of temperance and justice. Thus if there are, as the poets tell us, any inhabitants in the happy isles, to these a higher degree of philosophy, temperance, and justice will be necessary, as they live at their ease in the full plenty of every sensual pleasure. It is evident, therefore, that these virtues are necessary in every state that would be happy or worthy; for he who is worthless can never enjoy real good, much less is he qualified to be at rest; but can appear good only by labour and being at war, but in peace and at rest the meanest of creatures. For which reason virtue should not be cultivated as the Lacedaemonians did; for they did not differ from others in their opinion concerning the supreme good, but in imagining this good was to be procured by a particular virtue; but since there are greater goods than those of war, it is evident that the enjoyment of those which are valuable in themselves should be desired, rather than those virtues which are useful in war; but how and by what means this is to be acquired is now to be considered. We have already assigned three causes on which it will depend; nature, custom, and reason, arid shown what sort of men nature must produce for this purpose; it remains then that we determine which we shall first begin by in education, reason or custom, for these ought always to preserve the most entire harmony with each other; for it may happen that reason may err from the end proposed, and be corrected by custom. In the first place, it is evident that in this as in other things, its beginning or production arises from some principle, and its end also arises from another principle, which is itself an end. Now, with us, reason and intelligence are the end of nature; our production, therefore, and our manners ought to be accommodated to both these. In the next place, as the soul and the body are two distinct things, so also we see that the soul is divided into two parts, the reasoning and not-reasoning, with their habits which are two in number, one belonging to each, namely appetite and intelligence; and as the body is in production before the soul, so is the not-reasoning part of the soul before the reasoning; and this is evident; for anger, will and desire are to be seen in children nearly as soon as they are born; but reason and intelligence spring up as they grow to maturity. The body, therefore, necessarily demands our care before the soul; next the appetites for the sake of the mind; the body for the sake of the soul.

Chapter XVI

If then the legislator ought to take care that the bodies of the children are as perfect as possible, his first attention ought to be given to matrimony; at what time and in what situation it is proper that the citizens should engage in the nuptial contract. Now, with respect to this alliance, the legislator ought both to consider the parties and their time of life, that they may grow old at the same part of time, and that their bodily powers may not be different; that is to say, the man being able to have children, but the woman too old to bear them; or, on the contrary, the woman be young enough to produce children, but the man too old to be a father; for from such a situation discords and disputes continually arise. In the next place, with respect to the succession of children, there ought not to be too great an interval of time between them and their parents; for when there is, the parent can receive no benefit from his child's affection, or the child any advantage from his father's protection; neither should the difference in years be too little, as great inconveniences may arise from it; as it prevents that proper reverence being shown to a father by a boy who considers him as nearly his equal in age, and also from the disputes it occasions in the economy of the family. But, to return from this digression, care ought to be taken that the bodies of the children may be such as will answer the expectations of the legislator; this also will be affected by the same means. Since season for the production of children is determined (not exactly, but to speak in general), namely, for the man till seventy years, and the woman till fifty, the entering into the marriage state, as far as time is concerned, should be regulated by these periods. It is extremely bad for the children when the father is too young; for in all animals whatsoever the parts of the young are imperfect, and are more likely to be productive of females than males, and diminutive also in size; the same thing of course necessarily holds true in men; as a proof of this you may see in those cities where the men and women usually marry very young, the people in general are very small and ill framed; in child-birth also the women suffer more, and many of them die. And thus some persons tell us the oracle of Traezenium should be explained, as if it referred to the many women who were destroyed by too early marriages, and not their gathering their fruits too soon. It is also conducive to temperance not to marry too soon; for women who do so are apt to be intemperate. It also prevents the bodies of men from acquiring their full size if they marry before their growth is completed; for this is the determinate period, which prevents any further increase; for which reason the proper time for a woman to marry is eighteen, for a man thirty-seven, a little more or less; for when they marry at that time their bodies are in perfection, and they will also cease to have children at a proper time; and moreover with respect to the succession of the children, if they have them at the time which may reasonably be expected, they will be just arriving into perfection when their parents are sinking down under the load of seventy years. And thus much for the time which is proper for marriage; but moreover a proper season of the year should be observed, as many persons do now, and appropriate the winter for this business. The married couple ought also to regard the precepts of physicians and naturalists, each of whom have treated on these subjects. What is the fit disposition of the body will be better mentioned when we come to speak of the education of the child; we will just slightly mention a few particulars. Now, there is no occasion that any one should have the habit of body of a wrestler to be either a good citizen, or to enjoy a good constitution, or to be the father of healthy children; neither should he be infirm or too much dispirited by misfortunes, but between both these. He ought to have a habit of labour, but not of too violent labour; nor should that be confined to one object only, as the wrestler's is; but to such things as are proper for freemen. These things are equally necessary both for men and women. Women with child should also take care that their diet is not too sparing, and that they use sufficient exercise; which it will be easy for the legislator to effect if he commands them once every day to repair to the worship of the gods who are supposed to preside over matrimony. But, contrary to what is proper for the body, the mind ought to be kept as tranquil as possible; for as plants partake of the nature of the soil, so does the child receive much of the disposition of the mother. With respect to the exposing or bringing up of children, let it be a law, that nothing imperfect or maimed shall be brought up,..........As the proper time has been pointed out for a man and a woman to enter into the marriage state, so also let us determine how long it is advantageous for the community that they should have children; for as the children of those who are too young are imperfect both in body and mind, so also those whose parents are too old are weak in both: while therefore the body continues in perfection, which (as some poets say, who reckon the different periods of life by sevens) is till fifty years, or four or five more, the children may be equally perfect; but when the parents are past that age it is better they should have no more. With respect to any connection between a man and a woman, or a woman and a man, when either of the parties are betrothed, let it be held in utter detestation on any pretext whatsoever; but should any one be guilty of such a thing after the marriage is consummated, let his infamy be as great as his guilt deserves.

Chapter XVII

When a child is born it must be supposed that the strength of its body will depend greatly upon the quality of its food. Now whoever will examine into the nature of animals, and also observe those people who are very desirous their children should acquire a warlike habit, will find that they feed them chiefly with milk, as being best accommodated to their bodies, but without wine, to prevent any distempers: those motions also which are natural to their age are very serviceable; and to prevent any of their limbs from being crooked, on account of their extreme ductility, some people even now use particular machines that their bodies may not be distorted. It is also useful to enure them to the cold when they are very little; for this is very serviceable for their health; and also to enure them to the business of war; for which reason it is customary with many of the barbarians to dip their children in rivers when the water is cold; with others to clothe them very slightly, as among the Celts; for whatever it is possible to accustom children to, it is best to accustom them to it at first, but to do it by degrees: besides, boys have naturally a habit of loving the cold, on account of the heat. These, then, and such-like things ought to be the first object of our attention: the next age to this continues till the child is five years old; during which time it is best to teach him nothing at all, not even necessary labour, lest it should hinder his growth; but he should be accustomed to use so much motion as not to acquire a lazy habit of body; which he will get by various means and by play also: his play also ought to be neither illiberal nor too laborious nor lazy. Their governors and preceptors also should take care what sort of tales and stories it may be proper for them to hear; for all these ought to pave the way for their future instruction: for which reason the generality of their play should be imitations of what they are afterwards to do seriously. They too do wrong who forbid by laws the disputes between boys and their quarrels, for they contribute to increase their growth-as they are a sort of exercise to the body: for the struggles of the heart and the compression of the spirits give strength to those who labour, which happens to boys in their disputes. The preceptors also ought to have an eye upon their manner of life, and those with whom they converse; and to take care that they are never in the company of slaves. At this time and till they are seven years old it is necessary that they should be educated at home. It is also very proper to banish, both from their hearing and sight, everything which is illiberal and the like. Indeed it is as much the business of the legislator as anything else, to banish every indecent expression out of the state: for from a permission to speak whatever is shameful, very quickly arises the doing it, and this particularly with young people: for which reason let them never speak nor hear any such thing: but if it appears that any freeman has done or said anything that is forbidden before he is of age to be thought fit to partake of the common meals, let him be punished by disgrace and stripes; but if a person above that age does so, let him be treated as you would a slave, on account of his being infamous. Since we forbid his speaking everything which is forbidden, it is necessary that he neither sees obscene stories nor pictures; the magistrates therefore are to take care that there are no statues or pictures of anything of this nature, except only to those gods to whom the law permits them, and to which the law allows persons of a certain age to pay their devotions, for themselves, their wives, and children. It should also be illegal for young persons to be present either at iambics or comedies before they are arrived at that age when they are allowed to partake of the pleasures of the table: indeed a good education will preserve them from all the evils which attend on these things. We have at present just touched upon this subject; it will be our business hereafter, when we properly come to it, to determine whether this care of children is unnecessary, or, if necessary, in what manner it must be done; at present we have only mentioned it as necessary. Probably the saying of Theodoras, the tragic actor, was not a bad one: That he would permit no one, not even the meanest actor, to go upon the stage before him, that he might first engage the ear of the audience. The same thing happens both in our connections with men and things: what we meet with first pleases best; for which reason children should be kept strangers to everything which is bad, more particularly whatsoever is loose and offensive to good manners. When five years are accomplished, the two next may be very properly employed in being spectators of those exercises they will afterwards have to learn. There are two periods into which education ought to be divided, according to the age of the child; the one is from his being seven years of age to the time of puberty; the other from thence till he is one-and-twenty: for those who divide ages by the number seven are in general wrong: it is much better to follow the division of nature; for every art and every instruction is intended to complete what nature has left defective: we must first consider if any regulation whatsoever is requisite for children; in the next place, if it is advantageous to make it a common care, or that every one should act therein as he pleases, which is the general practice in most cities; in the third place, what it ought to be.

Book VIII

Chapter I

No one can doubt that the magistrate ought greatly to interest himself in the care of youth; for where it is neglected it is hurtful to the city, for every state ought to be governed according to its particular nature; for the form and manners of each government are peculiar to itself; and these, as they originally established it, so they usually still preserve it. For instance, democratic forms and manners a democracy; oligarchic, an oligarchy: but, universally, the best manners produce the best government. Besides, as in every business and art there are some things which men are to learn first and be made accustomed to, which are necessary to perform their several works; so it is evident that the same thing is necessary in the practice of virtue. As there is one end in view in every city, it is evident that education ought to be one and the same in each; and that this should be a common care, and not the individual's, as it now is, when every one takes care of his own children separately; and their instructions are particular also, each person teaching them as they please; but what ought to be engaged in ought to be common to all. Besides, no one ought to think that any citizen belongs to him in particular, but to the state in general; for each one is a part of the state, and it is the natural duty of each part to regard the good of the whole: and for this the Lacedaemonians may be praised; for they give the greatest attention to education, and make it public. It is evident, then, that there should be laws concerning education, and that it should be public.

Chapter II

What education is, and how children ought to be instructed, is what should be well known; for there are doubts concerning the business of it, as all people do not agree in those things they would have a child taught, both with respect to their improvement in virtue and a happy life: nor is it clear whether the object of it should be to improve the reason or rectify the morals. From the present mode of education we cannot determine with certainty to which men incline, whether to instruct a child in what will be useful to him in life; or what tends to virtue, and what is excellent: for all these things have their separate defenders. As to virtue, there is no particular in which they all agree: for as all do not equally esteem all virtues, it reasonably follows that they will not cultivate the same. It is evident that what is necessary ought to be taught to all: but that which is necessary for one is not necessary for all; for there ought to be a distinction between the employment of a freeman and a slave. The first of these should be taught everything useful which will not make those who know it mean. Every work is to be esteemed mean, and every art and every discipline which renders the body, the mind, or the understanding of freemen unfit for the habit and practice of virtue: for which reason all those arts which tend to deform the body are called mean, and all those employments which are exercised for gain; for they take off from the freedom of the mind and render it sordid. There are also some liberal arts which are not improper for freemen to apply to in a certain degree; but to endeavour to acquire a perfect skill in them is exposed to the faults I have just mentioned; for there is a great deal of difference in the reason for which any one does or learns anything: for it is not illiberal to engage in it for one's self, one's friend, or in the cause of virtue; while, at the same time, to do it for the sake of another may seem to be acting the part of a servant and a slave. The mode of instruction which now prevails seems to partake of both parts.

Chapter III

There are four things which it is usual to teach children-reading, gymnastic exercises, and music, to which (in the fourth place) some add painting. Reading and painting are both of them of singular use in life, and gymnastic exercises, as productive of courage. As to music, some persons may doubt, as most persons now use it for the sake of pleasure: but those who originally made it part of education did it because, as has been already said, nature requires that we should not only be properly employed, but to be able to enjoy leisure honourably: for this (to repeat what I have already said) is of all things the principal. But, though both labour and rest are necessary, yet the latter is preferable to the first; and by all means we ought to learn what we should do when at rest: for we ought not to employ that time at play; for then play would be the necessary business of our lives. But if this cannot be, play is more necessary for those who labour than those who are at rest: for he who labours requires relaxation; which play will supply: for as labour is attended with pain and continued exertion, it is necessary that play should be introduced, under proper regulations, as a medicine: for such an employment of the mind is a relaxation to it, and eases with pleasure. Now rest itself seems to partake of pleasure, of happiness, and an agreeable life: but this cannot be theirs who labour, but theirs who are at rest; for he who labours, labours for the sake of some end which he has not: but happiness is an end which all persons think is attended with pleasure and not with pain: but all persons do not agree in making this pleasure consist in the same thing; for each one has his particular standard, correspondent to his own habits; but the best man proposes the best pleasure, and that which arises from the noblest actions. But it is evident, that to live a life of rest there are some things which a man must learn and be instructed in; and that the object of this learning and this instruction centres in their acquisition: but the learning and instruction which is given for labour has for its object other things; for which reason the ancients made music a part of education; not as a thing necessary, for it is not of that nature, nor as a thing useful, as reading, in the common course of life, or for managing of a family, or for learning anything as useful in public life. Painting also seems useful to enable a man to judge more accurately of the productions of the finer arts: nor is it like the gymnastic exercises, which contribute to health and strength; for neither of these things do we see produced by music; there remains for it then to be the employment of our rest, which they had in view who introduced it; and, thinking it a proper employment for freemen, to them they allotted it; as Homer sings:

> "How right to call Thalia to the feast:"

and of some others he says:

> "The bard was call'd, to ravish every ear:"

and, in another place, he makes Ulysses say the happiest part of man's life is

> "When at the festal board, in order plac'd, They hear the song."

It is evident, then, that there is a certain education in which a child may be instructed, not as useful nor as necessary, but as noble and liberal: but whether this is one or more than one, and of what sort they are, and how to be taught, shall be considered hereafter: we are now got so far on our way as to show that we have the testimony of the ancients in our favour, by what they have delivered down upon education-for music makes this plain. Moreover, it is necessary to instruct children in what is useful, not only on account of its being useful in itself, as, for instance, to learn to read, but also as the means of acquiring other different sorts of instruction: thus they should be instructed in painting, not only to prevent their being mistaken in purchasing pictures, or in buying or selling of vases, but rather as it makes them judges of the beauties of the human form; for to be always hunting after the profitable ill agrees with great and freeborn souls. As it is evident whether a boy should be first taught morals or reasoning, and whether his body or his understanding should be first cultivated, it is plain that boys should be first put under the care of the different masters of the gymnastic arts, both to form their bodies and teach them their exercises.

Chapter IV

Now those states which seem to take the greatest care of their children's education, bestow their chief attention on wrestling, though it both prevents the increase of the body and hurts the form of it. This fault the Lacedaemonians did not fall into, for they made their children fierce by painful labour, as chiefly useful to inspire them with courage: though, as we have already often said, this is neither the only thing nor the principal thing necessary to attend to; and even with respect to this they may not thus attain their end; for we do not find either in other animals, or other nations, that courage necessarily attends the most cruel, but rather the milder, and those who have the dispositions of lions: for there are many people who are eager both to kill men and to devour human flesh, as the Achaeans and Heniochi in Pontus, and many others in Asia, some of whom are as bad, others worse than these, who indeed live by tyranny, but are men of no courage. Nay, we know that the Lacedaemonians themselves, while they continued those painful labours, and were superior to all others (though now they are inferior to many, both in war and gymnastic exercises), did not acquire their superiority by training their youth to these exercises, but because those who were disciplined opposed those who were not disciplined at all. What is fair and honourable ought then to take place in education of what is fierce and cruel: for it is not a wolf, nor any other wild beast, which will brave any noble danger, but rather a good man. So that those who permit boys to engage too earnestly in these exercises, while they do not take care to instruct them in what is necessary to do, to speak the real truth, render them mean and vile, accomplished only in one duty of a citizen, and in every other respect, as reason evinces, good for nothing. Nor should we form our judgments from past events, but from what we see at present: for now they have rivals in their mode of education, whereas formerly they had not. That gymnastic exercises are useful, and in what manner, is admitted; for during youth it is very proper to go through a course of those which are most gentle, omitting that violent diet and those painful exercises which are prescribed as necessary; that they may not prevent the growth of the body: and it is no small proof that they have this effect, that amongst the Olympic candidates we can scarce find two or three who have gained a victory both when boys and men: because the necessary exercises they went through when young deprived them of their strength. When they have allotted three years from the time of puberty to other parts of education, they are then of a proper age to submit to labour and a regulated diet; for it is impossible for the mind and body both to labour at the same time, as they are productive of contrary evils to each other; the labour of the body preventing the progress of the mind, and the mind of the body.

Chapter V

With respect to music we have already spoken a little in a doubtful manner upon this subject. It will be proper to go over again more particularly what we then said, which may serve as an introduction to what any other person may choose to offer thereon; for it is no easy matter to distinctly point out what power it has, nor on what accounts one should apply it, whether as an amusement and refreshment, as sleep or wine; as these are nothing serious, but pleasing, and the killers of care, as Euripides says; for which reason they class in the same order and use for the same purpose all these, namely, sleep, wine, and music, to which some add dancing; or shall we rather suppose that music tends to be productive of virtue, having a power, as the gymnastic exercises have to form the body in a certain way, to influence the manners so as to accustom its professors to rejoice rightly? or shall we say, that it is of any service in the conduct of life, and an assistant to prudence? for this also is a third property which has been attributed to it. Now that boys are not to be instructed in it as play is evident; for those who learn don't play, for to learn is rather troublesome; neither is it proper to permit boys at their age to enjoy perfect leisure; for to cease to improve is by no means fit for what is as yet imperfect; but it may be thought that the earnest attention of boys in this art is for the sake of that amusement they will enjoy when they come to be men and completely formed; but, if this is the case, why are they themselves to learn it, and not follow the practice of the kings of the Medes and Persians, who enjoy the pleasure of music by hearing others play, and being shown its beauties by them; for of necessity those must be better skilled therein who make this science their particular study and business, than those who have only spent so much time at it as was sufficient just to learn the principles of it. But if this is a reason for a child's being taught anything, they ought also to learn the art of cookery, but this is absurd. The same doubt occurs if music has a power of improving the manners; for why should they on this account themselves learn it, and not reap every advantage of regulating the passions or forming a judgment on the merits of the performance by hearing others, as the Lacedaemonians; for they, without having ever learnt music, are yet able to judge accurately what is good and what is bad; the same reasoning may be applied if music is supposed to be the amusement of those who live an elegant and easy life, why should they learn themselves, and not rather enjoy the benefit of others' skill. Let us here consider what is our belief of the immortal gods in this particular. Now we find the poets never represent Jupiter himself as singing and playing; nay, we ourselves treat the professors of these arts as mean people, and say that no one would practise them but a drunkard or a buffoon. But probably we may consider this subject more at large hereafter. The first question is, whether music is or is not to make a part of education? and of those three things which have been assigned as its proper employment, which is the right? Is it to instruct, to amuse, or to employ the vacant hours of those who live at rest? or may not all three be properly allotted to it? for it appears to partake of them all; for play is necessary for relaxation, and relaxation pleasant, as it is a medicine for that uneasiness which arises from labour. It is admitted also that a happy life must be an honourable one, and a pleasant one too, since happiness consists in both these; and we all agree that music is one of the most pleasing things, whether alone or accompanied with a voice; as Musseus says, "Music's the sweetest joy of man;" for which reason it is justly admitted into every company and every happy life, as having the power of inspiring joy. So that from this any one may suppose that it is necessary to instruct young persons in it; for all those pleasures which are harmless are not only conducive to the final end of life, but serve also as relaxations; and, as men are but rarely in the attainment of that final end, they often cease from their labour and apply to amusement, with no further view than to acquire the pleasure attending it. It is therefore useful to enjoy such pleasures as these. There are some persons who make play and amusement their end, and probably that end has some pleasure annexed to it, but not what should be; but while men seek the one they accept the other for it; because there is some likeness in human actions to the end; for the end is pursued for the sake of nothing else that attends it; but for itself only; and pleasures like these are sought for, not on account of what follows them, but on account of what has gone before them, as labour and grief; for which reason they seek for happiness in these sort of pleasures; and that this is the reason any one may easily perceive. That music should be pursued, not on this account only, but also as it is very serviceable during the hours of relaxation from labour, probably no one doubts; we should also inquire whether besides this use it may not also have another of nobler nature-and we ought not only to partake of the common pleasure arising from it (which all have the sensation of, for music naturally gives pleasure, therefore the use of it is agreeable to all ages and all dispositions); but also to examine if it tends anything to improve our manners and our souls. And this will be easily known if we feel our dispositions any way influenced thereby; and that they are so is evident from many other instances, as well as the music at the Olympic games; and this confessedly fills the soul with enthusiasm; but enthusiasm is an affection of the soul which strongly agitates the disposition. Besides, all those who hear any imitations sympathise therewith; and this when they are conveyed even without rhythm or verse. Moreover, as music is one of those things which are pleasant, and as virtue itself consists in rightly enjoying, loving, and hating, it is evident that we ought not to learn or accustom ourselves to anything so much as to judge right and rejoice in honourable manners and noble actions. But anger and mildness, courage and modesty, and their contraries, as well as all other dispositions of the mind, are most naturally imitated by music and poetry; which is plain by experience, for when we hear these our very soul is altered; and he who is affected either with joy or grief by the imitation of any objects, is in very nearly the same situation as if he was affected by the objects themselves; thus, if any person is pleased with seeing a statue of any one on no other account but its beauty, it is evident that the sight of the original from whence it was taken would also be pleasing; now it happens in the other senses there is no imitation of manners; that is to say, in the touch and the taste; in the objects of sight, a very little; for these are merely representations of things, and the perceptions which they excite are in a manner common to all. Besides, statues and paintings are not properly imitations of manners, but rather signs and marks which show the body is affected by some passion. However, the difference is not great, yet young men ought not to view the paintings of Pauso, but of Polygnotus, or any other painter or statuary who expresses manners. But in poetry and music there are imitations of manners; and this is evident, for different harmonies differ from each other so much by nature, that those who hear them are differently affected, and are not in the same disposition of mind when one is performed as when another is; the one, for instance, occasions grief 13406 and contracts the soul, as the mixed Lydian: others soften the mind, and as it were dissolve the heart: others fix it in a firm and settled state, such is the power of the Doric music only; while the Phrygian fills the soul with enthusiasm, as has been well described by those who have written philosophically upon this part of education; for they bring examples of what they advance from the things themselves. The same holds true with respect to rhythm; some fix the disposition, others occasion a change in it; some act more violently, others more liberally. From what has been said it is evident what an influence music has over the disposition of the mind, and how variously it can fascinate it: and if it can do this, most certainly it is what youth ought to be instructed in. And indeed the learning of music is particularly adapted to their disposition; for at their time of life they do not willingly attend to anything which is not agreeable; but music is naturally one of the most agreeable things; and there seems to be a certain connection between harmony and rhythm; for which reason some wise men held the soul itself to be harmony; others, that it contains it.

Chapter VI

We will now determine whether it is proper that children should be taught to sing, and play upon any instrument, which we have before made a matter of doubt. Now, it is well known that it makes a great deal of difference when you would qualify any one in any art, for the person himself to learn the practical part of it; for it is a thing very difficult, if not impossible, for a man to be a good judge of what he himself cannot do. It is also very necessary that children should have some employment which will amuse them; for which reason the rattle of Archytas seems well contrived, which they give children to play with, to prevent their breaking those things which are about the house; for at their age they cannot sit still: this therefore is well adapted to infants, as instruction ought to be their rattle as they grow up; hence it is evident that they should be so taught music as to be able to practise it. Nor is it difficult to say what is becoming or unbecoming of their age, or to answer the objections which some make to this employment as mean and low. In the first place, it is necessary for them to practise, that they may be judges of the art: for which reason this should be done when they are young; but when they are grown older the practical part may be dropped; while they will still continue judges of what is excellent in the art, and take a proper pleasure therein, from the knowledge they acquired of it in their

youth. As to the censure which some persons throw upon music, as something mean and low, it is not difficult to answer that, if we will but consider how far we propose those who are to be educated so as to become good citizens should be instructed in this art, and what music and what rhythms they should be acquainted with; and also what instruments they should play upon; for in these there is probably a difference. Such then is the proper answer to that censure: for it must be admitted, that in some cases nothing can prevent music being attended, to a certain degree, with the bad effects which are ascribed to it; it is therefore clear that the learning of it should never prevent the business of riper years; nor render the body effeminate, and unfit for the business of war or the state; but it should be practised by the young, judged of by the old. That children may learn music properly, it is necessary that they should not be employed in those parts of it which are the objects of dispute between the masters in that science; nor should they perform such pieces as are wondered at from the difficulty of their execution; and which, from being first exhibited in the public games, are now become a part of education; but let them learn so much of it as to be able to receive proper pleasure from excellent music and rhythms; and not that only which music must make all animals feel, and also slaves and boys, but more. It is therefore plain what instruments they should use; thus, they should never be taught to play upon the flute, or any other instrument which requires great skill, as the harp or the like, but on such as will make them good judges of music, or any other instruction: besides, the flute is not a moral instrument, but rather one that will inflame the passions, and is therefore rather to be used when the soul is to be animated than when instruction is intended. Let me add also, that there is something therein which is quite contrary to what education requires; as the player on the flute is prevented from speaking: for which reason our forefathers very properly forbade the use of it to youth and freemen, though they themselves at first used it; for when their riches procured them greater leisure, they grew more animated in the cause of virtue; and both before and after the Median war their noble actions so exalted their minds that they attended to every part of education; selecting no one in particular, but endeavouring to collect the whole: for which reason they introduced the flute also, as one of the instruments they were to learn to play on. At Lacedaemon the choregus himself played on the flute; and it was so common at Athens that almost every freeman understood it, as is evident from the tablet which Thrasippus dedicated when he was choregus; but afterwards they rejected it as dangerous; having become better judges of what tended to promote virtue and what did not. For the same reason many of the ancient instruments were thrown aside, as the dulcimer and the lyre; as also those which were to inspire those who played on them with pleasure, and which required a nice finger and great skill to play well on. What the ancients tell us, by way of fable, of the flute is indeed very rational; namely, that after Minerva had found it, she threw it away: nor are they wrong who say that the goddess disliked it for deforming the face of him who played thereon: not but that it is more probable that she rejected it as the knowledge thereof contributed nothing to the improvement of the mind. Now, we regard Minerva as the inventress of arts and sciences. As we disapprove of a child's being taught to understand instruments, and to play like a master (which we would have confined to those who are candidates for the prize in that science; for they play not to improve themselves in virtue, but to please those who hear them, and gratify their importunity); therefore we think the practice of it unfit for freemen; but then it should be confined to those who are paid for doing it; for it usually gives people sordid notions, for the end they have in view is bad: for the impertinent spectator is accustomed to make them change their music; so that the artists who attend to him regulate their bodies according to his motions.

Chapter VII

We are now to enter into an inquiry concerning harmony and rhythm; whether all sorts of these are to be employed in education, or whether some peculiar ones are to be selected; and also whether we should give the same directions to those who are engaged in music as part of education, or whether there is something different from these two. Now, as all music consists in melody and rhythm, we ought not to be unacquainted with the power which each of these has in education; and whether we should rather choose music in which melody prevails, or rhythm: but when I consider how many things have been well written upon these subjects, not only by some musicians of the present age, but also by some philosophers who are perfectly skilled in that part of music which belongs to education; we will refer those who desire a very particular knowledge therein to those writers, and shall only treat of it in general terms, without descending to particulars. Melody is divided by some philosophers, whose notions we approve of, into moral, practical, and that which fills the mind with enthusiasm: they also allot to each of these a particular kind of harmony which naturally corresponds therewith: and we say that music should not be applied to one purpose only, but many; both for instruction and purifying the soul (now I use the word purifying at present without any explanation, but shall speak more at large of it in my Poetics); and, in the third place, as an agreeable manner of spending the time and a relaxation from the uneasiness of the mind. It is evident that all harmonies are to be used; but not for all purposes; but the most moral in education: but to please the ear, when others play, the most active and enthusiastic; for that passion which is to be found very strong in some souls is to be met with also in all; but the difference in different persons consists in its being in a less or greater degree, as pity, fear, and enthusiasm also; which latter is so powerful in some as to overpower the soul: and yet we see those persons, by the application of sacred music to soothe their mind, rendered as sedate and composed as if they had employed the art of the physician: and this must necessarily happen to the compassionate, the fearful, and all those who are subdued by their passions: nay, all persons, as far as they are affected with those passions, admit of the same cure, and are restored to tranquillity with pleasure. In the same manner, all music which has the power of purifying the soul affords a harmless pleasure to man. Such, therefore, should be the harmony and such the music which those who contend with each other in the theatre should exhibit: but as the audience is composed of two sorts of people, the free and the well-instructed, the rude the mean mechanics, and hired servants, and a long collection of the like, there must be some music and some spectacles to please and soothe them; for as their minds are as it were perverted from their natural habits, so also is there an unnatural harmony, and overcharged music which is accommodated to their taste: but what is according to nature gives pleasure to every one, therefore those who are to contend upon the theatre should be allowed to use this species of music. But in education ethic melody and ethic harmony should be used, which is the Doric, as we have already said, or any other which those philosophers who are skilful in that music which is to be employed in education shall approve of. But Socrates, in Plato's Republic, is very wrong when he permits only the Phrygian music to be used as well as the Doric, particularly as amongst other instruments he banishes the flute; for the Phrygian music has the same power in harmony as the flute has amongst the instruments; for they are both pathetic and raise the mind: and this the practice of the poets proves; for in their bacchanal songs, or whenever they describe any violent emotions of the mind, the flute is the instrument they chiefly use: and the Phrygian harmony is most suitable to these subjects. Now, that the dithyrambic measure is Phrygian is allowed by general consent; and those who are conversant in studies of this sort bring many proofs of it; as, for instance, when Philoxenus endeavoured to compose dithyrambic music for Doric harmony, he naturally fell back again into Phrygian, as being fittest for that purpose; as every one indeed agrees, that the Doric music is most serious, and fittest to inspire courage: and, as we always commend the middle as being between the two extremes, and the Doric has this relation with respect to other harmonies, it is evident that is what the youth ought to be instructed in. There are two things to be taken into consideration, both what is possible and what is proper; every one then should chiefly endeavour to attain those things which contain both these qualities: but this is to be regulated by different times of life; for instance, it is not easy for those who are advanced in years to sing such pieces of music as require very high notes, for nature points out to them those which are gentle and require little strength of voice (for which reason some who are skilful in music justly find fault with Socrates for forbidding the youth to be instructed in gentle harmony; as if, like wine, it would make them drunk, whereas the effect of that is to render men bacchanals, and not make them languid): these therefore are what should employ those who are grown old. Moreover, if there is any harmony which is proper for a child's age, as being at the same time elegant and instructive, as the Lydian of all others seems chiefly to be-These then are as it were the three boundaries of education, moderation, possibility, and decorum.

www.ingramcontent.com/pod-product-compliance
Lightning Source LLC
Chambersburg PA
CBHW071718120626
46550CB00001B/286
* 9 7 8 8 0 2 7 2 7 3 3 1 7 *